The book of Joshua is an important book in the Old Testament. It marks the transition of the people of God delivered from Egypt to actually entering the promised land. Dr. Firth's commentary makes a fine contribution to the existing literature on this important book. What is offered in this commentary is a meticulous reading of the text highlighting the literary features as well as paying due attention to historical matters. Equally important is that the commentary also probes the theological significance of each unit. The commentary is well written with clear lines of thought. What is of particular importance is that Dr. Firth enters into a dialogue with the existing body of literature on the book of Joshua. Interested readers of the Bible, theological students, pastors, Old Testament scholars, and theologians will benefit a lot by reading this commentary and acquaint themselves with the intriguing book of Joshua.

—**S. D. Snyman,** *University of the Free State*

David Firth is one of the leading Old Testament scholars active today and he has turned his attention to the book of Joshua within the context of the canon. I enthusiastically recommend this commentary because of its sensitive literary reading of the book as well as its insightful theological analysis. Joshua is often ignored or avoided these days by Christians because of its violence, but Firth helps us appreciate its importance to our theology and faith.

—**Tremper Longman III,** *Westmont College*

David Firth's Joshua commentary reveals depth of scholarship married to a highly readable writing style that engages the text and its scholarship clearly and with economy. He opens up the book's difficulties as well as its surprises, attentive to historical context and narrative art. His approach to Joshua as a "bridge" book highlights its canonical connections, including connections to the New Testament as well as readers today. Accessible. Engaging. Faithful. A great addition to the study of Joshua; I'd recommend it to my seminary students, to pastors, and to interested laypeople.

—**Lissa M. Wray Beal,** *Providence Theological Seminary, Otterburne, Canada*

JOSHUA

JOSHUA

Evangelical Biblical Theology Commentary

General Editors

T. Desmond Alexander, Thomas R. Schreiner,
Andreas J. Köstenberger

Assistant Editors

James M. Hamilton, Kenneth A. Mathews,
Terry L. Wilder

David G. Firth

 LEXHAM
ACADEMIC

Joshua
Evangelical Biblical Theology Commentary

Lexham Academic, an imprint of Lexham Press
1313 Commercial St., Bellingham, WA 98225
LexhamPress.com

Print ISBN 9781683594406
Library of Congress Control Number 2020948488

General Editors: T. Desmond Alexander, Thomas R. Schreiner, Andreas J. Köstenberger
Assistant Editors: James M. Hamilton, Kenneth A. Mathews, Terry L. Wilder
Lexham Editorial: Derek Brown, Kelsey Matthews, Elliot Ritzema, Abigail Salinger, Abigail Stocker, Jessi Strong
Cover Design: Joshua Hunt
Typesetting: ProjectLuz.com

CONTENTS

GENERAL EDITORS' PREFACE

I n recent years biblical theology has seen a remarkable resurgence. Whereas, in 1970, Brevard Childs wrote *Biblical Theology in Crisis*, the quest for the Bible's own theology has witnessed increasing vitality since Childs prematurely decried the demise of the movement. Nowhere has this been truer than in evangelical circles. It could be argued that evangelicals, with their commitment to biblical inerrancy and inspiration, are perfectly positioned to explore the Bible's unified message. At the same time, as D. A. Carson has aptly noted, perhaps the greatest challenge faced by biblical theologians is how to handle the Bible's manifest diversity and how to navigate the tension between its unity and diversity in a way that does justice to both.[1]

What is biblical theology? And how is biblical theology different from related disciplines such as systematic theology? These two exceedingly important questions must be answered by anyone who would make a significant contribution to the discipline. Regarding the first question, the most basic answer might assert that biblical theology, in essence, is *the theology of the Bible*, that is, the theology expressed by the respective writers of the various biblical books *on their own terms* and *in their own historical contexts*. Biblical theology is the attempt to understand and embrace *the interpretive perspective of the biblical authors*. What is more, biblical theology is the theology of the *entire* Bible, an exercise in *whole-Bible theology*. For this reason biblical theology is not just a modern academic discipline; its roots are found already in the use of earlier Old Testament portions

---

[1] D. A. Carson, "New Testament Theology," in *DLNT* 810.

in later Old Testament writings and in the use of the Old Testament in the New.

Biblical theology thus involves a close study of *the use of the Old Testament in the Old Testament* (that is, the use of, say, Deuteronomy by Jeremiah, or of the Pentateuch by Isaiah). Biblical theology also entails the investigation of *the use of the Old Testament in the New*, both in terms of individual passages and in terms of larger Christological or soteriological themes. Biblical theology may proceed *book by book*, trace *central themes* in Scripture, or seek to place the contributions of individual biblical writers within the framework of the Bible's larger overarching *metanarrative*, that is, the Bible's developing story from Genesis through Revelation at whose core is *salvation* or *redemptive history*, the account of God's dealings with humanity and his people Israel and the church from creation to new creation.

In this quest for the Bible's own theology, we will be helped by the inquiries of those who have gone before us in the *history of the church*. While we can profitably study the efforts of interpreters over the entire sweep of the history of biblical interpretation since patristic times, we can also benefit from the labors of scholars since J. P. Gabler, whose programmatic inaugural address at the University of Altdorf, Germany, in 1787 marks the inception of the discipline in modern times. Gabler's address bore the title "On the Correct Distinction between Dogmatic and Biblical Theology and the Right Definition of Their Goals."[2] While few (if any) within evangelicalism would fully identify with Gabler's program, the proper distinction between dogmatic and biblical theology (that is, between biblical and systematic theology) continues to be an important issue to be adjudicated by practitioners of both disciplines, and especially biblical theology. We have already defined biblical theology as whole-Bible theology, describing the theology of the various biblical books *on their own terms* and *in their own historical contexts*. Systematic theology, by contrast, is more topically oriented and focused on contemporary contextualization. While there are different ways in which the relationship between biblical and systematic theology can be construed, maintaining a proper distinction between the two disciplines arguably continues to be vital if both are to achieve their objectives.

---

[2] The original Latin title was *Oratio de iusto discrimine theologiae biblicae et dogmaticae regundisque recte utriusque finibus.*

The present set of volumes constitutes an ambitious project, seeking to explore the theology of the Bible in considerable depth, spanning both Testaments. Authors come from a variety of backgrounds and perspectives, though all affirm the inerrancy and inspiration of Scripture. United in their high view of Scripture and in their belief in the underlying unity of Scripture, which is ultimately grounded in the unity of God himself, each author explores the contribution of a given book or group of books to the theology of Scripture as a whole. While conceived as stand-alone volumes, each volume thus also makes a contribution to the larger whole. All volumes provide a discussion of introductory matters, including the historical setting and the literary structure of a given book of Scripture. Also included is an exegetical treatment of all the relevant passages in succinct commentary-style format. The biblical theology approach of the series will also inform and play a role in the commentary proper. The commentator permits a discussion between the commentary proper and the biblical theology it reflects by a series of cross-references.

The major contribution of each volume, however, is a thorough discussion of the most important themes of the biblical book in relation to the canon as a whole. This format allows each contributor to ground biblical theology, as is proper, in an appropriate appraisal of the relevant historical and literary features of a particular book in Scripture while at the same time focusing on its major theological contribution to the entire Christian canon in the context of the larger salvation-historical metanarrative of Scripture. Within this overall format, there will be room for each individual contributor to explore the major themes of his or her particular corpus in the way he or she sees most appropriate for the material under consideration. For some books of the Bible, it may be best to have these theological themes set out in advance of the exegetical commentary. For other books it may be better to explain the theological themes after the commentary. Consequently, each contributor has the freedom to order these sections as best suits the biblical material under consideration so that the discussion of biblical-theological themes may precede or follow the exegetical commentary.

This format, in itself, would already be a valuable contribution to biblical theology. But other series try to accomplish a survey of the Bible's theology as well. What distinguishes the present series is its orientation toward Christian proclamation. This is the Evangelical Biblical Theology Commentary series! As a result, the ultimate purpose of this set of volumes is not exclusively, or even primarily, academic. Rather, we seek to relate biblical theology to our own lives and to the life of the church. Our desire is to equip those in Christian ministry who are called by God to preach and teach the precious truths of Scripture to their congregations, both in North America and in a global context.

The base translation for the Evangelical Biblical Theology Commentary series is the Christian Standard Bible (csb). The csb places equal value on faithfulness to the original languages and readability for a modern audience. The contributors, however, have the liberty to differ with the csb as they comment on the biblical text. Note that, in the csb, OT passages that are quoted in the NT are set in boldface type.

We hope and pray that the forty volumes of this series, once completed, will bear witness to the unity in diversity of the canon of Scripture as they probe the individual contributions of each of its sixty-six books. The authors and editors are united in their desire that in so doing the series will magnify the name of Christ and bring glory to the triune God who revealed himself in Scripture so that everyone who calls on the name of the Lord will be saved—to the glory of God the Father and his Son, the Lord Jesus Christ, under the illumination of the Holy Spirit, and for the good of his church. To God alone be the glory: *soli Deo gloria*.

DEDICATION

FOR EMMA INESON

ACKNOWLEDGMENTS

Writing a commentary such as this is simultaneously and individual and communal task. It is individual because a commentator must wrestle with all the dimensions of the text and come to conclusions about it. Although Joshua is widely regarded as a "difficult" text, I have found this to be an enriching process, even if much of this occurred in the isolation of my study. But it is also a communal task because each of us engages with and is supported by a range of people who encourage, pray and challenge us about the work we do. Although I will undoubtedly miss some who deserve my thanks it is right that at least some attempt is made to acknowledge those who have journeyed with me.

First, I need to acknowledge Ray McClenden and Chris Cowan who worked with me in the earlier stages of writing the commentary, especially to Chris who proof read the whole for me, making many suggestions about points that would make it more readable. Since the commentary moved to Lexham Press, Derek Brown has ably continued this work in ushering the work towards publication.

Second, I wish to thank the community at Trinity College Bristol and Bristol Baptist College. They welcomed me early in the writing phase and who supported me as I continued to research and write, including those students who took my classes on Joshua and helped me to work through some of my earlier conclusions and to clarify other points. But perhaps the most important element here was the way the faculty made me welcome so that I knew I had joined a community that was about academic rigor and faithful witness. Most notably, I need to thank our then principal, Dr Emma Ineson, who made Trinity such an encouraging place to work. Delays in publication because of a change of publisher meant that I was not able to give her a copy of this as she left to become Bishop of Penrith, but I hope that even if a little later than I would have hoped, the dedication of this to her can at least represent an appropriate word of thanks.

Finally, and aware that others could also be mentioned, I need to thank my wife Lynne who has continued to support and encourage me in my work. She embodies the truth that a prudent wife is a gift of God (Prov. 19:14).

David Firth
August 2020

LIST OF ABBREVIATIONS

ANE	ancient Near Eastern
BA	*Biblical Archaeologist*
BASOR	*Bulletin of the American Schools of Oriental Research*
BBR	*Bulletin for Biblical Research*
BHS	*Biblia Hebraica Stuttgartensia*, ed. Karl Elliger and Wilhelm Rudolph. Stuttgart: Deutsche Bibelgesellschaft, 1983.
BTB	*Biblical Theology Bulletin*
CBQ	*Catholic Biblical Quarterly*
cf.	compare
CSB	Christian Standard Bible
CTJ	*Calvin Theological Journal*
DCH	*The Dictionary of Classical Hebrew*, ed. D. J. A. Clines. 8 vols. Sheffield: Sheffield Academic Press, 1993–2011.
e.g.	for example
ESV	English Standard Version
ET	English translation
GKC	*Gesenius' Hebrew Grammar*, ed. E. Kautzch, tr. A. E. Cowley
HUCA	*Hebrew Union College Annual*
i.e.	that is
IEJ	*Israel Exploration Journal*
JBL	*Journal of Biblical Literature*
JBQ	*Jewish Bible Quarterly*
JESOT	*Journal for the Evangelical Study of the Old Testament*
JETS	*Journal of the Evangelical Theological Society*
JSOT	*Journal for the Study of the Old Testament*
lit.	literally

LXX	Septuagint (Greek) text of the Old Testament
mss	manuscripts
MT	Masoretic (Hebrew) text of the Old Testament
NIDOTTE	*New International Dictionary of Old Testament Theology and Exegesis,* 5 vols., ed. Willem A. VanGemeren (Carlisle: Paternoster, 1997).
NIV	New International Version
NIVAC	NIV Application Commentary
OG	Old Greek
OTE	*Old Testament Essays*
ResQ	*Restoration Quarterly*
Syr	Syriac
Tg	Targum
TynBul	*Tyndale Bulletin*
VT	*Vetus Testamentum*
v(v).	verse(s)
WBC	Word Biblical Commentary
WTJ	*Westminster Theological Journal*
ZAW	*Zeitschrift für die alttestamentliche Wissenschaft*

INTRODUCTION

T he book of Joshua stands at an important point of transition both in the life of Israel and within the canon that reflects on that life. Appreciation of this shared transition is crucial if we are to read this text and continue to hear it as Scripture today. These points of transition have also played an important role in how the book has been understood through the years, not only in recent critical interpretation but also in the history of Christian interpretation.

The transitional function of the book is flagged by its opening verses, declaring that Moses was dead and Joshua was therefore to lead Israel into the land God was giving them. Moses had been the pivotal human figure in the Pentateuch, the one who led Israel out from Egypt and through whom the great body of God's teaching at Sinai had been delivered. But Moses had died outside the land (Deut 34). Of the great promises to Abraham of blessing, a divine-human relationship, posterity, and land (which can be traced back to Gen 12:1–3), the promise of land remains unfulfilled by the end of Deuteronomy.[1] So do we read Joshua as the completion of the promises from the Pentateuch? If so, does it matter that we no longer have Moses as the key figure? Or do we read Joshua as initiating something new in Israel's life? If so, are we to read it primarily in terms of what follows?

The answers to these questions have largely shaped the interpretation of this book. Although there are no simple answers to the questions themselves, the view developed here is that Joshua is a bridge text. Janus-like,

---

[1] See David J. A. Clines, *The Theme of the Pentateuch* (Sheffield: JSOT Press, 1978), 29; and T. Desmond Alexander, *From Paradise to the Promised Land: An Introduction to the Main Themes of the Pentateuch* (Carlisle: Paternoster, 1995), 33–47.

it looks back to the Pentateuch and the themes developed there while regarding itself as a discrete work, and it also anticipates Israel's life in the land, planting seeds for a larger story while still being complete in itself. Overemphasizing either of these perspectives leads to a distortion in how this text is read. If we primarily look at its role in bringing the Pentateuch's themes to completion, we underplay its preparation for what follows. Conversely, if we primarily look at how it prepares for events that follow, then we underplay its important links to what has gone before. We need instead to read Joshua as a distinctive work that relates both to what has gone before and what comes after, but without subsuming it into either.

I. Date, Authorship, and Purpose

Although Jewish tradition assigned authorship of the book to Joshua himself,[2] there is clear evidence within the book that, even though Joshua is reported as having either written certain documents (Josh 24:26) or at least initiated their writing (18:1–10), the book itself must have been completed at a later date. Most obviously, the book records Joshua's death and also comments on the period after it (24:29–31). This cannot have come from Joshua himself since it clearly looks back on his time.

Moreover, there are sixteen times when the phrase "until this day" occurs in the book. Apart from instances where it is spoken by someone within the narrative (e.g., Caleb in 14:11), all occurrences of this statement exceed the horizon of Joshua's own life.[3] The actual date presupposed by these various statements is often quite vague, and for the most part is simply a time after Israel's entry into the land. However, the statement in 15:63 (= Judg 1:21) about the continued control of Jerusalem by the Jebusites ceased to be true following David's capture of the city (2 Sam 5:6–10).[4] If all the "until this day" statements came from one hand (a point not universally agreed upon), then at least an early edition of the book needs to have been completed by then. How much earlier than the time of David this could have been is not clear, but it is important to note that

---

[2] See *Baba Bathra* 15a; this position is still favored by Adolph L. Harstad, *Joshua* (St. Louis: Concordia, 2004), 8–9.

[3] See the table in Brian Neil Peterson, *The Authors of the Deuteronomistic History: Locating a Tradition in Ancient Israel* (Minneapolis: Fortress, 2014), 81–82.

[4] The phrase occurs a further six times in Deuteronomy and thirty times in Judges–2 Kings.

written materials in the book reach back into the second millennium. If these materials came from diverse hands, then the most we could say is that the source material behind Joshua 15 is relatively early. However, the statement in 13:13 could also be read as describing conditions prior to David's ascension to the throne of Judah (cf. 1 Sam 27:8), and so would indicate that several of the "until this day" statements must be fairly early. Moreover, since Joshua 13 and 15 seem to reflect different source materials, then it seems most likely that the same editorial hand has brought these comments together. Moving on to Josh 16:10, the reference there about Gezer ceased to be true by the time of Solomon (1 Kgs 9:15–16), though of course this would also have been true in the time of David. We cannot say anything more specific about the other uses of this phrase in Joshua, but since those we can locate indicate an early date for at least key source materials on which the author has drawn, the probability must exist that the other occurrences of this statement are also quite early.[5] If so, and recognizing that the "until this day" formula is scattered across the whole book and not just the sections associated with the land allocation that can be dated, then we have good reason to think that at least an early edition of the book existed by the time of David.

How much earlier than David this material existed is more difficult to determine, but there are clues that we should look to the early part of David's reign for the initial composition of the book. There are several features indicating the author was particularly familiar with the south of Israel but considerably less familiar with the north. The allotments for the tribes in the far north (Zebulun, Issachar, Asher, and Naphtali; 19:10–39) are all described quite vaguely, whereas those of Judah (15:1–63) and Benjamin (18:11–28) are outlined in great detail. The allotment for Dan (19:40–48) is also fairly vague, but this is because the book already knows of Dan's failure to take their allotment and that they had therefore moved to the far north. This movement must have been relatively early, yet still at some point after Samson (Judg 13–16) since his work as a judge is set in the area Dan was initially allotted. This information means we cannot place the book's composition too close to the entry into the land, especially since the statement in Josh 24:31 can also be taken as suggesting that the author knows about many of the events described in Judges.

[5] Indeed, Peterson, *Authors*, 91–96, argues that all of these references make the most sense by the time of David.

This combination—of awareness of the geography of the south but not the north and the need to allow for at least a significant portion of the events described in Judges to have passed—would bring us to the early period of the monarchy as the most likely point for initial composition. Such a conclusion fits with what I have noted about the phrase "until this day," while locating the author in either the central highlands or south of the country.[6]

Composition during the time of David may also be indicated by the interest the book shows in otherwise obscure locations that were important for his period in the wilderness (e.g., Hormah in Josh 15:29, cf. 1 Sam 30:30; Ziph in Josh 15:24, cf. 1 Sam 23:13). We might also note that the survival of the Archites (Josh 16:2), seemingly a Canaanite group, becomes important when Hushai the Archite emerges as an important figure in David's court (2 Sam 15:32–37; 16:15–17:16). Finally, the covenant with the Gibeonites (Josh 9) provides the crucial background to events in 2 Sam 21:1–14. Although Gibeon's importance emerges at other key points (e.g., Josh 10:1–5; 2 Sam 2:12–17; 1 Kgs 9:1–2), the covenant between Israel and Gibeon is of particular importance for David's reign. It is possible to speculate more precisely than this,[7] but the gains in doing so are slight and the evidence less secure. However, a reasonably secure conclusion is that at least an early edition of the book of Joshua came into being among those associated with David's court. Therefore, it provides important background to David's reign even as it also explores Israel's origins in the land.

Although these clues point to David's court as the most likely point of origin for the book, we should not assume that the book is simply an apology for David. It is clear from an overview of its contents that Joshua is concerned with much more than David's court. However, consistent with its bridging function noted above, it aims to show how the themes left incomplete from the Pentateuch are brought to their conclusion while also anticipating events that would be important for the time of

---

[6] H. J. Koorevaar, *De Opbouw van het Boek Jozua* (Heverlee: Centrum voor Bijbelse Vorming-Belgie, 1990), 255–61, argues that because the book displays no knowledge of the destruction of Shiloh, it cannot have been composed before this happened. Although the evidence considered here cannot conclusively rule this out, the extent of the interest in the David tradition suggests we need to date the book almost a century after this, especially as an argument from silence is always risky.

[7] E.g., the reference to Geshur and Maacah in Josh 13:13 can be linked to 2 Sam 3:3 and 13:37–38.

David. Further, as Peterson has argued, the circles in David's court that brought this material together probably established a pattern for continued reflection on it, something that can explain both the interrelated nature of the whole of Joshua–Kings and also the distinctive nature of each book within that collection.[8]

The clues noted above show that the book prepares us for events from David's reign. These, along with the migration of the tribe of Dan to the far north, are key elements in which the book looks forward.

The book's role in bringing the story of the Pentateuch to a close is perhaps better known, but it is worth noting that the book's current shape emphasizes the fulfillment of the land promise as God, through Joshua, grants Israel the land. Hence, Joshua 1 deliberately reflects on the land promise in light of Moses' death in Deuteronomy 34 while also looking back to events in Numbers 21. This chapter also shows awareness of other passages in Deuteronomy, but the key point to note at this point is that it intentionally joins Joshua to the Pentateuch. Likewise, the recital of Israel's earlier history in Joshua 24 deliberately reaches back to the patriarchs (Gen 12–50) to stress God's faithfulness in fulfilling the land promise. The one key promise that remained unfulfilled in the Pentateuch has thus come to its fulfillment, and Israel as a whole could commit themselves to this faithful God as a result. The covenant ceremony in Josh 8:30–35 thus brings the promise of the Pentateuch to a satisfactory conclusion while also reminding later generations of the fact that they too need to make this same decision to serve Yahweh alone, a reminder that is of particular importance after the sobering events from the period of the judges. Joshua fulfills its key purposes precisely because it is a bridging text.

This high level of integration thus suggests that, even if we cannot specifically name the author or authors of the book, it is clear that the final text is not simply a collation of sources, but rather an intentionally structured and presented whole, and it needs to be read as such.

II. Joshua and the Canon

Joshua's function as a bridging text has also led to two key ways in which scholars have read it relative to the works around it, one way primarily

---

[8] For a summary, see Peterson, *Authors*, 297–302.

looking back (as part of a Hexateuch) and the other primarily looking forward (as part of a Deuteronomistic History). Not surprisingly, there is value in both of these approaches, though neither fully addresses the function of the book. We need, however, to note each briefly before commenting on Joshua's connections to the wider canon in order to understand how it contributes to wider discussions in biblical theology.

A. JOSHUA AS THE CONCLUSION TO THE HEXATEUCH

Following the establishment of the Documentary Hypothesis as the dominant model for reading the Pentateuch in the late nineteenth century, one prevailing way of reading Joshua was to assume that the principal sources behind this model (JEDP) continued into Joshua. This is because it was thought unlikely that the main story line of the Pentateuch would end at the close of Deuteronomy, since by that point Israel had taken control of territory east of the Jordan, but not the land actually promised to its west.[9] Given that chapters 13–21 refer primarily to events recounted in Numbers (almost all P on this analysis), then these chapters could also be assigned to P. Chapters 1–12 were usually assigned to JE (since disentangling these sources here was too difficult), but with such significant editing by D that the value of this source analysis was rendered doubtful. Chapter 22 was also usually assigned to P (though verses 1–8 are more probably D on this analysis), while chapter 23 was D. Chapter 24, which is difficult to align with any of these sources, might represent material from another source.

The seeming triumph of Martin Noth's proposal of a Deuteronomistic History (see section B below) was largely seen to have overturned this model for reading Joshua. Given that the majority of contemporary pentateuchal critics no longer work with this model (most European scholars now seem content to divide the Pentateuch into P and non-P),[10] it might seem this approach is now passé. Moreover, the "Hexateuch" (i.e., Genesis–Joshua) has only ever been a scholarly construct, not something recognized in any system for organizing the canon of the Old Testament. There is, nevertheless, still good reason to note this approach even if

---

[9] Adrian H. W. Curtis, *Joshua* (Sheffield: Sheffield Academic Press, 1994), 15.

[10] This is not the place for an overview of current approaches to the Pentateuch. For a helpful overview, see Gordon J. Wenham, *Exploring the Old Testament Volume 1: The Pentateuch* (London: SPCK, 2003), 159–86.

only because it stressed the connections between Joshua and the rest of the Pentateuch.

Although he was broadly working with the source-critical model noted above, Gerhard von Rad took up the importance of reading Joshua in light of the Pentateuch with characteristic elegance.[11] A particularly noteworthy aspect of his study was that he gave attention to the final form of the Hexateuch, noting that the history recounted in this grand work was essentially a statement of Israel's faith, even if his larger concern was with how the Hexateuch developed. What particularly interested von Rad was the fact that the Hexateuch provided a "summary of the principal facts of God's redemptive activity."[12] What he appreciated, therefore, was the importance of seeing Joshua as the point where the promises of God to Abraham reached their conclusion.

Although seeing Joshua as part of a Hexateuch fell out of favor following the rise of Noth's theory of the Deuteronomistic History, it has been revived as a model for reading Joshua in recent years by Pekka Pitkänen.[13] Pitkänen dates the material in Joshua quite early. His main concern has been with the composition of this material, for which he has developed a complex model, rather than developing its theological elements.[14] Nevertheless, his approach demonstrates the continued importance of seeing Joshua in dialogue with the whole Pentateuch.

Reading Joshua in light of the Pentateuch is theologically helpful, but the category of a Hexateuch remains problematic in that it treats all six books as a single work. However, Joshua distinguishes itself from the Pentateuch even as it looks back to it. Joshua himself is told to meditate upon the Torah (1:8), accordingly regarding at least some pentateuchal material (in that the reference there might only be to Deuteronomy) as a separate and authoritative document. Likewise, when Joshua approaches the eastern tribes about crossing the Jordan to enable the western tribes to receive their allotment (1:13), or when Caleb approaches Joshua to

---

[11] Gerhard von Rad, "The Form-Critical Problem of the Hexateuch," in von Rad, *The Problem of the Hexateuch and Other Essays* (London: Oliver & Boyd, 1966), 1–78; and "The Promised Land and Yahweh's Land in the Hexateuch" in *The Problem*, 79–93.

[12] Von Rad, "Form-Critical Problem," 2.

[13] Pekka Pitkänen, "Reading Genesis-Joshua as a Unified Document from an Early Date: A Settler Colonial Perspective," *BTB* 45 (2015): 3–31; and Pitkänen, "Priestly Legal Tradition in Joshua and the Composition of the Pentateuch and Joshua," *OTE* 29 (2016): 318–35.

[14] For a helpful summary diagram, see Pitkänen, "Priestly Legal Tradition," 329.

receive his (14:6–12), this is done on the basis of an existing set of traditions found in Numbers. And, of course, it is these earlier promises that Joshua can insist were fulfilled (21:43–45; 23:14), though it is also possible to use these promises for looking to what God will do if Israel is unfaithful. These examples indicate that Joshua completes promises made in the Pentateuch, but is nevertheless separate from it in that it depends on the pentateuchal material as an authoritative source rather than as a direct continuation of it.

B. JOSHUA AS PART OF THE DEUTERONOMISTIC HISTORY

A far more common approach to Joshua now is to see it as part of a Deuteronomistic History, an approach that can largely be traced back to the influential study of Martin Noth.[15] Noth argued that Joshua–Kings, together with parts of Deuteronomy, comprised a single work of history that was completed in the exile, though drawing on older source materials, with the goal of explaining the Babylonian exile. Noth's original theory has been taken up and developed in a range of ways, with debates over whether the history was a largely unified work or has gone through various redactions (including questions about when it was completed), and whether it offers a pessimistic or hopeful evaluation of Israel's position in the exile.[16] One problem that emerges from these alternatives is that remarkably diverse approaches to reading these texts are all grouped together under the one label, held together by the fact that they look at how Joshua prepares for much that follows.

This is not the place for evaluating this hypothesis as a whole. As with the Hexateuch model, it does have some important strengths. Most obviously, as noted above, there are points where material in Joshua prepares for events told in later books. Apart from the points previously noted, we might also observe the curse that Joshua pronounces on the one who rebuilds Jericho (Josh 6:26), which finds a specific fulfillment in 1 Kgs 16:34. These examples show that although Joshua is narrated by

---

[15] Martin Noth, *The Deuteronomistic History*, 2nd ed. (Sheffield: Sheffield Academic Press, 2001). The German original appeared in 1943. An unfortunate side effect of the prominence given to this theory is that his work on the Chronicler's history, which was an integral part of his original work, was translated separately into English.

[16] The various theories are helpfully summarized by Peterson, *Authors*, 7–60. See also Thomas Römer, *The So-Called Deuteronomistic History: A Sociological, Historical and Literary Introduction* (London: T&T Clark, 2007) for a cautious evaluation of the theory.

looking back at the events of Israel's entry into the land, it also serves to look beyond that time and prepare for events later in Israel's story. Of course, this does not explain the literary relationship between these texts. If various elements in Joshua take us to the time of David, is the reference in Kings looking back to an existing text more or less the same as our Joshua, or is this evidence of continued writing in which material found in Joshua was composed to explain later events?[17]

Another strength of this model is that it looks to Deuteronomy as a key theological resource for Joshua—a key weakness in the Hexateuch model. That is, this model accepts the dependence of Joshua on existing pentateuchal materials, even if different approaches within this model sometimes treat the material in Deuteronomy as being composed for this history. It is, however, entirely possible to regard Deuteronomy as an existing body of material that Joshua references. This seems more consistent with how the book now functions, and there are certainly points where even its diction, and not only its theological themes, seem to emerge from Deuteronomy (e.g., Joshua 23). Deuteronomy is thus an undoubtedly important dialogue partner for Joshua, as are the remaining books in the Deuteronomistic History.

Nevertheless, there are significant weaknesses with this model that are particularly important for interpreting Joshua. Perhaps the most important (as already noted) is that the bulk of Joshua 13–21 has little if any interest in "Deuteronomistic" material, engaging instead with material from Numbers, while Joshua 24 (especially in the historical recital in vv. 1–12) draws on much of the Pentateuch, though without obvious reference to Deuteronomy. Joshua 22 does seem to draw on both, but in discrete sections, so that verses 1–8 draw on Deuteronomy but the rest of the chapter looks to Numbers. Such observations immediately cast doubt on the value of describing this material as "Deuteronomistic." Indeed, as Pitkänen has argued, this mixture of Priestly and Deuteronomistic material is unique among these books.[18] This raises the question of whether "Deuteronomistic" is a helpful label for describing Joshua, given that roughly half the book shows no particular interest in material that might reasonably be described by this label.

---

[17] This does not have to bear on the question of history; the dating of source materials that might have been used is a separate issue from the literary relationship of the texts as we now have them.

[18] Pitkänen, "Priestly Legal Tradition."

Moreover, this model has tended to flatten the different books of the Former Prophets so that their distinctiveness is not always seen, though there are clear differences between Joshua and the rest of Judges–Kings. Joshua has no interest in the Spirit of God or of wisdom, even though both of these are important themes in Judges–Kings, and there are points where the narrative style of Joshua is clearly different too.[19]

Reading Joshua within a Deuteronomistic History is thus helpful as a means of seeing it as part of a larger story into which it has been integrated, but it does not fully recognize the distinctive features of the book and therefore risks flattening its content and themes into one particular frame of reference. By contrast, seeing it as a bridging work that has been taken up into a larger story enables the benefits of both the Hexateuch and Deuteronomistic History models to be seen without either coming to dominate interpretation.[20]

C. JOSHUA AND THE WIDER CANON OF SCRIPTURE

Whereas discussions of the Hexateuch and Deuteronomistic History are largely concerned with understanding the initial setting of the book, reflection on Joshua in light of the wider canon (both OT and NT) is principally concerned with how material in Joshua is taken up in the rest of the Bible. This comes out of its bridging function while also noting that, in both the Hebrew canonical structure and the Greek one (which has shaped our English Bibles), Joshua is given prominence by being placed at the head of a larger story that knows of the significant material that precedes it. Whereas the Hebrew tradition reads Joshua as the first book of the Former Prophets, the Greek canon places it as the first volume in a series of historical books. Regardless of the canonical structure adopted, a key element is that Joshua immediately follows the events of the Pentateuch. Again, the bridging function is crucial.

Given the importance of the exodus in the theology of the Old Testament, it is not surprising that Joshua is a less prominent text for

---

[19] On some elements of narrative distinctiveness, see David G. Firth, "Disorienting Readers in Joshua 1.1–5.12," *JSOT* 41 (2017): 413–30. See also "Joshua as Narrative" below.

[20] For a slightly fuller treatment of literary criticism and Joshua while recognizing its contested nature, see J. Gordon McConville, *Joshua: Crossing Divides* (London: T&T Clark, 2017), 18–27. A model for reading Joshua not dissimilar to that proposed here is H. J. Koorevaar, "The Book of Joshua and the Hypothesis of the Deuteronomistic History: Indications for an Open Serial Model," in *The Book of Joshua*, ed. Ed Noort (Leuven: Peeters, 2012), 219–32.

reflection both there and in the New Testament. But reference to it is made at key points, demonstrating continued reflection on it. The traditions in Joshua are taken up in two key directions within the balance of the Old Testament—either to demonstrate the faithfulness of God in fulfilling his promises·or to highlight the sin of the generation that entered the land.

Emphases on the faithfulness of God can be seen in the Latter Prophets, Psalms, and Nehemiah. In Amos 2:9, God points out that he had destroyed the Amorite who had been before Israel. Although the sequence in Amos 2:9-11 is slightly odd (in that it seems to describe Israel's entry into the land before the exodus), this is probably because Amos wants to highlight God's faithfulness in the provision of the very land that Israel was now defiling.[21] Likewise, reference to Gilgal in Amos 4:4 and 5:5 demonstrates awareness of the importance of that site as a sanctuary, something that presumes knowledge of the crossing of the Jordan and the establishment of the cairn there (Josh 3–4).[22] Amos' point is that the northern kingdom had failed to live in light of the faithfulness of God in bringing Israel into the land and the mechanisms that God had provided for Israel to remember this. This is not an issue that was unique to the northern kingdom, because Mic 6:5 also remembers the crossing of the Jordan as evidence of God's faithfulness, something that Judah was ignoring.

The Psalms likewise remember themes from Joshua as evidence of God's faithfulness, though again the references are fairly brief. Although most are in the historical psalms, there is an important allusion in Ps 47:1-4. In these verses, the importance of Yahweh's reign over all the peoples is affirmed, with the gift of the land to Israel as particular evidence of his sovereignty. The claim of verse 8, that God reigns over the nations, is thus particularly rooted in the experience of Israel receiving the land. Similarly, Ps 114:3-6 reflects on the crossing of the Jordan as evidence that all the earth should tremble before the God of Jacob, who is Lord of all the earth. Pss 78:54-55; 105:44-45; and 135:11-12 all point to God's faithfulness in the provision of the land as a reason for Israel to continue in faithful obedience and praise. These references, along with Neh 9:24-25, all look to Joshua as a key point of reference that establishes

---

[21] So David Allan Hubbard, *Joel and Amos: An Introduction and Commentary* (Leicester: Inter-Varsity Press, 1989), 143.

[22] Arguably, a similar reference underlies Hos 6:7, but as the exegesis of this verse is much disputed it is not included here.

God's faithfulness, and thus provide reasons why Israel should also have been faithful.

Although Joshua can be used to point to the faithfulness of God, reference to it can also be made to stress the failures of the generation that entered the land. The possibility of understanding Joshua as part of a history of failure is already hinted at in some of the texts noted above. Ps 78:56–58 includes a summary of a history of provoking God that is probably intended to be traced back to the first generation in the land. Reference to the sanctuary at Shiloh presumes knowledge of Josh 18:1, though it is more concerned with events in 1 Sam 4:1b–7:1. More particularly, Ps 106:34–39 looks back to the failure of the first generation in the land to destroy (שמד) the previous inhabitants, while noting that Israel was gradually ensnared by the idols of the peoples there. This passage clearly reflects on the comments scattered through Joshua about the continued existence of some Canaanite groups (Josh 15:63; 16:10; 17:12–13; 19:47), while also reflecting on the challenge posed by Joshua to all those gathered at Shechem to remove foreign gods and serve Yahweh alone (Josh 24:1–28). Such a compressed treatment does not leave room for the possibility that foreign peoples could indeed be integrated into Israel while stressing that the danger was always with the worship of other gods.

Although there are no indisputable citations of Joshua in the New Testament,[23] there are key points where themes from Joshua are taken up. The patterns in the Old Testament noted above continue into the New. Thus, reflection on God's faithfulness through Joshua can be seen in Stephen's speech to the council in Jerusalem. In Acts 7:45 he points to the fact that Israel had brought the tabernacle with them into the land because God had driven out the nations, presuming some knowledge of Josh 3:13–17 and 18:1, though the reference is really broad enough to encompass much of the book. Like several of the texts noted above, Stephen draws on this to point to failures within Israel, so he draws on Joshua from within this wider tradition. Stephen also makes a more specific allusion to Josh 24:32 earlier in his speech when he notes Joseph's burial (Acts 7:16), though this reference too builds to his larger accusation.[24]

---

[23] Hebrews 13:5b could be a citation from Josh 1:5, but given that the text in Joshua is itself taken from Deut 31:6 the primary reference is probably to Deuteronomy (with, of course, echoes in Joshua).

[24] A more oblique reference to Josh 24:32 is found in John 4:5, but there it is presented as a simple statement of fact.

An intriguing allusion to Josh 7:19 occurs in John 9:24, where the Pharisees challenge the man born blind to "give glory to God." Joshua uses the same phrase when challenging Achan to tell the truth about his sin, the implication being that the man has hidden sin that needs to be revealed. However, in a typical Johannine irony it is the Pharisees who have unrecognized sin, as the man challenges them to explain how Jesus could have healed him if he were the sort of sinner they believed. In this instance, the Pharisees demonstrate that they know the content of the Scriptures but misapply them.

Just as the Old Testament could point to failures in the generation that entered the land, so also Heb 4:8 looks back to the partial nature of Israel's occupation of the land as a point where Israel did not fully achieve the rest God intended for them.

The most important development found in the New Testament's appropriation of Joshua is focused on the character of Rahab. She occurs first in Matthew's genealogy of Jesus (Matt 1:5) as one of a group of women (with Tamar, Ruth, and Bathsheba) who would appear to be inappropriate for the lineage of the Messiah and yet whose presence demonstrates the fact that God's grace in Christ encompasses all people. Indeed, within Matthew there is a balance between the international nature of Jesus' genealogy at the beginning of the Gospel and the commission to make disciples of the nations (Matt 28:16–20) at the end. Rahab is also an important example in Heb 11:30–31 on account of her faith that was expressed within the fall of Jericho. Here, the writer telescopes Joshua 2 and 6 by linking her faith in hiding the spies to her deliverance when the city walls collapsed. Intriguingly, the writer suggests that the others perished because of disobedience. This indicates a line of interpretation that understood destruction of the city to be the maximum possible punishment, but not a necessary one. This combination of Joshua 2 and 6 is also apparent in Jas 2:25, where James stresses the fact that Rahab's faith was shown by her actions in receiving the spies and sending them off by a different route.

These three New Testament books are united in making explicit something that is otherwise only implicit in Joshua itself—that there was always the possibility of the Canaanite population being integrated into Israel on the basis of faith. The continued presence of non-Israelites in the land by the end of Joshua was both a threat and an opportunity, and the reception of Joshua in the rest of Scripture continues to recognize that both of these possibilities continued to work themselves out in the life of Israel.[25]

III. The Genre of Joshua

Central to the task of interpreting any text is determining its genre. The nature of genre is a complex issue because it relates to a series of decisions any author makes when composing a text as well as those decisions an audience is capable of making when seeking to interpret that text. Moreover, genre is always fluid to some extent because changes in culture and language mean that scope exists for existing genres to develop in new ways that might not have been available to an earlier generation, even while remaining true to the basics of that genre.[26] Nevertheless, for a text to communicate there is always some interplay between it and its readers as they assign some genre to it. Although this is often done intuitively, a more effective approach is for readers to seek consciously to determine a text's genre. In this model, we acknowledge that the text's author is not accessible to us to answer the question of genre, but we assume that the text itself will contain sufficient clues for us to answer this question.

We must keep in mind that naming a text's genre is not the same as understanding it, and that different labels could be used to describe the genre even while there is (broad) agreement as to what the genre is. Although labels assist us in discussing genre, we should be ultimately concerned with how a particular text seeks to communicate. If we do not understand this, we can easily misinterpret a text by applying inappropriate criteria to determine meaning. For example, were we to read the parable of the two sons and the gracious father (Luke 15:11-32) outside of its narrative context, we might conclude that Jesus was speaking about an actual son who had claimed and squandered his inheritance before his father's death (in contrast to his brother). In that case, we would read the parable as being historically referential. Yet although the parable is *lifelike*, nothing is at stake if we conclude that the genre of parable does not describe *actual* events. Interpreting it as a parable directs us to read it differently from Luke 15:1-2, which does claim to be

---

[25] See also §2 below.

[26] On the issue of genre more widely, see the helpful study by Jeannine K. Brown, "Genre Criticism and the Bible," in *Words and the Word: Explorations in Biblical Interpretation and Literary Theory*, ed. David G. Firth and Jamie A. Grant (Nottingham: Apollos, 2008), 111-50.

historically referential and so provides a historical context from which to read the parable (though we also recognize that Luke has provided a literary context with his Gospel). In any case, we can recognize that the parable represents an ancient genre, even if it is one that continues to find echoes today.

Likewise, a crucial starting point for reading Joshua is to understand it as an ancient text; therefore, its genre will conform to ancient patterns rather than contemporary ones.[27] I will comment on its genre here by identifying its key features.

A. JOSHUA AS NARRATIVE

An obvious starting point is to observe that Joshua is a narrative. Distinguishing between story and narrative is important, even if in popular usage these two terms are sometimes used interchangeably. Strictly speaking, the *story* is what happens, while the *narrative* is how that story is told. In terms of narratology, it does not matter whether the story is something that actually happened because those who narrate it have made choices about what to include and how to present it. I will therefore consider the issues of Joshua as a narrative without reference to the question of history, but then reflect on the issue of history as a separate indicator of genre.

The features of the narrative texts of the Old Testament have been the subject of fairly intense study since the 1970s. Even though much has changed since its publication, the pivotal work on this topic in English remains Robert Alter's *The Art of Biblical Narrative*.[28] Alter demonstrates that, although Old Testament narratives are structured around the same elements as contemporary narratives (having plot, dialogue, characterization, scene, and a narrator), this is because these elements are essential for the existence of a narrative. What matters more is how these elements are deployed within a particular culture and time. Hence, although Joshua is clearly a narrative, it works within the constraints of the narrative patterns available to the writers of the Old Testament and should not be read through modern narrative conventions. Nevertheless, the tools of

---

[27] See especially John H. Walton and J. Harvey Walton, *The Lost World of the Israelite Conquest: Covenant Retribution and the Fate of the Canaanites* (Downers Grove, IL: IVP Academic, 2017), 7–12.

[28] Robert Alter, *The Art of Biblical Narrative* (New York: Basic Books, 1981).

narrative criticism (and narratology more generally) are useful to the
extent that they open up the narrative world of the text.

One problem with the success of Alter's work (and those that followed
over the next decade) is that narrative critics have tended to treat all
the books of the Old Testament in much the same way. Although this is
appropriate at a general level since ancient audiences needed enough
mutually intelligible information across these works to interpret them,
the distinctive nature of the different narrative texts of the Old Testament
has not always been recognized. Therefore, we need to understand the
particular ways in which Joshua employs available narrative conventions.

To begin, we can regard Joshua as a narrative in that it recounts a
story—the story of Israel's origins within the land promised by God.
Moreover, we can trace this narrative across the book as a whole as the
partial fulfillment of God's promise to Joshua in 1:3-5. This is a partial
fulfillment because, although by the end of the book Israel is clearly in the
land and the trustworthiness of God's promises is affirmed (Josh 21:43-45;
23:14-16), the book is also clear that much of the land remained to be
taken (13:1-7; 23:1-16). A way toward resolution of this apparent paradox
is provided by the covenant commitments made in 24:1-28. The process
by which this is worked out constitutes the plot of the book as a whole,
with the plot of the various narratives contributing to it. Scenically, we
trace this across the central highlands, into the south, then the north, and
back to the central highlands with a host of characters, though Joshua
himself is the central human figure. Some form of dialogue features in all
levels of narrative, and though it isn't nearly as prominent as in a book
like Ruth, it is an important feature of Joshua.

Observing that Joshua is a narrative text is only a first step. The book
works with the conventions of narrative in the Old Testament in some
distinctive ways, and these deserve some consideration. This is important
because, although there has been a proliferation of narrative studies of
the Old Testament overall, Joshua has largely missed out on this.[29] As a
result, diachronic explanations are often given for matters that can be
resolved by closer attention to Joshua's narrative poetics.[30] A key goal
of this commentary is to attend to Joshua's narrative features on the

---

[29] See Sarah Lebhar Hall, *Conquering Character: The Characterization of Joshua in Joshua 1–11*
(London: T&T Clark, 2010), 4–6. On narrative techniques more broadly, see André Wénin,
"Josué 1–12 comme récit" in *The Book of Joshua* (Leuven: Peeters, 2012), 109–38.

[30] Broadly, poetics are concerned with the study of how a particular genre works.

assumption that doing so will help readers understand it better; if it is better understood, then it can be better proclaimed. However, rather than provide a comprehensive introduction to Joshua's narrative poetics, I will comment on two key features that are of particular importance for it—focalization and anachrony.[31]

A key element to notice from the outset is Joshua's use of focalization. This is not something typically covered by books on the narratology of the Old Testament, and it is often confused with point of view. Developed initially by Gérard Genette, focalization is concerned with the extent to which a narrator provides readers with information needed to interpret the events recounted.[32] Genette proposes a sliding scale with three key reference points. First, with zero focalization, the narrator is not only omniscient (as a narrative concept) but is able to provide guidance to readers so that our knowledge exceeds that of characters in the narrative. Second, with internal focalization, the narrative focuses on a particular character, and as readers we know only what that character knows. Finally, in an externally focalized narrative, readers know less than the characters. As readers, we can only interpret on the basis of what we observe occurring within the narrative and not on the basis of other information provided by the narrator.

The majority of Old Testament narratives are zero focalized—the narrator knows what is happening and provides readers with the information needed to interpret events. For example, in the narrative of David's adultery with Bathsheba and murder of Uriah (2 Samuel 11), the narrator is present at a range of sites and knows more than the various characters, even if everything isn't disclosed in order for narrative tension to remain. Although a brilliant piece of narration, it follows the dominant pattern of zero focalization.

Internal focalization is less common, but still prevalent. For example, Nehemiah's response to news from Jerusalem (Neh 1:1–2:10) is presented

---

[31] Through the commentary I have generally followed the narratological convention of referring to the "narrator" rather than the "author." For much of Joshua, these terms can largely be regarded as interchangeable. Nevertheless, following Wolf Schmid, *Narratology: An Introduction* (Berlin: de Gruyter, 2010), 65, there is still value in examining the narrator as one present within the text whereas the author stands outside of it. Attention to this also enables a closer focus on narrative studies.

[32] Gérard Genette, *Narrative Discourse: An Essay in Method* (Ithaca: Cornell University Press, 1980), 189.

from his own perspective, and thus internally focalized. We know only what he knows, and so have no information other than what is available to him. The narrator of the book may know more, but by restricting our focus to what Nehemiah sees, our field of view is smaller. In the Old Testament, such internal focalization is typically embedded within a larger narrative.

By far the rarest mode in the Old Testament is external focalization. This factor alone makes Joshua's use of it worth noting. A striking feature of the book of Joshua is that its first five chapters are almost entirely externally focalized.[33] For example, when we come to the story of Rahab in Joshua 2, the narrator provides us with no guidance about how to interpret these events, especially Rahab's comments. Is the agreement made with Rahab a sin, since Israel was meant to destroy the Canaanites, or is it a moment of insight about how the people of God are being formed? At the end of this chapter, which is also particularly notable for how it characterizes Rahab and the scouts through dialogue, we simply do not know. Likewise, in the story of the crossing of the Jordan in Joshua 3–4, the narrator does not provide guidance for interpreting what is happening. As a result, we do not know why Joshua gives the instructions he does. The effect is that as we reach Jericho in Joshua 6, we do not know if Israel is in a right relationship with God or not. External focalization is used to provide information to readers, but not enough for them to interpret these events with confidence. This additional information is then provided in the following chapters. Indeed, in 6:1–2; 7:1; and 9:1–4 the narrator adopts an explicitly zero focalized perspective, providing guidance that had been left out previously. Even so, it is not until 11:15 that readers can be certain of the appropriateness of Joshua's actions. This technique then forces us to reread what has been recounted with the information provided there. This pattern of external focalization is resumed in Joshua 22, meaning that by the end of that narrative the narrator has not disclosed the exact reasons for various elements within it, probably because to do so would distract from the key goal of raising the question of the identity of the people of God.

A second feature that is important for understanding Joshua's narrative poetics is anachrony, an element seldom treated in the principal works on Old Testament narrative. We can define an anachrony as any

---

[33] See Firth, "Disorienting Readers in Joshua 1:1–5:12."

point where the order in which events are recounted differs from the order in which the narrative indicates they happened.[34] Although many narratives in the Old Testament follow a structure in which the order of recounting is the same as the order of events, this is not always the case. Joshua is not as distinctive as Samuel in its use of anachrony. But it is still worth noting that, just as Joshua uses changes in focalization to leave readers looking for additional information, so also it deploys various anachronies to increase reader involvement with the text.

For example, although the narrator clearly knows that the men crossing the Jordan (Josh 3–4) are not circumcised, there is no mention of this until 5:4—and even then it is after God has directed Joshua to make flint knives to circumcise the Israelite males. All of this is important because Israel was about to celebrate Passover, an event for which the narrator has deployed subtle clues through the earlier narratives. Thus as readers we receive a shock when we discover that the nation is in no condition to celebrate Passover, let alone take over the land promised. Likewise, although Achan clearly took the banned goods from Jericho during the events recounted in Joshua 6, we do not learn of this until chapter 7. Once again, Joshua employs these techniques as a mechanism for engaging readers with the text, creating additional suspense that draws readers into the narrative world it has created. Although Joshua arguably lacks the narrative sophistication of a book like Samuel, it nevertheless has its own techniques that need to be recognized and that indicate a high degree of sophistication.

B. JOSHUA AS HISTORY

Just as consideration of Joshua as narrative must consider the ancient context, so too must consideration of the book as history. This is particularly important in that the conventions by which history is recounted vary across cultures and time. For example, no contemporary historians would invent speeches for characters as a means of presenting both what they believe happened and how it is to be interpreted, although Herodotus had no problem doing this. We do not, however, regard him as writing anything other than history because of this (and not just because we trace the word back to him), even if there are numerous points where we might not regard him as a reliable source. But we read him within

---

[34] Genette, *Narrative Discourse*, 35.

the constraints of his own context, even if an important part of his work was indeed pioneering something new in Greece by writing history in prose rather than poetry. Likewise, in assessing Joshua as history we need to see it in light of the conventions that applied in its world. Failure to attend to this can mean misrepresenting the history the book presents.

Yet even before this we need to ask a more basic question: Does Joshua intend to recount events as history? Its narrative elements suggest that it also seeks to entertain—though there is no reason to assume that a book cannot both entertain and provide a historical account, especially if most of those who would access its content would do so through hearing it read rather than reading it themselves.

The question of whether a given text is a work of history is a complex one, and it does not depend entirely on whether what it says is true. A work can be intended as history but be wrong. In this case, assessment of the issue of truth is concerned with whether it is a good piece of history writing, not with the more basic question of whether it is history.[35] When determining whether a text is a work of history we are to some extent working with the question of the author's intention. But as noted above, we can only access that through the text. It has also been noted that works that are not intended to be historical can be lifelike, so simply finding this feature does not make it a work of history. However, it is possible to point to evidence within the text of Joshua that suggests it is intended as a work of history, though as with any history it is reported with the goal of challenging the views of a later generation.[36] In this light, it is helpful to distinguish between "history" as that which happened at some point in time and "historiography" as the selective writing about events from the past. The genre question is more strictly about historiography, but given that "history" and "historiography" are not often distinguished in popular discussion we can continue to use "history" here. Nevertheless, as Long has indicated, "historiography" is a useful term because it allows

---

[35] On this distinction, see David G. Firth, "The Third Quest for the Historical Mordecai and the Genre of the Book of Esther," *OTE* 16 (2003): 233–43.

[36] In this I agree with Lori L. Rowlett, *Joshua and the Rhetoric of Violence: A New Historicist Analysis* (Sheffield: Sheffield Academic, 1996), 11–12, though unlike her I see this history as something directed to the time of David rather than the late seventh century BC. Likewise, although Douglas S. Earl, *Reading Joshua as Christian Scripture* (Winona Lake, IN: Eisenbrauns, 2010), 14–48, is careful to show that myth is a category that can use history in establishing a foundational narrative, this approach seems to put too much weight on the historiographical goal of the text rather than its historical referentiality.

for the artistic representation of the past,[37] which in this case is evident in the literary skill deployed in Joshua.

The key marker of a work of history is that it in some way attempts to represent the past. Whereas a writer of fiction is free to invent what might happen, a historian is constrained by what is known of the past.[38] Demonstrating this is not simply a matter of pointing to certain pieces of archaeology because a writer of fiction might also draw on known events from history while still creating a work of fiction. Conversely, a writer might intend to create a work of history but misrepresent that same evidence. Rather, we need to look for evidence within the text itself that Joshua is intentionally referential—that it is constrained by the past inasmuch as it is known—in creating its record of Israel's origins in the land. Only if that condition is satisfied can we evaluate what it means to speak of Joshua as history.

Fortunately, the same evidence noted above as pointing to the origins of the book in the united monarchy also suggests that a key concern of Joshua is to represent the past. Most importantly, the frequent occurrence of the phrase "to this day" as evidence that events from the past continued to shape Israel's enduring experience indicates that Joshua is constrained by history. Similarly, observations about how Israel's life changed after the time of Joshua (such as 24:31) indicate that the book's record is shaped by the constraints of the past. As such, we can regard Joshua as a work of history.

But making this identification is only part of the process, because just as techniques and emphases in narration change over time, so also the nature of history writing changes. Evaluating Joshua as a work of history means considering its own methods (and this means reading it in light of other ANE materials that establish a context for it) but also examining its own modes of representing the past. Indeed, it is quite possible that attention to these features will address some of the often-noted problems of relating the book to the archaeological record.

Before noting the archaeological issues, it is worth highlighting the important work of K. Lawson Younger in establishing the extent to which Joshua follows some common patterns in ancient

---

[37] V. Philips Long, *The Art of Biblical History* (Leicester: Apollos, 1994), 63.
[38] Cf. Long, *Art of Biblical History*, 68.

historiography—conquest narratives in particular.[39] By looking at external evidence, he develops the key insight that many ancient conquest narratives routinely use hyperbole as a standard element, especially in the numbers they use and the extent of the victories they describe. This creates the possibility that Joshua might be written according to these conventions. Younger then provides clear evidence from the text of Joshua that it does indeed employ this technique. Thus the use of hyperbole as a rhetorical technique in ancient history writing is a presumed element in the relationship between author, text, and reader. Readers would expect it to be a feature of the text. This is assuredly not the case in history writing in the modern world, where the expectations are quite different. Evaluations of the historical intent of Joshua that do not take this into account project a false value onto the book, often creating a straw man when our values are not found in the text.[40]

Although the issues cannot be dealt with fully here, recognizing the ways in which Joshua conforms to the modes of its time may also help resolve some of the supposed contradictions between the book and the archaeological evidence, especially regarding the excavations at Jericho.[41] In the commentary on Joshua 6, I discuss the key issues, but here it is sufficient to note that perceived contradictions between Joshua and the archaeological evidence are shaped by a history of reading Joshua against a context different than its own; the book itself never claims Jericho was a significant site at the time.[42] At other points, we need to acknowledge that there is a variance between the apparent claims of the text and the dominant interpretation of the archaeological record (e.g., with Ai, Joshua 7), though in those instances it is worth noting that alternative interpretations of the archaeology also exist. Again, comment on the

---

[39] K. Lawson Younger, Jr., *Ancient Conquest Accounts: A Study in Ancient Near Eastern and Biblical History Writing* (Sheffield: JSOT Press, 1990).

[40] See also Iain Provan, V. Philips Long, and Tremper Longman III, *A Biblical History of Israel*, 2nd ed. (Louisville: Westminster John Knox, 2015), 203.

[41] Much here finally depends on the date we believe that Joshua entered the land. In my view, a commentary is not the place for this discussion. Suffice it to say that, of the two dates most commonly argued (c. 1400 BC or c. 1250 BC), my evaluation of the archaeological material relevant to Joshua has assumed that he was leading Israel into the land c. 1250 BC. For an accessible discussion, see Ralph K. Hawkins, *How Israel Became a People* (Nashville: Abingdon, 2013), 49–90.

[42] It is worth noting that Dame Kathleen Kenyon, who directed the key excavations, did not see a contradiction between Joshua and her work.

particulars are provided at the appropriate points, but the important thing to note here is that these are an attempt to read Joshua within its own context. When we do so, the supposed difficulties in reconciling Joshua with what we know from the history of the period are often greatly reduced. This is not to say that we can resolve all the historical problems posed on the basis of our current knowledge, but there is still good reason to believe that Joshua records events that did actually happen.

C. JOSHUA AS NARRATED HISTORY AND SCRIPTURE

Drawing the above discussion together, we can describe Joshua as a work of narrated history. Although it is common to speak of "historical narrative," this label arguably puts the terms in the wrong order. Reading Joshua as a work of history reminds us that, as with all history, it draws on the past to communicate something to a later audience. In other words, history is not recounted simply because it happened. Rather, history is recounted because it matters to a later generation. Yet it is *narrated* history—that is, it is told with artistry and selectivity. The elements of artistry have been noted above, but we need also to observe that this is a highly selective work.

The author of this book has not told us everything about Israel's origins in the land because that was not the goal, and this alone is a good reason why the language of "conquest" to describe the book is not altogether helpful, even if some (though not all) of the land was conquered.[43] We need only to note that Joshua 10 describes events in the far south of the land while Joshua 11 describes something similar in the far north without ever attempting to explain what happened in between. Caleb's statement about the forty-five years since Moses had promised him an inheritance in the land (14:10) indicates a gap of about five years since Israel had entered the land, though we would be hard pressed to find those years on the basis of what is presented. Finally, Joshua 24 reports an event at Shechem, though at no point are we told about Israel taking control of that region (even if 8:30–35 might hint at this).

Examples such as these can be multiplied, but such selectivity (which is not concerned to provide a full report on Israel's emergence in the land) indicates that although some elements of conquest are of interest, that is

---

[43] Cf. David Merling Sr., *The Book of Joshua: Its Theme and Role in Archaeological Discussions* (Berrien Springs: Andrews University Press, 1997), 177–81.

not the principal focus of the book. Rather, the mixture of elements that stress both the complete fulfillment of God's promises and the fact that much remained to be taken directs us to the issue of the identity of the people of God. This theme comes into particular focus in the closing chapters, but has been of increasing importance as the book has progressed. If Joshua was written in the time of David, then these questions would be particularly important given the divide between the north and the south that had emerged under Saul, with his clear preference for the tribe of Benjamin (1 Sam 22:6–10). Moreover, various Canaanite groups continued to be of importance. Understanding how God had shaped Israel's past would be significant, especially if that included both ethnic Israelite and Canaanite groups.

Ultimately, we do not read Joshua as simply a work of history or narrative (though it is both), but as Scripture, as one part of the word of God. Whether or not those who composed it were conscious of this, its place as Scripture is the most important reason it is read today. Reading it as such cannot mean sidestepping the complex challenges its interpretation presents.[44] But honoring it as Scripture means first understanding it as a historically situated message from which we continue to hear God.

IV. Joshua and the Problem of Violence

In light of the purpose and genre of Joshua, we come to what is often seen as the pressing problem with the book as a whole: its seeming destruction of the Canaanite population of the land.[45] This issue becomes especially important because of the focus on books like Joshua by modern critics of Christian faith like Richard Dawkins, who compares the accounts of Israel's entry into the land to various modern genocides.[46] This reading of Joshua is not unique to him, and indeed many modern believers (Christian and Jewish) struggle with the book in the same way.[47] An introduction

---

[44] Earl, *Reading Joshua as Christian Scripture*, 12.

[45] See further §6 below.

[46] Richard Dawkins, *The God Delusion* (London: Black Swan, 2006), 280.

[47] See Earl, *Reading Joshua as Christian Scripture*, 2–3; and McConville, *Joshua: Crossing Divides*, 69. One might also note that in the commentary of Matthias Eder, *Das Buch Josua* (Stuttgart: Verlag Katholisches Bibelwerk, 2017), roughly one-third of the introduction (pp. 47–69) is given to this issue. See also David G. Firth, *The Message of Joshua: Promise and People* (Nottingham: Inter-Varsity Press, 2015), 19–30.

to a commentary is not the place to resolve all of these issues, but it is possible to sketch some central themes for reflecting on this in light of the points made above about the genre of Joshua. We begin by reflecting on what it means that Joshua is an ancient text and that it conforms to ancient expectations, not modern ones (even if it also challenges both).

To begin with, Joshua does indeed describe a significant amount of war violence, though perhaps not as much as is sometimes suggested in popular discourse. Most of the violence is contained in chapters 6, 10, and 11, all of which describe aspects of Israel's military campaign in the land. As a proportion of text, and given the importance of Israel taking the land, this is not especially high. What tends to trouble modern readers far more are statements such as we find in 6:21: "They completely destroyed everything in the city with the sword—every man and woman, both young and old, and every ox, sheep, and donkey." Even if we understand the death of combatants in warfare, a line has been crossed with the deaths of noncombatants who have been killed simply for being where they were. This in turn is linked to the larger issue of the justice of God in giving to Israel a land already occupied by another people, which strikes many modern people as an example of colonialism. As one person put it to me recently, "Israel may have thought God was giving them the land, but that doesn't mean he was."

These are complex issues, but we can begin to address them by noting both Joshua's bridging function and its genre as narrated history that operates with its own period's conventions. As a bridging text, Joshua is structured to begin by having us reflect on Deuteronomy (Josh 1:1-9), but then it gradually introduces more of the Pentateuch, with reference to Numbers in the balance of Joshua 1. Since these are the two main points of reference for the book, this element is important. Nevertheless, Joshua 24 concludes the book by taking readers back to Genesis (Josh 24:1-12) before looking beyond the life of Joshua to the generations that followed (24:31). Joshua thus connects the Pentateuch to the rest of the books of the Former Prophets. With the mention of Abraham in the conclusion, readers are reminded of the need to understand Israel's place in the land in terms of the promise to him (Gen 12:7; 15:7-21). This promise is a crucial component of the whole story of the Pentateuch, and indeed from the time of Abraham's call the land is always central. And something acknowledged already in these earlier texts is that the land was occupied by the various Canaanite peoples.

A central idea of the Pentateuch, therefore, is that the land of Canaan does not belong to any one people. It belongs to God, and he has the right to give it to whomever he chooses.[48] In this case, the land he chose to give to Israel was the land of Canaan. The exodus, it should be noted, always had the goal of leading the people to the land. Even though Numbers 13–14 reports an initial failure on Israel's part in taking the land, the clear links between Josh 5:1–12 and the Passover account in Exodus 12 demonstrate that Israel's entry to the land was the fulfillment of the hope of the exodus. Joshua therefore forms part of a larger narrative that insists the land did not belong to the Canaanite peoples but rather to God, and that without Israel taking the land the exodus would be meaningless. The rest of the story of Israel in the land (Judges, Samuel, Kings) can thus look back on the events in Joshua and interpret Israel's life in light of God's faithfulness to the covenant and the implications of this for Israel.

Alongside this bridging function, we also read Joshua as an example of ancient narrated history, and in particular conquest narratives. As noted above, an important feature of this genre is its use of hyperbole. Examples of this are easily discernible within the text, and also have implications for how we understand words associated with the root חרם (usually rendered something like "destroy completely").

For example, according to Josh 10:37, Joshua "completely destroyed Hebron and everyone in it." Yet when Caleb wants to claim the city as his promised inheritance only five years later, it is clearly an inhabited and defended town (14:6–15). If the account in 10:37 means that the city was completely destroyed, then this would seem to contradict the later passage, since it is highly unlikely that there would once again be a populated and defended center only a few years later. But this is a problem only if 10:37 intends to communicate that there was no longer a city there. Once we consider the genre, it is far more likely that Joshua uses the language of total destruction to refer to a comprehensive victory.

As a modern analogy, I have heard football fans claim their team "totally destroyed" their opponents. But within the genre of modern sports banter, we know that no such thing has happened, and that this language means one team had a comprehensive victory, not that the opponents were left without any living players. If something like this

---

[48] Walton and Walton, *The Lost World of the Israelite Conquest*, 64–71, stress that the ability of a deity to give land to his or her people was a standard feature of the ANE.

was written down and then read by a new audience three thousand years later, they might believe that ours is a more violent society than it is. But for Israel, this language also provides reassurance, highlighted at key structural points in the book (10:14, 42; 23:3, 10), that God had fought for Israel. As a people who committed themselves to the covenant (24:1–28), Israel could know that God would continue to fight for them in a violent world where they too would suffer violence.[49] At the same time, the covenant reminded Israel that God could also take the land from them, just as he had taken it from the Canaanites.

V. Outline

I. Entering the Land (1:1–5:12)
  A. Preparations for Entering the Land (1:1–18)
    1. Directives to Joshua (1:1–9)
    2. Directives to the Leaders (1:10–11)
    3. Discussions with the Eastern Tribes (1:12–18)
  B. Rahab and the Spies in Jericho (2:1–24)
    1. Directives to the Spies (2:1a)
    2. Deceiving the King of Jericho (2:1b–7)
    3. The Oath with Rahab (2:8–21)
    4. The Report to Joshua (2:22–24)
  C. Crossing the Jordan (3:1–4:24)
    1. Initial Preparations for Crossing (3:1–6)
    2. Directives for Crossing (3:7–13)
    3. A Miraculous Crossing: Part 1 (3:14–17)
    4. Twelve-Stone Memorial: Part 1 (4:1–10a)
    5. A Miraculous Crossing: Part 2 (4:10b–18)
    6. Twelve-Stone Memorial: Part 2 (4:19–24)
  D. Circumcision and Passover (5:1–12)
    1. Canaanite Fear (5:1)
    2. Circumcision (5:2–9)
    3. Passover (5:10–12)
II. Taking the Land (5:13–12:24)
  A. Jericho (5:13–6:27)
    1. Joshua and the Commander of the Lord's Army (5:13–15)
    2. Instructions for Capturing the City (6:1–5)

---

[49] Ederer, *Das Buch Josua*, 67–69.

BIBLICAL AND
THEOLOGICAL THEMES

R eflection on biblical theology can move in two basic directions—from the general to the particular or from the particular to the general. That is, we can look at themes that are significant across the canon and then look for their presence in a particular text (general to particular), or we can identify the leading themes in a particular text and then explore the ways in which they are developed more broadly across the canon (particular to general). Although there ought to be some degree of cross-over between these approaches, since themes that occur more widely are likely to be present in a particular text, they each represent a different approach to the task of biblical theology.

The strength of the general-to-particular model is that it highlights the unity of the biblical witness, though at the risk of flattening the distinctiveness of the various texts.[1] Conversely, the particular-to-general model's strength is that it brings out what might be largely neglected themes in particular texts,[2] but may lose sight of the unity of the larger biblical witness. A dialogue between these approaches is certainly possible at the level of an overall biblical theology,[3] but in a work such as this it seems better to focus on the second model in order to highlight Joshua's

---

[1] This model is exemplified, e.g., in Walther Eichrodt, *Theology of the Old Testament*, 2 vols (London: SCM Press, 1961, 1967), and his use of "covenant" as a structuring center.

[2] As exemplified in Gerhard von Rad, *Old Testament Theology*, 2 vols. (London: SCM Press, 1962, 1965).

[3] As exemplified by Brevard S. Childs, *Biblical Theology of the Old and New Testaments* (London: SCM Press, 1992).

own themes, even though some of these will feature more broadly across the canon. Because these themes emerge from the exegesis of the book, the following sketches do not provide detailed support for the exegesis but assume readers will consult the relevant exegetical discussions in the commentary. Tracing these themes first from Joshua also means that each of them is to some extent related to the others, but there is value in considering them individually even if we must ultimately integrate them in both our reading of Joshua and of the wider canon.

§1 Faithfulness and Obedience

Readers of Joshua encounter the theme of faithfulness and obedience almost immediately. Having heard of Moses' death, we read God's words to Joshua requiring him to observe carefully all that had been passed on by Moses. Indeed, Joshua was to meditate on the book of God's instruction day and night in the knowledge that keeping these instructions faithfully provided assurance that he would succeed in claiming the land (1:6–9).

So important is the theme of obedience to God's word that it is given prominence at each major section of the book. As Joshua stood outside Jericho ready to launch Israel's first military campaign in the land, he received instructions from God explaining how to take the city: march around it for seven days with the priests blowing on ram's horns (6:1–5). In preparation for the land allocation, Joshua was told what to do (13:1–7): divide the land among the nine and a half tribes who would live west of the Jordan, even though much of that land remained to be taken. In the final section of the book, it is notable that Joshua's speech to the eastern tribes emphasized their faithful obedience while also stressing the need for their continued obedience (22:1–5). By this point, therefore, we have moved from Joshua's own obedience to that of the people as a whole.

This is because Joshua's obedience was representative of the greater demand that was placed on the people as a whole. This was already apparent when Joshua summoned the eastern tribes to fulfill their promise to assist their kin in taking the land west of the Jordan, with this summons leading to their own promise of obedience (1:10–18). This call to the nation continues in both of Joshua's great addresses (23:1–16; 24:1–28), demonstrating that continued obedience to God's word was to shape the people going forward.

In addition to statements stressing the importance of obedience to God's word at the head of each section, there are also important reflections on the nature of obedience in the summaries to each half of the book. In the summary of Israel's entry into the land, we are told that Joshua did everything that God had commanded through Moses (11:15). Indeed, so complete was his obedience that the narrator observes, "He left nothing undone of all that the Lord had commanded Moses." Similarly, in the summary after the covenant at Shechem, we are told that Israel had "served"[4] God throughout the lives of Joshua and the elders who outlived him (24:31). Faithfulness and obedience thus provide bookends to Joshua as a whole (as well as dividing it into its principal sections), something that is marked by the move from Joshua's personal obedience to that of the people as a whole.

But what does obedience look like in Joshua? We might be predisposed to think of obedience as precisely following a particular command. But this is merely a basic understanding of the concept, only directly relevant in Joshua to the making of flint knives and circumcising the Israelite men (5:2). We see a much broader understanding of obedience when Joshua is told to "meditate" on the Torah. Meditation involves more than simply memorizing Torah in order to carry out certain actions at definite points in time. Rather than a set of commandments designating specific actions, the Torah is better understood as a form of structured wisdom, something that gives shape to life and demonstrates the patterns of order God desires.[5] It was entirely possible to transgress this pattern of order by acting contrary to it, as in the case of Achan (Josh 7), but this does not mean that it mandated only a specific set of actions. What is true of Torah can also be true of more specific directives.

This is illustrated at several points in Joshua. At Jericho, Joshua was given specific instructions about how the city was to be captured (6:2–5). In fact, though, beyond the general process, Joshua was left to determine the exact means of how to accomplish this. He was required to do certain things, but how he arranged the people to march around the city was left up to him. Obedience involved faithfulness to required specifics (e.g., priests blowing horns), but it also included working out other elements to best

---

[4] CSB here has "worshiped," a not inappropriate sense of the verb עבד, but this rendering is probably too narrow at this point, and the broader sense of "served" is thus better.

[5] See John H. Walton and J. Harvey Walton, *The Lost World of the Israelite Conquest: Covenant Retribution and the Fate of the Canaanites* (Downers Grove, IL: IVP Academic, 2017), 89–98.

deploy the people and ensure they were faithful to God's requirements. At other points, such as crossing the Jordan, this element of figuring out how to obey God's directives was developed without knowing the exact goal. For example, in 3:7–8, Joshua knew that God was to exalt him but understood only that he was to command the priests to stand in the river when Israel reached its edge. What was to happen at the crossing was revealed only later. Obedience could entail faithfulness either to specifics or to general guidance, in which much was left for Joshua to work out.

This becomes particularly important for understanding events in which Canaanites not only survive but also become part of Israel, most notably in the cases of Rahab (2:1–21; 6:17, 21–23, 25) and the Gibeonites (9:1–27). If Israel was to destroy all Canaanites in accordance with Deut 7:1–6, then was not their survival evidence of disobedience? If we treat obedience only as the exact carrying out of a specified action, then we could certainly read it this way. But if so, then we are left with an apparent contradiction in Josh 11:15, which explicitly commends Joshua's obedience. In the case of the Gibeonites, we are even told that God determined that they would not be destroyed (11:19–20), though only after their incorporation into Israel. If obedience meant destroying all the Canaanites, then how could Joshua have known there was an alternative plan for the Gibeonites?

Taking the comments in 11:15–23 seriously in light of all that has happened to this moment in the book requires us to consider a different approach.[6] According to this passage, Joshua had fully obeyed, but he had not destroyed all the Canaanites. Indeed, 13:1–7 will make clear that many still survived. This suggests that obedience was a matter of faithfully reflecting on what God wanted to achieve through a directive and then working toward that goal. When we look at Deut 7:1–6, we see that the continued existence of the Canaanites could lead Israel away from faithfulness to God. But what if some Canaanites did not pose a threat? Indeed, what if they actually came to serve God or at least were not a stumbling block to those who did? Obedience in this case would require not destroying these people. Joshua's meditation on the Torah was meant to help him understand this and apply it. Obedience was thus faithfulness to what God was achieving through Israel in his mission. The

---

[6] I assume the unity of the book's focus. For more details, see the comments on those verses.

commandments were to be understood as shaping the general pattern of Israel's actions rather than requiring a mechanical application of directives. This does not mean "anything goes"; Achan stands as clear evidence that disobedience (sin) is a tragic possibility.

The importance of this model of obedience can be traced through the canon. Joshua stands as the first book of the Former Prophets in the Hebrew Bible, while Psalms most commonly stands as the first book of the Writings. There is a close parallel between the command for Joshua to meditate on Torah in 1:6–9 and Psalm 1, which indicates that such meditation is the way to a flourishing life for any Israelite. This is a consistent pattern in the book: this model of meditative obedience starts with Joshua himself but is then picked up by the people as a whole. Appearing at the beginning of both the Prophets and the Writings, the theme of obedience to the Torah receives prominence. Moreover, it is reinforced by the presence of this same theme in Mal 4:4–6, so that the Prophets as a whole[7] are bounded by the theme, which then continues in the Writings. Although the structure of the Old Testament canon in English (following the LXX and Vulgate) is different (and no one way of arranging the canon is definitive), the parallel between Joshua and Psalms is easily noticed. Obedience shaped by meditation is a vital component of the life of God's people.

The pattern can be traced further into the New Testament, with the obvious development that obedience is now shaped by a relationship to God in Christ. A particularly clear example of this can be seen in the Sermon on the Mount, in which Jesus made clear that he expected disciples not only to hear what he said but also to do it (Matt 7:21–23). Something of the shape of the obedient life is outlined in the antitheses where Jesus contrasted his teaching with earlier material (Matt 5:17–48)—some from the Old Testament and some consisting of rabbinic adaptations of the Old Testament. Notably, when he made a contrast with the Old Testament, Jesus' concern was to reflect on the heart of the commandment and to work out how that could be lived in a new context.

This is particularly evident in Jesus' antitheses about murder and adultery (Matt 5:21–30). In neither did he suggest that the new covenant abolishes the commandment. But he considered their intent and how they

---

[7] In the Hebrew Bible, Joshua–Kings (less Ruth) and Isaiah–Malachi (less Lamentations and Daniel) make up the Prophets.

could be lived out rather than focusing on obedience simply as completion of a given action (or in these cases, *not* completing an action). Both
of these commandments reflect a general concern in the Decalogue to
create a community of trust. A redeemed community needs to be able to
trust one another. But this cannot happen when our motivations are not
considered. Clearly, someone could keep the prohibition against murder
by refraining from illegal killing. Jesus, however, went to the heart of the
commandment, pointing to a much stricter interpretation of it, one that
considers our intentions, not just our actions.

Jesus' teaching comes from a profound reflection on the Torah. We
(like Joshua) need to meditate on God's word and understand that obedience to it is essential. But, rather than simply conforming our behavior to
specific acts, our obedience needs to be consistent with God's purposes
and developed through faithfulness in new contexts. Obedience is faithfulness that draws Scripture and life into a fresh dialogue.

§2 Identity of the People of God

Throughout Joshua, it is clear that God was giving the land of Canaan
to his people. But who were the people of God? Although at one level
the answer is "Israel," a careful reading of the book indicates that the
identity of the people is more complex than that. The people of God are
more appropriately defined as those who join God in his purposes (though
to a lesser degree those who do not oppose God's purposes may enjoy
the blessings of being among his people). Indeed, one of the key tasks of
Joshua is to challenge a facile idea of the identity of God's people.

The centrality of the issue is raised early in the book and is a pivotal element throughout. We see foreigners integrated into Israel, but
we also see Israelites excluded.[8] Joshua 1 establishes that Israel was
to take the land, with the implication that the inhabitants were to be
destroyed so that Israel could settle and not be led astray by false worship. Certainly Joshua 22–24 is concerned that Israel not be caught in
this trap. Nevertheless, the Israel that emerges at the end of the book is
not the same one that entered the land under Joshua. The people of God

---

[8] The importance of this is explored in more detail in David G. Firth, "Models of Inclusion
and Exclusion in Joshua," in *Interreligious Relations*, ed. Hallvard Hagelia and Markus Zehnder
(London: T&T Clark, 2017), 71–88.

are not identified on the basis of ethnicity but rather on the basis of a relationship with God.

The variations to ethnic Israel are established as soon as we encounter Rahab in Joshua 2. A Canaanite prostitute, we might imagine her to be precisely the sort of person that Israel should destroy. But actually she demonstrated the sort of faith to which any Israelite might aspire, assisting the scouts and obtaining a promise that she and her family would not be destroyed. The promise was fulfilled when Jericho fell (6:17, 22-23), so that Rahab's family continued to live among Israel (6:25). The declaration that Joshua accomplished all that God commanded through Moses (11:15) makes clear that Israel's actions toward Rahab were no mistake. Indeed, it is notable that the book gives as much space to the death of Achan and his family (Josh 7) as it does to Rahab's inclusion. Achan was an Israelite, but he incurred God's wrath for his decision to take from the items dedicated to God at Jericho (7:1). By this point of the book, in addition to seeing the capture of two relatively insignificant cities (Jericho and Ai), we have seen Canaanites becoming Israelites and Israelites becoming Canaanites.

The situation becomes more complex with the Gibeonites in Joshua 9, yet it is important to note the prominent place given to foreigners in the covenant ceremony recounted before Israel encountered the Gibeonites (8:30-35). Curiously, apart from Rahab's family, no other foreigners have been mentioned in the book, but clearly at this point there were foreigners sojourning within Israel (8:33, 35) who had committed themselves through the blessings and curses. The presence of foreigners as a significant group thus prepares us for the encounter with the Gibeonites.

According to 11:19-20, the Gibeonites were apparently moved to act because God had not hardened their hearts so that they would resist Israel. But according to 9:24, their own perception was that they acted because of their fear of what God had commanded Moses. Yet these two explanations are not incompatible with one another because divine sovereignty and human responsibility can go together. The Gibeonites were then placed in the sanctuary to carry out menial tasks. By the end of the battle reports, we thus have evidence of the continued existence of Canaanite groups. Their existence is not regarded as problematic, however, since they were integrated in different ways into the people of God.

The importance of foreigners is also stressed in the land allocation chapters (Joshua 13-21). Although Caleb is already well known to readers from the initial attempt to enter the land (Numbers 13–14), his Edomite heritage is stressed by noting that he is a Kenizzite (Josh 14:6). This man of foreign heritage demonstrated the sort of faith Israel was meant to display in claiming the land. Thus, Caleb becomes the paradigmatic figure for these chapters, just as Rahab had been in Joshua 1–12. Notable too is that Caleb is prominent at the start of this section, while foreigners more generally are noted when discussing the cities of refuge at its close (20:9). These foreigners were clearly intended to be people who understood the requirements of Torah, which is why they could claim refuge. They included various Canaanite groups mentioned as continuing to live among Israel (e.g., 15:62; 16:2, 10; 17:12–13).

Joshua 22–24 then becomes a reflection on the identity of the people of God in light of all that has gone before. Although Joshua 22 is at one level about Israel's internal identity, it makes clear that their identity was not defined by geography, since the eastern tribes lived outside the promised territory. In Joshua 23–24 Joshua spoke to the assembly. By this time, we know they are a mixed people, which is part of the reason Joshua had to exhort them to be faithful and obedient to Yahweh alone and not to the gods of their ancestors (24:22–24). This then becomes the definition of the people of God: a people committed to the service of Yahweh alone, with the possibility of all such people obeying God. Ethnic Israel was the vehicle by which this happened; non-Israelites were incorporated to varying degrees into Israel. But what defined the people of God was their commitment to him.

This theme appears through the rest of the Bible. Notably, Israel's first judge (Othniel in Judg 3:7–11) was a member of Caleb's family and, therefore, not ethnically Israelite. Yet he becomes the paradigm figure through which we read the rest of the stories of the judges. Conversely, in the dreadful events of Judges 19–21, we see an Israel that had lost sight of what it meant to be faithful. As a result, they devoted to destruction some of their own people to resolve a problem of their own making (Judg 21:11). An Israel that did not live in obedience to God became indistinguishable from the Canaanites and had no claim to being God's people.

In both Samuel and Kings, continued prominence is given to foreigners who were integrated into God's people. Although David is often portrayed as an ideal Israelite, it is notable that in 2 Samuel 11 Uriah the Hittite is more righteous because he lived for God. Israel was to be a people open to all who gave themselves to the service of God; this truth is particularly prominent in Solomon's prayer at the dedication of the temple in which he anticipated the foreigner coming to the sanctuary because of the need of all peoples to know God (1 Kgs 8:41–43). There is also an important shift in language compared to what we see in Joshua. In Joshua, the foreigner (Heb גֵּר) refers either to someone who had chosen to live within Israel or to a displaced Israelite. But in Kings, the foreigner (Heb נָכְרִי) refers to someone in his own land who yet would become part of the people of God. Naaman (2 Kgs 5:1–19) exemplifies this kind of foreigner within Kings. Perhaps surprisingly, this type of integration may even be alluded to in Esth 8:17, where many ethnic groups "professed themselves to be Jews" following Mordecai's elevation.

Other parts of the Old Testament also anticipate the point when God's people will be more clearly drawn from all peoples. In Isa 19:16–25, we see the hope that even Egypt and Assyria, the archetypal oppressors of Israel, would one day become part of God's people. This hope finds further expression in Isa 56:1–8 in its declaration that all who commit themselves to God's covenant will have a home in the sanctuary. Such a home does not mean a second-class status but rather being an integral part of God's people. Just as Joshua himself stressed in Joshua 24, the people of God are those who are committed to him.

It is no surprise to find this understanding of the people of God in Jesus' ministry. In all three Synoptic accounts of the cleansing of the temple (Matt 21:12–13; Mark 11:1–11; Luke 19:45–46), Jesus cited Isa 56:7, emphasizing that the temple was meant to be a place for all to worship. His anger was directed against those who exploited such people for their own benefit and who, therefore, did not obey God.

This concern for the inclusion of foreigners is also evident through Matthew's Gospel. Although Jesus at one point only sends his disciples to the "lost sheep of Israel" (Matt 10:6; cf. Matt 15:24), at key moments he recognizes foreigners who become part of the people of God and who demonstrate greater faith than ethnic Israelites (Matt 8:5–13; 15:21–28). The parable of the wedding banquet (Matt 22:1–14) fits this pattern, and those who celebrate the banquet have responded to God's call in obedience. All of this prepares for the well-known commission of Matt 28:16–20, with its directive to disciple the nations by baptizing and teaching them to obey all that Jesus commanded. Thus, the identity of God's people has clear continuity with what we have seen in Joshua. Our response to Jesus determines whether we are part of God's people.

The concern that the people of God should encompass all nations is expressed throughout the New Testament. Paul's language of "the obedience of faith" (Rom 1:5; 16:26) catches this well, identifying a characteristic to be found among all the nations. This is why the gospel is for all who believe (Rom 1:16–17). It involves not only belief but obedience, reflecting the pattern already seen in Joshua even as Paul's understanding of the righteousness of God is expressed through faith in Christ, which can be described as obedience. That God's people are made up of all those bought by Jesus is also reflected in the song of the elders (Rev 5:9–10), in which they affirm that Jesus' death was for "every tribe and language and people and nation." This possibility has its roots in Joshua and can be traced through the rest of the Bible. The people of God are those who live in faithful obedience to God—a faithful obedience that now finds its focus in Jesus.

§3 Joshua and Jesus

Even though there are relatively few direct links between Joshua and Jesus, there are still parallels between them and points where the presentation of Joshua feeds into the larger presentation of Jesus in the New Testament.[9] It is worth understanding these connections in order to appreciate the wide background of Old Testament sources that the New Testament writers draw on in presenting Jesus. A helpful entry point into this topic is to consider some christological titles and then reflect on ways in which Joshua relates to them. From that, we can consider the more specific connections drawn between Joshua and Jesus in the epistle to the Hebrews.

Although there are many important christological titles, two important ones relative to Joshua are "servant of the Lord" and "prophet." We cannot unpack every relevant New Testament passage on these titles, but we will explore how these titles are developed in Joshua and then

---

[9] Zev Farber, *Images of Joshua in the Bible and their Reception* (Berlin: Walter de Gruyter, 2016), 284–85, claims there is no Joshua–Jesus typology in the New Testament. However, although it is subtle and not a significant feature, the evidence suggests that when later Christian writers developed this theme more explicitly they were not creating something absent in the New Testament. Farber (pp. 286–309) helpfully traces it through the Epistle of Barnabas, the dialogues of Justin Martyr, and Tertullian).

in the rest of the Old Testament. This will be followed by a reflection on the links with Jesus in the New Testament.

A key goal of the book of Joshua is to present him as a "servant of Yahweh" (Josh 24:29). This is a title he receives only at the end of the book, whereas at the beginning he is still Moses' "assistant" (מְשָׁרֵת מֹשֶׁה). This was the standard designation of Joshua in the Pentateuch, going back to Exod 24:13 when he ascended the mountain with Moses and the elders. But at Joshua's death, he received the title "servant of Yahweh," the same title Moses received at his death (Deut 34:5). The importance of this title for Moses is underscored by its recurrence fourteen times in Joshua.[10] When Joshua also received the title, clearly he was deemed someone who had worked faithfully within God's purposes like Moses.

Whereas Moses and Joshua only received this title in retrospect, David was described as God's servant while still alive. It was first used when Abner spoke to the elders of Israel (2 Sam 3:18). Though we do not have another reference to this promise from God, it is not inconsistent with the wider presentation of David in 1–2 Samuel. The title was applied more directly to David by God when Nathan spoke to him about his plan to build a temple (2 Sam 7:5).

This trajectory from Moses to Joshua to David as God's servants leads us to the book of Isaiah, where "servant" language becomes particularly important. In Isa 20:3, Isaiah himself is given this title, but the focus shifts to an unnamed servant of Yahweh who most prominently appears in Isa 42:1–9; 49:1–6; 50:4–10; and 52:13–52:12. Scholarly discussion of the identity of this figure is massive and cannot be considered here.[11] Nevertheless, although Moses and David both influence the overall presentation of the servant, there are also allusions to Joshua. Most notable is the declaration of Isa 50:8–9, which points to how God helps the servant against his adversaries, a theme evident in Joshua. Perhaps more directly, God promised Joshua that he would "succeed" (תַּשְׂכִּיל; Josh 1:8), a term used to introduce the fourth of the so-called Servant Songs (Isa 52:13). Admittedly, Joshua is not a major influence on the presentation of the

---

[10] Josh 1:1, 13, 15; 8:31, 33; 11:12; 12:6 (x2); 13:8; 14:7; 18:7; 22:2, 4, 5. Moses also receives this title in 2 Kgs 18:12; 2 Chr 1:3; 24:6.

[11] For a helpful start, see H. G. M. Williamson, *Variations on a Theme: King, Messiah and Servant in the Book of Isaiah* (Carlisle: Paternoster, 1998), 113–66; Andrew T. Abernethy, *The Book of Isaiah and God's Kingdom: A Thematic-Theological Approach* (London: Apollos, 2016), 137–60.

servant in Isaiah, but he is one of many streams that come together in this figure. Within Isaiah we ultimately move from the "servant" to the "servants" (Isa 54:17), and their certainty of success when confronted by military might is also consistent with God's promises to Joshua (Josh 1:5).

The New Testament reflects at length on Jesus as the servant *par excellence*. We can only consider some key texts here. An important one for our purposes is found in Acts 8:26–40, when Philip encountered the Ethiopian eunuch reading Isa 53:7–8. Asked about the identity of this figure, Philip proclaimed Jesus from this text. This is consistent with the proclamation of Peter and John in Acts 3:13, in which they insist that God had glorified "his servant Jesus." Similarly, John indicates that the servant figure finds fulfillment in Jesus (John 12:38). Even where the language of the servant is absent, many passages allude to the servant texts, such as 1 Pet 2:21, in which discussion of Christ's suffering builds on Isaiah 53. Read against the background in Joshua, we see how Jesus, like Joshua, succeeds in the mission given to him by God, though in his case it transcends any geographical location.

Although it is not a major element in the book, Joshua is also presented as a prophet (Josh 3:9; 24:2–13). It is, perhaps, not surprising that his prophetic role and his designation as servant both find expression in the book's final chapter since it represents the pinnacle of his work. Joshua's prophetic role demonstrates that in this, too, he continued the work of Moses. In the Old Testament, Moses is the archetypal prophet, the one against whom all other prophets are assessed. At the point of the composition of Deuteronomy, it could be said that no prophet had arisen like him (Deut 34:9–12), though earlier in the book there is a promise that God would raise up a prophet like him (Deut 18:18). This text is best understood as referring to a continued series of prophets rather than just a single figure.[12] Although his role as a prophet does not rise to the level of Moses, Joshua is the first one God raised up to demonstrate this. Others like Samuel and Elijah would continue this tradition, each likened to Moses in various ways. Similarly, Jeremiah's call narrative (Jer 1:4–10) likens him to Moses and the Isaianic servant. Joshua thus stands within a stream of figures pointing to God's faithfulness in raising up prophets like Moses, even if none ever quite attain his status.

---

[12] J. G. McConville, *Deuteronomy* (Nottingham: Apollos, 2002), 303.

To speak of Jesus as a prophet is to consider one of his offices as traditionally defined—along with priest and king. Since Joshua was neither of these, the connection between Jesus and Joshua is more limited in this respect. Nevertheless, one of the key elements in New Testament Christology is its application of the office of prophet to Jesus. It is clear from the dialogue reported in John 1:19–28 that at least one of the expectations for the Messiah in Jesus' day was that he would be a prophet like Moses. Hence John the Baptist was asked, "Are you the prophet?" (John 1:21).[13] Denying this, John instead indicated that he was the forerunner who prepared the way. Later, Jesus claimed prophetic authority for himself, saying he spoke the Father's word (John 12:49), just as prophets spoke God's word, something consistent with Deut 18:18. A key test for the authentic prophet in Deut 18:21–22 is the reliability of the prophetic message, especially a word of judgment. We see this affirmed of Jesus in Luke 19:41–44, where his lament over Jerusalem indicated what would happen to the city in AD 70. Joshua was a prophet like Moses (Deut 18:18), so that he stands in the tradition that anticipated Jesus even as Jesus far exceeded him.

These connections between Joshua and Jesus are thus more than typological, and more than the simple fact that they share the same name.[14] They are grounded in key themes that run throughout the Bible and come to an explicit conclusion in Heb 3:1–4:13. The author of Hebrews there explores the way Jesus is greater than both Moses and Joshua. We are first shown how Jesus is greater than Moses because he is the Son, whereas Moses was a servant (Heb 3:1–6). But this in turn raises the question of succession: If Joshua succeeded Moses and was less significant than Moses, how do we evaluate Jesus against him?

The writer next makes a more explicitly typological move, one that is particularly notable in that he uses the name Ἰησοῦς to refer not to Jesus but to Joshua (Heb 4:8).[15] Joshua's key task (reflected through Psalm 95 in Heb 4:7–11) had been to grant Israel rest in the land. Although Joshua did indeed point to the gift of rest (Josh 21:44), this was not the last place at which rest was given in the Old Testament. Indeed, rest was

---

[13] 1QS IX, 9–11 and 1Q28a II, 11–21 can both be read as indicating that the Qumran community expected a prophetic messiah as well as a royal one.

[14] "Jesus" in English derives from Ἰησοῦς, which is how the name "Joshua" is presented in the LXX.

[15] Thomas R. Schreiner, *Commentary on Hebrews*, BTCP (Nashville: B&H, 2015), 143.

also given to another servant of the Lord, David, in 2 Sam 7:1–3.[16] That
this was necessary was already a hint that Joshua's rest was not final.
Thus, the writer points to the Sabbath rest that remains for the people
of God (Heb 4:4–11) and urges his readers to enter it—much as Joshua
had entered into the land. This rest that Jesus provides is greater than
what Joshua provided because it is eternal, not limited to a particular
time and place. Nevertheless, part of the pattern for experiencing the
rest that Jesus gives is modeled on the rest given by Joshua. Moses is a
more significant figure for the New Testament's presentation of Jesus,
but we cannot ignore Joshua.

§4 Land as God's Gift

Any reading of Joshua will note the importance of the theme of the land
as God's gift to Israel.[17] In Josh 1:2, God commanded Joshua to rise and
cross the Jordan to enter the land that he was giving them. The noun
אֶרֶץ (usually "land") occurs 107 times in the book, though somewhat
surprisingly its often near synonym אֲדָמָה occurs only twice (23:13, 15).[18]
In both of the latter references, אֲדָמָה is the place from which God would
remove Israel for their unfaithfulness, whereas אֶרֶץ typically refers to
what he was giving Israel. Care must be taken with such a small sample,
but Joshua seems to distinguish between the land as that which God was
giving (אֶרֶץ) and the land as that which Israel could lose (אֲדָמָה). Perhaps
the latter term is used to refer to the productive value of the land (it can
also mean "soil, dirt"), while the more common term is used to refer to
the land as a whole, though the use of אֶרֶץ at 23:16 suggests that this term
can also be used to refer to land that could be lost.

The more important element is the idea that the land was God's gift to
Israel, albeit one that Israel had to take. The verbal root נתן ("give") occurs
eighty-seven times in the book, with many of these instances referring
either directly to God's gift of the land or at least to some part of it (e.g.,
Jericho in 6:2). However, the gift is expressed in different ways. Twenty
times, this verb appears as a *qal* perfect, describing the gift as already

---

[16] In Hebrews, Psalm 95 is specifically cited as a word from David (Heb 4:7).

[17] It is thus something of a surprise that Walter Brueggemann's otherwise excellent *The
Land: Place as Gift, Promise and Challenge in Biblical Faith*, 2nd ed. (Minneapolis: Fortress, 2002)
does not provide a sustained treatment of Joshua.

[18] Excluding the homonym "Adamah," which occurs as a proper noun at 19:36.

given. Sometimes, this is because it refers to land already given east of the Jordan (e.g., Joshua 13), but at other points the verb describes what would happen under Joshua's leadership. For example, in 1:3 every place where Joshua's foot would tread was already given to Israel. Perhaps most remarkably, in 2:9 Rahab's confession asserts that God had already given Israel the land, which the scouts repeat to Joshua (2:24).

At other points, the *qal* infinitive construct is used, with seven of its nine occurrences associated with the gift of the land, always referring to something promised that could be anticipated or that had been fulfilled. This concept is evident in God's speech to Joshua (1:6), in the Gibeonites' explanation of why they had acted as they did (9:24), and in the narrator's comments on God's faithfulness in giving the land (21:43).

The imperative is used with reference to the land or some part of it three times (14:12; 15:19; 20:2), though in these instances the focus is always on how Israel was to allot the gift. The *qal* imperfect is used in 8:18 to describe Ai, and the *waw*-consecutive is used twenty-four times to describe either God defeating a particular city (e.g., 10:32) or Israel allotting some part of the land that God had given (e.g., 13:15; 17:4). In four instances, the *qal* participle is used to describe the gift as a process that was happening (1:2, 11, 15; 11:6). There is also one instance of a *niphal* (24:33), which refers to the town given to Eleazar, though of course this could only be given because it was part of the land God had already given.

We can sum this up by noting that Joshua variously understands the land as something already given in terms of God's promise or as a promise being fulfilled, until we reach the two summary statements (21:45; 23:14–16) that reflect on God's faithfulness in giving the land. However, even here there is still a future orientation present because although the land had been given, much of it still needed to be taken (13:1). But this tension in no way changes the reality that the land had been given.

Understanding the land as a gift must therefore be balanced by noting that the land was to be taken by Israel. The importance of this can be seen in the twenty-eight occurrences of the verb ירשׁ, which depending on context is either "possess" or "dispossess."[19] There is some variability here. In the *qal* (which is typically "possess") the verb tends to have Israel

---

[19] Technically, there are twenty-nine occurrences of the root. But since the infinitive absolute in 17:13 works in combination with its cognate there rather than on its own, these two occurrences are combined in the count above.

as the subject, noting that they have an active role in receiving the gift (e.g., 1:11; 13:1). The *hiphil* (typically "dispossess") may have either God or Israel as subject. If Israel is subject, it refers to taking possession of an occupied place (e.g., 8:7), or more commonly to their failure to take possession (e.g., 17:13). Where God is the subject, the emphasis falls on his active role in giving Israel the land (e.g., 13:6).

In reflecting on the possession of the gift, therefore, Joshua retains a balance between Israel's initiative and God's faithfulness, noting both Israel's role in taking up the gift and God's continued involvement in giving it. The land was always something given and something being given, something that Israel must possess and that God was enabling them to possess. Yet the land was also something that Israel often failed to possess (most obviously as reported for Dan in 19:47, where the verb ירש is applied to land outside the boundaries promised).

A key issue in Joshua is determining what the boundaries of the land are, something of particular importance because of the eastern tribes that settle outside the area that had been initially promised. However, in their case it is possible to look back to events recorded in Numbers (1:13; 22:2–4) and understand that this was still land given by God. Although the issue in Joshua 22 is ostensibly the altar on the bank of the Jordan, the deeper issue is determining which land belonged to the people of God (see §2 above, "Identity of the People of God"). What emerges is that the people of God were not bound by borders if they were faithful. More problematic is the settlement of Dan outside of the territory allotted to them (19:47). The implication is that even though the people of God are not defined by boundaries, a failure to live in the promise of the land as a gift means that Dan's territory, even though proverbially the north of Israel (in the phrase "from Dan to Beersheba"), is actually not part of the land. So, there was flexibility over what constituted the land, but it was only valid when affirmed by God.

We can draw these elements together by noting that in Joshua the land is always something that has been given and is in process of being given, always something to be possessed and something Israel may fail to possess. God was also prepared to grant more land to Israel, but it was not for Israel to determine this. Although these perspectives might be seen as contradictions, each was true. But the way in which it was expressed would depend on what Israel needed to know at any given point. Israel was always on the way toward full reception of the gift of the land. Though that gift was fully expressed in the time of David (2 Sam 8:1–13), the expulsion of Dan from their land already anticipated the loss of the northern kingdom (2 Kgs 17:6) and the exile of Judah (2 Kgs 24:10–17; 25:1–21). Israel possessed the land through faithful obedience but could lose it through disobedience.

The importance of the land as a theological theme across the Old Testament cannot be underestimated. The land defines Israel politically and is also the place where Israel could most clearly express itself as the people of God. Esther is unique among the books of the Old Testament in not showing interest in the land, but that is because it explores the nature of exile.

When we turn to the New Testament we notice that the land theme is at best a minor one.[20] At one level this should neither surprise nor trouble us; the center of the New Testament is not a place but a person, Jesus. Nevertheless, in the New we find important echoes of the Old Testament's rich theology of the land. Perhaps the most important of these is in Jesus' reading of Isaiah 61 in Luke 4:18–20. Although the theme of the land is not expressed directly here, the text is replete with allusions to the year of Jubilee (Lev 25:8–55). For this year to function, Israel's occupation of the land was central since people could only return to their family land once it had been allotted in Joshua. But here Jesus takes up the hope of Jubilee and makes clear that a greater hope is found in him. Closely related to this is the third beatitude in the Sermon on the Mount (Matt 5:5), in which Jesus said the meek would inherit the land, drawing from the language of Joshua. Readers in English, however, may miss the resonances with Isa 61:2 (lxx); the word for "mourning" in Matthew (πενθοῦντες) refers to the Isaiah text and through that to the Jubilee. The promise of the land is vital background to this, but it finds its focus in Jesus.

The development of the theme of the land as God's gift in the New Testament thus finds its principal outworking in its presentation of discipleship. This discipleship is, like the gift of the land, rooted in a life that we already have in Jesus but that we must possess—a life that is offered but not all take. It is a life shaped by obedience to Jesus and that God may bless in new and unexpected ways, but it is not a life where believers are free to determine their own patterns. It is a life that finds blessedness (μακάριοι) in unexpected ways but knows that hope is centered on Jesus

---

[20] Cf. Brueggemann, *The Land*, 160.

as the one in whom the gift of the land continues to find focus, even as we are called to disciple all the nations in obedience to him (Matt 26:16–20). Christian ministry is thus shaped by the pattern of Israel's relationship to the land in Joshua, but with our focus now on Jesus.[21]

§5 Leadership

The theme of leadership in Joshua is closely related to the theme of faithfulness and obedience (see §1). Indeed, one could argue that neither theme could exist without the other. Leadership was an important element of the life of the people of God in Joshua as they worked out what it meant to obey God. Obedience was expected of the people, but guidance was needed to work out the shape of obedience in any one circumstance. This relationship exists because, as noted in considering faithfulness and obedience above, there is always a dialogue between Scripture and life. In the same way that jazz musicians improvise within certain constraints, and do so because of a deep knowledge of music, so Scripture gives shape to obedience but does not always dictate the exact form it will take. To push the analogy with jazz one step further, even within an improvised set of music there is normally a leader who, understanding the constraints that apply, leads the band. We see something like this in Joshua, and we can trace this idea through other parts of the canon.

Although various types of leaders within Israel are mentioned in Joshua (e.g., 1:10; 23:2; 24:1), no attempt is made to differentiate them from one another. They represent either military or civil leadership, but beyond this the book largely assumes their functions rather than explains them. There is no one word in the book that means "leadership."[22] Rather,

---

[21] Careful readers will note that this discussion does not address the issue of whether there is a future land for Israel. This rather knotty issue is tied to different theological systems and the place they give to Israel. One need only compare dispensationalism with covenant theology to see how this draws on the question of the identity of God's people and how Israel is related to this. In fairness, I should make clear that my own view on this broadly matches that developed by Peter J. Gentry and Stephen J. Wellum in *Kingdom through Covenant: A Biblical-Theological Understanding of the Covenants* (Wheaton: Crossway, 2012), 683–94, so that there is only ever one people of God—those who have committed themselves to God. If so, there is no need for a future land for Israel, though I cannot rule that out.

[22] Strictly, this is true of the Old Testament as a whole, though there are a large number of words that come under this domain. See *NIDOTTE* 5:117.

as is true for the Old Testament as a whole, Joshua shows us leadership in action instead of providing a theoretical reflection on the concept.[23]

Within the book, three key figures stand out: Joshua, Caleb, and Phinehas. Joshua is, of course, a significant leader for the book, while Caleb is important in the land allocation chapters (Joshua 13–21) and Phinehas comes to prominence in the encounter with the eastern tribes (Joshua 22). Eleazar is also important for the land allocation, but his actions are linked with Joshua. Although we will not consider him, the fact that he is linked with Joshua in the land allocation (14:1–5; 19:51) indicates that there were limits to the role of any one leader. The importance of these figures for the book is evident from the fact that all except Caleb are mentioned in the book's close (24:29–33). Each one demonstrated leadership that brought what God had already revealed into dialogue with the new circumstances of the people.

In Joshua's case, we immediately see the importance of his reflection on the Torah (1:6–9) as central to his leadership. This reflection can easily be seen in the balance of Joshua 1, as his directives to the eastern tribes are saturated in the language of Numbers and Deuteronomy. The processes in chapter 1, however, begin to explore how his leadership might develop. Most notably, although there was an existing agreement that the eastern tribes would join the others in taking the land, there was no specific mechanism for how this would take place. Joshua's directives in 1:10–15 thus worked this out in light of Israel's circumstances. Because of this, the eastern tribes could commit themselves to his leadership, tying Joshua's work to that of Moses (1:16–18).

By contrast, Joshua followed no particular directive when sending the scouts to spy out the land in chapter 2. Although some have questioned the appropriateness of Joshua doing this, it is ultimately something that the book affirms when it declares that he did everything commanded through Moses (11:15–23). Setting these chapters in dialogue with each other is important if we are to understand its theology of leadership. What becomes clear is that where fairly clear guidelines were already

---

[23] Dennis J. McCarthy, "The Theology of Leadership in Joshua 1–9," *Biblica* 52.2 (1971): 168–69, argues that we see what themes are of interest through how the stories are told. His approach is thus similar to that adopted here. However, reading the book as a whole indicates that although his view (p. 175) that God develops his work through a leader he trusts and sustains is right as far as it goes, it needs to be extended to see a wider understanding of leadership across the book as a whole.

given, Joshua was expected to determine how to apply them, but there were points where such guidelines were lacking. Yet as long as he worked toward God's stated goals, Joshua had considerable freedom to lead. Whether in crossing the Jordan (Joshua 3–4), taking Jericho (Joshua 6) and Ai (7:1–8:29), or resolving the issue of the Gibeonites (Joshua 9), the key was always bringing current circumstances into dialogue with what God had revealed and ensuring that God's people were working toward fulfilling his purposes for them.

This relationship between understanding what God had promised and working out its application in new circumstances can also be seen in the book's presentation of Caleb and Phinehas. Caleb pointed to a promise received through Moses that he was to inherit a portion in the land (14:6–9), but the promise did not specify how it was to be received. Therefore, Caleb's confidence in claiming the promise (14:10–15) was dependent on his working with God to claim his land. In so doing, he provided a model for the other tribes who were still to claim their allocation (18:1–10). Caleb's pattern of leadership is closer to that of Joshua 1, where a specific promise could be claimed.

Phinehas' work in Joshua 22, however, is closer to the leadership displayed in Joshua 2, in which there was no promise to be claimed but rather a complex issue to be resolved. Just as Joshua ultimately received confirmation of God's gift of the land with the return of the scouts (2:24), Phinehas discerned what God was doing through his interaction with the eastern tribes (22:31). In both chapters 2 and 22, leadership involved discerning what God was doing in light of the general direction he had given for his people rather than claiming a specific promise.

At the end of the book, Joshua himself received the title "servant of the LORD" (24:29 ESV). This title, more than any other, was a commendation of his leadership. Perhaps more importantly, it demonstrated that the concept of servant leadership is not unique to the New Testament (even if Jesus gave it a particular shape; see Mark 10:35–45). Servant leadership from the perspective of Joshua requires the integration of (1) helping God's people understand what God has revealed, and (2) working out the implications as they move into new contexts.

This pattern can easily be traced across large parts of the Old Testament, though only a few examples can be considered here. For example, in 1 Samuel 1–12 the prophet Samuel was charged with leading the nation from one pattern of government to another. Samuel was not convinced of the virtue of the proposal for monarchy, but he accepted that this was something that God himself was ultimately bringing about. Samuel's role was to contribute to this (1 Samuel 8). But in doing so, he was careful to point the nation back to what God had done in the past and to insist that this should shape their future (1 Samuel 12).

Jeroboam failed to understand that what God had done in the past was meant to provide a pattern that Israel should follow in the future. This was central to him establishing his own sanctuaries, the sin that would mark the northern kingdom and cause its demise (1 Kgs 12:25-33). The goal of leadership is to lead the people of God into a deeper relationship with him by understanding how his revelation shapes the present and the future; this goal influences the assessment of various leaders in the Prophets (cf. Isa 7:1-17, Jer 22:11-30).[24] Most obviously, the book of Isaiah draws on this pattern when speaking of the servant of the Lord, who (like David) is marked by the Spirit and renders justice that is rooted in the Torah (Isa 42:1-9).[25]

The importance of the servant figure cannot be overestimated for our understanding of Jesus. As we have noted, Jesus' presentation of leadership based on the pattern of the servant has deep roots in the Old Testament, including the pattern of leaders suffering for their people. But the cruciform element of Jesus' leadership takes this beyond anything explicit within the Old Testament. Moreover, where the Old Testament designates crucial leaders as "the servant of the LORD," Jesus took the concept of servanthood and made it paradigmatic for leadership. Importantly, he contrasted his model with the dominant pattern in the Mediterranean world, whereby leaders lorded their status over their subjects (Mark 10:42-45). If servant leadership is ultimately cruciform, then leadership cannot be about the accumulation of status. It must instead be focused on enabling God's people to live the life he has for them.

Jesus' model seems to have shaped Paul's understanding of his role. He often designates himself as a "servant" (δοῦλος) in his letters (e.g.,

---

[24] See David G. Firth, "Leadership," in *Dictionary of the Old Testament Prophets*, ed. Mark J. Boda and J. Gordon McConville (Downers Grove, IL: IVP Academic, 2012), 501-5.

[25] See Williamson, *Variations on a Theme*, 130-46; S. D. (Fanie) Snyman, "A Structural-Historical Exegesis of Isaiah 42.1-9," in *Interpreting Isaiah: Issues and Approaches*, ed. David G. Firth and H. G. M. Williamson (Nottingham: Apollos, 2009), 250-60; Abernethy, *The Book of Isaiah and God's Kingdom*, 138-42.

Rom 1:1; Phil 1:1).[26] Elsewhere (2 Cor 4:5), he also highlights the importance of being a servant of God's people. Moreover, when encouraging the Philippians to strive for unity (Phil 1:27–2:12), he encourages them to follow Jesus' own pattern of servanthood (Phil 2:7). Similarly, when encouraging Timothy to develop his ministry, Paul grounds this in servanthood—that is, being prepared to suffer while enabling God's people to grow (2 Tim 2:22–26). Servanthood is not the only biblical image for leadership, but it is one to which Joshua makes a rich contribution and that Jesus developed through his teaching.

§6 Power and Government

Because Joshua is largely a book about Israel's entry into the land, often focused on military elements, one can easily miss the political dimension that is integral to this story. In part, missing this political dimension can also come from an interpretative focus on the Canaanites as gross sinners, though in fact this is not something that Joshua ever states.[27] Once we step away from an approach that is narrowly focused on military matters, we can recognize that Joshua does develop a theology of politics that challenges various views of power and government precisely because God's approach to politics is opposed to structures that oppress people.[28] It is important, therefore, that we consider this theme in Joshua and in the rest of Scripture because of the ways in which this has been portrayed in popular literature, especially in the work of the "New Atheists."[29]

Understanding this theme requires close attention once again to the troubling issue of the ban—devoting something to destruction (חרם).[30] In the introduction, I argued that we should not understand this as referring

---

[26] This same self-designation also occurs in 2 Pet 1:1 and Jude 1, demonstrating that the apostles and other early leaders understood this to be pivotal to their role.

[27] See Walton and Walton, *Israelite Conquest*, 137–56.

[28] I thank Richard S. Hess for a stimulating presentation at the Institute for Biblical Research "Unscripted" session at the SBL Annual Meeting in San Antonio in 2016, which made me reflect on this issue. Sadly, given the nature of "Unscripted" presentations, there is no published paper to which later reference can be made. However, the more general elements of his approach can be seen in Richard S. Hess, "War in the Hebrew Bible: An Overview," in *War in the Hebrew Bible and Terrorism in the Twenty-First Century*, ed. Richard S. Hess and Elmer A. Martens (Winona Lake, IN: Eisenbrauns, 2008), 27–30.

[29] E.g., Richard Dawkins, *The God Delusion* (London: Black Swan, 2006), 280.

[30] See "Joshua and the Problem of Violence" in the Introduction. This section should be read in conjunction with the discussion there.

to total destruction but rather to a comprehensive victory. Though it would be foolish to think that this never involved death, the actual levels of destruction described are considerably less than many people imagine because of the distance between the language of the text and how we might use similar language today. Nevertheless, we can see some of Joshua's key contributions to a theology of power and government if we note what is placed under the ban in Joshua, as well as what God excludes from it.

The verbal forms of חרם occur fourteen times in Joshua. The cognate noun occurs twelve times, mostly close to the verb, though all except three of these are associated with Achan's sin.[31] For our purposes, therefore, the verbal forms are most important. The verb is not widely distributed across the book as a whole, with all occurrences falling into chapters 1–12.[32] For convenience, these are tabulated here:

Reference in Joshua	Speaker	Place / Persons Devoted
2:10	Rahab	Sihon and Og
6:18	Joshua	Jericho and its contents
6:21	Narrator	Inhabitants and livestock of Jericho
8:26	Narrator	Ai
10:1	Narrator	Jericho, Ai, and their kings
10:28	Narrator	Makkedah, king, inhabitants
10:35	Narrator	Inhabitants of Eglon
10:37	Narrator	Hebron, king, inhabitants
10:39	Narrator	Debir, king, inhabitants
10:40	Narrator	Hills, Negev, and Shephelah and their kings
11:11	Narrator	Hazor and its king
11:12	Narrator	Northern cities and their kings
11:20	Narrator	Cities of Israel
11:21	Narrator	Anakim and their cities

---

[31] Josh 7:1 (x2), 11, 12 (x2), 13 (x2), 15; 22:20. The other three appear in the Jericho story leading up to Achan's sin: 6:17, 18 (x2).

[32] In Joshua, the verb always occurs in the *hiphil* perfect, imperfect, *waw*-consecutive imperfect, and infinitive construct, though variations in tense are essentially a function of narrative form rather than carrying significant theological meaning.

Some caution is needed in interpreting this table, particularly regarding the meaning of the verb חרם as "to defeat comprehensively" when read in light of Joshua's genre, rather than "totally destroy" or something similar (though for consistency, "devoted" is used here). But with this caveat noted, some intriguing patterns emerge. After the first two references, in which Rahab and Joshua are the speakers, the verb occurs in the context of either a report of a specific event or a summary of several. A more important pattern, however, is evident when we consider the place or persons devoted.

In all cases, we are dealing with a city and its king. In some instances, the presence of the king is not made explicit (e.g., 6:18), but subsequent narration gives attention to the kings (for Jericho in 10:1). Language of kingship here sometimes refers only to what might now be called local chieftains, but at other points a hierarchy of these kings is meant (10:1-5; 11:1-5, 10). This observation needs to be tied to the list of kings in 12:7-24, which includes several kings whose cities were not mentioned in the previous narrative. The list is included at this point in the book to show that the focus of devoting places and people was specifically on cities with kings. This observation in turn needs to be tied to the fact that the cities were invariably highly defensible, centers from which Israel might make themselves militarily secure. Three cities were burned—Jericho, Ai, and Hazor.[33] The first two were not large cities, so their burning is principally symbolic of the fact that Israel was not to find its security in fortified cities. Hazor (11:1-11), however, represented a special case, because it was such a large center that was militarily strong and exerted political power over the northern portion of the land. But the clear message here, especially given God's command to Joshua to hamstring the horses and burn Hazor's chariots, is that Israel was not to structure its common life along this pattern. Although the theme is less developed in the southern campaign (Joshua 10), the same motifs are present. Both the southern and northern campaigns focus on how God defeated foes who were far more powerful than Israel (10:12-14; 11:6-8). Thus, the ones devoted

---

[33] Ralph K. Hawkins, *How Israel Became a People* (Nashville: Abingdon, 2013), 117-19, notes that Dan was also destroyed in the period of Israel's emergence in the land, but this is recorded in Judges 18 and so falls outside of our consideration here. In addition, the fact that Dan is outside the land that God promised means the account in Judges 18 functions differently from the three noted here.

were those associated with Canaanite royal structures—the cities and the armed forces who resisted Israel by fighting for them.

In light of this, note the exceptional case of the Gibeonites. Although Gibeon was a large city, "like one of the royal cities" (10:2), it was apparently not governed by a king. We cannot say for certain that this is why God did not harden their hearts, but their response to Israel in Joshua 9 differs notably from that of the other kings (9:1; 10:1–5; 11:1–5). Kings—specifically Canaanite kings—thus emerge as a particular focus in the book. God opposed them and the trappings associated with them. In light of this, Rahab's reference to Sihon and Og in her confession (2:10) fits with the general pattern. We are not told what was wrong with these kings and their cities, so all we can do is infer. But notably both Sihon and Og (and also Balak in 24:9) opposed Israel in some way. Israel was, of course, to avoid anything associated with Canaanite religion, but perhaps a particular feature to be avoided was a tendency to place too much power in the hands of a king.

Israel's approach to power and politics was to be different. This was evident in the law of the king (Deut 17:14–20). The king was not to be elevated above his kin in power, wealth, or prestige; instead, he was to study and teach the Torah. This model of kingship is decisively different from the royal patterns observable in Joshua, in which the kings consistently opposed Israel and led their people to destruction. Read against Deuteronomy, we see a fundamental problem with Canaanite kingship, especially its tendency to aggregate power to individuals and disempower the rest of the people. Joshua thus created a context in which Israel could live out a very different political reality.

That is not to say that Israel consistently lived this out. By the time of Samuel, there were already those calling for a king "like all the nations" (1 Sam 8:5). The ambiguity of this statement is fundamental to the conflict that is resolved in these chapters. Although Deuteronomy had allowed for a king "like all the nations" (Deut 17:14), this king was not to function like the kings of the nations. The elders in Samuel's day were really asking for a king who would indeed function like the kings of the nations, rather than according to the pattern of Deuteronomy. This is what Samuel opposed (1 Sam 8:10–18), though in the end God demonstrated that he had a very different view of kingship (especially in 1 Samuel 12, where the problems of kingship come into focus). Nevertheless, the central point remains: Israel's politics were to be fundamentally different from those of the nations precisely because they were not to aggregate power to a central individual. Even before Israel had a king, Joshua made clear that a different model of power and government was needed.

In light of the Davidic covenant (2 Sam 7:1–17; cf. 2 Sam 23:1–7), the prophets develop the idea of how Israel was to model the issue of power and government. In Isa 11:1–9, we see a Davidic king who surpasses his predecessors in his understanding of justice and righteousness, demonstrating that government in Israel was to exercise power on behalf of the poor. Thus, Isa 32:1–8 speaks of the pattern of government that should be expected of kings, even though a coming one will transcend them all. By contrast, Jeremiah outlines the failings of David's descendants in his own time because justice was not central to their reigns (Jer 21:11–22:30). Josiah may have been an exception for Jeremiah, but the problem remained.

In the New Testament, of course, the hope of a kingdom with justice and opportunity for all is expressed in the language of the kingdom of God. The kingdom is central to Jesus' preaching from the beginning of the Synoptic Gospels (Matt 4:17; Mark 1:15). This theme in the New Testament is too large to consider here,[34] and of course we must see this in terms of its presentation of Jesus as the Messiah. But from the perspective of what it means for lived experience, we can perhaps consider Paul's observation that the kingdom is "righteousness, peace, and joy in the Holy Spirit" (Rom 14:17). Cited without its context, this could easily become a mere epigram rather than something that demands a different view of life. When we read it in the context of the need for all believers to support and encourage one another by walking in love (Rom 14:13–23), we realize that this vision of the kingdom is drawn from Jesus' teaching while also developing the alternative vision of power and politics we see at work in Joshua. The community of God's people is marked by love and a desire to see one another flourish through the work of the Spirit. Canaanite models of power and government are antithetical to this.

§7 Rest

As with many of Joshua's themes, rest first emerges in the opening chapter, though it will appear again at strategic points. Particularly important

---

[34] For a manageable introduction, see Thomas R. Schreiner, *Magnifying God in Christ: A Summary of New Testament Theology* (Nottingham: Inter-Varsity Press, 2010), 20–26.

is when Joshua explained to the eastern tribes why they needed to cross the Jordan with the western tribes (Josh 1:13). Joshua referred to God's promise to the eastern tribes (Num 32:20–22; Deut 3:18–20), assuring them of rest in their land east of the Jordan if they enabled the other tribes to claim their inheritance. Rest was thus available to all of the people of God, and it was not dependent on living within the boundaries initially promised but on the people's faithfulness to God. This use of the participle "will give rest" (מֵנִיחַ) in Josh 1:13 makes clear that rest was not yet something resolved for them.

Rest here is based on the verb נוח, which occurs nine times in the book. At some points, it occurs in a narrative and simply means, "to stop, to stand at a place," as for example when the priests entered the Jordan (3:13). Similarly, in 4:3, 8, the verb is used with reference to placing the stones that would form the memorial cairn for crossing the river. Texts such as these do not contribute significantly to the theology of rest, but the other occurrences of the verb explore the idea of rest as something related to a settled life in the land that God was giving. Notably, before the eastern or western tribes obtained rest, we learn that the scouts entered Jericho after its defeat, brought out Rahab and her family, and settled them (literally, "caused them to rest," וַיַּנִּיחוּם) outside the camp. Though they were outside the camp, nevertheless this clan achieved rest before any Israelites did, reflecting Rahab's own commitment to Israel (2:4–21).

After this, the root נוח is put aside, and the verb שקט is used at two pivotal points. The first of these is at 11:23 in a summary of the conquest traditions, which notes that "the land had rest from war." Whereas נוח is largely about rest as settlement, שקט refers to rest as the absence of war. Only Rahab and her clan had been granted rest in the form of settlement at this point. So, rest from war was a necessary step toward the rest of settlement of which Joshua had spoken (1:13–15). The land also had rest from war after Caleb claimed his territory (14:15). Again, this was good for the land, but it was not yet the rest that accompanied settlement in the land given by God.

Since rest through the absence of war had been realized, steps could be taken toward obtaining the full rest that God had promised. Therefore, subsequent references to rest return to the root נוח, since it represents the goal of the settlement process. Israel was not only to live in a land without war, but also each clan was to settle on the land that God was giving them. Thus, we are repeatedly told that the land was allotted to the tribes "by their clans" (e.g., 13:16). Rest as settlement means that everyone had their place as God's gift to them. That is why the narrator returns to the theme of rest in the summary statement of 21:43–45. God had given each clan a place to be settled; therefore, Israel could know that he had given them rest on every side.

The idea of rest on every side echoes Deut 12:11, which expresses this as the condition for Israel having a central sanctuary. To some extent, this had already happened when the tent of meeting was set up at Shiloh (Josh 18:1). At that point the land could be considered subdued (כבש) before them, with the verb describing the outcome of the absence of war noted earlier (11:23; 14:15). But language of rest is withheld until the summary statement in 21:43–45 because only then were God's promises proved reliable, including the promise of rest. Israel was now settled in the land that God had given, even if technically much of the land remained to be taken (13:1–7).

From this point (Josh 21:43–45), the references to rest spell out its implications. In 22:4, when Joshua sent the eastern tribes back to their territory, he affirmed that rest had been given to the western tribes. This implied that the eastern tribes would also enjoy rest once they returned, but it also made clear that this enjoyment was dependent on their continued faithfulness to God's commandments. Of course, the balance of that chapter shows how fragile Israel's grasp on rest was. The construction of an altar on the banks of the Jordan brought the nation to the brink of war, thus winding back even the more limited rest spoken of earlier (11:23, 14:15). Only with the (restored) absence of war at the end of that chapter could the narrator return to the theme of rest as an existing gift from God when introducing Joshua's speech in 23:1. Again, Israel's grasp of the rest was fragile and dependent on their continued faithfulness to God's commands.

Rest in Joshua can thus be summed up as something that emerges in stages. Settlement is a key goal, but to achieve it Israel first needed the absence of war. Only then could they have rest as a settled life, yet this settled life could be enjoyed only through continued faithfulness.

This pattern of rest in Joshua also finds expression in the life of David. Just as Israel had struggled because of the presence of war, so David's early years were marked by continued conflict with Saul. However, David's reign needs to be seen in contrast to the period of the judges. Characteristically, each judge was able to usher in a period of rest (שׁקט)—that is, an absence of war. But there was no settled life because of the continued disobedience of the nation. David's reign (though often greatly troubled) would finally see the more substantial rest of which Josh 21:43–45 had spoken.

After David's conflicts with Saul ended, he approached Nathan with the idea of building the temple (2 Sam 7:1–2). We are told that God had given him "rest on every side" (2 Sam 7:1). The close resemblance between this statement and those in Josh 21:44 and 23:1 is unlikely to be accidental. The rest achieved under Joshua, which was under continued threat because of Israel's disobedience, was (temporarily at least) experienced by David. Sadly, his sin (2 Samuel 11) meant this would not be a permanent experience (2 Sam 12:1–15a). David's own life thus embodied the experience of Israel in Joshua: rest as a settled life can be experienced, but this rest is always fragile, always under threat because of human sin.

For the Chronicler, it is important to show that this pattern of rest continued to be available to David's descendants, even if few of them enjoyed it to its fullest extent. When David spoke to Solomon about the temple and its construction, he referred to God's promise about Solomon being a "man of rest" (1 Chr 22:9), so that he could say God had given Solomon "rest on every side" (1 Chr 22:18). The conditions that led David to want to build the temple existed for Solomon, even if they no longer did for David. Indeed, when organizing the Levites, David pointed to this rest as something given to the nation (1 Chr 23:25). The rest was also experienced by his descendants in a more limited way. God's gift of "rest on every side" could be used as a rallying cry by Asa (2 Chr 14:7), though this was in the face of threatened war. Nevertheless, in a context of faithfulness, rest could be experienced under both Asa (2 Chr 15:15) and Jehoshaphat (2 Chr 20:30). A unifying feature of all these references to rest is that it was given by God. A truly settled life for God's people is experienced in faithfulness to God but only as God gives it.

Against this background we need to read Hebrews 4, which reflects on Joshua and on Psalm 95. God had sworn that the exodus generation would not enter his "rest," a noun derived from נוח (Ps 95:11, quoted in Heb 4:3). The psalm refers to Numbers 13–14 and the failure of the first generation to enter the land. For Christians, there is a rest that can be experienced already through the work of Jesus, and we enter into this rest through continued faithfulness (Heb 4:3, 11).

The writer also weaves Gen 2:2 into his discussion, introducing an element of rest associated with the verb שבת that does not feature in

Joshua. This is the rest that God takes on the seventh day. Although the writer uses the one Greek verb and its noun cognate (καταπαύω and κατάπαυσις) throughout this discussion, he was likely aware of the nuances that lay behind the different verbs in Hebrew because the "Sabbath rest" (σαββατισμὸς) of which he speaks is a rest that can take satisfaction in what has been done. This rest transcends the experience described in Joshua, yet at the same time the writer is well aware that the rest spoken of in Joshua was always fragile. Indeed, given the exhortation in the letter, the writer sees the same fragility even for believers. Rest is available, a rest that is more than the absence of conflict—and even more than a settled life. There is a rest in which full satisfaction is available, a rest found as believers enter through obedience to God's word, which remains sharper than any double-edged sword (Heb 4:12). The writer thus reflects deeply on Joshua, but he sees a significance in Jesus that exceeds the old experience.

§8 The Promise of God

As with the theme of land, the theme of God's promise is apparent almost from the start of Joshua. In part, this is because the preeminent promise within Joshua is the gift of the land, but it is not limited to that. The close link between promise and land is seen in 1:3, where Joshua is assured that God was giving Israel (the "you" here is plural) every place where the soul of their foot treads, just as he had promised Moses. The promise of God is thus introduced as a key motif in the book that can be traced as Israel received the land, culminating in the editorial statement in 21:43–45 and Joshua's reflections in 23:14–16. In Joshua, Yahweh is a promise-keeping God.[35]

Although this might seem self-evident when reading in English, there are some complexities to be noted. Most importantly, no word in Hebrew has the particular sense of "promise." This does not suggest that the

---

[35] Walter C. Kaiser, *The Promise-Plan of God: A Biblical Theology of the Old and New Testaments* (Grand Rapids: Zondervan, 2008) argues that "promise" forms the appropriate center for biblical theology. Such a large-scale reflection is more than can be attempted here and is related to the debate about whether or not a "center" for biblical theology is needed. My proposal is more modest: The promise of God is *an* important theme in biblical theology, even if it is central in Joshua. Nevertheless, Kaiser's work is important for tracing this particular theme through the whole Bible.

concept was not understood, for the presence of a concept in the thought-world of a given people is not restricted by the existence of a word for that concept in their language. Arguably, some way of expressing the concept is needed, but that is a slightly different matter.

Within Joshua, two key terms are used that point to the idea of God's promise. The first, and perhaps most important, is the use of the root דבר in either its verbal or nominal forms. This is actually one of the most common words in the Hebrew Bible. As a verb, it usually means "to speak," while the noun typically means "word" or "thing." But when the root refers to something previously spoken that is now fulfilled, it has the sense of "promise." This could refer to either human or divine speech, though it is doubtful this root is used in Joshua for any but divine promises. In Joshua, whenever something happens that God had previously spoken, we can understand this as a promise.

The other form of promise is associated with oath giving, something that one party has sworn to do. In Joshua, this always involves the *niphal* of the verb שׁבע or a cognate noun.[36] Again, this can refer to human promises (e.g., 2:12, 9:15) as well as divine ones (e.g., 1:6). Closely related to oath giving is the making of a covenant (e.g., 24:26), a process by which an agreement is formalized. Moreover, simple speech by God can be used to introduce new promises (e.g., 1:8–9), even though there is no specific vocabulary associated with promising. Rather, the form of the speech indicates that a promise was made. Taking these elements as our main clues, we can note that the theme of God's promise can be considered something made in the past and now fulfilled, or something that provided guidance for how Israel was to live as those who had received his promises.

Perhaps more important is how the theme of the fulfillment of God's promises is related to the structure of the book. Joshua 1–12 opens with God reminding Joshua of promises previously made (1:3, 6). Joshua could prepare to enter the land because God had promised to give it, a promise that reaches back to Genesis (Gen 12:7; 15:18–21). Although in Josh 1:3 the promise is traced to Moses, the oath sworn to the ancestors in Josh 1:6 refers to the patriarchs. So these opening statements place the events in Joshua in a larger story, highlighting a promise that goes back more

---

[36] This root, as a noun, can mean either "oath" or "seven." In Joshua, the noun is always the number "seven." The verb also occurs in *hiphil* in 23:7, where it is a synonym for "worship." The noun שְׁבֻעָה ("oath") occurs three times (2:17, 20; 9:20) but always with reference to a human promise.

than four hundred years. God was fulfilling his promise, and Joshua was to participate in this.

The fulfillment of God's promise is equally important in the land allocation (Joshua 13–21). The land allocation proper begins with the story of Caleb. Whereas Joshua was to lead the nation to the land and claim God's promise, Caleb approached Joshua and Eleazar to claim the promise God made to him through Moses (14:6–9). Whereas Joshua's response to God's promise is paradigmatic for the first half of the book, Caleb's is paradigmatic for the land allocation, especially since much of the land remained to be taken (13:1–7). Both these promises are referred to in the close of the land allocation (21:43–45), which affirms that none of God's good promises had failed (21:45). Yahweh is a promise-keeping God; this is good news for his people.

In the closing section of the book (Joshua 22–24), the theme of the promise of God focuses on Israel's future, a future shaped by knowledge of the past. In 22:4, the eastern tribes were sent back to their territory with a reminder that none of God's promises had failed, a reason for continued obedience to him. The altar conflict in 22:9–34 explores the need to remember God's faithfulness to his promises and, therefore, the need of the people to be faithful to him. The theme of the promise as something that should shape future behavior is also important in Joshua 23, which refers to God's promise four times (23:5, 10, 14, 15). There is a notable shift here from chapters 1–21, which had primarily looked at the promise as something fulfilled in what had happened. In chapter 23, the fulfilled promise is what enabled Joshua to look forward and stress that God's promise could also serve as a word of judgment if Israel broke the covenant. God is consistent in his promises. He promised to give the land, but he also promised to take it away for covenant violation (23:13, 15–16; cf. Deut 28). His promise was both a source of hope and also a word of warning. Therefore, Israel had to hold both of these elements together.[37]

God's fulfillment of his promise is a substantial theme in the balance of the Old Testament, though the accent falls on the promise as a word of judgment for unfaithfulness. This theme is central in the reflection on the fall of the northern kingdom (2 Kgs 17:7–23), which notes that

---

[37] Kaiser, *The Promise-Plan of God*, focuses on the hopeful promises, perhaps because these are the ones taken up directly in the New Testament, but both are important for a full understanding of the promises of God.

they were removed from the land because of their failure to keep God's commandments. The author of Kings notes that God exiled the northern kingdom "just as he had declared through all his servants the prophets" (2 Kgs 17:23). The summary of the preceding verses has numerous echoes of Joshua 23. Although the author of Kings refers to a series of prophets, we are probably right to think of Joshua as one of them. Furthermore, although English versions tend not to use the word "promise" in 2 Kgs 17:23 (largely because when speaking of God, "promise" tends to be used for more hopeful themes), the use of the verb דבר is consistent with "promising." God had indeed stated that this behavior would result in the loss of relationship with him and in exile from the land. Thus, since these conditions came to pass, this could be considered a promise fulfilled. Judah's exile can also be spoken of as the fulfillment of a promise from God (2 Kgs 24:13).[38]

This does not mean the Old Testament only knows of the promise of God as something experienced negatively. Exile was the fulfillment of God's promise, but so was the end of exile. Both 2 Chr 36:22–23 and Ezek 1:1–4 (which are similar) look back to God's word through Jeremiah, probably to his comments in Jer 29:10. But even here Jeremiah reflects on earlier promises from God (perhaps a combination of Deut 4:29–31 and the seventy-year message in Jer 25:11–14), which indicated that exile was not the final experience for Israel. All of this prepares for the words of consolation that make up Jeremiah 30–33, including the classic promise of the new covenant (Jer 31:31–34). The promise of God was both a word of warning if Israel transgressed his covenant and a word of hope since he would not abandon his people.

Whereas the accent in the Old Testament is on God's promise as a call for faithfulness in light of judgment rather than as hope for the future, the opposite is the case in the New Testament (though both elements are present). Greek does have a specific word meaning "promise" (ἐπαγγελία and its cognates). The term is sometimes used to refer to promises from God (e.g., Acts 26:6–7; Titus 1:2), but it would be wrong to reduce the concept to this word alone. The New Testament writers also drew on the Old Testament as promise simply by using the language of speech (e.g., Heb 4:4–10). When speaking of the promise, the New Testament writers

---

[38] CSB here renders the verb דִּבֶּר as "predicted," but once again this conforms to the conditions for a promise in which God does what he said he would.

are particularly concerned to stress the reality that God's promises find their fulfillment in Jesus (e.g., 2 Cor 1:20). This concern explains why the emphasis of the New Testament is on the current fulfillment of the promise and thus closely parallels the situation in Joshua where fulfillment of promises is stressed.[39] How the promise is fulfilled will vary.

Taking Psalm 2 as an example, we note that it has been fulfilled in Jesus (Acts 13:33; Heb 1:5), is being fulfilled in the life of the church (Acts 4:23–31), and will be fulfilled in Jesus' return (Rev 19:11–16). Jesus is the central focus of God's promise in the New Testament, but there is variety in how the promise is being fulfilled. Alongside this, there is (like Joshua 22–24) a minor-key melody in which the promise is a continued call to faithfulness because of the possibility of judgment, a theme evident in the letters to the churches (Revelation 2–3).

Throughout the Bible, therefore, the promise of God is a source of consolation and encouragement. Yet it is also a summons to faithfulness on the part of the people of God, precisely because God is one who keeps his promises. Joshua, perhaps more than any other book of the Bible apart from Revelation, holds these two elements together.

---

[39] The promise theme far exceeds anything that can be discussed here. For the positive elements of the promise in Jesus, see Kaiser, *The Promise-Plan of God*, 233–388.

EXPOSITION

I. Entering the Land (1:1–5:12)

A. Preparations for Entering the Land (1:1–18)

¹ After the death of Moses the Lᴏʀᴅ's servant, the Lᴏʀᴅ spoke to Joshua son of Nun, Moses's assistant: ² "Moses my servant is dead. Now you and all the people prepare to cross over the Jordan to the land I am giving the Israelites. ³ I have given you every place where the sole of your foot treads, just as I promised Moses. ⁴ Your territory will be from the wilderness and Lebanon to the great river, the Euphrates River—all the land of the Hittites—and west to the Mediterranean Sea. ⁵ No one will be able to stand against you as long as you live. I will be with you, just as I was with Moses. I will not leave you or abandon you.

⁶ "Be strong and courageous, for you will distribute the land I swore to their ancestors to give them as an inheritance. ⁷ Above all, be strong and very courageous to observe carefully the whole instruction my servant Moses commanded you. Do not turn from it to the right or the left, so that you will have success wherever you go. ⁸ This book of instruction must not depart from your mouth; you are to meditate on it day and night so that you may carefully observe everything written in it. For then you will prosper and succeed in whatever you do. ⁹ Haven't I commanded you: be strong and courageous? Do not be afraid or discouraged, for the Lᴏʀᴅ your God is with you wherever you go."

¹⁰ Then Joshua commanded the officers of the people, ¹¹ "Go through the camp and tell the people, 'Get provisions ready for yourselves, for within three days you will be crossing the Jordan to go in and take possession of the land the Lᴏʀᴅ your God is giving you to inherit.' "

¹² Joshua said to the Reubenites, the Gadites, and half the tribe of Manasseh, ¹³ "Remember what Moses the Lᴏʀᴅ's servant commanded you when he said, 'The Lᴏʀᴅ your God will give you rest, and he will give you this land.' ¹⁴ Your wives, dependents, and livestock may remain in

the land Moses gave you on this side of the Jordan. But your best soldiers must cross over in battle formation ahead of your brothers and
help them [15] until the LORD gives your brothers rest, as he has given you,
and they too possess the land the LORD your God is giving them. You
may then return to the land of your inheritance and take possession of
what Moses the LORD's servant gave you on the east side of the Jordan."
[16] They answered Joshua, "Everything you have commanded us
we will do, and everywhere you send us we will go. [17] We will obey you,
just as we obeyed Moses in everything. Certainly the LORD your God will
be with you, as he was with Moses. [18] Anyone who rebels against your
order and does not obey your words in all that you command him, will
be put to death. Above all, be strong and courageous!"

Context

Readers commencing Joshua should realize from the outset that, although
there are good reasons for seeing it as a distinct book,[1] it is also part of a
continuing narrative. That narrative begins with the creation account in
Genesis and, in various ways, continues through to the end of 2 Kings. Most
importantly, Joshua follows immediately from the end of Deuteronomy.
Indeed, the opening, "After" (1:1), represents a consecutive verb (וַיְהִי),
which usually requires it to be read in terms of what precedes. Although
this verb can introduce a book without making a direct connection with
what has gone before (e.g., Esth 1:1), the fact that it is here associated
with Moses' death makes clear that we are to read this chapter in light
of the closing chapter of Deuteronomy. Deuteronomy will thus provide a
key point of reference for reading Joshua and especially this chapter. In
fact, large parts of God's speech to Joshua verge on being a compilation
of references to Deuteronomy:

1. The statement of Moses' death (v. 2) recapitulates Deuteronomy 34.
2. Reference to every place "where the sole of your foot treads"
   (v. 3) is taken from Deut 11:24.
3. The promise that "no one will be able to stand against you" (v. 5)
   is taken from Deut 7:24 and 11:25, while the promise never to
   leave or forsake Joshua is taken from Deut 31:8 (having been first
   spoken to the nation in 31:6).
4. The command to "be strong and courageous" (vv. 6, 9, 18) is taken
   from Deut 31:7, 23.

---

[1] On the distinctiveness of 1:1–9 as an introduction to a new book, see H. J. Koorevaar, *De
Opbouw van het Boek Jozua* (Heverlee: Centrum voor Bijbelse Vorming-Belgie, 1990), 163–64.

A clear effect of this is that when we read of the "book of instruction" (תּוֹרָה) on which Joshua is to meditate in verse 8, we naturally think of Deuteronomy as the most obvious reference. Admittedly, the direct citations are taken from a small cluster of chapters in Deuteronomy (7, 11, 31, and 34), but the level of reference to Deuteronomy in a relatively short speech makes clear that it is a pivotal text for understanding this chapter.[2] But it would be wrong to focus only on Deuteronomy, because when we turn to both the directives to the leaders (vv. 10–11) and the subsequent discussions with the eastern tribes (vv. 12–18) the primary reference is to the book of Numbers, although we return to Deuteronomy in verses 16–18.[3] This follows the pattern of the book as a whole: chapters 1–12 refer primarily to Deuteronomy, chapters 13–21 use Numbers as their main point of reference, and chapters 22–24 again use Deuteronomy. Thus, it becomes clear that Joshua 1 is an intentional introduction to the book.

As we read this chapter, therefore, we are reminded that this is a story to be situated within a larger story—one where the past is crucial for its interpretation. But we are also offered a vision of what it means for Israel to progress and enter the land that God had promised, which takes us back to Genesis 15. The vision for going forward is rooted in the past, in texts that are themselves the basis for further reflection. At the same time, they are presented as a mechanism by which Israel can begin to see God's promises fulfilled. As we progress through the rest of the book, we will see that the processes by which Israel is to make sense of her past as a guide for her future are quite complex. This is so in part because Joshua will describe scenarios that are not expressly anticipated in the Pentateuch, yet it always remains the case that understanding the past is vital for Israel to understand her vocation and thus how she is to go forward.

---

[2] Joshua 1:1–9 is often treated as a literary bridge between Deuteronomy and Joshua. The processes by which this occurs are complex, as is evident in T. B. Dozeman, "Joshua 1,1–9: The Beginning of a Book or a Literary Bridge?" in *The Book of Joshua*, ed. E. Noort (Leuven: Peeters, 2012), 159–82. But focus on these verses in isolation means we miss the ways in which this chapter as a whole creates bridges in multiple directions. See further Terence E. Fretheim, *Deuteronomic History* (Nashville: Abingdon, 1983), 49–53.

[3] The ways in which Joshua engages with pentateuchal texts varies. But following J. J. Krause, *Exodus und Eisodus: Komposition und Theologie von Josua 1–5* (Leiden: Brill, 2014), 56–58, we can note three basic categories: Joshua can *appeal* to an earlier text, *allude* to it, or *explain* it. These categories are not mutually distinct from one another but are a useful set of reference points. Although vv. 12–15 do show close affiliation to Deut 3:18–20, they are also sufficiently different that the additional information provided by Numbers 32 is pivotal.

Exegesis

1:1. The opening of Joshua immediately situates the events of this chapter in the context of Deuteronomy 34 and its description of Moses' death. We are not told how long after Moses' death this is, but since Deut 31:14–23 made clear that Moses knew he was about to die and that Joshua had been commissioned as his replacement, we are probably to assume that these events are very close in time to the events of Deuteronomy 34. In any case, although Joshua had known that Moses was going to his death, he would not yet have known that he had died, so God's speech will make this clear to him.

The descriptions of both Moses and Joshua in this verse are important for the narrative as a whole. Moses is called God's "servant," a title that is otherwise associated with David and the enigmatic servant in the book of Isaiah. Deut 34:10–12 is clear that no one else exercised a ministry with the significance of Moses. Nevertheless, since Joshua is also called God's "servant" at the end of his life (24:29), we are assured that in at least some respects he continued the pattern Moses had laid down. But as we commence the book, Joshua is still known as Moses' attendant, the one who had served Moses, continuing a title used of him earlier (Exod 24:13; 33:11; Num 11:28). It is an important role, and in Num 11:28 it is particularly associated with the presence of God's Spirit. Indeed, the presence of the Spirit is expressly said to be a key reason for his designation as Moses' successor (Num 27:18). The evidence of this wisdom, combined with Moses' laying hands on him, was a key reason why Israel obeyed Joshua (Deut 34:9). Unlike the other books of the Former Prophets, the book of Joshua never mentions the Spirit, but the background to this chapter assumes that the presence of the Spirit is a key element in Joshua's role. This is therefore foundational background information against which we are to trace his transition from Moses' attendant to the Lord's servant.

As is more common in the Old Testament, he is here called Joshua, though his name was originally "Hoshea" (Num 13:16). Both forms of the name are variants of the concept of "salvation," except that "Hoshea" expresses this generically, whereas "Joshua" makes an explicit link with Yahweh. We do not know anything about his father Nun beyond his mention in the genealogy in 1 Chr 7:27.

1:2–5. God's speech to Joshua can be divided into two parts. In the first of these (vv. 2–5) God reminded Joshua of his promises and of their continued validity in spite of Moses' death, before exploring how Joshua and Israel can progress in verses 6–9. The speech thus sets the pattern to be followed by the chapter as a whole. Although as readers we are told of Moses' death in verse 1, it is only as God spoke that Joshua discovered this fact and his work as Moses' designated successor began.[4]

Rather than mourn Moses, Joshua and the people were to arise and prepare to cross the Jordan to the land that God was giving to the Israelites (drawing on phrasing that appears twenty-one times in Deuteronomy; reference to God giving the land occurs in each stage of this chapter). Lying behind this is the belief that all land ultimately belongs to God; therefore, he can give it as he wills. These two imperative verbs show that the focus is on the future. But Joshua needed a context for understanding that future, so the balance of the speech's first half recounts some of the key promises that God had made to Israel.

Although God is speaking to Joshua, the promises were directed both to Joshua and to Israel as a whole. Hence "your territory" is plural, since the boundaries described for the land belong to the nation, and this is consistent with the use of the plural through verses 3–4. On the other hand, the promises in verse 5 are in the singular, directed to Joshua in particular, even if Israel could take comfort from them.

Verses 3–4 thus describe the boundaries of the land that God had promised to Israel—broadly those described to Abram in Gen 15:18–21.[5] Here, though, "the wilderness" stands for the area around the "brook of Egypt" in Gen 15:18, and "the Hittites" stand for all the peoples of the land listed in Gen 15:19–20, meaning that the reference is to a Canaanite group rather than the better-known Hittites whose empire was based in Anatolia.[6] The "wilderness" represents the region of the Negev to the south, while Lebanon is the northern boundary, though this is also traced eastward to the Euphrates. The Mediterranean is a natural boundary to the west. As Hubbard has pointed out, these boundaries are more than

---

[4] As Sarah Lebhar Hall, *Conquering Character: The Characterization of Joshua in Joshua 1–11* (London: T&T Clark, 2010), 13, argues, the characterization of Joshua only makes sense in light of this function.

[5] G. Matties, *Joshua* (Harrisonburg, PA: Herald Press, 2012), 47, notes that the boundaries used here represent typical Egyptian descriptions of Canaan in the fourteenth and thirteenth centuries BC.

[6] See R. S. Hess, *Joshua: An Introduction and Commentary* (Leicester: Inter-Varsity Press, 1996), 70–71.

Joshua was ever realistically going to walk,[7] and it would not be until the time of David that Israel's boundaries would closely approximate these (2 Samuel 8). But the idea of walking them seems to relate to the idea that when land was exchanged the one acquiring it would walk the boundaries, something that might lie in the background of the removal of the sandal of the kinsman unwilling to act as levirate (Deut 25:9–10).[8]

Although the promise in verse 5 would have resonance for the rest of Israel, it is particular to Joshua. As the one called to lead Israel, he needed to know that no enemy would be able to resist him for the whole of his life, language that refers specifically to military opposition in Deut 7:24 and 11:25.[9] This promise has a clear time limit—one reason why we need to understand Israel's taking of the land as a one-off event in God's purposes. No one could later make this claim, which significantly undermines Nelson's assertion that Joshua here functions as a type for Josiah.[10] Although some broad parallels between them exist (as we would expect for significant leaders), this verse makes clear that no successor could automatically claim God's presence. God would not forsake Joshua because there was a specific task that he had ahead of him, something made clear by the fact that this promise follows on from the two imperatives that occur immediately after the news of Moses' death. Obedience to those commands is already the basis for fulfillment of the promises, both to Joshua and to Israel.

1:6–9. The second half of God's speech also begins with two imperatives ("Be strong and courageous"), though these two are effectively synonyms.[11] These imperatives follow logically from the promise of verse 5—if no one could resist Joshua, then there was no basis for fear. Instead, as leader he was to distribute the land that God had sworn to give to their ancestors (adapting phrasing found five times in Deuteronomy). The land is thus simultaneously God's gift and something to be claimed

---

[7] R. L. Hubbard Jr., *Joshua*, NIVAC (Grand Rapids: Zondervan, 2009), 78.

[8] This practice is expressly carried out for the allocation of land to nine tribes in Josh 18:8–10.

[9] This makes the claim of Earl, *Reading Joshua as Christian Scripture*, 122, that Joshua was not really interested in conquest sit oddly with the text's own posture.

[10] R. D. Nelson, "Josiah in the Book of Joshua," *JBL* 100.4 (1981), 531–40. For more wide-ranging criticisms of this thesis, see Butler, *Joshua 1–12*, WBC (Grand Rapids: Zondervan, 2014), 202–4.

[11] For the military background of this phrase, see Rowlett, *Joshua and the Rhetoric of Violence*, especially 156–80.

and allotted. Verse 7 provides a more specific focus for Joshua: He was to be strong and very courageous in carefully observing all the instruction (תּוֹרָה) that God had given through Moses. This was not simply a set of facts to be known but rather a life that was to be lived—and living this life would take effort. Drawing on the common metaphor of life as a journey, the idea is that Joshua should stay on the path that this instruction provides rather than take alternative routes, for this is the means by which he would succeed. This success is related to the task that God had given Joshua, so walking faithfully in the Mosaic instruction was the means by which Joshua could lead the people into the land that God had promised.

Joshua was to meditate (הָגָה) on this instruction. The verb, with a similar promise of success, also occurs in Ps 1:2 and means something like "growl" or "mutter." This verbal element is more apparent in Ps 2:1, where it is translated "plot." It is difficult to match this word to a single English verb since "meditate" is often thought of as a silent activity. That the instruction was to be in Joshua's "mouth" is an idiom that goes naturally with the verb. Thus, he would continue reflecting on its meaning, with such reflection being verbal. This relates to the fact that reading in the ancient world meant reading aloud. In the same way, reflection on it was verbal. But what matters in particular is that Joshua's life was to be shaped by faithfulness to God's instruction. At this stage in the book we might think of this as unproblematic, but as the ensuing chapters unfold it becomes clear that Joshua would need to wrestle with the intent of the instruction in order to determine how it was to be applied in a range of circumstances.[12] This would require seeing the instruction as guidance for situations that would be faced rather than as a comprehensive set of rules that could simply be applied. Joshua would need a deep knowledge of God's instruction, which meant both knowing its content and reflecting on how it could be applied. Therefore, it could not depart from his mouth, because only by continued recitation/meditation could he both know it and understand how to apply it. Psalm 1 then broadens out this possibility for all believers.

God's speech then concludes with a reminder of the command to be strong and courageous so that Joshua would understand there is no place for fear because Yahweh would go with him. Joshua could succeed and lead his people to success when he understood that his role as a leader

---

[12] See §1 ("Faithfulness and Obedience").

was to journey with God, know God's instruction, and shape his life by it. Success here does not mean something financial but to receive the things that God is giving. We might perhaps think of "success" as flourishing in the life God has prepared—which is the way it is developed in Psalm 1. Here, that flourishing would be military, as Israel received the land God gave.

1:10–11. God's command in verse 2 had been for Joshua to prepare the people to cross the Jordan. Joshua could not do this on his own, so the first stage involved him commanding the officers to go through the camp and tell the people to ready their provisions to cross the Jordan in three days to possess the land God was giving them. A key verb here is עָבַר, which is translated "go through," whereas when speaking of the Jordan it is translated "crossing." Use of this verb echoes God's command in verse 2 and also prepares for chapters 3–4, where it will function as a key word in the narrative (occurring twenty-two times). In this way, the narrative makes clear that Joshua was indeed obeying God.

The identity of the officers (שׁוֹטֵר) Joshua commanded is unclear, but it is possible they were military officers with some form of adjunct judicial role.[13] In any case, it shows a continuation of the pattern established in Exodus 18 and Num 11:16–30 of sharing leadership functions, even when there was a central leader. Joshua may have been the main leader, but he was not a solo figure. At this stage he seems to have anticipated a fairly rapid departure, though in fact there was nothing in God's speech that required it to be as soon as three days' time. Another period of three days is mentioned in Josh 3:2, and somehow we have to account for the time when the spies were in Jericho, not least because Rahab told them to hide for three days before returning to the camp (2:16). We can find ways to make these time periods match up,[14] but it is probably better to think of "three days" as an idiom not dissimilar in meaning to the English "a few days," permitting openness rather than providing chronological

---

[13] See P. S. Johnston, "Civil Leadership in Deuteronomy," in *Interpreting Deuteronomy: Issues and Approaches,* ed. D. G. Firth and P. S. Johnston (Nottingham: Apollos, 2012), 147.

[14] The best attempt at this is D. M. Howard Jr., " 'Three Days' in Joshua 1–3: Resolving a Chronological Conundrum," *JETS* 41.4 (1998): 539–50. Howard proposes a seven-day structure that allows the various periods to overlap with one another. His system does work, but it is difficult (albeit not impossible) to make the consecutive verb with which chapter 2 commences concurrent with events in this chapter.

exactitude. The point is that the nation needed to be ready to move when summoned by God to do so.

1:12–15. Although the land promised by God was west of the Jordan, the tribes of Reuben, Gad, and half the tribe of Manasseh had received their allocation of land in Gilead east of the Jordan in Numbers 32 (though the other half of Manasseh would settle west of the Jordan). This happened with the understanding that they would join the remaining tribes and not return to their territory until the land west of the Jordan was taken for their kinsfolk. These tribes needed to be reminded of that commitment because, although there would be divisions among them (as seen in chapter 22), the taking of the land was the task of all Israel. Unity was essential. Thus, Joshua summoned them to remember the command that God had given through Moses.

The words attributed to Moses in verse 13 are summaries of what he said in Num 32:20–22 and again in Deut 3:18–20. Joshua's quote is not exact but provides the essence of the earlier discussion. The quote itself is not the commandment, since it does not direct the eastern tribes to do anything but rather assures them that God had allotted the land east of the Jordan. Strictly, their territory was to the north of where Israel then was, but "this land" (v. 13) is more generally understood as the territory east of the Jordan. Rather, the command is the conclusion Joshua drew from the larger conversation between Moses and the eastern tribes in Num 32:16–27 in which they had accepted Moses' proposal—that their wives, children, and livestock remain in the east while they cross over and fight—as a command from him since they had promised to do so. The fighting men of the eastern tribes were to go over ahead of their kinsfolk, prepared for battle (see Josh 4:12).

Although it is not mentioned, the assumption is that the other men (those too old, too young, or who for some other reason could not fight) would have stayed with the women, children, and livestock. For the eastern tribes, this was a risky process since, militarily at least, all they had would be left vulnerable while they assisted their kinsfolk. But just as they had received rest in the land now allotted to them, so also their kinsfolk needed to receive rest in the land that God had promised. Only when that had happened could these tribes return to their territory (recounted in chapter 22).

1:16–18. The response of the eastern tribes was positive, accepting that Joshua's directive to remember Moses' words should be understood

as a command. Thus, they would leave their families and livestock east
of the Jordan and go where Joshua directed. Indeed, they equated their
earlier commitment to Moses with their present commitment to Joshua.
Given the various ways in which the Israelites had failed to obey Moses
during the period in the wilderness, this might not sound like the most
wholehearted of commitments. But if we understand this in terms of the
commitments made in Numbers 32, then it can be understood more positively, which is probably what is intended by the eastern tribes. However,
for the narrator there may well be a note of irony in this claim, especially
as there will be points in the book where such wholehearted obedience
seems to be lacking. That the eastern tribes intended it positively seems
borne out by their wish that God be with Joshua as he had been with
Moses and that therefore all should obey Joshua.

This obedience is forcefully expressed, referring to Joshua's "order"
(פֶּה), "words" (דָּבָר), and all that he might "command" (צוה). To some
extent, these three should be seen as synonymous, though the last represents a more formal directive than the other two. The repetition of
the concept is what matters most. Thus, regardless of how Joshua might
express a directive, it was to be obeyed, and failure to do so would constitute rebellion meriting the death penalty. Aaron had been put to death
for rebellion against God (Num 20:24), background that suggests the eastern tribes understood failing to obey Joshua in the upcoming campaign
as disobeying God. Since the verb for "rebel" here is not particularly
common, a reference to Aaron is probably intended, meaning that the
chapter begins and ends with reference to the deaths of the nation's two
most prominent leaders. We are probably to interpret this understanding
of rebellion as part of the background to the conflict between east and
west in chapter 22 when the western tribes were prepared to attack the
eastern because of a perceived failure to obey. Although that chapter will
demonstrate that obedience is more complex than is sometimes imagined,
what matters here is the intent.

The eastern tribes also expressed the wish that God would be with
Joshua as he had been with Moses (v. 17), the very thing that God promised Joshua in verse 9. Furthermore, they charged Joshua to be strong and
courageous (v. 18), echoing God's words in verse 9. Thus, they expressed
the mutual commitment that existed between them and Joshua, and the
echoes of God's words bring the chapter to a neat close, balancing their
words with his.

Bridge

As the introduction to the whole book, this chapter establishes a number of key themes that will be developed as it progresses.[15] First, we should note the ways in which it links the past, present, and future. Here, the text is anchored in Israel's past through the many references to Numbers and Deuteronomy. If Israel was to understand its position, then it had to be rooted in the past, in those points where the promises of God were made and expounded, where their own experience had shown the reality of those promises. Here, they are not explicitly referenced, but the constant engagement with passages from earlier parts of the Pentateuch shows that Israel needed this background. There were obvious reasons for this in their context. They needed to know that the land they were about to enter was the one God had promised. But they also needed to be reminded that this past was not all glorious success. Mention of Moses' death, and allusion to Aaron's in verse 18, means the chapter as a whole is bookended by references to points where even the great leaders of the past had failed. The past thus provided Israel with hope for going forward while at the same time showing that they could not simply assume God would go with them.

The past also shaped Israel's present. In Joshua's case this meant not only that he could be assured of God's presence, but also that his own life was to be shaped by continual reflection on God's instruction. This would provide him with the resources to know what a life of obedience to God—which included being strong and courageous—would look like. For the eastern tribes, this meant obeying Joshua as the one whom God had called. This reflection on past and present also provided an understanding of the future in which Israel could advance with confidence into the land that God was giving, living a life that was shaped by obedience.

This integration of past, present, and future is something that occurs at many places in the Bible—indeed, we return to it in Joshua's final addresses in chapters 23 and 24. But it is perhaps seen most clearly in the celebration of the Lord's Supper as the point when we remember Jesus' death, understand what it is to be part of his community as the church, and look to the future as we "proclaim the Lord's death until he comes" (1 Cor 11:26). The book of Joshua suggests that reflection on the past to

---

[15] See especially §1 ("Faithfulness and Obedience"), §4 ("Land as God's Gift"), and §5 ("Leadership").

understand the present and so illumine the future was fundamental to Israel's communal life, and the same continues to be true for the church.

A second key theme focuses on the nature of leadership. The reference to Moses and allusion to Aaron stress the point that all human leaders, no matter how great, will at times fail. Indeed, although Moses had accused the people of being rebels at Meribah (Num 20:10), the reality is that he and Aaron had rebelled against God there. Neither, therefore, had entered the land. But God's speech to Joshua makes clear that what mattered most was continuing the work God had set before his people. Of first importance was not the leader but rather the task to which God had called the leader. Joshua's status at this point is clearly less than that of Moses, but he will eventually obtain the title "servant of the Lord" because of his faithfulness to the work. Leadership is thus not about accumulating authority but about faithfully doing what God calls one to do. As with Moses, Joshua shared the work with others because leadership is not about aggregating tasks to oneself so that people are dependent on a particular leader but rather recognizing the proper giftedness of each person so that they all contribute to the work God has set out.

Leadership is an important theme in the book.[16] Though Joshua would not always be a successful leader, the heart of his leadership is found in his continued reflection on God's instruction. Psalm 1 makes it clear that this is not restricted to leaders, since all believers can profitably do so, but it is particularly important that leaders are shaped by such reflection. By the time of the New Testament, we may note the extent to which Paul's ministry was shaped by his continual reflection on the Scriptures. Although there is no doubt that Paul's gifts and experience of the Spirit played their part in this (and as I have noted, Joshua's own experience of God's Spirit is in the background here too), his grounding in the Scriptures and continued reflection on them is a clear contributor to his ministry's effectiveness. This may also be one reason why he was keen that leaders not be new converts (1 Tim 3:6), since those without a grounding in the Scriptures were more likely to be "puffed up with conceit."

Finally, we can note the theme of the presence of God. God assured Joshua of his presence with him (vv. 5, 9), while the eastern tribes

---

[16] See especially D. J. McCarthy, "The Theology of Leadership in Joshua 1–9," *Biblica* 52.2 (1971): 165–75.

expressed this as a wish for Joshua (v. 18). God's presence throughout the chapter is linked to obedience, perhaps because obedience is the means by which God's people truly discover what the reality of his presence is like. This theme is picked up by the writer to the Hebrews (in 13:5, a text that is similar to Deut 31:6 and Josh 1:5 without quite being a quote from either[17]) and applied to the church in general, but it is most fully understood through Jesus' promise at the end of Matthew's Gospel (Matt 28:16–20). A church that joins in God's mission is a church that most fully experiences God's presence.

B. Rahab and the Spies in Jericho (2:1–24)

[1] Joshua son of Nun secretly sent two men as spies from the Acacia Grove, saying, "Go and scout the land, especially Jericho." So they left, and they came to the house of a prostitute named Rahab, and stayed there.

[2] The king of Jericho was told, "Look, some of the Israelite men have come here tonight to investigate the land." [3] Then the king of Jericho sent word to Rahab and said, "Bring out the men who came to you and entered your house, for they came to investigate the entire land."

[4] But the woman had taken the two men and hidden them. So she said, "Yes, the men did come to me, but I didn't know where they were from. [5] At nightfall, when the city gate was about to close, the men went out, and I don't know where they were going. Chase after them quickly, and you can catch up with them!" [6] But she had taken them up to the roof and hidden them among the stalks of flax that she had arranged on the roof. [7] The men pursued them along the road to the fords of the Jordan, and as soon as they left to pursue them, the city gate was shut.

[8] Before the men fell asleep, she went up on the roof [9] and said to them, "I know that the LORD has given you this land and that the terror of you has fallen on us, and everyone who lives in the land is panicking because of you. [10] For we have heard how the LORD dried up the water of the Red Sea before you when you came out of Egypt, and what you did to Sihon and Og, the two Amorite kings you completely destroyed across the Jordan. [11] When we heard this, we lost heart, and everyone's courage failed because of you, for the LORD your God is God in heaven above and on earth below. [12] Now please swear to me by the LORD that you will also show kindness to my father's family, because I showed kindness to you. Give me a sure sign [13] that you will spare the lives of my father, mother, brothers, sisters, and all who belong to them, and save us from death."

---

[17] See T. R. Schreiner, *Commentary on Hebrews* (Nashville: B&H, 2015), 413–14.

¹⁴ The men answered her, "We will give our lives for yours. If you don't report our mission, we will show kindness and faithfulness to you when the Lord gives us the land."

¹⁵ Then she let them down by a rope through the window, since she lived in a house that was built into the wall of the city. ¹⁶ "Go to the hill country so that the men pursuing you won't find you," she said to them. "Hide there for three days until they return; afterward, go on your way."

¹⁷ The men said to her, "We will be free from this oath you made us swear, ¹⁸ unless, when we enter the land, you tie this scarlet cord to the window through which you let us down. Bring your father, mother, brothers, and all your father's family into your house. ¹⁹ If anyone goes out the doors of your house, his death will be his own fault, and we will be innocent. But if anyone with you in the house should be harmed, his death will be our fault. ²⁰ And if you report our mission, we are free from the oath you made us swear."

²¹ "Let it be as you say," she replied, and she sent them away. After they had gone, she tied the scarlet cord to the window.

²² So the two men went into the hill country and stayed there three days until the pursuers had returned. They searched all along the way, but did not find them. ²³ Then the men returned, came down from the hill country, and crossed the Jordan. They went to Joshua son of Nun and reported everything that had happened to them. ²⁴ They told Joshua, "The Lord has handed over the entire land to us. Everyone who lives in the land is also panicking because of us."

Context

This chapter needs to be read with chapter 1 as part of a thematic double introduction to the book of Joshua, neither of which is complete in itself.[18] While chapter 1 introduces Israel, its people, and leadership, this chapter now brings readers to encounter the Canaanites, the people who lived in the land that God was giving to Israel. This provides a vital framework for understanding the land's existing inhabitants. A people who are never actually encountered are easy to demonize as people who "get what they deserve." But whenever we actually meet people and have to understand them, such a process is made much more difficult. It would be possible to read Joshua 1 and understand the Canaanite population in an entirely negative way—after all, God was giving their land to Israel. Although there is an important tension that runs through the book between God

---

[18] This point resolves the problem of R. G. Boling, *Joshua* (Garden City, NY: Doubleday, 1992), 150, who feels the chapter sticks out "like a sore thumb." It is distinct from chapter 1, but this is because the narrator needs us to consider key themes not developed in chapter 1.

giving the land and Israel taking it, the assumption that runs throughout is that the land is to be Israel's. Since Deut 9:4–6 makes clear that God was expelling the Canaanites because of their wickedness (though it also warns Israel that they are receiving the land because of God's faithfulness to his promises, not Israel's righteousness), it could be possible to keep the Canaanites faceless and thus never make Israel confront what it means to take a land where someone else is resident, even if it is God's gift.

But rather than keeping the Canaanites faceless, Joshua takes the far more difficult path of forcing readers to encounter them and thus to ponder questions about their nature and identity. This is particularly focused in the character of Rahab, someone who seems at first to be precisely the sort of person Israel should destroy; she was a Canaanite prostitute, and thus we would expect her to lead Israel astray. And yet, she showed herself loyal to the spies, took risks on their behalf, knew something of Israel's story, gave the spies information that they were incapable of obtaining themselves, and even made a confession of faith in Yahweh that would have done the most orthodox Israelite proud. In short, any stereotypes readers might have held about Canaanites after chapter 1 are challenged as Rahab functions as a reverse of the foreign women in Num 25:1–5.[19] Thus, rather than playing the harlot, Israel was saved by one.

Nevertheless, the narrator is careful throughout never to comment on the actions of all the characters, so at this stage in the narrative we cannot know whether the decision of the spies to swear an oath to Rahab is right or wrong. Deuteronomy 7:2 says that Israel is to make no covenant with the Canaanites, so at one level we might think the spies have made a major mistake.[20] Such a reading might, in the end, conclude that Rahab is a "shrewd woman who prevails" over the spies.[21] But the narrator's refusal to comment, leaving open the question of how to interpret this

---

[19] For the importance of this connection, see. J. J. Krause, "Aesthetics of Production and Aesthetics of Reception in Analyzing Intertextuality: Illustrated with Joshua 2," *Biblica* 96.3 (2015): 416–27. Key to this point is the association of the toponym Shittim ("Acacia Grove"), which occurs narratively in these two texts and otherwise only in Josh 3:1, though it is echoed in Joel 3:18 (MT 4:18) and Mic 6:5. This important point weakens the alternative claims of H. Seebass, "Das Buch Josua als literarisch nicht zu erwartende Fortsetzung des Buches Numeri" in *The Book of Joshua*, 251–52.

[20] This view is developed most fully by L. Daniel Hawk, *Every Promise Fulfilled: Contesting Plots in the Book of Joshua* (Louisville: Westminster John Knox, 1991), 71–72.

[21] L. Daniel Hawk, *Joshua* (Collegeville, MN: Liturgical Press, 2000), 35.

encounter, means we cannot know this. Although some have wanted to read Rahab as a trickster who simply did what was necessary to survive,[22] it is also possible to see the oath sworn to her as "negotiated exception to the policy of extermination of Canaanite population groups."[23] This latter reading is certainly more consistent with the New Testament's application of Rahab's story (Matt 1:5; Heb 11:31; Jas 2:25), but it is not a conclusion we can yet draw. We need more information than this chapter alone provides. The key point at this stage is that we have encountered a Canaanite and now have to think about her position.

Related to the need to encounter the Canaanites is the need to understand that God was indeed giving Israel the land. We might have met a resident of the land who surprises us in many ways, but this does not change the fact that the land is something that God was giving to Israel. The importance of this gift as an element that binds Joshua 1 and 2 together to form the introduction to the book as a whole can be seen in how this theme functions to bookend these chapters. In 1:2 God told Joshua to prepare to enter the land, a rest that was required for all Israel in 1:15. When the spies returned to Joshua in 2:24, they declared that God "has handed over the entire land to us." The participle "giving" (נֹתֵן) of 1:2 is now a verb announcing a completed action (נָתַן). Most remarkably, this was first announced by a Canaanite prostitute in verse 9.[24] But her speech in turn becomes the means by which Israel's most incompetent spies discover, and so can announce, what God is doing—even though at this stage the narrator's refusal to comment on any of this means we do not know if her interpretation is correct. As readers, we will need to wait until the account of Jericho's capture (5:13–6:27) to learn this. Thus, it is only as second-time readers (which the New Testament writers surely were) that we can realize she is not only correct but also presents an exception to the destruction of the Canaanites as a people.

---

[22] See Cristina García-Alfonso, *Resolviendo: Narratives of Survival in the Hebrew Bible and in Cuba Today* (New York: Peter Lang, 2010), 39–62, who offers a positive postcolonial reading.

[23] Nicolai Winther-Nielsen, *A Functional Discourse Grammar of Joshua: A Computer-Assisted Rhetorical Structure Analysis* (Stockholm: Almqvist & Wicksell, 1995), 162.

[24] On the unexpected nature of this, see J. J. Krause, *Exodus und Eisodus: Komposition und Theologie von Josua 1–5* (Leiden: Brill, 2014), 177.

Exegesis

2:1a. The Old Testament is familiar with spy narratives. The most notable among these is that recorded in Numbers 13–14, in which Joshua and Caleb were themselves among the spies. Awareness of this may lie in the background here (perhaps through its summary in Deut 1:19–25), though if so it is only at a generic level. Indeed, there are numerous contrasts between the two accounts. For example, there are only two spies here instead of twelve. Beyond that, the earlier spies were clearly competent at doing what Moses had asked them to do even if the majority had not believed God's promises. These spies did not actually do anything Joshua asked, were very nearly caught, and yet came back convinced of the truth of God's promise concerning the land.

One key distinctive here is that Joshua sent the spies secretly, something not said of Moses. Since it is redundant to speak of this being a secret from the Canaanites, it can only mean that Joshua did not tell the Israelites.[25] As is typical of this chapter, we are not told if this was appropriate or not. Accordingly, some interpreters are critical of Joshua here, claiming he has followed a discredited approach.[26] But there is no contradiction in the Bible between trusting God and making proper plans since wisdom is a gift from God.[27] And given the ways in which this spy narrative will be so unlike others, especially its use of burlesque humor, it is perhaps more likely that we are to regard this as acceptable planning on Joshua's part even if we cannot conclude it was valid until the end of the chapter when the spies reported back.

Joshua here is called "son of Nun," repeating the patronym used at 1:1, and he will receive this full title again in verse 23 when the spies return.[28] The patronym is used ten times in the book, usually at key points of transition, and its function here provides another indicator that this chapter is to be read in conjunction with chapter 1. Mention of the spies leaving

---

[25] J. J. Krause, "Vor wem soll die Auskundschaftung Jerichos geheim gehalten warden? Eine Frage zu Josua 2.1", *VT* 62.4 (2012): 454–56.

[26] Hawk, *Every Promise Fulfilled*, 61; A. Sherwood, "A Leader's Misleading and a Prostitute's Profession: A Re-Examination of Joshua 2," *JSOT* 31.1 (2006): 51.

[27] Similarly, H. N. Rösel, *Joshua* (Leuven: Peeters, 2011), 42: "According to biblical concept, divine action does not exclude human action." See also Hall, *Conquering Character*, 32–36, on why sending the spies was appropriate.

[28] This, and other features, leads J. H. Stek, in "Rahab of Canaan and Israel: The Meaning of Joshua 2," *CTJ* 37 (2002): 39–38, to posit a chiastic structure for the chapter, though only his proposals for vv. 8–14 are fully persuasive.

from Acacia Grove links this narrative to Num 25:1–5 (see above), since there is no particular need to mention it. It is sufficient to know that Israel was on the plains of Moab. Joshua's instructions to the spies are quite specific: They were to scout out the land, especially Jericho. Israel was not a people with significant military experience, certainly not of siege warfare, and since at this stage Joshua has received no indication of how Jericho was to be captured, it was quite natural that he would want to know more about the city. However, since these were two of the most incompetent spies of all time (part of the narrative's humor), they would not do anything like this. Indeed, though they would return with no significant militarily information, they would still come back with awareness of what God was doing.

2:1b–3. In spite of the specific nature of Joshua's directions, the next thing we know about the spies is that they were in the house of a prostitute (זוֹנָה) named Rahab (the only named person apart from Joshua), where they stayed. This is presumably because unknown men visiting a prostitute would not attract attention. In spite of various attempts through history to make Rahab (whose name means "broad," though that does not have the connotation in Hebrew that it sometimes has in English) an innkeeper rather than a prostitute,[29] the normal meaning of the word used here is "prostitute."

Moreover, the narrator employs double entendres, using verbs that are used as euphemisms for sexual activity but without ever indicating that something inappropriate actually happened. Indeed, both the verbs "to come in" (בא) and "to lay down, stay" (שכב) are used in verse 1, generating a frisson of sexual tension given Rahab's profession. Of course, the text says nothing about her background or why she ended up in this work—there were few career options for women who needed to support themselves, and poverty was often a primary reason.[30] On the whole, the narrative is only interested in her current profession as it prepares for her profession of faith. But the use of terms that are elsewhere employed as euphemisms seems intentional, especially when these verbs are repeated in the subsequent dialogues. Indeed, the verb "to come in" is repeated

---

[29] See D. J. Wiseman, "Rahab of Jericho," *TynBul* 14 (1964): 8–11. This interpretation goes back at least as far as Josephus, *Ant.* 5.7–8.

[30] Though R. B. Coote, "Joshua," in *The New Interpreter's Bible*, ed. Leander E. Keck (Nashville: Abingdon, 1998), 592–96, makes this central to his reading.

in the report to Jericho's king, which notes that the men had come to investigate the land.

We do not know how this information was discovered, but that it happened so soon indicates that the spies were not particularly good at keeping their task secret. Given that Jericho was most likely a fairly small town (see comments on 6:1), it is not surprising that the men's arrival was noticed. But the accuracy of the report to the king (in effect a local chieftain, since מֶלֶךְ has a wider semantic range than the English "king"), along with the fact that this report came the night they arrived, might indicate that they had not been especially secretive. So, as Joshua had sent the spies in verse 1, the king sent his officers to Rahab in verse 3. They demanded that she bring the men out from her house, though the triple use of "come in to" with reference first to Rahab herself, then to her house, and then the land, would suggest that they expected some sexual transaction to have occurred. In any case, the king's message makes clear that he knew the spies had come to investigate (לַחְפֹּר) the land. Whatever the king might imagine to have happened in Rahab's house, he was at least right in his interpretation of why the men were there.

2:4–7. Verse 4a is a flashback to events before the king's men arrived at Rahab's house, indicating that she had made her decision to help the spies before the king's men arrived. By the time the king's men came, she had already hidden both scouts.[31] With this information in place, we then resume the main narrative as she responds to the king's demand knowing that she was acting favorably toward the spies. The background to this visit, where the earlier language describing her had at least hinted at double entendre, becomes more focused here as Rahab's speech plays with the expectations of the men who had arrived.[32] The king's demand assumes that the men had come for sexual activity, so her speech coquettishly plays this up, affirming that the Israelite spies had indeed "come to" her. Her interlocutors thought that these men went to her as a prostitute, so she was prepared to use such language in response. Her claim that she did not "know" where the men had come from also reflects another euphemism, even if this time it is simply used to claim a lack of knowledge. The implication is clear: A prostitute has a particular function, and

---

[31] The MT reads וַתִּצְפְּנוֹ, "she had hidden him," but CSB is correct to follow LXX, Tg, and Syr and read "hidden them."

[32] See Nelson, *Joshua*, 43–44.

inquiring into why men might have come to her is not common practice. Indeed, it might even be thought that such an inquiry would be contrary to what was expected of a prostitute. Her speech thus shows considerable skill in playing to the flawed expectations of those who were sent to her. Since she was a prostitute, they saw her solely in sexual terms, and she was not interested in correcting their attitude. Instead, she claimed that the men had left at nightfall, the time just before the city gate would be locked—a perfectly natural time for her visitors to depart. And just as she had not known where they had come from, neither did she know where they were going. However, she indicated that, even though she did not know where they had gone, the king's men would be able to catch them if they pursued.

Having recounted the conversation with the king's officers, the narrative returns to Rahab's hiding of the spies in verse 6, making clear that they had not gone as she had told the officers but rather that they were hidden on the roof of her house under some flax she had laid there. Since it is unlikely that cultivated flax was grown in the area at the time, this was probably the wild flax collected in the early part of the northern spring, which is consistent with the references to the Jordan being in flood in 3:15. The stalks would not have provided sufficient cover had the king's officers entered the property to search, but would presumably have provided enough cover to conceal them from neighbors whose dwellings might overlook her roof. Instead of searching her house, the king's officers charge off after the spies, heading toward the Jordan. To this point, the encounter between Rahab and the officers has been pure slapstick comedy, but here we have the sudden and jarring note that, after the officers left on their impossible chase, the gate was closed. The spies were trapped in the city and utterly dependent on Rahab's goodwill.

But should Rahab have told the truth to the officers? That she lied to them has troubled many interpreters over the years,[33] and this is made especially problematic by her commendation in Jas 2:25, though the lie itself is not explicitly mentioned. While the Bible does encourage truthfulness, this seems to be a story in which Rahab's status as an underdog,[34] someone who can only use her wits since she has only a limited knowledge

---

[33] See especially the helpful excursus in David M. Howard Jr., *Joshua* (Nashville: B&H, 2008), 106–12.

[34] See O. Horn Prouser, "The Truth about Women and Lying," *JSOT* 61 (1994): 29.

of what God requires, means she is assessed on the basis of her intentions more than anything else. Within her frame of reference (and she can hardly be expected to follow normative biblical models here), she showed great fidelity to the spies, taking the risk that the officers would search her house and find them, or that her actions on their behalf would lead to her arrest and probable execution.[35] It should be noted that at this point she has not received any promises from the spies, so she is not acting on the basis of a reward. Instead, for reasons we only discover in the subsequent verses, she committed herself to Israel. As is typical of the narrator in this chapter, no comment is made on her actions—we simply have to observe them and decide on their appropriateness. Indeed, the absence of any comment on the truthfulness of her response may be the point—the narrator leaves it to us as readers to decide how appropriate her speech was within the context of her actions, and we have to judge that on the larger outcomes of the book, not on this chapter alone.

2:8–13. Since verse 7 ended with the closing of the city gate, we have to assume some time had passed before Rahab joined the spies on her roof. csb interprets יִשְׁכָּבוּן as a reference to the men going to sleep. Although the verb more commonly means "to lie down" (and is another verb used euphemistically for sex), this is most likely correct, as the men would have been lying down if they were covered by the stalks of flax. So, it is now the end of the day, and Rahab went up to the roof once again, though by now she would have been covered by darkness.

The coquettish language to date might lead readers to wonder what will happen, but it is unlikely that any reader would expect what actually happens. Whatever her profession has been, Rahab now makes a profession of faith of which any Israelite would be proud. A Canaanite prostitute expresses her understanding of Yahweh in a way that shows a profound understanding of his character. The language of the confession is probably intended as a summary of her speech rather than a direct quotation, which would explain in part the nature of her language, but that her profession is written up in an Israelite style does not change the wonder of it.[36]

---

[35] See the parallel in Donald H. Madvig, "Joshua," in *The Expositor's Bible Commentary*, ed. F. E. Gaebelein (Grand Rapids: Zondervan, 1992), 260.

[36] This would also explain the possible allusions to the Decalogue noted by Joshua Berman, "Law Code as Plot Template in Biblical Narrative (1 Kings 9.26–11.13; Joshua 2.9–13)," *JSOT* 40 (2016): 344–49.

Her opening statement in verse 9 is an affirmation of knowledge, not just something vaguely believed. She knew that God had given the land to Israel. Rahab does not define "this land"—it could be the region around Jericho alone, though more likely we are to understand this as the same land as God had outlined to Joshua in 1:4. She makes no claim of any right of the Canaanite peoples to the land, accepting that God has the right to give the land to another people. The implication of God's gift of the land is that the terror of the Israelites has fallen upon its inhabitants. This terror is anticipated in the Song of the Sea (Exod 15:16), and God had promised to send his terror before Israel as they entered the land (Exod 23:27). Because of this terror, the land's inhabitants were panicking, providing another link to the Song of the Sea, which anticipates this panic (Exod 15:15). These allusions provide the background to the first great act of Yahweh that Rahab and her fellow inhabitants had heard of, which is the drying up of the Red Sea (more literally the "Sea of Reeds") when Israel came out of Egypt. She thus demonstrates awareness of what God had done in the exodus.

Rahab's knowledge of God's mighty acts was not restricted to the more distant past, as she also affirms that they had heard about what Israel had done to Sihon and Og, the two Amorite kings who had lived east of the Jordan. Their defeats are presented as paradigmatic evidence of God's gift of the land to Israel in Deut 2:26–3:11, though their actual defeats are recorded in Num 21:21–35. Their defeats as recorded in Numbers are complete, though Rahab adds that Israel "completely destroyed" them.

This term (from the root חרם) mostly refers to activity described in Joshua, but it was used to describe what Israel had done to the Canaanite king Arad in Num 21:1–3, and perhaps more importantly for the present context reflects Deut 3:6.[37] It represents a concept, difficult to represent in English, in which something is devoted to God and thus removed from common use. This does not have to mean destruction. For example, in Mic 4:13 it is more likely that the devotion of the wealth of the nations to God means it was given over to the treasury rather than destroyed.[38] This would be consistent with the fact that in Joshua 6:19 the items from

---

[37] For a convenient overview of this word and its usage, see Jackie A. Naude, *NIDOTTE* 2:276–77. A fuller but still accessible treatment is provided by J. P. U. Lilley, "Understanding the HEREM," *TynBul* 44 (1993): 160–77.

[38] Though HCSB does render the relevant portion "set apart their plunder to the LORD for destruction."

Jericho that are so designated go "into the LORD's treasury."[39] These clearly are not destroyed but rather given over wholly to God.

In warfare, however, the term means the consecration to destruction of those defeated, although as we go through the book of Joshua we see that this is applied to varying degrees, with Jericho as the strictest interpretation of it. The concept is not uniquely Israelite, so Rahab's use of the term is not altogether surprising. It suggests she saw the defeat of these kings as evidence that Israel's occupation of the land God was giving them had begun (even though they were across the Jordan), since their defeat was a sacral act. Moreover, the defeat of Sihon and Og represented a recent victory for Israel. When this was combined with the exodus, Rahab effectively summed up the forty years since Israel's departure from Egypt—all of which has apparently been reported in Canaan. Israel's approach is no surprise, and neither is the fact that God has been at work in it. But though this summary was good news for Israel, it was not received as such by the Canaanite community, their hearts melting and their courage failing.

Rahab's observation was not only rooted in the summary of what God had done but also indicated something about the character of Yahweh. Although Rahab spoke of him as "your God," this is because she addressed the spies as Israelites. Her declaration that he is "God in heaven above and on earth below" effectively identified him as the only God, or at least the only valid one. She thus modeled for her compatriots a different response to this God. What she had heard indicated there was only one God to whom she could be committed.

Accordingly, she asked the spies to swear an oath that, as she had shown "kindness" (חֶסֶד) to them, so they would show kindness to her family. The seriousness of this is that it would be an oath sworn before Yahweh. She apparently knew that she stood under the ban but asked for it not to be applied to her because of her kindness, which might also be understood as loyalty. The point is that she had gone beyond what might reasonably be expected, risking her own life for the Israelites even as she confessed a profound understanding of who God really is.

In the ancient world, people were deemed to be part of a wider community and not just individuals. Rahab's request to spare her family

---

[39] See also Num 18:14 and Ezek 44:29 for similar usage. It is arguable that this is also the intent of Lev 27:28.

prepares us for the altogether more tragic story of Achan's family in chapter 7, where the link between family and individual is also evident. The father's house was the smallest level of the family in ancient Israel. This typically covered two or three generations who lived together, though Rahab only included two generations (her parents and siblings).

She asked for a sure sign (אוֹת אֱמֶת), reliable evidence that the spies would indeed protect her and her family and not put them to death, though none is forthcoming. Astute readers may well be uncomfortable at this point, given that Deut 7:2 explicitly rules out making any covenants with Canaanites, and an oath at this point looks suspiciously like a covenant.[40] Did Rahab ask for what could not be granted? Or was she, in effect, the first Canaanite convert to Yahweh, and thus in effect an Israelite?[41] This question will be answered affirmatively in chapter 6, but here it is left unresolved.

2:14–21. Whatever misgivings readers might have, the spies apparently did not share them, pledging their own lives for those of Rahab and her family. They stipulated only that Rahab could not tell anyone about their agreement, though that presumably would not include her family. Based on that condition, when God gave Israel the land they would act with kindness (חֶסֶד) and faithfulness (אֱמֶת) toward her. Although this speech is expressed formally, it is not strictly an oath, but the spies would still have understood it that way in verse 17. But this again raises questions about the actions of all involved. Rahab had apparently asked for what could not be given, and though the spies described what they had done as an oath, none of the formulas associated with an oath are present. Most notably, Rahab had asked them to swear by Yahweh, but there is no evidence the men did this. Have they been taken in by Rahab's declaration of faith to make an oath they should not have made? Have they taken in Rahab by feigning an oath? Or has everyone acted with good faith? The narrator refrains from making any comment, so at this point we do not have clear answers to these questions.

---

[40] See K. M. Campbell, "Rahab's Covenant: A Short Note on Joshua ii 9–21," *VT* 22 (1972): 243–44, though some of his covenant features are out of sequence.

[41] So Hess, *Joshua*, 92; Howard, *Joshua*, 97. A slightly softer position in which this narrative argues in favor of the integration of non-Israelites is offered by Krause, *Exodus und Eisodus*, 151–52. By contrast, B. L. Crowell, "Good Girl, Bad Girl: Foreign Women of the Deuteronomistic History in Postcolonial Perspective," *Biblical Interpretation* 21 (2013): 1–18, unconvincingly sees her as part of a pattern promoting suspicion of foreignness.

What is clear is that Rahab acted on the assumption of the spies' good faith and let them down from a window in her house. Although Jericho is often pictured as a fortress, it is more likely that it was a small town where the houses of the poor formed a sort of terrace that also functioned as an outer wall (see on 6:1). This would allow the men to be let out of Rahab's window.

Remarkably, Rahab and the spies seem to have a conversation as they were climbing down the wall of her house to make their escape. Rahab's directive is clear: The men are to go to the hills and, thus, away from the Jordan. There they are to hide for a few days (as at 1:11, "three days" is probably an idiom for an undefined period) to allow those who pursued them to the fords of the Jordan to return before trying to return to Joshua. Yet as the spies are hanging on a rope outside her window, we find them attempting to renegotiate the terms of their agreement.[42] This would ordinarily be rather surprising, but it is not inconsistent with their general characterization throughout the chapter.

They insisted they would be free from the oath that they claimed Rahab forced them to swear unless a crimson cord was tied to her window. It is difficult to see how they were forced to swear an oath unless they regarded Rahab's actions on their behalf as compulsion, so Hawk's assertion of the validity of this claim seems to over-read it.[43] Rather, it was simply a bargaining chip that allowed them to insist on the crimson cord. Since it is "this" crimson cord in verse 18, it might even have been the rope used to lower them. What tying the rope in the window would achieve is difficult to see, beyond marking out Rahab's house so that those in it would be safe when Israel entered the land. Otherwise, Israel would not know which house to protect (of course, at this point they did not know how Jericho actually would be captured). The cord thus protected the spies if any members of Rahab's family were killed because they were out of the house. But the rope itself could not signify that Rahab would indeed keep the agreement secret. So although the spies claimed they would be free from the oath if she told anyone of their arrangement or the spies' mission, the presence of the cord in the window could not actually validate this. It should be noted in passing that although the image of

---

[42] NIV (1984) treats this as a flashback, but the conditions required for a pluperfect sense are absent, so CSB (and NIV 2011) is right to present it so that the spies negotiate from the wall.

[43] Hawk, *Joshua*, 48. However, his observations on the chiastic structure of their comments are well made.

the crimson cord has often been used allegorically in reference to the death of Christ, the color "scarlet" is not normally associated with blood in the Old Testament, and in any case there is nothing in the narrative as it stands to suggest any particular symbolism in the color beyond the fact that it would stand out so that Israel could see it.[44]

Whatever the uncertainties of the spies' renegotiation, Rahab agreed, tying the cord in the window when the spies had gone. There may be a parallel between verse 1, in which Joshua sent the spies to find out about the land and Jericho, and Rahab sending them here, indicating that they now accepted orders from her. But this is not made explicit.

2:22–24. The rest of the narrative is told briefly. The spies went and hid in the hill country, an area with plenty of caves, until their pursuers had returned to Jericho without finding them. The spies then came down from the hill country, crossed the fords of the Jordan, returned to Joshua, and recounted all that had happened. The narrator is not interested in the details but rather their conclusion: God had given Israel the land, and the inhabitants were panicking because of Israel's approach. Reference to the panic betrays the source of the information, repeating what Rahab had reported in verse 9. Nevertheless, the information they brought was what Joshua had requested, even though they did not actually fulfill their role as scouts. Indeed, they were able to report this almost in spite of their incompetence.

Only when we reach the end of chapter 6 do we know that their assessment is correct; at this point the narrator has refrained from telling us this. They have, in effect, repeated Rahab's comments, but does the oath they swore to her mean that Israel was at risk? Although it will become clear that they were not and that Rahab's assessment is correct, first-time readers do not know this. So, at the end of this chapter we are left with both hope that God's promises are about to be fulfilled and also a nagging worry that the sworn oath of the spies might just have put everything at risk.

---

[44] There may be an echo of the Passover narrative, in which Israelite houses were marked by the blood of the lamb (Exod 12:7), something noted by N. P. Lunn, "The Deliverance of Rahab (Josh 2, 6) as the Gentile Exodus," *TynBul* 65 (2014): 14–15. But if so, color is not the issue.

Bridge

The fulfillment of promises is always important. Anyone who receives a promise, especially one that will take time to be fulfilled, appreciates evidence that the promise will indeed be fulfilled.[45] No one wants to stake their trust on hollow words. The scouts in this chapter, in thoroughly irregular ways, were able to come back with a declaration that God's promises were being fulfilled. Their encounter with Rahab made clear to them that the land's inhabitants were in a state of panic because they had already heard what God was doing. The spies appear barely competent (part of the humor of the chapter), and yet in spite of this they still discover what was needed, albeit from someone unpredictable.

Joshua had wanted to know more about the land, and Jericho in particular, since this was a place where Israel had not previously been. Since at this stage there was no intimation of how Jericho actually would fall, this is a perfectly reasonable military strategy and consistent with what Joshua had done when Israel had first reached the land in Numbers 13. But Joshua actually received information that was far more important, the key thing the spies of his generation had not brought back: Yahweh was indeed giving the land. In spite of all their failings, the scouts were able to affirm this. But, importantly, at this stage we do not know if this is correct. There is certainly reason to believe it; after all, why else would Rahab take such a risk? But a first-time reader cannot be sure that she has told the truth. Was she simply looking for a way to save her own life? We know she lied to the king's officers. Might she also have lied to the spies?

Preachers will, therefore, need to be sensitive to their hearers' familiarity or unfamiliarity with this text. First-time readers need to appreciate the genuine uncertainty here, while repeat readers who are also familiar with the ways in which the New Testament takes up this story need briefly to suspend their knowledge that all will indeed work out. This is because the narrator has told the story without resolving key points of uncertainty precisely so that we will read on and gradually discover if this assessment is correct. Once we know this, we can return as second-time readers who know how the story ends.

This approach is important because it means the narrative reflects the world as we experience it. God's promises in Jesus are indeed in the process of being fulfilled, but we can only see the signs of what God is

---

[45] See Firth, *The Message of Joshua*, 43–44.

doing when we look back. The story is thus told to place us as readers in this same position—knowing the reality of God's promises and their future fulfillment, but not knowing what constitutes a sign from God or what effect our sin might have on how the promises are fulfilled. When we discover the truth of any sign, though, it enables us to become second-time readers of our own experience. Second-time readers can then see how Rahab truly is an example of faith in action: someone who put herself at risk for the people of God, and through whom we see truly what God is doing.

In addition, this chapter takes a great risk in bringing us face to face with a Canaanite. In part, this is because Rahab will be the opposite of the previous encounter with foreign women (Num 25:1–5), showing (to a second-time reader) that not all foreign women are dangerous. A Canaanite and a prostitute, she may look exactly like the sort of person who should be given over to destruction, but she will prove to be quite the opposite. She is the one who understands more clearly what God is doing and what commitment to him should look like than anyone else in the narrative. Suddenly, even before Israel has entered the land, the Canaanites look different. Rather than demonizing them, we need to think in different terms, seeing some as precisely the sort of people who should be included among God's people, even if this seems unlikely on first appearances. God will, it turns out, include people whom we might choose to exclude. Those who give themselves to him now have the chance to live, provided that commitment remains true. We need to read on to discover what happens to Israel and to Rahab and her family, because at this stage their survival is only a possibility. But in the meantime, we have to be open to the possibility that God will use the very people we would exclude in order to bring about his purposes.

C. Crossing the Jordan (3:1–4:24)

3 ¹ Joshua started early the next morning and left the Acacia Grove with all the Israelites. They went as far as the Jordan and stayed there before crossing. ² After three days the officers went through the camp ³ and commanded the people, "When you see the ark of the covenant of the Lord your God carried by the Levitical priests, you are to break camp and follow it. ⁴ But keep a distance of about a thousand yards between yourselves and the ark. Don't go near it, so that you can see the way to go, for you haven't traveled this way before."

⁵ Joshua told the people, "Consecrate yourselves, because the Lord will do wonders among you tomorrow." ⁶ Then he said to the priests, "Carry the ark of the covenant and go on ahead of the people." So they carried the ark of the covenant and went ahead of them.

⁷ The Lord spoke to Joshua: "Today I will begin to exalt you in the sight of all Israel, so they will know that I will be with you just as I was with Moses. ⁸ Command the priests carrying the ark of the covenant: When you reach the edge of the water, stand in the Jordan."

⁹ Then Joshua told the Israelites, "Come closer and listen to the words of the Lord your God." ¹⁰ He said, "You will know that the living God is among you and that he will certainly dispossess before you the Canaanites, Hethites, Hivites, Perizzites, Girgashites, Amorites, and Jebusites ¹¹ when the ark of the covenant of the Lord of the whole earth goes ahead of you into the Jordan. ¹² Now choose twelve men from the tribes of Israel, one man for each tribe. ¹³ When the feet of the priests who carry the ark of the Lord, the Lord of the whole earth, come to rest in the Jordan's water, its water will be cut off. The water flowing downstream will stand up in a mass."

¹⁴ When the people broke camp to cross the Jordan, the priests carried the ark of the covenant ahead of the people. ¹⁵ Now the Jordan overflows its banks throughout the harvest season. But as soon as the priests carrying the ark reached the Jordan, their feet touched the water at its edge ¹⁶ and the water flowing downstream stood still, rising up in a mass that extended as far as Adam, a city next to Zarethan. The water flowing downstream into the Sea of the Arabah—the Dead Sea—was completely cut off, and the people crossed opposite Jericho. ¹⁷ The priests carrying the ark of the Lord's covenant stood firmly on dry ground in the middle of the Jordan, while all Israel crossed on dry ground until the entire nation had finished crossing the Jordan.

4 ¹ After the entire nation had finished crossing the Jordan, the Lord spoke to Joshua: ² "Choose twelve men from the people, one man for each tribe, ³ and command them: Take twelve stones from this place in the middle of the Jordan where the priests are standing, carry them with you, and set them down at the place where you spend the night."

⁴ So Joshua summoned the twelve men he had selected from the Israelites, one man for each tribe, ⁵ and said to them, "Go across to the ark of the Lord your God in the middle of the Jordan. Each of you lift a stone onto his shoulder, one for each of the Israelite tribes, ⁶ so that this will be a sign among you. In the future, when your children ask you, 'What do these stones mean to you?' ⁷ you should tell them, 'The water of the Jordan was cut off in front of the ark of the Lord's covenant. When it crossed the Jordan, the Jordan's water was cut off.' Therefore these stones will always be a memorial for the Israelites."

⁸ The Israelites did just as Joshua had commanded them. The twelve men took stones from the middle of the Jordan, one for each of

the Israelite tribes, just as the Lord had told Joshua. They carried them to the camp and set them down there. ⁹ Joshua also set up twelve stones in the middle of the Jordan where the priests who carried the ark of the covenant were standing. The stones are still there today.

¹⁰ The priests carrying the ark continued standing in the middle of the Jordan until everything was completed that the Lord had commanded Joshua to tell the people, in keeping with all that Moses had commanded Joshua. The people hurried across, ¹¹ and after everyone had finished crossing, the priests with the ark of the Lord crossed in the sight of the people. ¹² The Reubenites, Gadites, and half the tribe of Manasseh went in battle formation in front of the Israelites, as Moses had instructed them. ¹³ About forty thousand equipped for war crossed to the plains of Jericho in the Lord's presence.

¹⁴ On that day the Lord exalted Joshua in the sight of all Israel, and they revered him throughout his life, as they had revered Moses. ¹⁵ The Lord told Joshua, ¹⁶ "Command the priests who carry the ark of the testimony to come up from the Jordan."

¹⁷ So Joshua commanded the priests, "Come up from the Jordan." ¹⁸ When the priests carrying the ark of the Lord's covenant came up from the middle of the Jordan, and their feet stepped out on solid ground, the water of the Jordan resumed its course, flowing over all the banks as before.

¹⁹ The people came up from the Jordan on the tenth day of the first month, and camped at Gilgal on the eastern limits of Jericho. ²⁰ Then Joshua set up in Gilgal the twelve stones they had taken from the Jordan, ²¹ and he said to the Israelites, "In the future, when your children ask their fathers, 'What is the meaning of these stones?' ²² you should tell your children, 'Israel crossed the Jordan on dry ground.' ²³ For the Lord your God dried up the water of the Jordan before you until you had crossed over, just as the Lord your God did to the Red Sea, which he dried up before us until we had crossed over. ²⁴ This is so that all the peoples of the earth may know that the Lord's hand is strong, and so that you may always fear the Lord your God."

Context

After the dual introduction of chapters 1–2, the narrative focuses on the process of entering the land that God had promised, requiring Israel to cross the Jordan since this was its most recognizable boundary. Chapter 1 has already established that the whole of Israel would not live there since Reuben, Gad, and half the tribe of Manasseh would settle east of the river. But the place of settlement for the remaining tribes is across the river. As a result of the encounter with Rahab in chapter 2, the spies could return to Joshua and affirm that God had indeed given Israel the land.

Preparing to cross the Jordan was highlighted as vital in God's speech to Joshua in 1:2 and had accordingly been central to Joshua's directives to the officers in 1:11 and to the eastern tribes in 1:14. These preparations were consistently focused on crossing in preparation for taking the land, which is why Rahab's confession of faith was so important in confirming the reality of the land as a divine gift (2:8–13). The two scouts must have successfully crossed the river to go to Jericho, though only their crossing back to Joshua was reported (2:23).

Given that the scouts seemed to have no difficulties, we might imagine that Israel would simply walk across at the fords near Jericho. But attentive readers may be aware that the reference to stalks of flax being dried in Rahab's house means it must be the early spring.[46] The implications of this, and in particular the effects of the spring thaw on the Hermon range, will be drawn out as we discover that the Jordan is in flood (3:15), an annual spring event. Indeed, these various hints about the date come together in the comment of 4:19 that Israel crossed the Jordan on the tenth day of the first month, which is the date on which the animal for Passover was selected (Exod 12:3). The preceding chapters have thus carefully brought together the themes of giving the land[47] and crossing the Jordan, all of which is tied to a careful dating structure that prepares for the celebration of Passover in 5:10–12. Chapters 3–4 thus bring these various elements to their climax while also preparing for events that will follow.

But it would be a mistake to think of Joshua 3–4 only as a conclusion to the earlier elements, because these chapters now develop them in new directions. The most obvious element is the close parallel between Joshua and Moses. God promised to begin exalting Joshua so Israel would know he was with him just as he was with Moses (3:7), something achieved when Israel crossed the Jordan (4:14). This exaltation came about because God's actions through Joshua were so similar to those he achieved through Moses. The most obvious example is the parallel between the crossing of the Jordan and the crossing of the Sea of Reeds. The reference to crossing on dry land (3:17, חָרְבָה, which alludes to Exod 14:21) hints at this, but it is made explicit in the reflection to be passed on to children in 4:23–24. The

---

[46] According to the Gezer Calendar, a document from about the tenth century BC, wild flax would be harvested around February/March.

[47] See further §4 ("Land as God's Gift").

stated purpose—that all might know of God's power (4:24)—is reminiscent of key statements about the plagues (Exod 7:5; 9:14–16), thus providing another link between Moses and Joshua. Finally, note that the nature of the questions the children are expected to ask in 4:21 is patterned on Deut 6:20, again connecting Joshua with Moses. The process of exalting Joshua is important for readers coming out of chapters 1–2 because the narrator's consistent policy of not commenting on the actions of various characters might raise questions about Joshua. Most notably, should he have sent spies to Jericho without any directive from God? I noted above that the whole of Joshua 2 leaves (first-time) readers with a range of unanswered questions. But the divine affirmation of Joshua in chapters 3–4 at least begins to address these issues, even as it provides information that Joshua himself could not previously have known about the means by which the Jordan would be crossed.

The provision of new information as needed highlights the fact that these two chapters continue the practice of not providing additional interpretative information other than through comments from God about what is happening. As readers, we discover key information at the same time as Israel within the narrative. So even though God must have revealed things to Joshua prior to this narrative, we do not discover what is to happen before Israel does. One effect of this is that the narrative seems at key points to repeat itself, as Israel appears to have crossed the Jordan in 3:17 only to complete it again at 4:18 (indeed the verb עָבַר, "to cross over," occurs some twenty-two times in the narrative, while the Jordan is named twenty-eight times). Likewise, both 4:4–9 and 4:19–20 seem to describe the process of selecting twelve stones to form a memorial of the crossing. This has led to numerous theories of textual displacement,[48] but it is possible to understand this as part of a coherent narrative strategy that makes use of the motif of repetition in order to emphasize key elements.[49]

---

[48] Most comprehensively in E-W. Lee, *Crossing the Jordan: Diachrony versus Synchrony in the Book of Joshua* (London: T&T Clark, 2014), who posits a range of literary layers that can be traced through a comparison of the LXX and MT. I cannot review the various proposals here, but the differences among them are significant in terms of the number of layers and their purposes, and this in itself raises questions about their value.

[49] See Winther-Nielsen, *Discourse Grammar*, 175–82, and Hall, *Conquering Character*, 61–64. This does not rule out the possibility of various sources being brought together (on which see E. Asis, "A Literary Approach to Complex Narratives: An Examination of Joshua 3–4" in *The Book of Joshua*, ed. E. Noort [Leuven: Peeters, 2012], 401–14, who shows that a literary approach to the finished text does not have to deny the presence of sources), but it does

In this case, the repetitions are employed in order to emphasize key motifs in the narrative that help readers make the connections between this account and the various passages in Exodus, while also stressing the importance of remembering this event along with those of the exodus. The entry into the land is thus shown to be every bit as important as the exodus since the goal of the exodus was always the "eisodus" when Israel entered the land that God had promised. Repetition is employed in conjunction with dischronologized narrative[50] as catechesis,[51] to show this linkage to the exodus so that Israel might remember the importance of what happened here. Indeed, these features allow the emphasis on memory (to which the whole narrative builds) to emerge.

Exegesis

3:1. As with the previous chapter, this story finds Israel at Acacia Grove, showing that there has been no movement while the spies were absent. Since in terms of plot this chapter follows more directly from chapter 1, the otherwise redundant reference to Acacia Grove reminds readers that we are also picking up from events in chapter 2, another sign that the opening chapters form a paired introduction to the book. Joshua's early start here indicates his keenness to begin the process of entering the land now that he has both the commitment from the eastern tribes and the reassurance from the spies. Leaving Acacia Grove was intended to be part of the journey into the land since it involved breaking camp and coming to spend the night on the banks of the Jordan in preparation for crossing over. Joshua knew at this stage that he was to prepare to cross the river (1:2), but he did not know the means by which this would be achieved. Preparation to cross was thus an act of obedience to the charge he had

---

remind us that the narrators of Joshua are working with patterns that they believed to be coherent, even though they may not be the forms used by critics today. Some of these patterns can be seen in B. Peckham, "The Composition of Joshua 3–4," *CBQ* 46 (1984): 418–23, though one need not accept his distinction in deuteronomistic layers. Robert L. Hubbard, "'What Do These Stones Mean?': Biblical Theology and a Motif in Joshua," *BBR* 11 (2001): 1–12, draws on the literary theory of G. Genette to explore the means by which the narrative's repetitions ("frequency" in Genette's terminology) generate emphasis.

[50] Hence, E. Ballhorn, "Die Gestaltung des Gilgal (Josua 3–4): Das Buch Josua als Heterptopie," in *The Book of Joshua*, 415, points to the unclear chronology as a principal problem in the narrative, though he also believes (417) that the various elements can be integrated by drawing on M. Foucault's concept of "heterotopia." For an alternative view, see Boling, *Joshua*, 159.

[51] Similarly, Butler, *Joshua 1–12*, 290.

received from God, as well as faith that God would enable this to happen. Joshua was joined in this by all Israel, thus highlighting the theme of the unity of Israel from 1:10–18, and introducing a key motif that runs through the whole of this narrative (3:1, 7, 17; 4:1, 11, 14). Joshua is the leader through whom God is working, but entry into the land fulfills his promise to all the people.

3:2–4. Sometime after their arrival at the Jordan, the officers introduced in 1:10 passed through the camp. Again, "after three days" should be understood as shorthand for "a few days" rather than a specific period of time, in effect indicating that they instructed the people soon after arrival and before anyone had time to settle in at the new location. That they "went through the camp" fulfills Joshua's earlier command to them in 1:11, though the verb עָבַר ("went through") is also the keyword that elsewhere refers to the actual crossing of the Jordan. As such, their action in obedience to Joshua's command foreshadows the experience of the whole nation.

The officers' command for the people introduces a new and so far unexpected element into the story: the central role to be played by the ark of the covenant. The ark will be mentioned seventeen times in this story, and though there are six variations in its naming (including the lengthy "ark of the covenant of the Lord of the whole earth" in 3:11), these variations add color to the narration more than anything else. The key concern for the people was that they be prepared to act. As soon as they saw the priests carrying the ark, they were to break camp (תִּסְעוּ, the same verb rendered "left" in v. 1) and follow it. The ark, a wooden chest covered with gold, had several functions in the Old Testament. It contained the tablets of the Decalogue, Aaron's rod that budded, and a jar of the manna from the wilderness (Exod 16:32–33; 25:16; Num 17:7–8; Deut 10:1–5; Heb 9:4).[52] The ark also served as a means of discerning God's will and as a symbol of God's presence in battle.

In Joshua its primary function is to lead Israel as a symbol of God's presence in their capture of the land, with all but three of the thirty references in the book occurring either in this story or in the capture of Jericho (chapter 6). There is no attempt here to explain the nature of

---

[52] See Deuk-Il Shin, *The Ark of Yahweh in Redemptive History: A Revelatory Instrument of Divine Attributes* (Eugene, OR: Wipf & Stock, 2012), 45–51.

either the ark or the Levitical priests[53] who carried it (see Num 4:4–15), since it is assumed that both those who heard the command and later readers would know these details. The focus is on the awareness required of Israel to break camp and follow the ark when they saw it taken up. No other command to leave was needed. However, a gap of one thousand yards was to be kept between the people and the ark. Although one might think this was related to the holiness of the ark (cf. Uzzah in 2 Sam 6:6–7), this is not the emphasis here. Rather, the gap is a function of Israel's lack of knowledge of the terrain, though the use of the ark shows clearly that God knew the way.[54] Since the exact location of Acacia Grove is unknown, it is impossible to be precise about this, but the distance was likely necessary because of the jungle of the Jordan that grew in this area, and also because of the Jordan's two banks, the upper bank and the true bank.[55] If so, it means the people could stand on the upper bank and see the direction the ark was taking, at least as far as the river, and so know the route to take.

3:5–6. These verses consist of a pair of directives given by Joshua. First, there is the command to the people to consecrate themselves because God was about to do something wondrous among them the next day. Consecration typically refers to ritual acts that demonstrate the holiness of the person concerned, indicating that the person so consecrated can appropriately be in God's presence (Exod 19:22; Lev 11:44; 20:7; Num 11:18). Although consecration might be carried out by an individual, it could also be a corporate activity. Israel is thus reminded that they are called to be God's holy people because they are to see something wondrous from him. At this point, we do not know that this refers to the crossing of the river, still less that the crossing will represent a close rerun of the crossing of the Sea of Reeds (Exod 14:21–31). But we know that, although Israel is already God's holy people, there was a need for them to be especially prepared to be in his presence. There may also be a parallel with Exod 3:20, in which God promised to do something wondrous in the midst of Egypt (meaning, of course, the exodus itself), while now,

---

[53] This is the only point in the narrative of the crossing that they are called "Levitical priests." Otherwise they are only "priests," suggesting that the reason for the combined title here (elsewhere typical of Deuteronomy) is to stress their legitimacy for the role of carrying the ark.

[54] Hubbard, *Joshua*, 151.

[55] See M. H. Woudstra, *The Book of Joshua* (Grand Rapids: Eerdmans, 1981), 81.

as we reach the goal of the exodus, he would do something wondrous in the midst of Israel.

The second directive is to the priests, telling them to take up the ark and go ahead of the people. The verb "go ahead" (עָבַר) here is intentionally ambiguous. CSB's "go on ahead" is consistent with the verb's usage to this point and so perfectly correct, but it masks the fact that this key verb will primarily refer to the actual crossing of the river (except perhaps in v. 11). So the priests are indeed to go ahead, but more specifically to cross ahead, of the people. That Joshua tells them to take up the ark means that a day must have passed between verses 5 and 6, as this now signals the point at which the preparations ended and the crossing could begin.

3:7–8. Although we now expect the crossing to begin, the narrative defers this to focus on a new message from God to Joshua. This commences a process—running throughout the crossing—of delaying the development of the narrative to provide information on how to interpret these events through speeches from God to Joshua and from Joshua to the people. God's speech to Joshua makes explicit something that has been hinted at previously: God would begin to exalt Joshua in the sight of Israel for the specific purpose of showing Israel that he was with Joshua just as he had been with Moses. That it was to "begin" here indicates that it would not be complete in the crossing of the river but rather would be an ongoing process. The parallel between the crossing of the river and the crossing of the sea is only one aspect of the Moses typology that runs through the book of Joshua. The sending of the spies in chapter 2 has echoes of Moses sending the spies in Numbers 13–14, while the encounter with the commander of God's army in Josh 5:13–15 clearly echoes Moses' encounter with God at the burning bush in Exodus 3. But because the references to Moses across chapters 3–5 are explicit, they show clear evidence of how God exalted Joshua.

This exaltation was not for Joshua's benefit, though. Rather, it was for the benefit of the people, that they might know God was present with Joshua as he had been with Moses. They would accordingly have confidence to continue with him as they entered the land, even though they did not know the specific challenges they would face. This exaltation begins immediately in the directive that Joshua was to give to the priests carrying the ark. When they entered the Jordan, they were to stand there. As a command, this is clear enough, but it does not explain why they were to do this.

3:9–13. Although the priests were given no reason for standing in the Jordan, Joshua explained it to the people. Since he announced a message from God, Joshua functioned as a prophet, in itself an echo of Moses, who was the model for all subsequent prophets in Israel (Deut 18:18). Joshua's ability to announce a message from God validated by subsequent events shows him to be, like Moses, an authentic prophet. However, this was a secondary function of his message. Its primary goal was to inform the people about coming events so that Israel would know that the living God was in their midst (the designation "living God" otherwise occurs only in Pss 42:2; 84:3; Hos 2:1—though a closely related form using אֱלֹהִים rather than אֵל is slightly more common).

Joshua's summoning of the people to draw near is unusual for prophetic speech, but it perhaps signifies the importance of this message being heard, since the announcement provided evidence not only of God's presence but also that he was giving them the promised land even though it was occupied. The seven groups mentioned in verse 10 do not cover all of the Canaanite peoples, but this is a fairly standardized list intended to be broadly inclusive. The same groups are listed in 24:11 (although in a slightly different order), while other lists have selections from those mentioned in verse 10 (5:1; 7:9; 9:1; 11:3: 12:8). Exact divisions between these groups are difficult to discern, not least because at points both "Canaanites" and "Amorites" are used as generic labels for the inhabitants (2:10; 16:10). Since Israel is said to have not gone this way before, and the narrative consistently adopts the position of Israel's knowledge, it is likely that these labels are intended as a general summary of the peoples of the land rather than specifically identifiable ethnic markers, though presumably they do point to ethnic groups that Israel knew. The point is that whoever the inhabitants of the land are, God was dispossessing them before Israel. The evidence for this will be seen when the ark enters the Jordan.

CSB omits Joshua's initial "behold" (הִנֵּה), though this is an important rhetorical element. We as readers are asked imaginatively to see through the eyes of Israel and watch the ark as it passes through the nation and enters the Jordan. The importance of the ark is seen in its title here. Although CSB has "ark of the covenant of the Lord of the whole earth," the

Hebrew is constructed as two phrases in apposition, so we might better translate as "the ark of the covenant, the Lord of the whole earth." This suggests that the ark itself is seen as embodying the presence of God among his people,[56] and God is also Lord of all the earth.

Verse 11 links the previous directive to the priests (v. 8, which ended without an explanation of what was to happen) with this explanation to the people. Thus, the priests effectively received the information they needed to understand what they were doing even as the people received information needed to interpret the miracle (since miracles are not themselves self-explanatory). Although we might expect the miracle itself to be described, there is a further delay as Joshua directs the people to select twelve men, one from each tribe. The function of these men is not yet explained, so that just as the priests had to enter the water with the ark without an explanation, so the people had to choose twelve men without knowing why. Only with these elements in place did Joshua explain the wonder for which we have been waiting since verse 5. When the priests entered the Jordan carrying the ark, the waters of the river coming from upstream would be cut off. Thus, as the waters came down, they would stand as a single heap, effectively damming the river. This heaping of the waters echoes the crossing of the sea in Exod 15:8, providing further evidence of Joshua's exaltation through the parallel with Moses.

3:14–17. With Joshua's speech completed, the narrative moves toward the crossing. In verse 14 the people broke camp as directed when the ark went before them to cross the Jordan. Verses 15–16 are a complex sentence that CSB helpfully reorders and divides for the sake of clarity in English. The comment about the Jordan overflowing its banks in spring (harvest season) occurs in the second half of the Hebrew of verse 15 where it functions as an aside between the first half of verse 15 and its continuation in verse 16. Although the harvest in many parts of the world occurs in autumn, Israel's harvest is in spring because its wet season occurs in the winter. Since the winter is warm enough for crops to grow, a harvest can be obtained in the spring. By contrast, the summer is hot and dry, making it difficult to grow crops.[57] But in early spring, the temperatures rise, creating a snow melt on the Hermon range from which the Jordan

---

[56] Similarly, Deuk-Il Shin, *The Ark of Yahweh*, 56.

[57] See I. H. Eybers, *A Geography of Biblical Israel and Its Surroundings* (Pretoria: NGK Boekhandel, 1988), 137–45.

flows down to the Dead Sea. This, along with the late rains in March and early April, results in the flooding of the Jordan described here. For much of the year, the Jordan is actually not a great barrier because of its fords,[58] but for this short period it is very difficult to cross. The aside about the flooding is thus important information, and it links well with the mention of the flax drying on Rahab's roof (see comments on 2:4–7), making clear that the Jordan could not be crossed in the ordinary manner.

Only at this point, therefore, do we discover the nature of the miracle announced in verse 5: the waters of the flooded river were cut off as soon as the priests carrying the ark entered the water. We are not told if Joshua had briefed the priests about what to expect, but as readers our position is the same as that of the Israelites, who only now discover the means for crossing the river. The standing up of the waters in a heap reflects Exod 15:8, which likewise mentions the waters standing in a heap. This heap of water, effectively a dam, is naturally upstream of where the priests had entered and so stopped the flow of water down to the Dead Sea. Although the drying out would take some time, even with a fast-flowing river, the emphasis here is on the immediacy of the process, which happened as soon as the priests entered the water.

The dam either formed at Adam, a town roughly nineteen miles north (CSB note), or with the water extending there (CSB text). The issue hangs on an internal scribal variant in the MT that is difficult to resolve, though slight preference should be given to CSB's main text on the basis of the number of manuscripts that have this reading. It is worth noting, however, that an earthquake in 1927 resulted in the Jordan being blocked in this same region. It would not be inconsistent with an emphasis on the miraculous nature of this crossing if a local tremor caused something similar, because the key element stressed within the narrative is its timing. But at the same time, we cannot use this later event to determine how this happened.

The narrator's sole focus is to make clear that this was a wondrous act from God that enabled Israel to cross the river opposite Jericho. Since the waters were blocked because the ark represented God's presence, the priests carrying the ark remained in the middle of the river until all the people had crossed. In a further link with the crossing of the Sea,

---

[58] See the helpful photo in R. J. Faley, *Joshua, Judges* (Collegeville, MN: Liturgical Press, 2011), 14, which shows this clearly.

the fact that the priests stood on dry ground (חָרְבָה) echoes Exod 14:21. The crossing of the Jordan is thus a repetition of the crossing of the Sea, demonstrating that God was indeed with Joshua as he had been with Moses.

4:1–3. At one level, we might think that the crossing narrative is complete. However, in 3:17 the priests were still in the middle of the river. This is related to the compositional technique of returning to earlier unresolved parts of the narrative to take them up again as a basis for further reflection. Just as the directive to the priests in 3:6 was left unresolved until 3:16, so also the directive to the people in 3:12 only begins to find its resolution here. While 3:16 stressed that the water dried up as soon as the priests entered the river, here the emphasis is on the fact that God spoke to Joshua as soon as the people had finished crossing and before the priests had left the river. Indeed, the priests are left standing there until 4:11. Joshua was told to choose twelve men, one per tribe, and to tell them to take twelve stones from the middle of the Jordan. Since 3:12 has indicated that the people were to do this, we are probably meant to assume that Joshua effectively validated their earlier choice. The stones were to be taken from the place where the priests' feet were, recognizing that the river had dried up as soon as their feet entered the water. Although no reason is yet given for this, the men were to place the stones at the place they would spend the night, which for the first time was west of the Jordan.

4:4–7. The function of the stones was left unexplained in God's speech to Joshua, just as the function of the twelve men had been left unexplained in 3:12. But before we receive an explanation of the stones, we are told of Joshua's obedience as he told the men to go take twelve stones from the river bed. That these were to be placed on their shoulders suggests they were substantial stones. More than this, the text emphasizes that these twelve men and stones matched the tribes of Israel. The stones were to be a sign in the midst of Israel, and to be a truly representative sign it needed the participation of each tribe.

Joshua then projected himself to a future time when later generations of Israelites would see the stones, presumably arranged as a cairn, and ask about their significance. Israel was then given an answer to pass on, summing up the narrative to this point—that the waters of the Jordan were cut off before the ark. This is a different emphasis from the second reflection on the stones, which will focus on Israel's crossing (vv. 20–23). Obviously, the two are linked, as the crossing could not have happened without the waters being dried up. But it is appropriate to note both elements in the miracle. While the second reflection considers Israel's experience, the emphasis here is on the divine initiative. The stones were thus a perennial reminder of the cutting off of the waters before the ark. Because of the close identification between God and the ark in 3:11 and 13, it is a way of saying the waters were cut off before God himself. As a memorial they served as a continual means of helping Israel remember that they had entered the land only because of what God had done.

4:8–10a. As Joshua had to obey God's command (vv. 1–3), the people now had to obey Joshua's—and in obeying Joshua they were also obeying God. The twelve men each took a stone from the midst of the Jordan. The representative nature of this action is again stressed as we are reminded this was in accordance with the number of Israel's tribes. The stones were placed at Israel's lodging place for their first night in the land. Because this cairn was west of the Jordan, it would be easy to imagine that only the tribes who lived in the land were to remember this, but the constant reference to all twelve tribes points out that the cairn would also be a memorial for the eastern tribes. Consistently, the book of Joshua emphasizes the inclusivity of Israel. Although the Jordan was a boundary (and chapter 22 will show it to be an important one), it was not to exclude those living outside it.

Verse 9 poses some significant challenges. CSB makes the twelve stones mentioned here a separate group from those brought up by the twelve men,[59] whereas the CSB note treats it as a flashback. Taken as the CSB text presents it, we have a second twelve-stone memorial that remained in the river bed at the point where the priests had stood. Although not grammatically impossible, the MT does not require this, and there is much to be said for the CSB note. Notably, the sentence does not commence with a consecutive verb, thus breaking the chain from verse 8. As a marked aside, therefore, and one with an unusual construction, we should not force it into a consecutive sequence. Nor do we need to make the small emendations found in the LXX to make sense of the text, though it is difficult. What the aside does is provide us with the new information: The stones the twelve men took up had already been placed near the priests' feet by Joshua. These, therefore, are the stones that the twelve men brought out to the initial lodging place and that remained until the

---

[59] The "also" of the CSB text comes from the LXX, not the MT.

time the text was written.[60] That verse 9 is an aside seems confirmed by its continuation in verse 10, which reminds us that the priests carrying the ark continued standing in the middle of the river until all that God had commanded Joshua was complete. This additional note is important because it stresses the importance of obedience to God's word, a central theme in the book.

God's word to Joshua was consistent with that given by Moses. Joshua's obedience to God's word through Moses is picked up again in 11:12–15, where the narrative reflects on the capture of the cities of the land. That reflection matches this one from the point where Israel enters the land. Joshua had been told he must be careful to do all that God had commanded through Moses (1:7), and this text provides a first example of this. It also shows that Joshua's obedience contributed to the means by which God exalted him so that the people would know God was with him as he had been with Moses.

4:10b–14. With the people across the Jordan, the narrative perspective shifts to within the boundaries of the land. The priests carrying the ark then left the river, though we return to this in verse 17. As is typical, the point at which the priests left the river is synchronized to the point where the people had finished crossing. The ark symbolized God's presence, so the priests needed to stay in the river until all were across to show that God had enabled the crossing. Since this narrative is content to provide flashbacks and employ other techniques to break chronology, we have another flashback in verse 12. The importance of the twelve-tribe structure of the nation has been emphasized throughout, as has the importance of obeying God's commands through Moses. This point is reinforced by the note here that the eastern tribes, Reuben, Gad, and half of Manasseh, had gone over at the head of the Israelites in battle formation, confirming that they too had obeyed the command of Moses (1:14).

Mention of the forty thousand who crossed (v. 13) is a reminder of the fact that this was a significant body of people. However, given the flexibility with which the word "thousand" (אֶלֶף) is used in the Old Testament,[61] it is possible that we should think of this as "forty larger military units" since the largest of these was called a "thousand" even though it may have been considerably smaller than that. Certainly, it is the military

---

[60] See also Howard, *Joshua*, 136.

[61] See J. W. Wenham, "Large Numbers in the Old Testament," *TynBul* 18 (1967): 24–34, 40–41.

context that is dominant here, and this may tip the balance in favor of this interpretation. However, on either reading, a significant body of people crossed the river.

In 3:7, God had told Joshua that he would begin to exalt him so that the people would know he was with him as he had been with Moses. We are now told in verse 14 that this process was complete. The various allusions to the crossing of the Sea in the exodus have made clear the association between Joshua and Moses and have thus given the people the evidence to conclude that God was with Joshua as he had been with Moses. This does not mean Joshua is yet accorded the same status as Moses, since Moses remains as Joshua's point of reference. But it does mean the people revered him as they had Moses, something that would continue for the rest of his life. Although the verb "revered" is often translated as "fear," either in the worship of God or some form of dread, used of a leader it indicates a willingness to trust him, something to which the rest of the book gives ample confirmation, even if there still remained points of challenge.

4:15–18. Although we were told in verse 11 the priests left the river bed, verse 15 introduces another flashback to indicate an example of the reverence given to Joshua. At the same time, the sequence of events here is important. It is God who first commanded Joshua to tell the priests to come up from the river, a command that Joshua relays. Joshua is a leader whom Israel would revere, but there remains an important order. He can only be revered because he is himself faithful to the command of God.

Then, in another of the exact synchronizations that are characteristic of these chapters, as the priests carrying the ark step onto solid ground, the river resumes its flow and begins once more to overflow its banks. Just as the timing of the waters being cut off was linked to the point where the feet of the priests reached the water, so here the resumption of the river's flow is timed to the point where their feet left the river.

The ark throughout has represented God's presence, and its movement is thus clear evidence to Israel that God performed this miracle. Likewise, the people are right to revere Joshua as the one through whom God revealed the timing of the miracle. Joshua's orders had at no point brought the miracle about. Through all of this, the Israelites knew that it was only because of God's actions on their behalf that they could enter the land.

4:19–24. Although the narrative has made clear that the events took place in spring, the significance is only made clear when we learn that Israel crossed on the tenth day of the first month, the day of preparation for Passover on which the lamb would be selected (Exod 12:3). The consequence of this in Israel's immediate experience will be noted in 5:10–12, but here it is important to note a further parallel to the exodus. Just as Passover represented the point at which the exodus proper began, so here entry into the land is part of the same salvation movement as the exodus. We cannot separate exodus from eisodus, going out from coming in. Passover, even more than the crossing itself, makes this link.

Israel's point of entry into the land is called Gilgal,[62] on the eastern limit of Jericho, that is, on the bank of the Jordan. The significance of the name (or at least one aspect of it) will be noted in 5:9. Here it is important to observe that this was the location of the twelve-stone cairn mentioned in verse 8. But whereas verse 8 says the men set down their stones, verse 20 tells us Joshua set them up in a recognizable form. Joshua also explained the significance of the cairn, returning to the anticipated children's question from verse 6, with the additional element that they were envisaged as speaking to their fathers (v. 21).

However, the answer this time is quite different. Previously, the answer focused on the cutting off of the waters (v. 7). But in verses 22–23, the focus is on Israel's crossing. The crossing could not, of course, have taken place without God's actions, and that point is rehearsed again, though with some small changes in terminology—notably that God had "dried up" the waters to enable Israel to cross on dry ground. Less evident to readers in translation is that the word for "dry ground" here (יַבָּשָׁה) is different from that of 3:17 (חָרָבָה), in part because it is cognate to the verb here, but also because it is even more typical of the language of the crossing of the Sea from the exodus (Exod 14:16, 22, 29; 15:19) in preparation for the explicit link that Joshua makes with the crossing (Josh 4:23). This is what Israel is to make known to their children, with the cairn acting as a trigger for the discussion.

The function of the cairn as a memorial (cf. v. 7) is not simply to say that these events happened. Rather, memory is something that needs to be shared, following the pattern Deut 6:20–25 had envisaged for the

---

[62] The MT has "the Gilgal," which might suggest this is not a proper noun, though perhaps the article is used to indicate the particular Gilgal meant since several places have this name.

Passover.[63] It is not enough that these things happened. Instead, there needs to be a means of reminding subsequent generations of both the event and its significance.[64] The cairn on its own could not do this, but by passing this on each generation could learn about both event and meaning. Moreover, as Joshua made clear, this meaning is not restricted to Israel alone. Rather, the purpose was "so that all the peoples of the earth may know" about God's power and so that Israel might fear him (Josh 4:24).

This declaration has connections to the events of the exodus, when God's actions were an announcement of his power to all the earth (Exod 9:18) and to Israel (10:1–2). This subsequently anticipated David's declaration to Goliath about the significance of his imminent victory over him (1 Sam 17:45–47), being a witness to all the earth and also Israel. The statement provides a crucial reflection on the purpose of the exodus and eisodus, an important reminder that although the book of Joshua is concerned with how God's purposes were being worked out for Israel at this particular moment, those purposes always looked beyond Israel. In this we thus have the first hint that the spies' deal with Rahab in chapter 2 may indeed have been part of God's greater purpose for the nations.

Bridge

Because this is such a rich narrative, there are numerous themes that can be developed today. However, because they are also tightly woven into a complex narrative, they are not "standalone" elements. Rather, they are integrated into one another.

A key element that emerges from both the content of the narrative and also the ways in which it is told is the importance of memory. Israel needed to remember what God had done, and this required the existence of mechanisms to enable this memory. The importance of this is seen in the fact that the account spends more time explaining the significance of aspects of the miracle through flashbacks than it does describing the miracle itself. If the only concern was to recount that Israel miraculously crossed the flooded Jordan, the story could have ended at 3:17. But the narrative makes clear that a miracle itself is not self-interpreting.

---

[63] On this, see David G. Firth, "Passing on the Faith in Deuteronomy," in *Interpreting Deuteronomy: Issues and Approaches*, 157–76.

[64] Which is exactly what Mic 6:5 does in its directive to remember these events.

Numerous clues in the account link it to the exodus and the crossing of the Sea.[65] But more than that is needed, which is why chapter 4 then provides a series of reflections, each adding a new layer of insight that helps us understand the meaning of the events.[66] Hence, the first reference to the memorial stones makes clear that Israel is to pass on the fact that it was God who stopped the waters, whereas the second reference stresses that it was God who brought Israel across the river as part of his witness to all the earth. The memorial cairn is needed within Israel so that it might trigger an important question (Why would there be a cairn of twelve stones by the Jordan?), and this question was to be answered in a way that ensured each generation would know both the reality of what happened and also its significance.

Although the terminology might be anachronistic, one might say that biblical literacy is therefore not to be reduced to knowing facts about the Bible. A knowledge of the core facts remains important, but simply knowing them does not mean we know the God whose story is revealed in them. Rather, it is expected that children will learn of the reality to which the story points in the larger narrative of God's mission. Each generation is to pass this on, and each generation needs triggers that will allow this thoughtful reflection. In the New Testament, reflection on the Lord's Supper clearly fulfills a similar function in that it involves a deep remembering of events linked to the need to understand the meaning of Jesus' death (1 Cor 11:23–26). Only when this is so can we truly say that eating the bread and drinking the cup proclaims the Lord's death until he comes.

A second theme that can be developed is the completeness of God's salvific purpose. We see this in the various ways in which this narrative links itself to what has gone before in the exodus while also anticipating the greater work that God will do. This is an important counter to the common trend of treating the exodus as an end in itself rather than as the first stage of a larger salvation story in which God was always taking Israel to the land. But this focus also means that we do not treat the particularity of this moment as an end in itself. Israel needed to enter the land because that was part of God's purpose for them, but even as

---

[65] The account of Elijah being taken up in 2 Kgs 2:1–14, meanwhile, deliberately alludes to this story, further extending the pattern of such miracles.

[66] See further J. J. Krause, "Der Zug durch den Jordan nach Josua 3–4: Eine neue Analysis," in *The Book of Joshua*, 397–400.

Israel remembered that truth, they were to know that this was part of God's larger plan that encompassed all the earth. This larger purpose, which includes all peoples, becomes a key element in the reflection on this event, one that continues to await the moment when peoples from every nation, tribe, and tongue will worship before the Lamb (Rev 7:9). Only by noting the ways in which this moment of salvation is linked to the greater story can we truly appreciate its significance.

Finally, we can note again the importance of Joshua's leadership. Leadership is not, as such, a theme that the Bible consciously demonstrates.[67] Rather, it is content to show examples of good leaders to us. Nevertheless, leadership is of some importance here because of God's declaration that he would begin to exalt Joshua like Moses (3:7) and the completion of that process (4:14). What is striking, though, is that Joshua simply does what God tells him to do, even though at key points he is given no reason as to why he should do so (e.g., 3:12). And just to reinforce this point, when we are told that God had exalted Joshua like Moses, Joshua again received a directive from God that he had to relay to others.

What then does leadership look like? At one level, for the Old Testament as a whole it looks like Moses, since he is always the key human paradigm, and that paradigm has one fundamental element—faithfulness to God. Good leadership may take many forms, and those forms will vary because of the particular circumstances, but at its heart leadership is about faithfulness to God. Joshua's leadership is, in many ways, quite different from that of Moses. But what these two leaders have in common is faithfulness to God, and this must be the defining mark of any leader among God's people.

D. Circumcision and Passover (5:1–12)

¹ When all the Amorite kings across the Jordan to the west and all the Canaanite kings near the sea heard how the Lord had dried up the water of the Jordan before the Israelites until they had crossed over, they lost heart and their courage failed because of the Israelites.

² At that time the Lord said to Joshua, "Make flint knives and circumcise the Israelite men again." ³ So Joshua made flint knives and circumcised the Israelite men at Gibeath-haaraloth. ⁴ This is the reason Joshua circumcised them: All the people who came out of Egypt who were males—all the men of war—had died in the wilderness along the

---

[67] Though see §5 ("Leadership").

way after they had come out of Egypt. [5] Though all the people who came out were circumcised, none of the people born in the wilderness along the way were circumcised after they had come out of Egypt. [6] For the Israelites wandered in the wilderness forty years until all the nation's men of war who came out of Egypt had died off because they did not obey the Lord. So the Lord vowed never to let them see the land he had sworn to their ancestors to give us, a land flowing with milk and honey. [7] He raised up their sons in their place; it was these Joshua circumcised. They were still uncircumcised, since they had not been circumcised along the way. [8] After the entire nation had been circumcised, they stayed where they were in the camp until they recovered. [9] The Lord then said to Joshua, "Today I have rolled away the disgrace of Egypt from you." Therefore, that place is still called Gilgal today.

[10] While the Israelites camped at Gilgal on the plains of Jericho, they observed the Passover on the evening of the fourteenth day of the month. [11] The day after Passover they ate unleavened bread and roasted grain from the produce of the land. [12] And the day after they ate from the produce of the land, the manna ceased. Since there was no more manna for the Israelites, they ate from the crops of the land of Canaan that year.

Context

Israel had entered the land. The crossing of the Jordan in chapters 3–4 was both a miracle that mirrored the crossing of the Sea in the exodus and a source of reflective memory from which Israel could continually be nurtured. Since readers have been reminded several times that God was giving the land to Israel (e.g., 1:2, 11, 15; 2:9, 24) we naturally expect that Israel will commence the process of taking the land. Indeed, that 5:1 recounts as fact what Rahab had previously reported (2:9–11) further fosters this impression. However, two patterns that have been carefully built up through the narrative to this point combine to defer this. These have been enabled by the consistent use of a narrative technique of not reporting anything in advance of the event. As readers, we only know what is happening as it occurs, meaning we experience similar emotions (in this case, surprise and perhaps disappointment) to the Israelites in the narrative. This means that, although the narrator clearly knows what is about to happen, the significance of subtly integrated themes can become clear only at this point.

The first pattern is the use of a delay immediately after a point at which an advance is expected, though in effect we only realize the existence of this pattern now that Israel has entered the land but does not immediately move toward Jericho. Joshua 1 had prepared us for an account of Israel's entry into the land. God's promise of the land had been affirmed, and all the tribes had committed themselves to claiming the land as one nation. But Joshua 2 had unexpectedly deferred this event while the two spies went to Jericho. As noted above (see "Context" on Josh 2:1–24), Joshua 1 and 2 together form a dual introduction to the book, each in a distinctive manner affirming that Israel was to receive the land. The advance into the land then began in chapters 3–4, again creating an expectation of an immediate taking of the land, especially in light of the claim of God's power in 4:24. But this expectation is deferred as Israel unexpectedly pauses to circumcise the males and then celebrate Passover. It is also notable that the texts with the preparation for advance (chapters 1, 3–4) and the delays (2:1–24; 5:1–12) are marked by points of shared vocabulary. So, in addition to the frequent repetition of the verb עָבַר (basically, "cross over" but used in a range of senses) in chapters 1, 3, and 4, we should also note the presence of the armed men from the eastern tribes in 1:14 and 4:12–13. By contrast, apart from reporting the return of the spies in 2:23 (and, so, *away* from the land), the verb עָבַר is wholly absent from the delay narratives. Instead, note the close correlation between the language of Canaanite fear in Rahab's speech and the narrator's comment in 5:1. Both the advance and the delay segments are linked by shared vocabulary and themes that show how they mutually interpret one another.

The second pattern runs across both the advance and delay segments. This is the careful use of references that point to the northern spring as the time when Israel was entering the land. Joshua 2:6 mentioned that Rahab hid the spies under drying flax stalks, pointing to a date in spring. This is confirmed by the comment about the flooding of the Jordan in 3:15, which moved this more specifically to the time of harvest (which in Israel happens in spring). All of this is then clarified by the note in 4:19 that the people entered the land on the tenth day of the first month, which is the date of preparation for Passover. This dating process is less emphasized than the points generating an expectation of advance, but their gradual increase in specificity is an important element, with 4:19 forming an important climax. Given that this has left only four days until Passover, is this enough time to capture Jericho?

Although 5:1 initially encourages readers to think this can be done, it turns out this is the wrong question because we discover that Israel was not in the proper relationship to God to advance. This is the one issue that has been carefully kept back until this point. The crossing of the Jordan makes clear that God does indeed have the power to lead Israel into the land, but that power is to be matched with an Israel that lives out the distinctiveness of its calling under the covenant. So, this second delay is crucial because it provides the opportunity to put right this relationship. Only then can the advance into the land continue. The mode for putting the relationship right is the principal focus here, a focus that is sharpened by the possibilities hinted at by 5:1.

Exegesis

5:1. This verse links this part of the narrative with what has gone before. As a result, many scholars join it primarily to the previous narrative.[68] However, its language provides the pattern for 9:1; 10:1; and 11:1, each of which introduces a new segment of narrative. This suggests that, although it works as a hinge between narrative segments, its primary function is to introduce a new stage in the story[69]—in this case, the beginning of Israel's life in the land.

The narrator now recounts the effect of the crossing of the Jordan—particularly God's drying it up—on the kings in the land. Unlike the seven-nation list of 3:10, only two groups (Amorites and Canaanites) are mentioned in v. 1, though they are apparently understood as representing all the peoples of the land. The Amorites were more or less immediately west of the Jordan, and the Canaanites were by the Mediterranean, though both "west" and "sea" are the same word (יָם) in Hebrew, with context determining meaning. Hebrew does not have fixed terms for the cardinal points; they are determined by imagining someone facing east (toward the sunrise), so that "west" might be either "behind" or "sea" since the Mediterranean is then behind the person. But that the Canaanites are near the sea indicates that they are further west than the Amorites, though there is no exact division. Each group is understood as having a plurality of kings, largely because each town had its own ruler who would claim the title מֶלֶךְ (king). These kings stood in graded power relationship with other kings, so that the ruler of a larger city would be king over those kings. Jabin, king of Hazor (11:1), is an example of a king who ruled other kings. Others would rule only very small communities as local chieftains.

---

[68] E.g., Butler, *Joshua 1–12*, 311.
[69] Similarly Hall, *Conquering Character*, 66.

However, these kings are not distinguished at this point, and irrespective of their status their response is the same, losing heart and having their courage fail because of Israel. This statement confirms Rahab's testimony, though the crossing of the Jordan has intensified it.

The new element here is that, whereas previously it was hearing about God drying up the Sea in the exodus that caused the people to lose heart and have their courage fail, this time it is hearing about God drying up the waters of the Jordan. Rahab's report had described the response of the people to older events, whereas the event that has affected these kings is the most recent. God's mighty acts are consistent, as is their effect. Since the previous report from Rahab led to confidence in God's gift of the land (2:24), we naturally expect that the same will be true here. But this confidence is laid out for us only to establish the contrast with what follows.

5:2–3. The account of crossing the Jordan frequently synchronized events with one another, and that pattern continues here as God's speech to Joshua is linked to the point where the kings have lost heart. At the very point where we expect God to tell Joshua to advance, we instead read of him telling Joshua to make flint knives. Indeed, there are three imperative verbs here, with the second pair dependent on the first.[70] Joshua is to make these knives and "circumcise the Israelite men again." Taken at face value, this is an odd statement since a man can only be circumcised once. There may be a clue in the use of the verb שׁוּב, which csb collapses into שֵׁנִית as "again" rather than "a second time."[71] But if we give the verb its full weight as an imperative rather than treating it as periphrasis, as do most translations, then the sense might be that Joshua was once again to institute the practice of circumcision. Certainly, this seems to be the sense of it as outlined in verses 4–7, where the narrator feels constrained to explain this otherwise odd statement. Flint is probably used because it is hard, sharp, and more reliable under the circumstances than metal knives—rather than because of a cultic preference for stone over metal, though it may also have been a traditional method (cf. Exod 4:25). Israel

---

[70] See *GKC* 120g on the coordination of imperative verbs here.

[71] The lxx presumes יָשַׁב ("sit"), but the mt should be retained as the more difficult reading. There are, indeed, a cluster of text-critical issues through this passage when one examines lxx and 4QJosh[a] (see Nelson, *Joshua*, 73–74, for a helpful summary), but csb's instinct to remain with the mt is generally sound. Although his comments apply only to vv. 10–12, I agree with Krause, *Exodus und Eisodus*, 336, that we should see the lxx here as a first interpreter of the mt rather than as a source for emendation.

at this time was still in the Bronze Age, and bronze cannot be made as sharp as flint, especially if it is obsidian, which was particularly well-suited to this task.[72] Of course, this is still a cultic act because circumcision was required of all Israelite males as a sign of their membership in the covenant community (Gen 17:9–14).

More importantly, because of the Passover background that has gradually emerged, the fact that no uncircumcised male could eat the Passover (Exod 12:48) means a crucial moment in Israel's life was about to commence with men unable to participate. Joshua's obedience to God's command is then simply described, noting that he made the knives and circumcised the men at Gibeath-haaraloth, a place name that means "hill of foreskins" (no doubt why most translations consign this point to a footnote rather than the main text). Since its location is related to that of Gilgal, which we cannot identify beyond the general region, we cannot identify this site either. However, since Gilgal was a camp and not a town, and since this hill was used only at this point, it is unlikely that we would be able to identify it. Nevertheless, the place name is a graphic reminder of what happened.

5:4–7. The need for circumcision comes as a complete surprise, as the book has not previously indicated that this was an issue. Since the requirement of male circumcision could be traced back to Abraham, we would expect that all would have been circumcised as infants. Accordingly, the narrator includes what would today probably be an explanatory footnote, explaining why this was needed. Although the men who had come out of Egypt in the exodus had been circumcised, they had all died in the wilderness. This summary statement ignores Joshua and Caleb, whose continued presence in Israel was allowed because of their faithfulness when the spies entered the land from Kadesh-barnea (Numbers 13–14; Deut 1:34–40). But since Joshua is addressed here this exception is implicit. The fact that the males who had come out of Egypt are expressly referred to as "men of war" is probably ironic, given their failure to believe God's promises resulting in their death in the wilderness (Num 14:20–25; Deut 1:34–40). These Israelites are labeled in verse 6 as a גוי (nation), a term that frequently has pagan overtones and that Deut 7:1 uses to describe the Canaanites. However, it was an acceptable term for Israel in Josh 3:17 and 4:1 (and again in 5:8), so it is probably

---

[72] See Hess, *Joshua*, 119.

used more to refer to Israel as a political entity than anything else even though they did not yet have land.[73]

By contrast, those born in the wilderness had not been circumcised. This failure was not noted before, making the surprise here even greater. Various forms of rebellion are described in Numbers 13–20, but none involved this basic marker of Israelite identity. However, in spite of the failures of the previous generation, a new generation now stood with a toehold on the land God was giving. The narrator identifies with this generation, noting that God had sworn to give this land flowing with milk and honey to "us" (v. 6), distinguishing those who now read this text from the generation that died in the wilderness. csb rightly renders an ambiguous Hebrew text as, "He raised up their sons" (v. 7), whereas hcsb had "Joshua" as the subject. The point then is that although God had allowed one generation to die in the wilderness, he continued to be faithful to Israel by raising up a new generation. Although this new generation had not been circumcised during the journey to the land, they were now circumcised by Joshua.

5:8–9. After the explanatory note, the main narrative set aside at verse 3 is now resumed. There are, however, still important links to the explanatory note, most obviously in the repetition of the verb תָּמַם. In verse 6 it refers to the completion of the exodus generation, meaning their death, whereas here it is used to refer to the completion of the circumcision of the nation. For one group, it had meant their exclusion from God's purposes because of their failure to believe, whereas here it refers to the inclusion of a nation that once again listens to God as circumcision is reinstituted. But that inclusion came with a cost: Israel could not immediately proceed to take the land. Instead, the nation needed to remain at Gilgal while the men who had been circumcised recovered.

While they recovered, we hear another message from God to Joshua in verse 9, so that divine speeches provide the boundaries for this section. God declared that he had "rolled away the disgrace of Egypt," to which the narrator attaches a note explaining why the place was called Gilgal. The name Gilgal was used in 4:19 but no explanation of the name was then given, suggesting that the narrator used the name on the basis of

---

[73] Butler, *Joshua 1–12*, 335, notes the difference between "people" (עַם) in verses 4–5 and גּוֹי here. But given the flexibility of these terms, it is probably better to see them as intentional variants for effect rather than contrasts.

common usage while delaying an explanation. "Gilgal" is related to a verb meaning "to roll"; on this basis some have thought the stones might have been arranged in a circle. Though not impossible, the text makes no such claim. But here there is a connection between God rolling away the disgrace of Egypt and the name (albeit through a play on words rather than the sort of scientific etymology found in dictionaries today). Amos makes a similar play when, having told Israel not to go to Gilgal (Amos 5:5), he summons Israel to let justice "roll down like waters" (5:24 ESV).[74] Here in Joshua, the name "Gilgal" becomes a memorial to God's action in removing the disgrace of Egypt. The exact nature of the disgrace is not mentioned,[75] but presumably it covers Israel's enslavement there and all that went with it. But now Israel is a nation prepared for God's purposes in a way the previous generation was not, and both God's speech and the name "Gilgal" attest to this.

5:10. With the men circumcised, Israel was in a condition to celebrate Passover on the fourteenth day of the first month (also called "Nisan"). This means the circumcision took place between the tenth day of the month, when Israel had crossed the river, and this day. Although a range of practices are associated with Passover (cf. Deut 16:1–8), none of these are recounted[76] since circumcision was the unique element of preparation for celebrating this first Passover in the land.

This celebration also completes the bridge with the exodus that was particularly clear in Joshua 3–4. Israel's first major experience in the wilderness was passing through the Sea, and their last major event was passing through the river. Similarly, their last major act in Egypt was celebration of Passover, which is their first act in the land. But just as Passover had pointed to something larger that God was about to do through Israel in the exodus, so also here the narrative sees this Passover as the first stage of something more. This is stressed by noting that Israel was "camped" at Gilgal on the plains of Jericho. Camping implies temporary habitation, as had been Israel's experience in the wilderness. But they were now in the land that God was giving them, a place where they were to find rest (1:15) and thus permanent settlement. Moreover, that they are on the plains of Jericho points to Jericho as the first significant site in the land,

---

[74] csb has "flow" rather than "roll down." This captures the sense well but misses the wordplay.

[75] Krause, *Exodus und Eisodus*, 310, calls it a "cryptic dictum" (my translation).

[76] Note especially the prohibitions on eating in Lev 23:9–14, which have to be assumed here.

something already indicated by the encounter of the spies with Jericho. Israel has looked back to the exodus in this celebration, and this act of looking back has prepared them to go forward with God into the land.

5:11–12. The first hint of this next step into the land is provided by the note about the food Israel ate the following day: unleavened bread and roasted grain. Unleavened bread is, of course, associated with Passover, but its production requires some form of grain to make flour, and this was not a feature associated with manna. This means Israel had been able to collect grain, a fact reflected in the roasted grain (probably barley, which was growing in the area since its harvest was also closely linked to Passover). This was not simply something they had gathered while across the river; the narrator specifies that it was from "the produce of the land" (v. 11).[77] This Passover is thus both a celebration of God's act of delivering Israel from Egypt and a first anticipation of life in the land of promise. This is then reaffirmed in the note that manna ceased on the day that Israel first ate from the produce of the land (v. 12). Israel had thus left the wilderness behind; from this point they are "in the land." Manna had been a temporary provision for the time in the wilderness (since Exodus 16), but the produce of the land was God's continuing provision. Israel's arrival at the beginning of the harvest meant they were able to eat the food of the land for all that year, so that the timing of their arrival was also part of God's provision.

Bridge

Appreciating the contrast established between verse 1 and verses 2–12 is vital to an understanding of this passage. Verse 1 establishes a setting that, on a superficial level, would suggest Israel can move straight in and take the land. After all, God was giving the land and had brought them across the Jordan while the inhabitants of the land were melting with fear. But the narrator has held back crucial information that suddenly makes the various hints as to the time of year in the preceding chapters much more important than they might otherwise have seemed. It is the time of Passover, and Israel needs to pause and celebrate this most important of festivals, thus completing the links that have been made between the exodus and the entry into the land. Israel needs to live by a different set

---

[77] The word for "produce" (עֲבוּר) plays with the verb "pass over" (עָבַר) which was so prominent in chapters 3–4. Similarly, Rösel, *Joshua*, 86.

of principles in which honoring God was primary. The opportunity to advance could not, on its own, be enough.

This situation is made even more complex by revealing that Israel's men needed to be circumcised. Not only was Israel not to advance immediately to claim the land God had promised, they were in effect to make themselves vulnerable because throughout the period of the Passover they would lack a fighting force.[78] Yet what mattered most was not claiming the promise of God but rather ordering their life such that they were in a right relationship with him by putting proper worship at the heart of who they were. There are instances later in Israel's history when approval needed to be given for non-orthodox worship practices,[79] but Israel here has the chance to do the right thing, and that is the priority. An Israel that did not put the worship of God at the center of its being would lose its distinctiveness. This makes clear that creating a people of faithful worship is central to the message of the book of Joshua.

There are obvious connections that can be made with the New Testament. For example, note Jesus' comments to the woman of Samaria that the Father seeks those who will worship him in spirit and in truth (John 4:16–26). An obvious focus here is that true worship is centered on understanding who Jesus is. We could also note Stephen's sermon in Acts 7 with its focus on showing that the form of worship matters less than the life that lies behind it. Both of these passages develop the themes of this passage. We should be careful, however, not to individualize this worship but to realize that in all of these passages the concern is with the worship of the people of God as a whole.

What becomes clear is that the worship God honors is the worship that prioritizes faithfulness to him. This is especially apparent in God's response to the circumcision in verse 9 and the provision of food from the land in verses 11–12.[80] As Israel seeks to worship truly, they discover God's promise being fulfilled. It is not that we seek to claim the promises of God. Rather, as we worship faithfully, and at times in costly ways, we begin to see the promises of God fulfilled.

---

[78] Note, e.g., what Simeon and Levi were able to do to Shechem in Gen 34:24–25.

[79] Such as Hezekiah's celebration of Passover in the second month as an emergency measure in 2 Chronicles 30.

[80] In light of this, we should also note the way Paul links circumcision and the baptism of believers in Col 2:11–12. Baptism, not circumcision, is the mark of the Christian community, but the pattern of faithfulness he develops in the balance of Colossians 2 can helpfully be compared with what we find here in Joshua.

II. Taking the Land (5:13–12:24)

A. Jericho (5:13–6:27)

5 ¹³ When Joshua was near Jericho, he looked up and saw a man standing in front of him with a drawn sword in his hand. Joshua approached him and asked, "Are you for us or for our enemies?"

¹⁴ "Neither," he replied. "I have now come as commander of the Lord's army."

Then Joshua bowed with his face to the ground in homage and asked him, "What does my Lord want to say to his servant?"

¹⁵ The commander of the Lord's army said to Joshua, "Remove the sandals from your feet, for the place where you are standing is holy." And Joshua did that.

6 ¹ Now Jericho was strongly fortified because of the Israelites—no one leaving or entering. ² The Lord said to Joshua, "Look, I have handed Jericho, its king, and its best soldiers over to you. ³ March around the city with all the men of war, circling the city one time. Do this for six days. ⁴ Have seven priests carry seven ram's-horn trumpets in front of the ark. But on the seventh day, march around the city seven times, while the priests blow the ram's horns. ⁵ When there is a prolonged blast of the horn and you hear its sound, have all the troops give a mighty shout. Then the city wall will collapse, and the troops will advance, each man straight ahead."

⁶ So Joshua son of Nun summoned the priests and said to them, "Take up the ark of the covenant and have seven priests carry seven ram's horns in front of the ark of the Lord." ⁷ He said to the troops, "Move forward, march around the city, and have the armed men go ahead of the ark of the Lord."

⁸ After Joshua had spoken to the troops, seven priests carrying seven ram's horns before the Lord moved forward and blew the ram's horns; the ark of the Lord's covenant followed them. ⁹ While the ram's horns were blowing, the armed men went in front of the priests who blew the ram's horns, and the rear guard went behind the ark. ¹⁰ But Joshua had commanded the troops, "Do not shout or let your voice be heard. Don't let one word come out of your mouth until the time I say, 'Shout!' Then you are to shout." ¹¹ So the ark of the Lord was carried around the city, circling it once. They returned to the camp and spent the night there.

¹² Joshua got up early the next morning. The priests took the ark of the Lord, ¹³ and the seven priests carrying seven ram's horns marched in front of the ark of the Lord. While the ram's horns were blowing, the armed men went in front of them, and the rear guard went behind the ark of the Lord. ¹⁴ On the second day they marched around the city once and returned to the camp. They did this for six days.

¹⁵ Early on the seventh day, they started at dawn and marched around the city seven times in the same way. That was the only day they marched around the city seven times. ¹⁶ After the seventh time, the priests blew the ram's horns, and Joshua said to the troops, "Shout! For the L ORD has given you the city. ¹⁷ But the city and everything in it are set apart to the L ORD for destruction. Only Rahab the prostitute and everyone with her in the house will live, because she hid the messengers we sent. ¹⁸ But keep yourselves from the things set apart, or you will be set apart for destruction. If you take any of those things, you will set apart the camp of Israel for destruction and make trouble for it. ¹⁹ For all the silver and gold, and the articles of bronze and iron, are dedicated to the L ORD and must go into the L ORD's treasury."

²⁰ So the troops shouted, and the ram's horns sounded. When they heard the blast of the ram's horn, the troops gave a great shout, and the wall collapsed. The troops advanced into the city, each man straight ahead, and they captured the city. ²¹ They completely destroyed everything in the city with the sword—every man and woman, both young and old, and every ox, sheep, and donkey.

²² Joshua said to the two men who had scouted the land, "Go to the prostitute's house and bring the woman out of there, and all who are with her, just as you swore to her." ²³ So the young men who had scouted went in and brought out Rahab and her father, mother, brothers, and all who belonged to her. They brought out her whole family and settled them outside the camp of Israel.

²⁴ They burned the city and everything in it, but they put the silver and gold and the articles of bronze and iron into the treasury of the L ORD's house. ²⁵ However, Joshua spared Rahab the prostitute, her father's family, and all who belonged to her, because she hid the messengers Joshua had sent to spy on Jericho, and she still lives in Israel today.

²⁶ At that time Joshua imposed this curse:

The man who undertakes
the rebuilding of this city, Jericho,
is cursed before the L ORD.
He will lay its foundation
at the cost of his firstborn;
he will finish its gates
at the cost of his youngest.

²⁷ And the L ORD was with Joshua, and his fame spread throughout the land.

Context

Although God had promised Joshua that he had given him every place where his foot would tread as far back as 1:3, at this point Israel possesses no more than a toehold in the land with their camp at Gilgal. God's initial speech to Joshua in chapter 1 created an expectation of Israel entering and claiming the land, but that has been continually deferred. Initially the crossing of the Jordan was delayed as the spies scouted out Jericho. Then, having crossed the Jordan in chapters 3–4, there was a further delay as the men were circumcised and Passover celebrated in 5:1–12. However, these delays end as Israel claims Jericho, the first substantial point in the land that they will hold.

Even so, the delays are not set aside, because each of the previous narratives in some way reaches a conclusion here. Thus, the Jericho account both begins the taking of the land and ends the entry into it. This effect of closing off the previous narratives is achieved by reference to each of them. Just as the ark had been prominent in crossing the Jordan (chs. 3–4), so also it is prominent here (ch. 6)—a prominence it has nowhere else in the book (it is mentioned elsewhere only in 7:6 and 8:33 [2x]). In both former narratives, the ark is something to be followed in a cultic procession, whereas in the latter two passages it is a marker of God's presence. These are not mutually exclusive functions, but there is a clear difference in emphasis. The clearly cultic nature of the procession also emerges out of the account of circumcision and celebration of Passover in 5:1–12. Chapter 2 had recorded the oath sworn to Rahab, and the result of that oath is now recorded here (6:22–25). Chapters 1 and 2 form a double introduction to the book, and there are also direct links here to chapter 1, most obviously in God's promise that no one would be able to resist Joshua (1:6), which finds its initial fulfillment here (even if that promise will be troubled at Ai). Less obvious in translation is that the verb עָבַר (variously, "cross over" or "pass through"), which was so prominent in chapters 1 and 3–4 is also prominent here, describing the task of the priests (6:7–8). God's promise to be with Joshua as he was with Moses (1:3) is reflected in the statement of divine presence in 6:27, as well as in Joshua's enigmatic encounter with the commander of the Lord's army and its clear echoes of Moses' encounter with God at the burning bush (Exod 3:1–6). The promises of God, in spite of the delays within the narrative, thus come together in this account, showing that in many ways it concludes the entry into the land.

Nevertheless, although the narrative makes clear links to what has gone before, there are key features that indicate its primary function is to initiate the process of Israel taking the land God had promised. Most obviously, the Jericho narrative recounts the first place Israel captured, even if God did not intend for them to retain anything from it for themselves. Israel might not have a place to settle at the end of this chapter, but they did control a key point of entry into the land, control that let them advance into the central hill country. The narrative's forward focus is also made clear by the reference to the city's goods being devoted to God. The trouble that this will bring prepares us for the events that will be associated with Achan and the naming of the Valley of Achor ("Valley of Trouble").

Yet an important change in narrative technique is also deployed in this passage, one that will continue to the end of chapter 12. Up to this point, the narrator has taken the position of an observer who recounts events as they happen and who provides no information about how we are to interpret them. We do not know, for example, if the oath sworn to Rahab was a sin in which Israel failed to recognize that all the peoples of the land are under the ban, or if it was a moment of profound insight in which the scouts realized that Israel was really made up of those who committed themselves to God regardless of ethnicity. This particular issue will receive further attention in the next narrative as we see Achan and his family, all ethnic Israelites, placed under the ban themselves because of their failure to follow the stipulations of the ban. Until now the narrator has held back from providing interpretive comments, either through narrative intrusions or reported speech from God, but that changes here. In each of the accounts associated with taking the land, the narrator adopts a position of narrative omniscience and so is able to explain in advance what is happening and to interpret events for readers.

In 5:13–6:27, this effect is achieved through a divine speech that guarantees the capture of the city (6:2–5), but at other points this can be achieved through direct commentary (e.g., 7:1). The previous narratives left a series of issues unresolved: Could Israel succeed if they had sworn an oath to a Canaanite? Could a nation that effectively crippled its soldiers by circumcision really hope to capture the land? But now we are given the means to understand these events and see how they contribute to a richer comprehension of what it meant to be Israel and to live out the demands of being the people of God. What has mattered throughout is obedience to God; the question left unanswered before is what that obedience might look like. To that we now turn, in a passage that explores what it means to be a worshiping and obedient people, as Israel is commanded to follow a strategy that makes no military sense.

Exegesis

5:13–15. Israel's base at Gilgal was already close to Jericho, but the importance of this location is emphasized by the note in verse 13 that Joshua was near the city. Although the Hebrew could be read as saying Joshua was in Jericho, the preposition used can also mean "by" and so stress the general region rather than a particular place. However, the intent is clearly to place Joshua at a point close to the city as the first step toward the city's capture. While there, Joshua "saw a man standing in front of him." As this brief and somewhat enigmatic account progresses, it will emerge that this is considerably more than just a man, but the narrative assumes Joshua's perspective, reporting what he sees.[81] The man was clearly a warrior prepared for battle with a drawn sword in his hand.[82]

In spite of the apparent threat such a warrior might pose, Joshua approached him even though he clearly did not recognize him. Joshua's question to the man is simple and direct ("Are you for us or for our enemies?") but presumes that the man is not an Israelite. The question itself is interesting for what it reveals about Joshua's understanding of Israel's relationship to non-Israelites. The query shows an openness to the possibility that a non-Israelite could work with Israel, a subtle hint that the oath sworn to Rahab was acceptable, if she was committed to Israel's purposes. But the question also assumes that this binary structure represented the only options available.

Yet the man's terse response, "Neither,"[83] immediately makes clear that there is a third alternative. He had come as commander of the Lord's army. The phrasing of the Hebrew emphasizes his role by placing it first in the sentence. The timing of this numinous encounter is important, for the commander has come "now"—that is, at the point when Israel needed to fight God's battle as they prepard to take the city. The fact that the

---

[81] The word הִנֵּה (untranslated in CSB and also absent from LXX, Syr, and Tg, but often rendered "behold") is frequently used in Hebrew narrative to mark a switch to the perspective of a character within the narrative. Matties, *Joshua*, 127–28, points to analogies with Abraham's encounter with the three men in Genesis 18, which may lie in the background here.

[82] Heavenly figures with drawn swords also appear in Num 22:23, 31 and 1 Chr 21:16, but such parallels only emerge once the reader knows more clearly who this "man" is.

[83] Many manuscripts along with the LXX and Syr assume a slightly different text here, reading לוֹ ("to him") for the MT לֹא ("neither" in CSB, though it could be a blunt "No"). But the alternative reading looks like a correction of a difficult text, and the terse and awkward phrasing of the MT should stand.

man was not necessarily for Israel means it was possible for them in some way not to join God in his battles. The presence of the commander of this army, presumably angelic (though the text is silent on exactly what this army was like), makes clear that God was prepared to fight. But it is also clear that Israel needed to join God's battle rather than wage their own.

Joshua responded by prostrating himself before the man, an act of homage that can be understood as an act of worship (so csb), but that is probably better understood as the deference expected before one's social superiors in that culture. Such homage is reflected in his question to the commander, whose status he recognizes by calling him "Lord."[84] There is a further mysterious feature when the commander directed Joshua to remove his sandals because he was standing (and thus no longer prostrate) on holy ground. This is a clear allusion to Moses and his encounter with God at the burning bush (Exod 3:1–6), yet another parallel between Moses and Joshua. Such parallels ultimately contribute to Joshua receiving the title "Servant of the Lord" (Josh 24:29) and demonstrate God's promise to be with Joshua as he had been with Moses (1:3). Thus, references to God's presence with Joshua function as bookends to the whole Jericho narrative (5:15; 6:27).

With the brief note that Joshua removed his sandals, we then leave this strange encounter. One might presume that there is a good deal more that could be said, but enough has been provided so that this encounter provides a frame through which we read the rest of the Jericho narrative.[85] God is present, and because this land is holy it already belongs to him. This is good news for Israel, but his presence does not mean Israel can presume he will support them in whatever they choose. Rather, Israel must follow the path that God sets before them if his army is to fight for them.

6:1. This verse is an aside that prepares us for what follows by describing the nature of Jericho as a site Israel needed to capture. The narrator's description of the city is thus pivotal to our understanding of the narrative as a whole, not least because of the historical issues that have plagued its interpretation. We are told the city was tightly shut up because of the presence of the Israelites through a pair of related

---

[84] It is probably better to leave this uncapitalized (i.e., "lord") to make clear that this is not the form of address for God.

[85] The various attempts to treat this section as a fragment of something larger that we no longer have, helpfully summarized by Krause, *Exodus und Eisodus*, 375–85, are thus unnecessary.

participles, סֹגֶרֶת וּמְסֻגֶּרֶת—both of which are based on the root סגר ("to shut")—but they make no reference to any degree of fortification.[86] CSB's "strongly fortified" therefore appears to represent the text of LXX, which changes the second participle to suggest fortification. This appears to be an interpretative change that presumes Jericho must have been a major city, perhaps the earliest evidence of this line of interpretation. But nothing in the Hebrew suggests anything along these lines. Indeed, that the city could be circumambulated seven times in one day makes clear that it could not have been particularly large. This would not, of itself, preclude heavy fortification, especially if Jericho was used more as a fort by some of the nearby cities in the hills to guard the fords of the Jordan. But if Jericho was a more or less independent city, then the text would not indicate the degree of wealth needed to support such fortifications. The city could be closed off; the Rahab story indicates that its gate could be shut to prevent movement in and out (Josh 2:5, 7). But none of this indicates any degree of fortification. All that we are told is that the city could be closed off to prevent movement in and out.

Attention to these details is important when we examine the text and the archaeological evidence in light of one another. Since Kenyon's excavations (1952–1958), the archaeology of Jericho (Tell es-Sultan) has generally been held to show that the biblical account cannot be rooted in history, though Kenyon herself did not come to this conclusion. Subsequent excavations have not significantly altered the interpretation of the site, and though there have been attempts to reinterpret her evidence, on the whole most archaeologists agree with the general tenor of her interpretation.[87] Basically, whether we have an early arrival of Israel (c. 1400 BC) or a later one (c. 1250 BC), we have to note that the evidence Kenyon found provides little evidence of occupation in the Late Bronze Age when the narrative is set. However, she did find some evidence of limited occupation of the site, which is actually consistent with the testimony of the text. There is considerable erosion of the site from this period, and if mud brick construction was used, we would not expect to find significant remains. However, there was a significant central house

---

[86] Nicholas P. Lunn, "Allusions to the Levitical Leprosy Laws in the Jericho Narratives (Josh 2 and 6)," JESOT 4.2 (2015): 136, notes the importance of this verb in the leprosy laws (e.g., Lev 13:4–5) in which it is used for quarantine. The point is separation, not fortification.

[87] For a helpful survey of the current archaeological evidence and its interpretation, see Ralph K. Hawkins, How Israel Became a People (Nashville: Abingdon, 2013), 91–105.

apparently occupied in the Late Bronze Age and some ash, which suggests destruction in this period too.

A likely scenario, therefore, is a small city of a couple of acres, the wall of which was formed by joining the houses of the poor into a terrace as an outer ring, with a gate joining those points where the terrace did not join. This would be consistent with Rahab's house being in the city wall (2:15), though it would not preclude there being points where the remains of the wall from the old Middle Bronze Age city might have been used. In short, the Jericho described by the text is a small settlement with some limited security—not a major city. The view that the story is unhistorical is rooted in the belief that Jericho was a major city, but in rejecting this on the basis of the archaeology,[88] it is really a history of interpretation—not the text itself—that is rejected.

But if Jericho was not a major site, why give it such importance in the story? Does this not diminish the miracle described here? These are natural questions if we have always assumed that Jericho was a large city, but we have to attend to what the text actually says and why. It is worth noting that the next story focuses on Ai as so small that only a small force was required to capture it (Josh 7:3). That assessment will prove to be misplaced, but only because of Israel's disobedience. These two narratives need to be read in light of one another (see discussion of context for 7:1–8:29). The initial failure at Ai highlights an important element already hinted at in Joshua's encounter with the commander of the Lord's army: Israel can succeed only when living in obedient faithfulness to God. Without this, even small opponents will overwhelm them. So here, Israel has to capture a city that, if left, would provide a basis for raids against them. But even though it is a small city, Israel's lack of experience in siege warfare and their need to depend on God alone means the only way they can capture the city is by obeying one of the strangest military stratagems ever devised. Together, these elements make clear what was already indicated in God's speech to Joshua in 1:3: God gives the land, and Israel is never to believe that their own strength achieved the victory. For the story to function in this way, we need both a small city and a miraculous defeat of it, and that is precisely what we

---

[88] E.g., Rösel, *Joshua*, 46, 97.

have. The city was shut up so Israel could not go in, but God would take them in and give the city to them.[89]

6:2–5. If verse 1 is an aside, it is possible that these verses are a direct continuation from 5:13–15 but with God's speech reported directly rather than through the commander. Such a continuation would mean that we have a fuller answer to Joshua's question in 5:14.[90] However, it is also clearly set off from that segment by the aside in verse 1, which is perhaps why we now have direct speech from God. The opening of the speech in verse 2 particularizes the more general statement of 1:3, in which God said he had given all the land to Israel. The statement here applies that general truth to the specific case of Jericho. But since the city was inhabited and Israel would face opposition, we learn that, not only the city, but also its king and fighting men had been given over to Israel.

The surprise comes in the instructions issued in verses 3–5. Israel had no experience of siege warfare, but we can reasonably assume they would not have come up with a plan like this.[91] The directives are simple but have the effect of taking what at first looks like a battle account and changing it to an extended act of worship. The men of war were to march around the city once a day for six days. The priests bearing the ark were also to circumambulate Jericho, with seven priests going ahead of the ark carrying ram's horn trumpets.[92] Nothing is said about the purpose of carrying the trumpets[93] (which would produce a blast of sound rather than something melodic) until the seventh day, on which everyone was to circle the city seven times while the priests blew the trumpets. However, the assumption is that the trumpets would be sounded each day, and that is certainly how the directive is applied in verse 8.

On the seventh day there was to be an extended blast on the horns. When the people heard this, they were to give a great shout. In response

---

[89] Hence, Dale Ralph Davis, *No Falling Words: Expositions of the Book of Joshua* (Grand Rapids: Baker, 1988), 51, trenchantly heads this passage, "Joshua Did *Not* Fight the Battle of Jericho."

[90] This possibility is explored quite thoroughly by Sarah Lebhar Hall, *Conquering Character: The Characterization of Joshua in Joshua 1–11* (London: T&T Clark, 2010), 79–82.

[91] This did not stop the crusaders at Jerusalem in 1099 who, in spite of their military training, attempted to apply this strategy to the city's capture with a signal lack of success.

[92] Several different terms are used to describe these, but they are probably stylistic variants rather than evidence of sources.

[93] So psychological readings, such as those of Madvig, "Joshua," 278, or Hélène Dallaire ("Joshua" in *The Expositor's Bible Commentary*, rev. ed., ed. Tremper Longman III and David E. Garland [Grand Rapids: Zondervan, 2012], 896) are unnecessary.

to this, God promised that the city walls would fall and Israel would advance into the city. What Jericho had sought to do in verse 1 is declared to be impossible because God would break down the barrier that kept Israel from entering the city. But the means by which this would be done would forever make clear to Israel that they had not done this on the basis of their strength or military skill. Israel simply had to obey, though they apparently had the freedom to work out how certain aspects of God's commands were to be applied.

6:6–7. Joshua's full patronym ("son of Nun") is used only ten times in the book; this is the last time it appears before the land allocation begins. Typically, this fuller form of his name occurs at key points in a narrative, as here where he begins to initiate God's plan for the city's capture. A key element of this whole account is Joshua's obedience to all that God commands. Just as he had obeyed the directive of the commander to remove his sandals (5:15), so also here he does exactly what God required.

There is a small chiasm in relation to God's commands in that they started with the men of war followed by the priests (vv. 3–4), while Joshua started with the priests followed by the men of war (vv. 6–7). The instructions closely match God's earlier directives,[94] with some priests told to take up the ark and seven others told to go before the ark with ram's horn trumpets. Joshua then spoke to the people[95]—a term probably meant to include everyone and not just the warriors since the armed group is treated separately—telling them to go around the city but with the warriors to go ahead of the ark. Joshua's instructions thus form the paradigm of obedience, which is so central to this narrative.

6:8–11. Although God's instructions outlined a seven-day structure for Israel, the narrative abbreviates its account of Israel's obedience, here providing the first of the six standard days as an example of their obedience. As soon as Joshua had finished speaking to the people, the seven priests bearing the ram's horn trumpets passed through the people and blew their horns. The ark followed. Consistent with God's instructions, the armed soldiers went ahead of the priests blowing the trumpets, with the rest of the people following as a rearguard. Although omitted by the

---

[94] The whole of Joshua's speech to the priests in v. 6 is missing from the Old Greek in spite of the introductory verb. It seems likely a scribe has gone to the same verb at the start of v. 7. If the scribe's manuscript was one that had the plural verb there (as opposed to the singular of Qere and many other manuscripts) then this slip is even more likely.

[95] Here csb correctly follows Qere and numerous manuscripts with the singular verb.

CSB, the MT could suggest that there were also those among the rearguard who were blowing trumpets,[96] though perhaps more likely the reference is to the continued blowing of the horns. There was nothing priestly about blowing such trumpets. This action was not specifically legislated by God's earlier speech in verses 2–5, nor was it precluded.

Shouting, however, was precluded by God, and Joshua prohibited it in his speech in verse 10. This is probably to be understood as a flashback to his directions in verses 6–7, the report of which has been delayed until now, in order to contrast with the blowing of the horns. The horns could be blown, but no speech was acceptable until Joshua commanded them to shout. The importance of this is underlined by the three different ways in which Joshua enjoined silence on the people. God's earlier speech indicated that the people were to shout when the long blast on the horn was heard, but this is a role Joshua assumed. Yet these texts do not contradict each other. Rather, Joshua took responsibility to note when the long blast was heard amid all the other noise and to give the directive to shout.

This shout could be a shout of acclamation in worship (e.g., Ps 96:1–2) or a war cry (e.g., 1 Sam 17:52), showing that worship and battle are joined. It was an act of leadership by Joshua, part of the process by which Israel had to work out how to apply God's command in practice. With this background information in place, verse 11 provides a simple summary, noting that the ark was taken around the city once and then, as commanded, returned to the camp for the night. Israel obeyed Yahweh's commands, though they had freedom to determine exactly how that obedience was to be worked out.

6:12–14. A briefer summary report is provided for the second day, before noting that this pattern was followed each of the remaining days. Joshua was apparently a frequent early riser since we are told six times in the book that he rose early, though given that this is again mentioned for the seventh day (v. 15) we are probably to understand that he did so each day at Jericho. Use of this motif typically occurs at points when Joshua was to provide significant leadership (e.g., 3:1; 7:16); therefore, it is perhaps as much an idiom associated with leadership as it is a report

---

[96] Nelson, *Joshua*, 88, believes those in the rearguard blew the trumpets, claiming this is evidence of confusion in the narrative and thus multiple sources. This is grammatically possible, though NIV may well be correct to interpret the clause more generally as referring to the continued blasts on the horns, in which case there is no confusion.

of his sleep habits. The report of the day in verses 12–13 is effectively a précis of what was described on the first day. Likewise, the summary in verse 14a matches the summary of the first day in verse 11. This was accomplished for each of days 1–6 (v. 14b).

6:15–19. The telescoping of the narrative reaches its focal point on the seventh day so that more attention can be given to it. This time everyone rose early, with "early" specified as dawn, and they circled the city seven times. Since obedience is central here, the text notes that this was the only day they did this. Just as the seventh day is a point of focus, so also is the seventh circumambulation. On this lap the priests sounded the horns and Joshua gave the command to shout. Joshua's speech is more than just the command to shout,[97] because he added that God had given the city over to them. Although this is an additional element introduced by Joshua, it is entirely consistent with God's word to him in verse 2. Thus, Joshua's announcement is both an act of obedience and an act of prophecy, declaring God's word to his people. It is an example of leadership that takes God's command seriously and also appreciates that God gave scope for how the command was to be applied.

Verse 17, however, introduces new information: The city and everything in it is "set apart to the LORD for destruction" (חֵרֶם; see on 2:10 for general comments on this concept). This represents one of the most difficult aspects of the Old Testament for most modern readers. Thomas Mann, for example, considers this to be a barbarous practice that Christians must reject.[98] Even Christians who would not wish to reject any part of Scripture struggle with it.[99] We cannot address all aspects of the problem

---

[97] Nicolai Winther-Nielsen, *A Functional Discourse Grammar of Joshua: A Computer-Assisted Rhetorical Structure Analysis* (Stockholm: Almqvist & Wicksell, 1995), 200, plausibly makes this a flashback. But the more important point is to interpret the saying at this point in the narrative.

[98] Thomas W. Mann, *The Book of the Former Prophets* (Eugene, OR: Cascade, 2011), 22.

[99] See, e.g., Christopher J. H. Wright, *The God I Don't Understand: Reflections on Tough Questions of Faith* (Grand Rapids: Zondervan, 2008), 80–88, or the different views in Stanley N. Gundry, ed., *Show Them No Mercy: Four Views on God and the Canaanite Genocide* (Grand Rapids: Zondervan, 2003). The treatment of J. P. U. Lilley, "Understanding the ḤEREM," *TynBul* 44 (1993): 160–77, remains the most accessible treatment, while Christian Hofreiter, "Genocide in Deuteronomy and Christian Interpretation," in *Interpreting Deuteronomy: Issues and Approaches*, ed. David G. Firth and Philip S. Johnston (Nottingham: Apollos, 2012), 240–62, provides a helpful overview of the different ways Christians have dealt with it. See also Butler, *Joshua 1–12*, 383–85; Jannica A. de Prenter, "The Contrastive Polysemous Meaning of חרם in the Book of Joshua: A Cognitive Linguistic Approach," in *The Book of Joshua*, ed.

here beyond noting that, although perhaps not widespread, it was not unique to Israel. This makes Douglas Earl's otherwise attractive suggestion that it should be read mythologically[100] less persuasive since it seems to represent a more widespread practice that is particularly associated with warfare.

One important point is that although destruction is clearly a possibility in the application of this concept, it is not a necessary part of it, as can be seen in the fact that the metal items found at Jericho were to go into God's treasury. Since chapter 2 left the status of the spies' vow to Rahab ambiguous, the narrative has deferred for as long as possible any mention of her. Only in verse 17 do we discover that the vow can indeed be acted upon, even though the scarlet cord has played no part in the city's capture.[101] Moreover, that Rahab and her family were exempt from destruction means that it did not have to apply to other Canaanites either. Thus, as Zehnder has shown, application of the ban was always conditional,[102] and therefore contemporary reference to this as "genocide" is misplaced.[103] As Moberly has argued, the concept is primarily a metaphor for giving absolute allegiance to God,[104] but it does allow for the possibility of destruction for those who choose to resist God's claim.

E. Noort (Leuven: Peeters, 2012), 473–88; Gordon Mitchell, *Together in the Land: A Reading of the Book of Joshua* (Sheffield: JSOT Press, 1993), 52–65; Barna Magyarosi, *Holy War and Cosmic Conflict in the Old Testament: From the Exodus to the Exile* (Berrien Springs: Adventist Theological Society, 2010), 136–53; and Terence E. Fretheim, *Deuteronomic History* (Nashville: Abingdon, 1983), 68–75.

[100] Earl, *Reading Joshua as Christian Scripture*. A more accessible example of his approach can be found in his book (which includes a response by Christopher J. H. Wright) *The Joshua Delusion? Rethinking Genocide in the Bible* (Cambridge: James Clarke & Co, 2010).

[101] Though the absence of any textual evidence has not stopped Shubert Spero, "Why the Walls of Jericho Came Tumbling Down," *JBQ* 34 (2006): 86–91, from imaginatively constructing a link.

[102] Markus Zehnder, *Umgang mit Fremden und Israel und Assyrien: Ein Beitrag zur Anthropologie des »Fremden« im Licht antiker Quellen* (Stuttgart: Kohlhammer, 2005), 483–87.

[103] Markus Zehnder, "The Annihilation of the Canaanites: Reassessing the Brutality of the Biblical Witness," in *Encountering Violence in the Bible*, ed. M. Zehnder and H. Hagellia (Sheffield: Sheffield Phoenix, 2013), 263–90. For a more detailed exploration of this, see Paul Copan and Matthew Flanagan, *Did God Really Command Genocide? Coming to Terms with the Justice of God* (Grand Rapids: Baker Academic, 2014).

[104] R. W. L. Moberly, *Old Testament Theology: Reading the Hebrew Bible as Christian Scripture* (Grand Rapids: Baker Academic, 2013), 53–71. See also Ludger Schwienhorst-Schönberger, "Josua 6 und die Gewalt," in *The Book of Joshua*, ed. E. Noort (Leuven: Peeters, 2012), 433–72.

The New Testament moves such judgment into the realm of escha-
tology, but clearly we cannot create a facile contrast between the Old
Testament and the New on this basis, since God's judgment on those
who continue to resist him remains an important element of the biblical
witness. Here, that judgment is immediate, but its deferral elsewhere does
not make it less real. The example of Rahab and her family demonstrates
that destruction is a maximum, but not necessary, understanding of the
concept of חֵרֶם since she had hidden "the messengers." Although these
men are considered spies in chapter 2, the description "messengers" in
verse 17 perhaps indicates that they always had the potential to offer
terms to those who responded to God's initiative.

If the Canaanite prostitute Rahab could move from this status to one
of life, Israel had to be aware of the reverse possibility. If they took what
now belonged to God alone, they could become devoted to destruction
themselves and set Israel's camp apart to destruction. Although this point
is introduced within the Jericho story, it prepares for the account at Ai
(Josh 7) in which the implications of Achan taking devoted items are
explored.[105] This also indicates that the concept of חֵרֶם is not one of ethnicity. Instead, it is always about devotion to God alone. What belongs to
God, whether goods or animate beings, cannot be claimed by humans, for
to do so is to move to a status of being devoted (possibly to destruction)
irrespective of one's ethnicity. Exactly what the Lord's "treasury" was
is unclear. It could reflect an updating of language for people familiar
with the temple (especially in v. 24), but it might equally relate to the
tabernacle. Regardless, it was a means of holding that which belonged
irrevocably to God.

6:20–21. Although it is common to speak of the "Battle of Jericho,"
the text actually gives very little space to it, perhaps because it would
distract readers from the fact that God won the battle, not Israel.[106] The
text itself is quite awkward, with the first part of verse 20 effectively
picking up from verse 16, while the second half repeats key information
and clarifies points that might not have been clear at first.[107] The people
shouted when commanded by Joshua, and the walls collapsed so that

---

[105] Lxx adds the element of coveting here, creating a stronger link with Achan's story (see Josh 7:21), but this is probably an interpretative addition.

[106] So Howard, *Joshua*, 174.

[107] See Winther-Nielsen, *Discourse Grammar*, 200–202, on the grammatical issues involved.

the people could advance exactly as God had indicated in verse 5. The omission of any reference to fighting emphasizes that this is God's victory.

What mattered was that Israel was obedient to God's command, so they devoted every living person or creature in the city to destruction. The victory was God's, but even the expression of his judgment on those who resisted him involved Israel. We might find it shocking that this included the young as well as the old.[108] Nothing will make this easy, but the contrast established with Rahab and the deliverance of her whole family, even though only Rahab actually hid the spies, makes clear that this was not a necessary outcome. People were seen in their corporate relationships rather than as individuals. Moreover, there is good reason to believe that the language here uses deliberate hyperbole as a way of expressing total victory that would have been understood in the ancient world but that modern readers do not recognize. See the comments on 10:20 for evidence of how this can be seen in the text of Joshua.[109]

6:22–25. Although verse 21 has described the general result for Jericho's population, Rahab and her family stand as an important contrast. In verse 22 Joshua commands the two spies to bring her and her family out in fulfillment of their vow to her. Joshua does not name Rahab, referring to her instead as "the prostitute" and "the woman." The point of such descriptions is probably to stress how unsuitable her deliverance would seem. The scouts, of course, could verify the house and also that Rahab was present, but they would depend on her to identify the others. We are not told how many were there, though given the relatively small size of the city and the importance of the extended family in that culture, it is not impossible that they represented a sizable proportion of the city's population.

In chapter 2, the narrator deliberately refrained from commenting on the appropriateness of the spies' vow. Since it did not impact Israel's ability to carry out God's command (unlike Achan in chapter 7), the vow indeed represented an authentic possibility. Any Canaanites who committed themselves to Yahweh, irrespective of their background, would cease

---

[108] Richard Dawkins, *The God Delusion* (London: Black Swan, 2006), 280, uses this as a reason why no thinking person should use the Bible to shape their ethics.

[109] See also "Joshua and the Problem of Violence" in the introduction.

to be devoted to destruction and find life within Israel. Mercy always remained a possibility.[110]

True to Joshua's directive, the scouts (called "young men" in v. 23) brought out Rahab, her family, and all her possessions. Although reference to her immediate family in the first half of verse 23 might suggest only her immediate family was intended, reference to her "whole family" (מִשְׁפָּחֹת) in the second half of the verse suggests a larger kin group since this typically refers to an extended family or even a clan (though of course it is impossible to say how large the group was). In verse 25 it is described as her "father's house," usually an extended family of several generations—a significant group, but perhaps not more than a few dozen individuals.

Rahab and her family were initially placed outside the camp, perhaps treating them as something unclean. Since this was normally a temporary action, and the narrator notes that she lived among Israel "to this day" (v. 25), we are probably to understand that she and her family were integrated into Israel. Since the book of Joshua looks back on all these events, this likely refers to the descendants of Rahab and the larger household to which she belonged. In contrast to Rahab and her family, the rest of the city was burned, one of only three cities of which this is said (the others are Ai and Hazor), except for those metal items that were placed in God's treasury.

6:26–27. Since God decreed the destruction of the city, Joshua declared a curse on anyone who would attempt to rebuild it (v. 26). Jericho is the most severe expression of devotion to destruction in the book of Joshua. In other instances, spoil is a possibility for Israel. But in this case, any attempt to profit from what God had done was prohibited. No one in Israel could gain wealth from Jericho, either at the point of its capture or in the future. The city was to remain as a permanent reminder of what could happen for an Israel that obeyed and for a Canaan that resisted.

Joshua's curse, which stipulates the death of the oldest and youngest child of the one who rebuilds, is expressed in poetry, indicating its solemnity. Although others would use Jericho as a base (it is even mentioned in 18:21 as a city allocated to Benjamin), it could not be reestablished and

---

[110] L. Daniel Hawk, *Joshua in 3-D: A Commentary on Biblical Conquest and Manifest Destiny* (Eugene, OR: Cascade, 2010), 73. This is a more open reading of Rahab than he had offered in his earlier work; see Hawk, *Every Promise Fulfilled: Contesting Plots in the Book of Joshua* (Louisville: Westminster John Knox, 1991), 59–71.

become a point for the accumulation of wealth. Hiel transgressed this prohibition in 1 Kings 16:34 when he rebuilt the city and tragically brought
the effects of the curse on himself, further demonstrating Joshua's prophetic status.

By contrast, the note of God's continued presence with Joshua makes
clear that there was a different way forward, one of obedience to God
rather than seeking wealth and power for oneself. God's promise to be
with Joshua is thus being fulfilled, and his fame spread throughout the
land (v. 27). Of course, various groups would respond differently to that
fame, and this in part lies behind the different responses to Israel in
chapters 9–11.

Bridge

Any reflection on this passage needs to integrate the themes of God's
faithfulness to his promises and the corresponding expectation of obedience on the part of his people.[111] In short, God's people can discover
the reality of God's promises as they are obedient to him—even when,
as here, that obedience leads to practices that seem surprising. Who,
after all, would devise a plan for capturing a city that involved marching
around it and shouting? Even an Israel that lacked experience in siege
warfare was unlikely to have proposed that idea. But this is central to the
narrative because it ties worship to the obedience of God's people. The
combination of warfare and worship is not common in the Bible, but it
does recur in Psalm 149, which sees this as an honor for God's people.[112]
In every case though, Israel could only wield the sword because in reality
it was God's sword.

The New Testament, however, takes this warfare in a different direction. Christ is the warrior who overcomes the foes of his people so that
they can live in faithfulness to him, perhaps because the church of the
New Testament is not tied to a particular place. Nevertheless, just as
God gave Israel the victory at Jericho, so also Paul makes clear that it
is God who gives believers victory over sin and death in Jesus Christ
(1 Cor 15:55–57). The practice of spiritual warfare is likewise something that believers achieve only by putting on the full armor of God
(Eph 6:10–17), though Paul also links it to worship as he stresses the

---

[111] See further §1 ("Faithfulness and Obedience") and §8 ("The Promise of God").
[112] See also 2 Chronicles 20.

importance of prayer for our own perseverance and also for his own work for the gospel (Eph 6:18–20). Unlike Israel in Joshua, Christians do not claim any land today, but we do advance the work of the gospel as a worshiping and obedient people, and in this we discover how God's promises continue to find fulfillment among us today.

Careful reflection is needed, though, on the nature of obedience. We might think of obedience to God as a straightforward process in which God tells his people what to do and they simply do it without much thought. But actually, careful reading of this narrative makes clear that obedience is more complex than that. God's instructions to Israel were clear, but there was also a great deal left unsaid. Part of Joshua's task as a leader was to work out how God's instructions were best put into practice. Although some have seen the variations between God's directives in 6:3–5 and their application later in the story as evidence of conflicting sources, it is better to note the distinction between what God says and the narrator's report of how Joshua and Israel worked this out. What we see then is that Joshua had considerable scope for how he arranged the people, perhaps even who would blow the horns, and how he would ensure that everyone knew the right time to shout. Even the timing of when information would be revealed (such as items under the ban and the rescue of Rahab's family) was apparently left for Joshua to resolve.

We might then think of obedience as something like a multi-lane highway that must head toward a specific goal but allows considerable latitude as to the lane to be followed. Paul's strategy of mission in Acts seems to work on this pattern, too. Although he was set apart for the work to which God had called him (Acts 13:1–5) and there were points at which he responded to specific guidance (Acts 16:6–10), for much of the time he worked out the best way to obey God's call on his life. Paul could depend on the work of the Spirit in a way not open to believers in the Old Testament, but the general principle remains the same.

Through all of this, we must also keep in focus the trustworthiness of God and his faithfulness to his promises. This is clearly seen in his presence with Joshua, fulfilling his earlier promises to him. The capture of the city is itself a first sign of the fulfillment of God's promises about the land, though this still required faith (Heb 11:31). The presence of God, of course, is something now available to all believers (Matt 28:20). But God's trustworthiness also manifests itself in the rescue of Rahab and her family because she had committed herself to God by hiding the spies, a theme that provides the basis for her commendation in the New Testament (Heb 11:31; Jas 2:25). The God who promises is faithful to his promises, and so he calls his people to live in the light of those promises. The next chapter, however, will warn us of what happens when God's people choose a different path.

B. Achan and Ai (7:1–8:29)

7 ¹ The Israelites, however, were unfaithful regarding the things set apart for destruction. Achan son of Carmi, son of Zabdi, son of Zerah, of the tribe of Judah, took some of what was set apart, and the Lord's anger burned against the Israelites.

² Joshua sent men from Jericho to Ai, which is near Beth-aven, east of Bethel, and told them, "Go up and scout the land." So the men went up and scouted Ai.

³ After returning to Joshua they reported to him, "Don't send all the people, but send about two thousand or three thousand men to attack Ai. Since the people of Ai are so few, don't wear out all our people there." ⁴ So about three thousand men went up there, but they fled from the men of Ai. ⁵ The men of Ai struck down about thirty-six of them and chased them from outside the city gate to the quarries, striking them down on the descent. As a result, the people lost heart.

⁶ Then Joshua tore his clothes and fell facedown to the ground before the ark of the Lord until evening, as did the elders of Israel; they all put dust on their heads. ⁷ "Oh, Lord God," Joshua said, "why did you ever bring these people across the Jordan to hand us over to the Amorites for our destruction? If only we had been content to remain on the other side of the Jordan! ⁸ What can I say, Lord, now that Israel has turned its back and run from its enemies? ⁹ When the Canaanites and all who live in the land hear about this, they will surround us and wipe out our name from the earth. Then what will you do about your great name?"

¹⁰ The Lord then said to Joshua, "Stand up! Why have you fallen facedown? ¹¹ Israel has sinned. They have violated my covenant that I appointed for them. They have taken some of what was set apart. They have stolen, deceived, and put those things with their own belongings. ¹² This is why the Israelites cannot stand against their enemies. They will turn their backs and run from their enemies, because they have been set apart for destruction. I will no longer be with you unless you remove from among you what is set apart.

¹³ "Go and consecrate the people. Tell them to consecrate themselves for tomorrow, for this is what the Lord, the God of Israel, says: There are things that are set apart among you, Israel. You will not be able to stand against your enemies until you remove what is set apart.

¹⁴ In the morning, present yourselves tribe by tribe. The tribe the Lord selects is to come forward clan by clan. The clan the Lord selects is to come forward family by family. The family the Lord selects is to come forward man by man. ¹⁵ The one who is caught with the things set apart must be burned, along with everything he has, because he has violated the Lord's covenant and committed an outrage in Israel."

¹⁶ Joshua got up early the next morning. He had Israel come forward tribe by tribe, and the tribe of Judah was selected. ¹⁷ He had the clans of Judah come forward, and the Zerahite clan was selected. He had the Zerahite clan come forward by heads of families, and Zabdi was selected. ¹⁸ He then had Zabdi's family come forward man by man, and Achan son of Carmi, son of Zabdi, son of Zerah, of the tribe of Judah, was selected.

¹⁹ So Joshua said to Achan, "My son, give glory to the Lord, the God of Israel, and make a confession to him. I urge you, tell me what you have done. Don't hide anything from me."

²⁰ Achan replied to Joshua, "It is true. I have sinned against the Lord, the God of Israel. This is what I did: ²¹ When I saw among the spoils a beautiful cloak from Babylon, five pounds of silver, and a bar of gold weighing a pound and a quarter, I coveted them and took them. You can see for yourself. They are concealed in the ground inside my tent, with the silver under the cloak." ²² So Joshua sent messengers who ran to the tent, and there was the cloak, concealed in his tent, with the silver underneath. ²³ They took the things from inside the tent, brought them to Joshua and all the Israelites, and spread them out in the Lord's presence.

²⁴ Then Joshua and all Israel with him took Achan son of Zerah, the silver, the cloak, and the bar of gold, his sons and daughters, his ox, donkey, and sheep, his tent, and all that he had, and brought them up to the Valley of Achor. ²⁵ Joshua said, "Why have you brought us trouble? Today the Lord will bring you trouble!" So all Israel stoned them to death. They burned their bodies, threw stones on them, ²⁶ and raised over him a large pile of rocks that remains still today. Then the Lord turned from his burning anger. Therefore that place is called the Valley of Achor still today.

8 ¹ The Lord said to Joshua, "Do not be afraid or discouraged. Take all the troops with you and go attack Ai. Look, I have handed over to you the king of Ai, his people, city, and land. ² Treat Ai and its king as you did Jericho and its king, except that you may plunder its spoil and livestock for yourselves. Set an ambush behind the city."

³ So Joshua and all the troops set out to attack Ai. Joshua selected thirty thousand of his best soldiers and sent them out at night. ⁴ He commanded them, "Pay attention. Lie in ambush behind the city, not too far from it, and all of you be ready. ⁵ Then I and all the people who are with me will approach the city. When they come out against us as

they did the first time, we will flee from them. ⁶ They will come after us until we have drawn them away from the city, for they will say, 'They are fleeing from us as before.' While we are fleeing from them, ⁷ you are to come out of your ambush and seize the city. The Lᴏʀᴅ your God will hand it over to you. ⁸ After taking the city, set it on fire. Follow the Lᴏʀᴅ's command—see that you do as I have ordered you." ⁹ So Joshua sent them out, and they went to the ambush site and waited between Bethel and Ai, to the west of Ai. But he spent that night with the troops.

¹⁰ Joshua started early the next morning and mobilized them. Then he and the elders of Israel led the people up to Ai. ¹¹ All the troops who were with him went up and approached the city, arriving opposite Ai, and camped to the north of it, with a valley between them and the city. ¹² Now Joshua had taken about five thousand men and set them in ambush between Bethel and Ai, to the west of the city. ¹³ The troops were stationed in this way: the main camp to the north of the city and its rear guard to the west of the city. And that night Joshua went into the valley.

¹⁴ When the king of Ai saw the Israelites, the men of the city hurried and went out early in the morning so that he and all his people could engage Israel in battle at a suitable place facing the Arabah. But he did not know there was an ambush waiting for him behind the city. ¹⁵ Joshua and all Israel pretended to be beaten back by them and fled toward the wilderness. ¹⁶ Then all the troops of Ai were summoned to pursue them, and they pursued Joshua and were drawn away from the city. ¹⁷ Not a man was left in Ai or Bethel who did not go out after Israel, leaving the city exposed while they pursued Israel.

¹⁸ Then the Lᴏʀᴅ said to Joshua, "Hold out the javelin in your hand toward Ai, for I will hand the city over to you." So Joshua held out his javelin toward it. ¹⁹ When he held out his hand, the men in ambush rose quickly from their position. They ran, entered the city, captured it, and immediately set it on fire.

²⁰ The men of Ai turned and looked back, and smoke from the city was rising to the sky! They could not escape in any direction, and the troops who had fled to the wilderness now became the pursuers. ²¹ When Joshua and all Israel saw that the men in ambush had captured the city and that smoke was rising from it, they turned back and struck down the men of Ai. ²² Then men in ambush came out of the city against them, and the men of Ai were trapped between the Israelite forces, some on one side and some on the other. They struck them down until no survivor or fugitive remained, ²³ but they captured the king of Ai alive and brought him to Joshua.

²⁴ When Israel had finished killing everyone living in Ai who had pursued them into the open country, and when every last one of them had fallen by the sword, all Israel returned to Ai and struck it down with the sword. ²⁵ The total of those who fell that day, both men and women, was twelve thousand—all the people of Ai. ²⁶ Joshua did not

draw back his hand that was holding the javelin until all the inhabitants of Ai were completely destroyed. ²⁷ Israel plundered only the cattle and spoil of that city for themselves, according to the LORD's command that he had given Joshua.

²⁸ Joshua burned Ai and left it a permanent ruin, still desolate today. ²⁹ He hung the body of the king of Ai on a tree until evening, and at sunset Joshua commanded that they take his body down from the tree. They threw it down at the entrance of the city gate and put a large pile of rocks over it, which still remains today.

Context

Although it is not as well-known as the story of Jericho's capture in chapter 6, the story of Ai, and in particular of Achan and his family,[113] forms an intentional pair with it. Indeed, just as chapters 1–2 formed an intentional pair that reflected on the means by which Israel was to take the land, so these two stories form an intentional pair that reflects on the nature of the people who are to take the land. The pattern of paired narratives can be outlined as follows:

1. Chapters 1–2: Israel reassured of God's gift of the land through God's promise (ch. 1) and Rahab's confession (ch. 2)
2. Chapters 3:1–5:12: Israel's entry into the land as end of the exodus through water crossing (chs. 3–4) and circumcision and Passover (5:1–12)
3. Chapters 5:13–8:29: Israel defined as those committed to a covenant relationship with God. Israel lives covenant faithfulness at Jericho and so does the Canaanite Rahab and her family (ch. 6). But at Ai (ch. 7:1–8:29), Israel initially acts like the Canaanites because of Achan's sin; only when sin is addressed can they proceed.

It becomes clear when outlined like this that the numinous encounter with the commander of God's army in 5:13–15 is crucial for understanding both the Jericho and Ai narratives. When Joshua asked him if he was for Israel or their enemies, the commander declined to take sides. He was there to command God's army, implying that he was not automatically for Israel. Rather, God's forces would fight for the people committed to

---

[113] Although technically one could separate the stories of Achan and the capture of Ai, a common source critical approach, Winther-Nielsen, *Discourse Grammar*, 216 (cf. 227–28), is right to insist that Achan's story needs to be seen as an embedded narrative, meaning we have to hold the two together.

do his will. As readers, we can easily assume that the victory at Jericho would lead to an unending series of victories. Indeed, this expectation has been fostered by the narrative to this point, since we have heard God's promise to give the land (1:3) and Rahab's confession leading to the message of assurance brought back by the scouts (2:24). Events at Jericho have shown that accepting a Canaanite who was prepared to give her loyalty to God would not hinder Israel's progress. In addition, the narrator has also reported on the dread experienced by the land's inhabitants in 5:1. Even Israel's need to reestablish covenant faithfulness through circumcision and stopping to celebrate Passover has not hindered their progress. The capture of Jericho made very clear that military prowess, hardly Israel's strong suit, was not the key issue in taking the land. What mattered was obedience to God, even if the terms of that obedience still needed to be worked out. Under those circumstances, one can assume that the commander of God's army would indeed fight for Israel.

However, we have seen before that the narrator in Joshua has a habit of providing information that leaves us unsure of our bearings. We could not, at first, be sure that Rahab had spoken the truth, and neither had we any inkling that Israel's men were not circumcised (5:2–9) or the difficulties that would be faced in celebrating Passover (5:10–12). So, although the narrator has created an expectation of continuing victory, we find a note in 6:18–19 requiring that Israel not touch any of the devoted items. Doing so would set Israel apart for destruction (חֵרֶם) and bring disaster (from the verb עכר, the same root as the name "Achor," the name the valley gains in 7:26). Although the Jericho narrative was careful to show how God's commands for the capture of the city were followed, no mention was made of the devoted items. But with the capture of Jericho and the deliverance of Rahab's family, we discover that Israel had not kept faith with these things. As a result, God's anger was directed against Israel. Rather than fighting for Israel, God fought against them because their sin made them liable for destruction.

The commander's answer in 5:14 is thus crucial. God does not fight for a nation as such; he fights for a people who are committed to him. Israel had to first learn what it meant to stand outside God's purposes before they could again discover him working for them. What this makes particularly clear is that entry into the land was not a matter of God playing national favorites. Rather, he was waging war against sin. Indeed, the language of warfare will be particularly important in both the identification of Achan and, finally, in Ai's capture.

Exegesis

7:1. As with the Jericho narrative, the narrator here adopts the position of narrative omniscience and so provides readers with interpretative clues in advance of recounting the events themselves. Here, we are told that Israel had been unfaithful (מעל) concerning the devoted things, referring back to 6:18–19. The verb "be unfaithful" is a rare one, occurring only four times in the book (and nowhere else in the Former Prophets, though it is fairly common in Chronicles), with the other three all in chapter 22, a narrative with close links to this one. Although we quickly focus on Achan, the narrator makes clear that his actions affect the whole nation. Just as Rahab's confession was sufficient for her whole family to be delivered, so also Achan's sin is sufficient to affect the whole nation. Sin is not an isolated act, something done in private without effect on others. Instead, the individual's sinful decision impacts the whole community. That is why we are told Israel had been unfaithful with the devoted things before our focus is directed to Achan.[114]

We are given an extended genealogy for Achan because the process by which he is identified as the perpetrator of the sin involves following this genealogy in reverse in verses 16–18. Although the other names in his genealogy are formed normally, Achan's name is difficult to associate with a known Hebrew root. Since it is formed with the same consonants as the word "Canaan," it is possible that this is effectively a derogatory nickname, suggesting that he truly has made himself a Canaanite.[115] If so, we may not know his actual name. But more important than his name is the simple statement that he took from the devoted things so that God's anger

---

[114] Joshua Berman, "The Making of the Sin of Achan (Josh 7)," *Biblical Interpretation* 22 (2014): 126–28, sees Achan as representative of the wider social milieu in Israel. This is plausible, but if so, Achan's sin was still a deliberate choice rather than a general attitude, and thus qualitatively different.

[115] Cf. Hawk, *Joshua in 3-D*, 87. In 1 Chr 2:7 his name is given as Achar (and always in LXX), which might also suggest that Joshua has deliberately distorted his original name. Rösel, *Joshua*, 111, thinks this is a secondary assimilation to the root from עכר, the root of the name of the valley of Achor, but since the Chronicler often records forms of names that may be more original (e.g., Merib-baal for Mephibosheth) when they have been distorted for rhetorical purposes, then we should consider this as evidence of a different source. An alternative is Ochran, a name that comes from the correct root and that is attested in Num 1:13.

burned against the Israelites—again stressing the corporate effect of the individual's sin. The motif of God's anger burning against the Israelites because of sin is common in the Old Testament (e.g., Num 11:1, 33) and indicates that God is about to act in judgment against them.

7:2–5. With Jericho secured, Israel could begin to explore the land. Since it was not an area they knew, it was entirely natural that Joshua should send spies into the hills above the town to scout out the area. Although the narrator says Joshua sent the men to Ai, Joshua's speech simply indicates they were to scout the area, suggesting that, rather than Ai being an intended destination, it was simply the point they reached. Although the exact location of Ai is a matter of dispute, the general area is clear, lying about ten miles west of Jericho on a natural route that leads to Bethel. It is linked with Beth-aven (v. 2), and though elsewhere that it is derogatory nickname for Bethel (Hos 4:15), here (and Josh 18:12) it is plainly another town associated with Bethel and Ai.

For some time, Bethel has almost universally been identified with modern Beitin, thus making et-Tell the site for Ai—a site that is problematic since there is no indication of it being occupied at the time of Joshua. But a long-standing problem with this is that Beth-aven cannot be identified with confidence. Following an earlier study by David Livingston,[116] Bryant Wood has argued that these sites have been misidentified and that Beth-aven is actually Beitin, with Bethel therefore at nearby el-Bira and Ai at Khirbet el-Maqatir.[117] There is a danger of circularity in Wood's argument, since he holds to a fifteenth-century-BC date for the exodus and conquest and therefore seeks evidence consistent with that—something that Hawkins has shown is unnecessary.[118]

Even allowing for this, though, the issues he raises with the now-traditional locations remain cogent but need further evidence if they are to become the standard view. Moreover, care must be taken not to presume that our exegesis is correct and then look for archaeology that supports it. However, Wood claims to have found evidence supporting

---

[116] D. P. Livingston, "Location of Bethel and Ai Reconsidered," *WTJ* 33:20–44.

[117] Bryant G. Wood, "The Search for Joshua's Ai," *Critical Issues in Early Israelite History*, ed. Richard S. Hess, Gerald A. Klingbeil, and Paul Ray Jr. (Winona Lake, IN: Eisenbrauns, 2008), 205–40.

[118] Hawkins, *How Israel Became a People*, 49–66.

his view that Khirbet el-Maqatir is Ai.[119] The evidence is intriguing and offers the potential for a solution to a long-standing problem, but it needs to be published in contexts where there can be more scholarly evaluation of it. It is tentatively adopted here, yet the alternative view of the more traditional location of Bethel and Ai, with Ai used more or less as a staging post for Bethel, remains possible.[120] On either interpretation, the oft-made argument that the archaeology of Ai disproves the biblical claims cannot be sustained.[121]

Whereas considerable attention is given to the spies in Jericho, here we completely bypass their journey beyond the note that they scouted Ai before returning to Joshua. Their report is supremely confident, noting that Ai is a small town and that only a small force is needed. As is often the case, it is unclear whether אֶלֶף should be translated as "thousand" or "military unit" (see CSB note), though it is also possible that the text is deliberately ambiguous, something that would be consistent with the use of hyperbole at key points. The claim that taking a larger force to Ai would wear the people out is not merely due to the steep climb from Jericho but because of the assumption that it would require a siege and keep too many people engaged in unnecessary activity. Since the town had a small population, a comparatively small force would more than suffice.

Although this report indicates that these spies were considerably more effective than the two who scouted Jericho in chapter 2 (since they returned with militarily helpful information), it is notable that they did not mention God. We can miss this easily enough since they gave apparently needed information, but as events transpire it gradually emerges that this is a significant gap. Indeed, we are probably not meant to notice this at first, so that we feel the same shock as Israel when their force of three thousand was easily defeated by the inhabitants of Ai. Thirty-six Israelites were killed as the men of Ai chased them down a hill to some

---

[119] Bryan Windle, "Biblical Sites: The Lost City of Ai ... Found," *Bible Archaeology Report*, April 21, 2019, https://biblearchaeologyreport.com/2019/04/12/biblical-sites-ai.

[120] See Hess, *Joshua*, 157–59, for a helpful summary. Leonard Allen, "Archaeology of Ai and the Accuracy of Joshua 7:1–8:29," *ResQ* 20 (1977): 41–52, also points to significant areas of the site that have not been excavated, though more has been excavated since he wrote.

[121] See, e.g., Rösel, *Joshua*, 109. A closely related issue is the suggestion that the name Ai (which is always *the* Ai in Hebrew) means "the ruin." But Howard, *Joshua*, 179 (cf. Ziony Zevit, "Archaeological and Literary Stratigraphy in Joshua 7:1–8:29," *BASOR* 251 [1983]: 26), has shown that this linguistic claim is suspect.

local quarries (unless Shebarim is a proper noun[122]). Instead of Canaanite hearts melting and becoming like water, as in 2:11 and 5:1, Israel lost courage. Israel was shocked, because both the victory at Jericho and the confident spy report led them to expect an easy victory here too. But the note from the narrator at 7:1 has prepared readers for a different interpretation of events, and this is now explored.

7:6–9. Joshua and the elders were stunned by the initial defeat at Ai, having clearly expected another victory. Unlike readers, they were unaware of Israel's unfaithfulness through Achan's taking from the devoted things. Their responses, tearing their clothes and throwing dust on their heads, are typical marks of mourning in the Old Testament (Gen 37:34; Ezek 27:30), as also is Joshua's act of prostrating himself (2 Sam 13:31). What is unusual is that Joshua prostrated himself before the ark, a reference that provides a clear link between this story, the crossing of the Jordan, and the fall of Jericho. This is the only time a person is said to have done this, though in 1 Sam 5:3–4 we are twice told that the Philistine god Dagon did so. Apart from the ceremony mentioned in Josh 8:30–35, the ark is not mentioned again in Joshua. Whereas in both the Jordan and Jericho narratives the ark functioned as something Israel was to follow, both here and in the later ceremony it is a symbol of God's presence. In this case, that presence provided Joshua with a focus for his prayer.

Joshua's prayer is, in fact, based on a misunderstanding of events to this point, assuming that God had in some way failed to keep his covenant with Israel, bringing them across the Jordan to hand them over to the Amorites for destruction.[123] Prayers of lament that accuse God occur often enough in Psalms (e.g., Psalm 44), so there is nothing wrong with Joshua praying as he did since he (as with any of us) could only pray on the basis of what he believed to be true. Joshua was unaware of Israel's sin, so he assumed that God has somehow failed—and, if so, it would have been better for Israel to have remained across the Jordan. Joshua recognized that Israel had been treated in this battle as God had promised the land's

---

[122] So ESV. The word comes from a root meaning "break," hence CSB's translation. Since place names in the Old Testament often describe the place, if Shebarim is a proper noun, it quite likely means there were quarries there.

[123] Hall, *Conquering Character*, 121, suggests that Joshua should have recognized the cause of the problem because he was present the last time Israel was defeated, but the links to Numbers 13–14 are too slight for this to be a substantial point.

inhabitants would be. In absolute terms, thirty-six casualties are not that significant, but losing people as well as a battle was a new experience, so the shock was even greater.

Joshua, as the one called to lead Israel, felt the blow acutely and recognized that a defeat would lead to God being viewed differently by the Canaanites. He acknowledged the difficulty he would face in knowing what to say (presumably to Israel) to explain why they had been defeated instead of their enemies (1:5). By contrast, the Canaanite population would be encouraged—reversing Rahab's confession (2:9) and the narrator's comment (5:1)—and so would now attack Israel. Joshua's fear that the Canaanites would be able to wipe out Israel assumes that the Amorites of Ai had overcome God. Hence, the focus of Joshua's prayer is reached in his closing question. In light of all this, what would Yahweh do about his great name—his reputation? Although Joshua's understanding of why he needed to pray was flawed, the goal of his prayer (God's reputation) was still appropriate.

7:10–15. Since the problem with Joshua's prayer was his assessment of why Israel had been defeated, God immediately addressed this issue, telling Joshua to stand up and asking why he had prostrated himself (rhetorically this also functions to direct him to stand). God had not been unfaithful; rather the problem lay with Israel. God explained this in a series of short statements, each progressively clarifying the problem.

The first statement is general: "Israel has sinned" (v. 11). This immediately reorients Joshua, showing that the content, if not the goal, of his prayer was wrong. The problem was with Israel, not God. The nature of the sin was then clarified: Israel had violated the covenant, meaning that their sin was a breach in their relationship with God. This is in turn defined by a third statement: They had taken from the devoted items, breaking the command of 6:18, which stipulated that they were to keep themselves from these things. Such an action is defined as theft, and thus a breach of the eighth commandment, because the devoted items belonged to God and could not be claimed by any human. Doing so involved deception, principally because this could not be done openly, and this deception was shown by the fact that they had put the devoted things with their own belongings.

Although verse 1 specified Achan as the perpetrator, his action affected the whole nation so that Israel as a whole was guilty of this sin. The result was an inability to prevail over their enemies. Israel had fled at

Ai, and they would continue to do as long as they had the devoted things since possessing them meant they were set aside for destruction. This is exactly as stipulated in 6:18; the actions of an individual who took the devoted things would render the whole camp liable to destruction. But verse 12 goes beyond 6:18 by adding that God would no longer be with Israel. By taking the devoted items from Jericho, Israel had effectively put themselves in the position of the Canaanites, nullifying the promise of 1:5. They were now among those who could not resist what God was doing. Israel was thus devoted to destruction, just like the Canaanites. Nevertheless, just as Rahab was able to align herself with God's purposes, Israel could do the same by removing what was set apart, possibly by destroying (שמד) those things.[124]

Having outlined the real problem, God then showed the means by which it could be resolved, telling Joshua to consecrate the people (v. 13). Exactly what such consecration meant varied, but it was (as in Exod 19:14–15 where it specifically meant an avoidance of sex) intended to prepare the people for an encounter with God. The emphasis was not on the means of consecration but rather on its purpose, which in this case is dealing with the presence of the devoted things within Israel, since their presence meant that Israel could not stand before their enemies. Only their removal could change the situation. All this, Joshua was to tell the people, along with the means by which this was to happen.

The encounter with God would happen in the morning when he would gradually reveal the one responsible by identifying the guilty tribe, clan, and household until the man was identified. This process thus reversed the order of the full genealogy with which Achan was introduced in verse 1. The term "select" (לכד) is unusual in that it more commonly means "capture," suggesting that God was engaging in warfare against the one who had sinned within Israel. The means by which this would take place is not explained, but the similar situation in 1 Samuel 14:41 could suggest that the Urim and Thummim were involved.[125]

The one identified was to be burned, along with all he had, because he had transgressed the covenant, committing an outrage in Israel. This outrage (נְבָלָה) can also be understood as a form of folly since the word

---

[124] Deut 13:12–18 already allowed for the possibility of sections of Israel being devoted to destruction, and that may lie in the background here. See Mitchell, *Together in the Land*, 75.

[125] This is explicit in the LXX, whereas the MT only asks that God give the right decision.

elsewhere has this sense,[126] indicating this is something anyone would recognize as wrong. Although we might initially think only the man and his possessions would be burned, verses 24-25 make clear that this included his whole family. Just as Rahab's whole family was saved because of her faithfulness, so also Achan's family would be destroyed because they all to some degree were involved in his sin.

7:16-21. The act of consecrating the people is passed over. Instead we move straight to the next day when Joshua again rose early, always a sign that he was about to engage in God's work, and initiated the process by which Achan would be identified. Obeying God's instructions in verse 14, Joshua brought the tribes forward, beginning a pattern in which we follow Achan's genealogy in reverse until he is taken after his tribe, clan, and household were identified. There is no mystery for the reader in this, since verse 1 has already revealed his identity, but one can feel the tension rising for Achan as the circle gradually tightens around him until he is selected.

Once Achan was identified, Joshua urged him to make a full confession of what he had done. Since this was above all a crime against God, he directed him to give glory to Yahweh, the God off Israel. Joshua's initial address to Achan was pastoral, calling him "my son," but pastoral awareness did not mean he avoided the real challenge Achan's actions posed. Giving glory to God involved a full confession since doing so would make public what God already knew. The phrase Joshua used when urging Achan to confess is more commonly associated with thanksgiving.[127] "Confession" is probably the better translation, not least because Joshua made this an explicit request, but it is a confession framed as a thanksgiving. This might seem an odd concept, but the idea is probably that Achan was now freed to tell the truth, and this was something for which he could give thanks. Since it was a thanksgiving for the chance to reveal what God already knew, a full confession with nothing hidden was necessary, and this is what Joshua urged.

Achan accordingly confessed to his crime, acknowledging that he had sinned against Yahweh, God of Israel, by taking things that belonged to him. But it was insufficient simply to accept that sin had occurred; a full confession needed to outline what was done. It began with what

---

[126] Most obviously in Abigail's speech to David about Nabal in 1 Sam 25:25.

[127] CSB note suggests "praise," but thanksgiving is the specific mode of praise here.

Achan had seen in the spoil[128] at Jericho: a beautiful cloak from Babylon, two hundred shekels of silver (roughly five pounds), and a bar of gold weighing fifty shekels (roughly a pound). He coveted them, breaching the tenth commandment (Exod 20:17; Deut 5:17; cf. Deut 7:25). Part of the commandment's concern is with coveting that leads to wrongful taking (cf. Mic 2:2), though all coveting leads to a breakdown in community relationships. Achan coveted what belonged to God and was, therefore, excluded from human association, with his coveting leading to taking. The completion of his confession required that he indicate the location of these goods, so he revealed that they were buried under his tent. The tragedy for Achan was that Jericho was the only time when the ban was applied in its severest form—in subsequent accounts, the Israelites were permitted to take spoil.

7:22–26. Joshua sent messengers to Achan's tent to test the truthfulness of his confession. The urgency of the situation is shown by their running to the tent. Having found the items, the messengers brought them back to Joshua and all Israel, making clear that, just as Achan's identification had been public, so the evidence of his guilt was to be public. Moreover, since God had revealed Achan's guilt and was the one sinned against, the goods were also presented before him. The verb translated "spread out" (hi. יצק) in verse 23 more often refers to pouring out liquids, often in cultic contexts (e.g., Gen 28:1–2), and that may lie behind its usage here since it is done before God. Israel in effect acknowledged that these goods belonged to God, though doing so also means they were open to inspection by God.

With this confirmation of Achan's guilt, Joshua (along with all Israel, again pointing to the public nature of this case) took Achan along with all his family and possessions to the Valley of Achor (v. 24). The listing of so many items (ox, donkey, sheep, tent) suggests that Achan was already relatively wealthy for an Israelite, highlighting that he had no need to covet.

The exact location of the Valley of Achor is disputed, but 15:7 indicates that it was on Judah's northern border. It may be El-Buqei'a, to the west of Qumran, but if so Joshua brought Achan about fifteen miles to an area whose capture had not been recounted unless it was subsumed

---

[128] Technically, since it belonged to God, it was not spoil, but this term might be used to describe how Achan saw it as something from which he could take for himself (see Madvig, "Joshua", 288). Earl, *Reading Joshua as Christian Scripture*, 149, thinks that Achan's confession was therefore deficient, confirming the death sentence.

into the capture of Jericho. On the other hand, since some place names are repeated for multiple sites in Joshua (e.g., the Debir of 15:7 may be different from that of 15:13), we are probably to assume another location in the vicinity of Jericho.

The more important point is the name "Achor," which means "trouble" and seems to derive from Joshua's question to Achan about why he had troubled Israel, as well as to be linked to Achan's name (see on v. 1). Joshua declared that God would trouble him—that is punish him for his sin. Joshua 6:18 had indicated that bringing the devoted goods into the camp would bring "trouble" onto Israel, making them liable to destruction. So, Achan was put to death by being stoned, treating him like the rebellious son of Deuteronomy 21:21. Achan's family was put to death with him, showing how sin affects more than just the individual and also providing a contrast to Rahab, whose family was saved. Perhaps also this functioned as a form of quarantine since the whole family would have come into contact with the banned goods and been made liable for destruction.[129] Achan the Israelite had become like a Canaanite, so he and his family were destroyed. But the Canaanite Rahab, because of her faithfulness, had become like an Israelite and was saved with her family.

The severity of this punishment is shown by the fact that the bodies were burned, which was not common, bringing the treatment of Achan into alignment with that of Jericho (6:24). Although it is possible to read verse 25 as describing two separate instances of Achan being stoned, the second time after the bodies were burnt, the different verbs indicate that these are not describing the same thing. csb's decision to link the second instance to the process by which the cairn was raised over their bodies is probably correct.[130] As with the stones at 4:9, these were a continuing reminder of this story when the book was written (this is the first of two cairns in the account, the second marking the fall of Ai in 8:29). Only then, when sin was fully addressed, was God's burning anger averted. Both the stones and the name continued to testify to the meaning of the story to subsequent generations.

8:1–2. With Achan's sin addressed, the narrative returns to the capture of Ai. But whereas the first account reported Israelite military action without reference to God, this time God took the initiative, bringing

---

[129] So Boling, *Joshua*, 288.
[130] Similarly Hess, *Joshua*, 155.

this account back into line with Jericho. On this occasion, however, God offered a more traditional military campaign.

God's initiative is apparent from the verbs in verse 1. Two opening prohibitions directed Joshua to stop being afraid or discouraged. These prohibitions are effectively the opposite of 1:6, suggesting that the failure at Ai meant Joshua was no longer living in accord with the directives there. Although similar language is used in 10:7 and 11:6, those instances refer to points of potential fear, whereas this time Joshua's response to the initial failure to capture Ai made his fear clear (cf. Josh 7:9–10). These prohibitions are followed by a string of four imperatives each of which tells Joshua what to do while reaffirming promises. Joshua was to take the whole military force, rise (untranslated in csb but collapsed into the next verb), and go attack Ai. All of this is God's initiative, and Joshua could simply obey, though it does indicate that the small force previously deployed was probably a sign of overconfidence. The fourth imperative, "Look," required Joshua to come to a new perspective in which, contrary to the expectations of his prayer in 7:9–10, he was to understand that God had indeed handed over the king of Ai, his people, city, and land to Israel.

Although the verbs at the start of verse 2 are not imperatives, they are dependent on those in verse 1, and so rightly represented as imperatives in csb. Israel was to treat Ai and its king as they had treated Jericho and its king: destroy them. However, an important exception is introduced that makes Achan's actions even more tragic—this time, Israel could claim the spoil and livestock for themselves. With this qualification, God returned to the imperative mode, telling Joshua to set an ambush behind the city. Israel were to fight at God's command and follow his battle plan.

8:3–9. As with Jericho's capture, Joshua had to obey God's command, but at the same time he had freedom to work out the means of his obedience. One might say that God's command gave the strategy for Ai's capture, but God left Joshua free to work out the tactics. Joshua's obedience is emphasized by the opening verbs of verse 3, which are from the same roots as the middle two imperatives of verse 1. In addition, the fact that the military force went with him shows obedience to the first imperative on verse 1. Evidence of his obedience to the fourth imperative is held back until his speech to the people in verse 7.

Joshua's need to work out the means of obedience is clear from the fact that his first action after setting out was to select a body of thirty thousand fighting men to send out by night—a force ten times the size the spies had suggested was needed to capture the city. As discussed in verse 3, אֶלֶף could refer to thirty large military units rather than a strict numerical count. As God had commanded Joshua, Joshua commanded the people. But his commands were an outworking of God's commands. "Pay attention" (v. 4) is the same verb translated "look" in verse 1 (רָאָה) and points to a basic understanding the troops would need. They would serve as the ambush behind the city, ready for the moment when the trap would be sprung, but still needing to keep a reasonable distance from the city. Joshua would approach the city with the remaining people, intending to draw the city's inhabitants out from behind their walls by pretending to flee once more. Previously, Israel had been overconfident, but this time Joshua imagined the residents of Ai as the overconfident ones, pursuing the fleeing Israelites and creating the opportunity for the ambush.[131]

In verse 7 Joshua referred to God's final imperative from verse 2. God's promise stands; he had already handed Ai over to Israel. But as we have seen before, God's promise still had to be claimed, and Israel had to follow through on God's strategy to take the city. As with Jericho (6:24), Joshua ordered that the city be burned. Although God had not outlined all the details of the plan, everything that Joshua said was consistent with it. This is why he could tell the troops that they were to obey God's word and understand this in terms of obedience to what he had commanded. With the command given, the ambush deployed west of Ai, between Ai and Bethel, while Joshua stayed the night with the rest of the people.

8:10-13. If we read these verses as describing what happened after verse 9 we will invariably find them confusing since they seem to introduce new elements that could contradict what has just been outlined. It makes more sense to read verses 11-13 as a flashback that provides additional information to readers. So, verse 10 continues from verse 9, with Joshua and the elders leading the people to Ai. But verse 11 introduces a circumstantial clause that breaks the chain of consecutive verbs. A new series is introduced in verse 14, following verse 10.[132] Once this

---

[131] Joshua seems to draw on a standard battle plan. A similar approach is used with the capture of Gibeah in Judg 20:1-48, an account with many similarities to this one (see Christopher T. Begg, "The Function of Josh 7,1-8,29 in the Deuteronomistic History," *Biblica* 67 [1986]: 329-30). But since it falls within the command given by God, there is no contradiction between his ingenuity in applying this to the situation and his obedience.

[132] Similarly, Howard, *Joshua*, 200-201; Butler, *Joshua 1-12*, 415. Cf. Woudstra, *The Book of Joshua*, 137.

is recognized, we no longer have the apparent problem of the troops spending two nights in the ambush, a situation in which it would be almost impossible for them to remain unobserved. Understood this way, the events described in verses 11–13 happened after verse 3 at the point when Israel had reached Ai.

In verse 12 we are told that Joshua selected five thousand troops for the ambush, whereas verse 3 mentions thirty thousand (again, the Hebrew for "a thousand" is probably the largest military unit). Howard thinks the number in verse 3 might be a textual corruption,[133] but it is difficult to explain how such a corruption would occur. Although still awkward, it is more likely that the thirty thousand represented the total force involved in the capture of the city, while five thousand constituted the actual ambush.[134] The earlier passage distinguishes between those sent out and those who stayed with Joshua, but we can still understand the whole force as being sent out, even if the five thousand are not specifically identified at that point. So, Joshua would have had a force of twenty-five thousand with him when he camped on a hill to the north of the city, while the remaining five thousand camped to the west, between Ai and Bethel. Joshua's activity in the night is also difficult to understand since the main body was on a hill, and the word for "valley" in verse 13 is different from that of verse 11. Perhaps this was a valley other than that between the main force and the city, though from there he would then have returned to the main body for his early start and mobilization of the troops described in verse 10.

8:14–23. The events of verse 14 are coordinated with those of verse 10, describing the response of Ai's king when he saw Joshua moving Israel's forces up to the city, though the king's response is subsumed into that of the people. Their sense of urgency is emphasized as they went out to confront Israel at a suitable place before the Arabah. This suggests a site toward the Rift Valley of the Jordan and, thus, toward Jericho—east of the city and away from the ambush.

In the second half of verse 14 the narrator returns to Ai's king. His haste means he had not considered the area west of the city, so he was unaware of the ambush waiting there. Moreover, he had abandoned the additional security of the city in his rush to confront Israel. What Joshua

---

[133] Howard, *Joshua*, 203–4.
[134] So Hess, *Joshua*, 162.

could not have predicted, that the king would lead his forces out of the city making it vulnerable to ambush, came about because of the king's hubris, which validates God's plan for the city's capture.

With Ai's forces drawn out, Joshua and Israel feigned a retreat toward the wilderness, presumably the area north of the Dead Sea, though they did not have to travel far. The effect was to give the inhabitants of Ai further misplaced confidence so that they were drawn away from the city. Indeed, none of the troops in Ai or Bethel (linked in v. 17 with those of Ai)[135] remained in their respective cities, though the exposure of Ai was crucial since it was left open to the ambush. Although these cities are related to one another, they are distinguished in the book, and each had its own king (12:9, 16). Bethel is treated as captured in 12:16, but there is no account of this, indicating that the record in Joshua is selective.

With Ai left open, the narrative returns to Joshua (v. 18), who then received a directive from God to signal the ambush to enter the city. The exact nature of the weapon in Joshua's hand is uncertain, since the word occurs only nine times in the Old Testament, three of which are in this passage. It is also mentioned twice in Goliath's weaponry (1 Sam 17:6, 45) as something that could be slung between the shoulders, which suggests "javelin" (so csb) might be meant, though "scimitar" is also possible. Whatever it is, it needed to be visible to the ambush and prearranged, so that the timing was left to God since he had given the city to Israel. It is unclear how this signal would have been visible at such a distance, but if the weapon was a javelin then some sort of banner could have been attached.

At the time directed by God, Joshua stretched out the weapon, and the ambush responded as required, capturing the city and setting it on fire. The verb "capture" (לכד) forms an important link with the story of Achan, where this same verb is used eight times in 7:14–18 to describe the process by which he was "taken." Thus, both Israelites and Canaanites who opposed God's purposes were taken. Moreover, just as Achan's body was burned, so also the city of Ai was burned, making it one of only four cities of which this is said.[136]

---

[135] Boling, *Joshua*, 240, suggests that Bethel should be understood as the Aiite sanctuary (taking the place name as a common noun, "house of god"). Although this would resolve the question of what Bethel was doing in this story, we would expect a pronominal suffix here, so it is more likely that this was the town name.

[136] The others were Jericho, Hazor, and Dan (Laish).

The attention of Ai's troops was caught by the rising smoke of the city, which left them disoriented and unable to flee. The Israelites who had seemed to flee before them suddenly became their pursuers. The rising smoke of the burning city discouraged Ai's troops but became a source of encouragement to Israel as they attacked. As a result, Ai's men were trapped between the two Israelite forces, with all struck down and no survivor or fugitive left save for the king who was captured. Although the language of "leaving no survivor" sounds absolute to a modern reader, this is likely stereotypical language emphasizing total victory rather than indicating everyone was killed, since hyperbolic language is clearly used in the book (see on 10:20).

8:24–29. With Ai's forces defeated in the open country, Joshua was able to lead Israel to the city, putting it to the sword. Again, this should be understood as an idiom referring to total victory rather than a literal description of what happened, especially if the "twelve thousand" in verse 25 refers to those engaged in military activity against Israel—thus, twelve large military units. Women would not ordinarily participate in battle, but it was not impossible for them to do so, so they could be understood as combatants, though presumably the men who had pursued Israel in the first place were the main fighting force.

Joshua's role in the victory is particularly emphasized (v. 26), noting that he did not withdraw his hand holding the weapon until the inhabitants of Ai had been devoted to destruction. This may be intended to parallel the point when Joshua himself had fought Amalek in Exod 17:8–16 and Moses had held high a banner that signified God's victory.

Although Ai was devoted to destruction, this time God permitted Israel to claim the city's cattle and spoil for themselves (v. 27), meaning this was a less strict application of the ban than had been applied at Jericho—again highlighting the tragedy of Achan's choice to take from the devoted things. There is also an important parallel between Joshua and the people, as each is obedient to God's commands for them.

Verses 28–29 provide an inclusio with verses 1–2, since Ai and its king were treated in the same way as Jericho. The city was burned, leaving it as an enduring ruin,[137] and the king was killed. The king's execution

---

[137] CSB has "permanent ruin" here, but this goes beyond the evidence of the Old Testament since Ezra 2:28 (= Neh 7:32) indicates later occupation, something supported by the archaeology of the site irrespective of whether we think it is et-Tell or Khirbet el-Maqatir. The word עולם can be time limited.

may have occurred during the battle, with his body hung on a tree until evening as a public announcement, or the hanging may have been the means of execution. In either case Joshua was careful to follow Deuteronomy 21:22-23, requiring that the body of a condemned person not be left on a tree overnight. The point behind this is that the body of the condemned is not to be abused. In this case, the king was buried at Joshua's command under a pile of rocks at the entrance to his city. This parallels the cairn where Achan was buried (Josh 7:24-26), with both pointing to the implications of resisting God's purposes. By contrast, the stones piled up at Gilgal (4:1-24) told a different story, of how God had brought Israel across the river into the land. The stones themselves were silent, but each story needed to be told for Israel to continually learn their significance.[138]

Bridge

Many modern readers will find this a long and difficult story, not least because of the violence it describes. There will also be a temptation to divide it into two separate accounts: the story of Achan and the capture of Ai. But the two are inextricably linked within the narrative. The fact that each concludes with reference to burning and the creation of a stone cairn is clear evidence that we are to read these as parallel narratives, each understood in light of the other. Moreover, there are other key words and themes that show these are to be read together. Achan's story represents a failed attempt by Israel to capture Ai when they had disobeyed and not sought God's guidance, whereas the successful ambush and battle at Ai occurred when Israel was once again obedient to God. Achan's cairn was a declaration to Israel of what happens when they opposed God's purposes, while that of Ai's king reminded Israel that they could, as an obedient people, once more succeed. Sin invariably damages God's people and its consequences cannot be reduced to an individual, but a people who deal with sin can once more see God's promises to them being worked out.[139]

That Israel was itself aware of this reality comes to the fore in Josh 22:16-20, when the western tribes mention Achan's sin to those who lived east of the Jordan. There Israel would discover that the eastern

---

[138] On this motif, see especially Robert L. Hubbard, Jr., "'What Do These Stones Mean?': Biblical Theology and a Motif in Joshua," *BBR* 11 (2001): 1-26.

[139] See further §2 ("Identity of the People of God").

tribes had not sinned as had been assumed, but it shows that events here left a deep wound on Israel's conscience for some time.

The pattern of an individual's sin and its impact on the nation is not restricted to this story. Both Kings and Chronicles demonstrate a close link between the faithfulness of the king and the extent to which the people as a whole experienced God's blessing. Clearly the king (both in Judah and Israel) stood in a special relationship to God that is not matched by every individual today. But to the extent that the king was representative of his people, his sin affected the nation. Neither is this concept limited to the Old Testament. Twice, Paul draws on the image of a little leaven affecting the whole lump of dough (1 Cor 5:6; Gal 5:9). In both instances, his point is that one example of sin will affect the whole church. Sin is not "contained," as if one person's sin has no effect on the wider community, something seen in Paul's comments in 1 Corinthians 11:30. The extent to which this happens will vary. Our modern Western world tends to insist that we all make free choices and that no one can criticize those choices, provided they do not self-evidently harm others. However, both this narrative and Paul's comments insist that this is not the case. We are always part of a community. When one part of that community sins, the whole will be affected in some way.

Sin, however, does not have to have the last word. When the Israelites realized their sin and addressed it, God once again provided a way forward for them. This, too, is a theme that runs through the Bible. David, after his adultery with Bathsheba and murder of Uriah (2 Sam 11), could still be the one through whom God's promises would be fulfilled. More important for this passage are those instances in which God responded to the repentance of his people as a whole, such as the various points when he raised up judges. The corporate dimensions of repentance are also evident in the New Testament, such as in 2 Cor 7:10–12, where Paul reflects on the godly grief of the congregation leading to repentance and at least the beginning of restoration.[140] Although we may (rightly) emphasize the importance of individual repentance at the point of entering into the Christian faith, we must not lose sight of the fact that repentance can also be a corporate response to God. As this story demonstrates, there is a future for God's repentant people.

---

[140] An excellent study of repentance, tracing it through the whole Bible, is Mark J. Boda, "Return to Me": A Biblical Theology of Repentance (Nottingham: Apollos, 2015).

This story also raises important questions about the identity of God's people. Appreciating this is essential if we are to wrestle with the issue of violence we see here. After the victory at Jericho, we might assume a fairly simplistic position in which all Canaanites (apart from Rahab's family) are rejected by God and thus only fit for destruction. But this story immediately makes this theory problematic. Achan, by his failure to obey God at Jericho, made himself liable to destruction. He had, in effect, made himself (and his family) Canaanites because of his failure to obey God. As noted in the exegesis above, obedience is something that needs to be worked out within the framework God gives, rather than something entirely fixed.[141] Nevertheless, obedience still needs to be within this framework. Achan's decision to take from the devoted items was clear disobedience to God's command. He thus became an immediate contrast to Rahab. One was a Canaanite who by committing herself to God was effectively treated as an Israelite, whereas the other was an Israelite who by his failure to obey God effectively became a Canaanite.

This demonstrates that the people of God are not defined by ethnicity but by their commitment to God's purposes. God opposes and judges those who are opposed to his purposes. This means that in the Old Testament, as in the New, it is a faith relationship with God that defines the people of God, a faith relationship that is ultimately focused on Jesus Christ. The people of Ai could have responded like Rahab, and Israelites could reject their status as God's people through sin. The violence we see in this chapter, therefore, is not about ethnicity. Moreover, as we have noted, there is good evidence from within the book that much of the language is an idiomatic way of describing a complete victory. Thus, God's judgment carried out through Israel is more focused than we might otherwise imagine, though it was still directed against a people who resisted his purposes.

Lest we think this understanding of the people of God has ended, we are reminded in the story of Ananias and Sapphira that God still punishes those who resist him (Acts 5:1–10). Moreover, when James insists that God opposes the proud (Jas 4:6), he does so in a context in which he urges God's people to turn away from friendship with the world—essentially Achan's problem. God's people are thus called to live a distinctive life in commitment to God's purposes, a life shaped by obedience and the

---

[141] See also §1 ("Faithfulness and Obedience").

blessing of God because—whether in history or eschatologically—God will oppose the proud.

C. Renewal at Mount Ebal (8:30–35)

[30] At that time Joshua built an altar on Mount Ebal to the Lord, the God of Israel, [31] just as Moses the Lord's servant had commanded the Israelites. He built it according to what is written in the book of the law of Moses: an altar of uncut stones on which no iron tool has been used. Then they offered burnt offerings to the Lord and sacrificed fellowship offerings on it. [32] There on the stones, Joshua copied the law of Moses, which he had written in the presence of the Israelites. [33] All Israel—resident alien and citizen alike—with their elders, officers, and judges, stood on either side of the ark of the Lord's covenant facing the Levitical priests who carried it. Half of them were in front of Mount Gerizim and half in front of Mount Ebal, as Moses the Lord's servant had commanded earlier concerning blessing the people of Israel. [34] Afterward, Joshua read aloud all the words of the law—the blessings as well as the curses—according to all that is written in the book of the law. [35] There was not a word of all that Moses had commanded that Joshua did not read before the entire assembly of Israel, including the women, the dependents, and the resident aliens who lived among them.

Context

Following the battle narratives of Jericho and Ai, this account may come as something of a surprise. Up to this point, Israel has consistently faced a problem that needed to be addressed (such as ensuring the tribes remained unified, crossing the Jordan, or capturing Canaanite towns). Even in chapters 6 and 7, in which either God or the narrator announced in advance the outcome, there was always an arc of tension to be resolved. But none of that is present here. Instead of a narrative in the classic sense, this brief passage has no discernible plot, being instead a recounting of Israel's actions at Mount Ebal. At no point is there a sense that Joshua would fail to read Yahweh's Torah. So this passage is narratively distinct from what has gone before and, indeed, from what will follow.

What many readers may miss is that this passage is also geographically distinct from what has gone before. The events of 6:1–8:29 have been focused on the area immediately across the Jordan from Shittim and the hills due west of there. Even if the exact site of Ai is disputed, it is about twelve miles west of Jericho. Israel's activity has focused on a very small part of the land. But suddenly in 8:30 we are more than twenty miles

north of there in the vicinity of Shechem, a town that lies immediately
east of Mount Ebal and Mount Gerizim. Shechem itself is not mentioned
in a narrative sense until 24:1, though it is noted as defining the boundary
of Manasseh in 17:7, while 20:7 notes that it was a city of refuge and 21:21
says it was a Levitical town.[142] Though it is not mentioned here, those said
to be standing in front of the mountains would need to be more or less
in Shechem. Rather than the town, the focus is on the two mountains
since they are mentioned in Deuteronomy 27. There, instructions were
given for an altar to be built on Mount Ebal from which the Levites were
to pronounce the curse on those in breach of the Torah. The geographical puzzle is what Israel is doing this far north at this point in the book,
especially since Josh 9:6 indicates that Israel was based at Gilgal. There
are several sites in Israel with this name, so it does not have to be the one
mentioned in 4:19–20 in the Jordan Valley,[143] but the best alternative (a
little to the north of Bethel) is still quite far from Shechem. Whichever
Gilgal is meant, we are left without any clear information about how Israel
came from there to the region of Shechem to conduct an extensive ceremony when there has been no mention of the defeat of local Canaanites.

These two features, the narrative and geographical distinctiveness,
thus distinguish this short passage from what has gone before. Indeed,
events in chapter 9 take us back several miles south of Ai and Bethel and
resume the types of narration from the earlier passages of the book. This
naturally raises questions about the purpose of this passage. Certainly, its
distinctiveness has been felt for some time and can be seen in the textual
tradition that has variously relocated it.[144] At Qumran (4QJosh[a]), it seemingly appears after 5:1 (there are uncertainties about the fragments) and
has Joshua carrying out the ceremony immediately after Israel's entry
into the land. But this is almost certainly a scribal correction based on an
overly literal reading of Deuteronomy 27:2. In the LXX, it occurs after 9:2.
Although this is plausible, it would then be a response to the gathering

---

[142] A Shechem is also mentioned in 17:2, but this is a clan ancestor in Manasseh
not the town.

[143] And as Hawkins shows in *How Israel Became a People*, 179–84, "Gilgal" might describe
a type of settlement.

[144] The fact of these variances does not, however, compel us to follow the lead of J. Alberto
Soggin, *Joshua: A Commentary* (London: SCM Press, 1972), 221, 241–44, and move the whole
passage to chapter 24 because of the location at Shechem. None of the variations in the
tradition move the text as drastically as that, and in any case this approach does not explain
why a passage located in Shechem would have been dislocated here.

of the Canaanite kings mentioned there, again making it more likely that this is a scribal correction of a difficult text. To be sure, it is precisely its awkwardness that makes it most likely that the MT records the original location of the passage. And it is this distinctiveness that indicates the importance of the passage as a form of reflection on the story to this point.

All of the above suggests that this passage is not told in chronological sequence relative to what has preceded and what follows. Although Joshua is, in general terms, related in chronological sequence, there is no reason why passages might not be told out of sequence in order to emphasize certain themes that are of particular importance.[145] If we were able to determine the exact sequence of Israel's entry into the land (and Joshua does not provide us with all the information needed to do this since that is not the book's primary concern), we would probably place this passage fairly late, perhaps as late as the events of chapter 24, with which this passage is clearly linked since it needs to occur at a point when Israel controlled the region. The introduction of the passage here shows that the book is more concerned to stress key theological themes that have become particularly important in light of the stories of Rahab and Achan—and their implications for understanding the place of the Torah in Israel.[146] Furthermore, the passage prepares for elements in the narratives to follow.[147]

Of particular importance here is the stress on the Torah, mentioned four times in this passage, with only five other occurrences in the rest of the book. However, the distribution of those other five references are important as each occurs at a crucial point in the book. In 1:7–8 the Torah is the text on which Joshua shall meditate. Obedience to it is a pivotal element in two of Joshua's three farewell addresses (22:5; 23:6). The covenant made in chapter 24 is written into the book of the Torah in 24:26. The book of Joshua as a whole is bounded by references to the Torah. But apart from this current passage it is not mentioned by name within the central part of the book, though there are references to obedience to all that Moses had commanded in 11:12–15, a concept parallel to that of performing the Torah. But as we have noted, the stories of Rahab

---

[145] E.g., 11:23 speaks of Joshua giving the land by tribal allotments, but the process of this is only described in chapters 13–21, and chapters 18–19 indicate that this was a protracted process.

[146] For the sense of Torah as more than law alone, see on 1:8.

[147] See also Hall, *Conquering Character*, 147; Winther-Nielsen, *Discourse Grammar*, 168n13.

and Achan have raised questions about what it means to faithfully do what Torah requires. Even here Joshua (see below, 8:32–33) makes subtle adaptations to Deuteronomy 27 because of his own circumstances. If Deuteronomy 7 precludes arrangements with any Canaanites, then why were Rahab and her family delivered? And why was Achan treated as a Canaanite given that the particular circumstances of his story were not envisaged in the Torah?

We cannot answer these questions until 11:12–15, which will address them directly. At this point it is enough to note that, although the book is aware of these questions (and will address them in chapter 11), the centrality of Torah indicated by 1:7–8 has not been set aside, and Joshua is in the process of showing how it is to be interpreted.[148] Indeed, where knowledge of the Torah was initially focused on Joshua himself, we now see that this is transferred to the people as a whole.

Beyond this, the current passage also prepares for the story of Gibeon, not only by insisting on the importance of Torah for Israel (and so raising new questions for readers of that narrative) but also by establishing the only legitimate altar mentioned in the book and so providing a place where the Gibeonites might work, even if the central sanctuary for the book will finally be at Shiloh (18:1). Perhaps more important in light of the inclusion of Rahab's family, this ceremony has included foreigners (גֵּר) as well as native Israelites, suggesting that Israel's identity is defined by commitment to the Torah, and through it to Yahweh, rather than by ethnicity.

Exegesis

8:30–31. In light of the contextual distinctiveness noted above, the opening in verse 30, "At that time" (אָז), needs to be understood fairly generally, referring to the period of Israel's entry into the land rather than the specific events at Jericho and Ai. The importance of Joshua building this altar as something dedicated to Yahweh, the God of Israel, as opposed to the gods of Canaan, should not be missed. Although Abraham, Isaac, and Jacob had all built altars within the boundaries of the land (Gen 12:7–8; 22:9; 26:25; 33:20; 35:7), these were in response to specific encounters with

---

[148] Cf. Nathan Chambers, "Confirming Joshua as the interpreter of Israel's *Tôrah*: The Narrative Role of Joshua 8:30–35," BBR 25 (2015): 147–53.

God. But this altar represents a larger claim: this land now belonged to Israel as God's people, and he alone was the God to be worshiped.

The altar was built at Mount Ebal, near Shechem, because this was where Deuteronomy 27:1–8 required Israel to construct an altar when they entered the land. The link to this passage is made explicit by the comment in verse 31 about Joshua's faithful fulfillment of Moses' command and the reference to the use of whole, uncut stones and absence of metal tools (Deut 27:5–6). This indicates that, as is most common in Joshua, the "book of the law" is Deuteronomy. The site is also important because Mount Ebal was not only the tallest mountain in Israel's north (Mount Gerizim is not much shorter), but it also controlled important trade routes through the region, which is probably why Abram passed through there in Genesis 12:6.

It is always difficult to make a specific association between a particular archaeological artifact and the biblical text, but an Iron Age site found on Mount Ebal appears to date to the time of Israel's arrival in the land and could be an altar, though it is unlike others from the period. The acoustics of the site would make it suitable for a large-scale public speech such as described here, and the animal bones found around it are consistent with Israelite practice. Although other interpretations of the site have been offered (e.g., that it was a farm), it is more probable that it represents an early altar, yet one that was only in use for a relatively short period.[149] It is thus possible this is indeed the altar described here.

Since the primary function of an altar was to offer sacrifice, it is not surprising that Joshua offered both burnt offerings (those in which the animal was completely burned, Leviticus 1) and fellowship offerings (those in which the priests and people ate from the offered animal, Leviticus 3). These sacrifices functioned to bring Israel before God in worship and as a people who recognized their need for atonement, a need that was particularly acute in light of events at Ai.

8:32–33. According to Deuteronomy 27:2–3, the stones at Mount Ebal were to be covered with plaster so that the words of the law could be written on them. It is possible this means the altar stones, though more likely both Deuteronomy and Joshua refer to some other stones that were

---

[149] For accessible summaries of the evidence, see Hawkins, *How Israel Became a People*, 184–87; Richard S. Hess, *Israelite Religions: An Archaeological and Biblical Survey* (Nottingham: Apollos, 2007), 216–21

set up for the writing.[150] The text mentions no plaster, yet we are consistently told that Joshua's actions were consistent with what Moses had commanded. Therefore, we should presume the stones were plastered, as this would have enabled Joshua to write on them.

Exactly what Joshua copied out is not clear. It is unlikely there would have been space to write out the whole Pentateuch, so the reference is probably either to Deuteronomy or perhaps to excerpts such as the Decalogue. The act of writing out a copy of the law is also mandated for the king on his accession (Deut 17:18), but this was to be a scroll that the king would keep to provide guidance through his reign, whereas Joshua's copy was left behind as a public testimony to the people. Literacy levels in Israel were not particularly high, so only a small portion of the population could read the text on these stones. But this was still a means of publishing the text, making it available to the wider community so that the literate could access it and in turn explain it to those unable to read. Although csb takes the last part of verse 32 as referring to Moses writing out the law before the people, it is perhaps more likely it refers to Joshua since transcribing text onto the stones would have been a public act.

In verse 33, Israel is defined as containing both foreigner and citizen alike. Were it not for the story of Rahab and her family, we might have thought that Israel would be made up only of those whose ethnicity meant they could trace their lineage back to Abraham. But actually, the Old Testament consistently makes clear that, although Israel was the people through whom God was bringing blessing to all the clans of the earth (Gen 12:3), Israel was never defined solely by ethnicity.[151] For example, when Abraham received the covenant of circumcision in Genesis 17, that was also applied to all those born in his house or who came into it (Gen 17:12). Moreover, the group that left Egypt in the exodus is said to have been ethnically diverse (Exod 12:38). As we progress through the book of Joshua we encounter more people who, though not ethnically Israelite, joined themselves to Yahweh and committed themselves to his purposes. Although their specific identity is not indicated here, these people form part of the body participating in this ceremony. Conversely, the story of Achan shows that native Israelites also needed to be committed to

---

[150] Similarly, Howard, *Joshua*, 216.
[151] See further, §2 ("Identity of the People of God").

God's purposes. As such, the stories of both Rahab and Achan provide the background needed to understand this event.

The nation was also organized into its various groups of leaders. The officers were prominent in 1:10 and 3:2; the elders played a significant role at 7:6 and 8:10; and the judges have not been mentioned previously and only occur later in standardized lists of leaders (23:2; 24:1). More importantly, these groups stood on either side of the ark of the covenant (the last time it is mentioned in the book), facing the Levites responsible for carrying it. The people were arranged into two groups, half before Mount Ebal and half before Mount Gerizim (consistent with Deut 27:11–13). The tribal division listed in Deuteronomy is not repeated but assumed, since all was done consistent with Moses' command.

One significant deviation from Deuteronomy 27 is that there is only the pronouncement of blessing on the people. In Deuteronomy only those on Mount Gerizim were to pronounce the blessing, while those on Mount Ebal were to announce the curse. Since all is said to be consistent with Moses' command, the curse pronouncement for covenant disobedience probably was declared, but within the narrative arc of Joshua the events at Ai have already shown the reality of the curse. Since they are a people for whom atonement has been made, the emphasis can thus fall on the blessing as the better way forward. Nevertheless, when he read the law, Joshua still read the curses as well as the blessings (v. 34).

8:34–35. Joshua's next task was to read the law to the people. Reading in the ancient world was normally done aloud,[152] but Joshua's reading here was more akin to the sort of public reading that would take place at a large worship event, and it was certainly a longer reading than would be typical of worship services today. The closest parallel is probably the reading of the law in Nehemiah 8:1–8 when Ezra read from early morning to midday. The initial emphasis had been only on the blessing (v. 33), but this time both blessings and curses are included (v. 34), since it is not possible to read the text without including both. That Joshua read the whole text (again, most likely Deuteronomy) is emphasized by noting that there was "not a word" that he left out (v. 35).

---

[152] Note Augustine's surprise that Ambrose would sit and read silently in the *Confessions*, book 6, chapter 3, though his surprise might have been that Ambrose would do this publicly, not just that he read silently.

As with the copying of the law, this reading was done before the whole
assembly of Israel. However, the definition of that assembly differs this
time. In verse 33, the distinction was between native and foreigner, with
the leaders of the people particularly noted. This time, the emphasis is
on the women, children, and foreigners who were present. The point is
that Israel was always to be an inclusive community, one that recognized
those who might be pushed to the margins in other communities. The
law was made available to all, not just to the elite, demonstrating another
way in which Israel was to be distinctive from the communities around
them. This act of inclusion showed precisely the sort of national character that had revealed Yahweh's presence in their midst to Rahab. Paul's
baptismal formula in Galatians 3:28 shows that the church continues to
be just such an inclusive people.

Bridge

Reflection on this passage needs to take into account its function within
the narrative of Joshua to this point and also its preparation for what
follows. At heart, it describes a pivotal moment of worship for the first
generation in Israel. This worship draws together key themes from the
past, especially evident in the repeated emphasis on faithfully doing
what Moses had commanded (vv. 31, 33, 35). This, in turn, links back
to the command that God had given Moses in 1:8 and, through it, to
Deuteronomy 27, a key text for this event. Israel's life was to be shaped
by obedience to the law given through Moses. The importance of this law
was not restricted to Joshua and the nation's leaders, but was extended
to the whole community. The publishing of the law by writing it on the
stones symbolically announced to all that they could access this key
text. Although Joshua had a special responsibility to shape his life and
leadership around the law, it is clear that this is something passed on
to the people as a whole.

In turn, this prepares for the evaluation of Joshua's leadership of the
nation (Josh 11:15–20) in terms of his faithfulness to what Moses had
commanded. The theme of a life shaped by obedience to God's word is
a vital one throughout the Bible. We cannot treat all references to this
theme, but it is worth noting that from the perspective of the Psalms
(e.g., Pss 1; 19; 119) such obedience is not a burden but rather a delight
(e.g., Pss 1:2; 19:8, 10; 119:97). This is because the law was never given

as a means by which Israel could be saved but rather a means by which a people redeemed by God could live as his covenant people. In the Old Testament as in the New, salvation is by grace; ethics is gratitude. We need this framework in place if we are not to misunderstand Paul's discussion of the law in Galatians. He is clearly addressing a situation in which teachers were claiming that obedience to the law was necessary for salvation, something that subverts the function of the law. If, instead, the law is understood as shaping the life of a community that has experienced God's deliverance, then it is possible to understand how Paul uses the law to guide Christian behavior in light of our salvation in Christ (e.g., Rom 12:1–15:13; Gal 5:14 citing Lev 19:18). But for such a pattern of behavior to be understood, there needs to be access to God's word, which of course is precisely what Deuteronomy 27 required and Joshua provided.

A vital element of the worship described here is its inclusive nature. The community of Israel is described twice. In verse 33, it is defined as "resident alien and citizen," while in verse 35 it covers women, children, and foreigners. Mention of these divisions is important in this setting because it provides important links back to earlier passages while preparing for what follows. For a book that focuses on the expulsion of the Canaanites, Joshua is remarkable for the fact that it gives so much attention to the foreigner. Rahab, of course, has been particularly prominent. She and her family are the only foreigners mentioned to date, but others will become important (most obviously the Gibeonites in chapter 9). Israel was to include the foreigner, not grudgingly, but by bringing them into worship, the heart of the nation. Worship gave a special place to women and children, sections of the community that were frequently marginalized in antiquity. Rahab, indeed, has been the only woman directly noted to this point, so she provides an interesting example.

Children have been mentioned in 4:6 and 4:21 (admittedly, a different word is used, but the concept remains) because Israel's worship was meant to provide a means of teaching them. By contrast, the children mentioned in 6:21 and 7:24–25 were destroyed because they were among those who rejected obedience to God's word. Although God's word does announce judgment, and the curse is announced here with the blessing, its purpose is to enable all to know God and what he requires. The means by which such knowledge would be passed on varies as we go through Scripture. To take only one example, in Titus 2, Paul encourages various groups within the congregation to pass on what they know of God's word in light of our hope in Jesus Christ so that we can live out what it means to be the people of God (Titus 2:14), precisely the task Joshua assumed here.

D. The Gibeonite Deception (9:1–27)

[1] When all the kings heard about Jericho and Ai, those who were west of the Jordan in the hill country, in the Judean foothills, and all along the coast of the Mediterranean Sea toward Lebanon—the Hethites, Amorites, Canaanites, Perizzites, Hivites, and Jebusites— [2] they formed a unified alliance to fight against Joshua and Israel.

[3] When the inhabitants of Gibeon heard what Joshua had done to Jericho and Ai, [4] they acted deceptively. They gathered provisions and took worn-out sacks on their donkeys and old wineskins, cracked and mended. [5] They wore old, patched sandals on their feet and threadbare clothing on their bodies. Their entire provision of bread was dry and crumbly. [6] They went to Joshua in the camp at Gilgal and said to him and the men of Israel, "We have come from a distant land. Please make a treaty with us."

[7] The men of Israel replied to the Hivites, "Perhaps you live among us. How can we make a treaty with you?"

[8] They said to Joshua, "We are your servants."

Then Joshua asked them, "Who are you and where do you come from?"

[9] They replied to him, "Your servants have come from a faraway land because of the reputation of the Lord your God. For we have heard of his fame, and all that he did in Egypt, [10] and all that he did to the two Amorite kings beyond the Jordan—King Sihon of Heshbon and King Og of Bashan, who was in Ashtaroth. [11] So our elders and all the inhabitants of our land told us, 'Take provisions with you for the journey; go and meet them and say, "We are your servants. Please make a treaty with us."' [12] This bread of ours was warm when we took it from our houses as food on the day we left to come to you; but see, it is now dry and crumbly. [13] These wineskins were new when we filled them; but see, they are cracked. And these clothes and sandals of ours are worn out from the extremely long journey." [14] Then the men of Israel took some of their provisions, but did not seek the Lord's decision. [15] So Joshua established peace with them and made a treaty to let them live, and the leaders of the community swore an oath to them.

[16] Three days after making the treaty with them, they heard that the Gibeonites were their neighbors, living among them. [17] So the Israelites set out and reached the Gibeonite cities on the third day. Now their cities were Gibeon, Chephirah, Beeroth, and Kiriath-jearim. [18] But the Israelites did not attack them, because the leaders of the community

had sworn an oath to them by the Lord, the God of Israel. Then the whole community grumbled against the leaders.

¹⁹ All the leaders answered them, "We have sworn an oath to them by the Lord, the God of Israel, and now we cannot touch them. ²⁰ This is how we will treat them: we will let them live, so that no wrath will fall on us because of the oath we swore to them." ²¹ They also said, "Let them live." So the Gibeonites became woodcutters and water carriers for the whole community, as the leaders had promised them.

²² Joshua summoned the Gibeonites and said to them, "Why did you deceive us by telling us you live far away from us, when in fact you live among us? ²³ Therefore you are cursed and will always be slaves—woodcutters and water carriers for the house of my God."

²⁴ The Gibeonites answered him, "It was clearly communicated to your servants that the Lord your God had commanded his servant Moses to give you all the land and to destroy all the inhabitants of the land before you. We greatly feared for our lives because of you, and that is why we did this. ²⁵ Now we are in your hands. Do to us whatever you think is right." ²⁶ This is what Joshua did to them: he rescued them from the Israelites, and they did not kill them. ²⁷ On that day he made them woodcutters and water carriers—as they are today—for the community and for the Lord's altar at the place he would choose.

Context

This chapter is the first of three that are linked by the same opening phrase (וַיְהִי כִשְׁמֹעַ), which could (rather woodenly) be translated "now when [x] heard," though csb varies the translation each time. The phrase recalls the opening words of 5:1, an association that is closest here given its reference to the kings across the Jordan as a group, whereas both 10:1 and 11:1 refer to a specific king who exercised authority over other kings in his region. But a significant change is now introduced. At 5:1, the kings heard about the crossing of the Jordan and lost heart, thus demonstrating the truth of Rahab's earlier assertion (2:11). What these kings heard this time apparently gave them new resolve to ally themselves against Israel. What this would mean in terms of their resistance is deferred until chapters 10 and 11, with the listing of defeated kings in chapter 12 showing their final failure. This phrase thus links these chapters as a tightly bound unit, albeit one that pictures a clear change in Israel's position in light of more recent events.

However, although the opening establishes a clear set of connections, this chapter defers any reference to these alliances to follow another account, that of the Gibeonites, a Canaanite (specifically Hivite, according to v. 7; cf. 11:19) group who found a way to avoid destruction and join Israel by means of deception. Although their own story is complete in itself within this chapter, they are actually another means by which this block of chapters is held together, since the alliance of southern kings attacked (10:1–5) in response to the Gibeonite agreement with Israel and since the Gibeonites are central to the evaluation of Joshua's actions in 11:19.

The Gibeonites also function to complicate the nature of Israel and what it means to be the people of God. Rahab, along with her family, had demonstrated that a Canaanite who was prepared to commit herself to Yahweh could join Israel. Conversely, Achan had demonstrated that an Israelite, along with his family, who set himself against Yahweh could be excluded from the nation. Moreover, the ceremony in 8:30–35 had emphasized the presence of the foreigner as part of Israel, even though Rahab and her family are the only foreigners to this point who have joined Israel. One could formulate a fairly simple definition of the people of God as those who commit themselves to fulfilling God's purposes; therefore, anyone not committed to this is excluded. For anyone who thought that Israel was defined ethnically, this was already a surprising position. But that simple view is further troubled here, for the Gibeonites (through deception) opt for a position of not resisting God's purposes rather than actively supporting them (as Rahab had). As a result, they were able to make a treaty (בְּרִית) with Israel. Although this treaty is problematic in several ways (see comment on vv. 14–15), it is allowed to stand and the Gibeonites are progressively moved closer to the sanctuary, with their place at the altar (v. 27, also referring back to 8:30–35). This story thus holds the whole of chapters 9–12 together while providing a further reflection on chapters 1–8 and the issue of Israel's identity.

Exegesis

9:1–2. As noted (see Context), reference to the kings west of the Jordan hearing something alludes to 5:1, except that instead of losing heart this time the kings formed an alliance to fight Israel. Exactly what they heard is not said—csb has "about Jericho and Ai," but this is an interpretative addition. Given that these kings gained heart from the news, it is more likely that only the news about Ai is intended here (the events of 8:30–35 are unlikely to be meant), unlike the Gibeonites who were influenced by both Jericho and Ai (v. 3). The gravity of the challenge Israel faced is emphasized by the listing of the regions in the land and the peoples who formed the alliance. The regional description moves from east to west, the "hill country" describing the mountains that rise steeply from the Jordan Valley, and then the "Judean foothills" (or Shephelah, though this term when not used as a proper noun means "lowlands") as the ground slopes down to the coastal plain and onto the Mediterranean cost. The alliance could also be measured from south to north, running to Lebanon in the north. The news they heard was, therefore, not restricted to the central highlands, but rather had reached the whole of the promised land.

This geographic listing is then provided with an ethnic map, describing the whole of the land by listing six of the seven groups typically used to define the indigenous peoples of the land (cf. 3:10). Only the Girgashites are omitted (though included by the LXX). The Gibeonites will later be listed as Hivites (v. 7), indicating that the list is general, a means of showing that resistance to Israel was now spread across the whole country even if not every person within each group was part of this resistance. Nevertheless, the hierarchical structure of Canaanite kingdoms, in which the king of one city would be under the authority of a more powerful king, shows that the decision of the Gibeonites involved a considerable risk on their part, as will become clear in 10:1–5. So, although Israel had entered the land and faced kings lacking the will to fight, the problems at Ai triggered a different context in which the kings were now prepared to join together to fight their common enemy, Israel.

9:3–5. Although readers have been made aware of the alliance against Israel, it is left aside until 10:1. Instead, we focus on the inhabitants of Gibeon because their response stands in marked contrast to the others. Based on what Joshua had done to Jericho and Ai, the Gibeonites devised a plan to make a treaty with Israel rather than seeking to oppose them. *Hearing* therefore continues to play a significant role, but what they heard convinced them not to oppose Israel, showing that some continued to demonstrate the type of response Rahab had indicated (2:9–13). This suggests that their awareness of the events at Ai had to include its capture and destruction, not just the initial successful resistance offered by the city.

Gibeon itself was an important town, the size of which becomes significant at 10:2. It would later be allocated to Benjamin (18:25) and become a Levitical city (21:7). It is generally identified with el-Jib, a site about eight miles northwest of Jerusalem and much the same distance southwest of Ai. This is near enough to where events narrated so far have taken place that the Gibeonites would have heard about them fairly soon. The site was excavated by a team led by James Pritchard from 1956 to 1962. Unfortunately, some of the site had been damaged in the First World War, making stratigraphy difficult, but Pritchard's team found evidence of Bronze Age occupation and also jar handles that bore the town's name. Material recovered from Bronze Age tombs also indicates the possibility of considerable wealth in the city, perhaps from the sale of wine since the Iron Age remains show that this was a significant industry there.[153]

Notably, there is no mention of a king here, so apparently the decision about how to respond to Israel was made by the town's inhabitants. Given the ubiquity of kingship in the region (the Philistines and Hittites in Anatolia being obvious exceptions), one could assume there was a king, but if so he was sidelined by his town's inhabitants.[154]

The focus instead is on the processes by which they deceived Israel. Although CSB announces their deception almost from the outset ("they acted deceptively"), verse 4 is actually highly ambiguous, at least on a first reading. We are told they acted with עָרְמָה, a word that can be either positive or negative. Negatively it can mean "crafty" (as in Exod 21:14, referring to someone who plots against another), but positively it can mean "prudence" (as in Prov 1:4, where it is a legitimate goal for wisdom instruction; cf. Prov 8:5, 12).

Complicating this is the *hapax* וַיִּצְטַיָּרוּ, which has been variously understood as "act as an ambassador" or "disguise oneself." One feature of the *hithpael* stem (used here) is that it can refer to someone feigning something, which might suggest on either interpretation that there was something deceptive (hence "They went disguised as ambassadors" in CSB note). But this is not a necessary feature of the stem. Given that we have no instances of it occurring elsewhere, a clear interpretation is difficult. CSB prefers to follow some variant manuscripts and read וַיִּצְטַיָּדוּ instead, a very small change and easily explained by confusion between the similar letters ד and ר, so that they "gathered provisions" instead. The virtue of this reading is that provisions will appear in the subsequent narrative, with this variant root featured in the noun rendered "provisions" in verse 11. Given that both are from comparatively rare roots, it is easy to

---

[153] For a helpful summary of the archaeology of Gibeon, see Pekka M. A. Pitkänen, *Joshua* (Nottingham: Apollos, 2010), 214–16.

[154] Many have used the lack of reference to a king to suggest they had no king, but there is insufficient information to decide this with certainty. The fact that Josh 10:2 describes it as "like a royal city" suggests that it was not royal and hence had no king.

see how the confusion would have arisen. But it still seems likely that this variant reading represents the sort of correction an informed scribe might have made to a difficult text, so preference should be given to the MT as it stands.[155]

If so, then we are to understand those who came to Israel as presenting themselves as ambassadors, but with the element of deception (and therefore of craftiness) held back until the narrative unfolds further. This is important, because readers know that ambassadors are expected to be prudent and will, therefore, carefully ration the truth. Only with hindsight do we know the Gibeonites have acted deceptively, though the possibility is present from the outset. We might capture the ambiguity by translating the first part of verse 4, "So they acted prudently, and they came and presented themselves as ambassadors," leaving to the reader to work out what this prudence means. However, we do quickly discover the nature of their ruse. They took worn-out sacks for their donkeys and old wineskins that had cracked and been mended to show the age of their provisions. Moreover, the old, patched sandals and threadbare clothing suggested a long journey, something that could be substantiated by the dry and crumbly bread.[156] However, although we are told about these things, the narrator leaves it to the Gibeonites to explain the reasons for this odd collection of materials. At the end of verse 5, we simply know that these items are part of their prudence as ambassadors, but we do not know their function.

9:6–7. Only in verse 6 do we begin to see how their prudence would display itself as they came to Joshua and the men of Israel at Gilgal.[157] Since Gilgal is a common place name, this does not have to be the site where Israel first entered the land (4:19). Indeed, this is highly unlikely given the travels they have already made. Deuteronomy 11:30 mentions another Gilgal in the region of Mount Ebal, which is the most likely option,

---

[155] Similarly, Nelson, *Joshua*, 121–22.

[156] Deut 8:4 stresses that Israel's clothes did not wear out in the wilderness, so the narrative here probably offers an ironic reflection on this fact.

[157] The MT here has the awkward "man of Israel" (אִישׁ יִשְׂרָאֵל). This has been the basis for various redactional theories (see, e.g., Ray K. Sutherland, "Israelite Political Theories in Joshua 9," *JSOT* 53 [1992]: 65–74, who identifies three strata, each reflecting a different period), but the term can be read collectively, something recognized by diverse witnesses in the textual tradition, making these unnecessary.

though another mentioned in 15:7 on the Judah–Benjamin border is also possible.[158]

Whichever Gilgal is meant, readers know that it is within the land of Israel, and so the first thing said by the Gibeonites—that they have come from a distant country—is untrue. At this point, we know that prudence is craftiness. Nevertheless, if the ambassadorial role is to negotiate the best outcome for one's people, then immediately asking for a treaty (בְּרִית) shows that even if they were not honest brokers, they were trying to represent the best interests of their people. Their request immediately raises questions, but it is again prudent.

According to Deuteronomy 20:10–18, Israel was not to make a treaty with any of the cities of the land, though they could do so with a city outside the land and then put that city's inhabitants to forced labor.[159] By presenting themselves as coming from a distant land, the Gibeonites have thus deceptively indicated that they fall into the group of cities with whom Israel can make a treaty. But the Israelites are at least suspicious, and the narrator provides additional reason for this suspicion by calling the Gibeonites "Hivites" and thus showing that they are one of the peoples of the land with whom Israel could not make a treaty. The Israelites' question identified the key problem: The Gibeonites have claimed that they are from a distant land, but how can Israel know? After all, for all the Israelites knew, they could have been locals. Hence, by asking how they could make a treaty with them, they were really asking for the evidence to enable this to occur.

9:8–13. Where the Israelites spoke corporately with the Gibeonites in verse 7 after they had initially addressed both Joshua and Israel in verse 6, in verses 8–13 the conversation is only between Joshua and the Gibeonites, though of course Joshua represents Israel throughout. Rather than answering the Israelites' question, the Gibeonites focus their attention on Joshua, identifying themselves as his servants. Ironically, what is here nothing more than a polite form of address anticipates their final situation. This is the first of six times that servant language is used in the balance of the chapter, with the concept of servanthood being gradually

---

[158] See Howard, *Joshua*, 224. Another Gilgal mentioned in 2 Kgs 2:1 is north of Bethel, but is unlikely here.

[159] Mitchell, *Together in the Land*, 85, says, "It is almost as though the Gibeonites have read the text in Deuteronomy."

resolved as we progress,[160] though for the Gibeonites it would mean they end up with a menial role in the central sanctuary. But at this point, the claim is purely formal and has no substance.

Accordingly, Joshua returns to the issue raised by the men of Israel, asking who the Gibeonites were and where they had come from. The Gibeonites' response is again deceptive, carefully mixing outright falsehood with things that a people from outside the land might have known, while never directly answering the question of their identity. So, again they repeat the claim to have come from a distant land, though this time it is "very distant" (csb "a faraway land," v. 9). They also adopt a more menial position than before, referring to themselves in the third person in order to continue to style themselves as servants. The Gibeonites' language again shows their prudence in presenting their case, as does their statement that they had come because of God's "reputation" (v. 9). This is literally because of his "name," but since this commonly refers to his reputation, csb's slight paraphrase is appropriate.

Their speech continues to develop the theme of hearing, which has been so central (indeed, the word translated "fame" in verse 10 comes from the root meaning "to hear"). The stories they recount are all from outside the land—the exodus from Egypt and the defeat of Sihon and Og (Num 21:21–35)—thus largely mirroring the stories reflected in Rahab's confession (see more on 2:9–13). There may be a small slip in their language in referring to these kings as "beyond the Jordan," something that might suggest they were people who lived west of the Jordan. But if so, Joshua and Israel did not notice this. The important point is that these are historical references a people from outside the land might have heard. They are careful not to mention anything more recent, even though verse 3 makes clear they are responding to the events at Jericho and Ai, since that would almost certainly have revealed them as indigenous to the land.

Thus, they acknowledge the earlier events as having led their elders and the inhabitants of the land to direct them to take provisions, go to Israel, claim the position of servants (i.e., a subservient people), and request a treaty. Reference to the provisions prepares readers to explore the lengthy list from verses 3–5. Reference to the treaty returns to the

---

[160] Rösel, *Joshua*, 144, points to the importance of this motif across the chapter as evidence against attempts to divide it into two essentially separate texts (divided at v. 16). This is not to deny that the narrator here draws on multiple traditions, but rather to stress (with Butler, *Joshua 1–12*, 440) that they are integrated in order to provide a positive assessment of Joshua.

request of verse 6, though since this time the treaty is mentioned in terms of the directive from the elders, the polite language from earlier is dropped. Only after this digression do they come back to their provisions, which are now proffered as evidence that they had indeed traveled a long way.

So, they show Israel the crumbly bread (claiming it was warm on the day they set out), the cracked wineskins (claiming they were new when filled), and their clothing and sandals (claiming they had been worn out by the long journey). Readers already know that the Gibeonites had selected these provisions because of their condition, though only now do we know why they had chosen them. In reality, none of the evidence they offer actually proves anything about their claims since Israel has no means of checking what these items were like when they set out, but for readers this statement is further evidence of their deceptive words.

9:14–15. With their case presented, the Gibeonites fell silent. It is notable that we are not told of anything Joshua or Israel said in response. It is as if they were silenced by the Gibeonites' loquaciousness. Instead, they took from the Gibeonites' provisions, showing they had been taken in by their argument. This account is, perhaps, similar to a situation in which someone hears only what they are told by a well-drilled salesperson and are unable to break out of the world as defined by the sales patter. The wisdom literature is well aware of this possibility, most notably in the observation of Proverbs 18:17, "The first to state his case seems right, until another comes and cross-examines him." Although the proverb's primary reference is to the law court, it clearly has a wider application. Israel was unable to move into a proper cross-examination, so that even the act of sampling the provisions means they had already accepted the basic premise of the Gibeonites.[161]

At this point, the narrator cannot resist making an evaluative comment, something rare in the book of Joshua, observing that although they sampled the Gibeonites' provisions, they did not seek God's counsel. Indeed, the sentence structure in the second half of verse 14 emphasizes this point by bringing God's counsel to the beginning of the clause. Israel

---

[161] F. Charles Fensham, "The Treaty between Israel and the Gibeonites," *BA* 27 (1964): 96–100, is typical of those who suggest that the sampling of the food was a covenant meal. But as Hall, *Conquering Character*, 153, points out, this was not appropriate food for such an event. Moreover, Fensham ignores the importance of the observation that Israel relied on physical evidence rather than inquiring of God.

could have avoided what follows by the simple expedient of asking God, but the one thing that was meant to distinguish them as a nation did not happen.

As a result, Joshua made peace with the Gibeonites, going beyond what they had explicitly requested, though consistent with it. This peace was enshrined in a treaty that permitted them to live. The word translated "treaty" is בְּרִית, elsewhere translated "covenant," and represents precisely the sort of agreement Deuteronomy 7:2 had indicated Israel was not to make with the people of the land. The solemnity of this is made clear by the oath that the leaders of the community swore to the Gibeonites. A simple lack of prayerfulness, or even the use of other devices such as the Urim and Thummim that God had given to determine his will, meant that Israel was deceived by a simple ruse. When the spies swore their oath to Rahab, there was at least evidence that she was prepared to commit herself to God, but there is no indication here that the Gibeonites were prepared to do this. So, has Israel made a fundamental mistake? It was clearly wrong to make the treaty without inquiring of God, but have they done something even more damaging? Or is there a means by which this too can be seen within God's larger purposes for his people?

9:16–21. The question raised by the treaty is not immediately resolved. Rather, just as the questions raised about the oath sworn to Rahab were answered over the succeeding chapters, so also the ambiguities surrounding the Gibeonites are worked out over the next three chapters. To some extent the significance of their position continues through the rest of the Former Prophets (see, e.g., 2 Sam 21:1–14).[162] In the immediate context, Israel deals with it in stages. The first comes about in verse 16 as Israel discovers that the Gibeonites were in fact indigenous to the land. The three-day period specified in verse 16 should be understood as an idiomatic reference to a short but indeterminate period (see comments on 1:11). Israel's hearing about Gibeon here parallels the earlier hearing of the Canaanite kings (9:1) and the Gibeonites (9:3) about Israel. Once again, there is no indication of how this news was heard. All that matters is that Israel realized they had been deceived, and the treaty was therefore suspect.

---

[162] For evidence of the antiquity of the traditions of Joshua 9 relative to 2 Sam 21:1–14, though with an overly complex literary formation, see Jörn Halbe, "Gibeon und Israel: Art, Veranlassung und Ort der Deutung ihres Verhältnisses in Jos IX," VT 25 (1975): 631–35.

These verses also show clear divisions between the Israelites and their leaders. Joshua himself is not mentioned until verse 22, perhaps suggesting that he was in some way separate from the other leaders, but this is probably not a distinction to be pushed. More important is the conflict between the Israelites and their leadership. There is no indication of the leadership suggesting that Israel should go to the Gibeonite cities (Chephirah, modern Khirbet Kephirah, and Kiriath-jearim were southeast of Gibeon, while Beeroth is most likely a little to the south). Together, these cities controlled access to the Sorek Valley—one of the best routes between the highlands and the coast. The importance of this will become more evident in the next chapter.

The surprise here is to discover that Gibeon was in fact the principal city in a league that opted to work together. Although the cities were fairly close to one another, Israel would presumably have camped against only one of the cities since they would be unlikely to try and attack several at once. However, no attack was launched because of the oath sworn by the leaders, an oath we are specifically told was in the name of Yahweh, the God of Israel. But this was not an oath that sat comfortably with the Israelites as a whole, as is clear from their grumbling. The echoes of the wilderness period that this opens (e.g., Exod 15:24; 16:2–3) might suggest that their grumbling is problematic.

The people as a whole were prepared to attack, seeing the Gibeonites as a people liable to destruction, but the leaders saw their oath as a barrier to this. The importance of the oath for the leaders becomes clear in their speech in verse 19. Their statement that they had sworn an oath in the name of Yahweh, God of Israel, repeats the point made by the narrator in verse 18, but it is expressed in a way that further emphasizes the gap between the people and their leaders. Their speech includes an emphatic pronoun (אֲנַחְנוּ) that is not technically necessary and so not represented in translation, but it functions to emphasize the fact that it was the leaders who had sworn this oath. Given this, there is some initial ambiguity in their statement "we cannot touch them." This could mean that the leaders could not act because of their oath, implying that the rest of Israel could. In this case, the "we" refers to the leaders. Alternatively, it could be an inclusive "we," meaning all Israel. Although it is perhaps more likely that this was what the leaders intended, the fact that the Gibeonites were only delivered after Joshua's intervention suggests that some were prepared to understand the prohibition on killing them in a more limited way.

If this division between people and leaders remains, then the leaders' continuation of their statement in verses 20–21 represents their preferred option, but not yet one that Israel as a whole would embrace. The leaders believed that the Gibeonites should be permitted to live. To break their oath would result in Yahweh's wrath falling on them since it would effectively compound the previous sin. Something similar would seem to lie behind Isaac concluding that he could not revoke his blessing on Jacob, even though it too had been gained through deceit (Gen 27).[163] The point is that an oath was meant to be unbreakable and therefore had to be kept, even if it was entered into on the basis of deception. Nevertheless, this was not to be a life of freedom. Instead, the Gibeonites would have a menial position within Israel, cutting wood and bearing water, something Deuteronomy 29:11 allowed as a position for foreigners living within Israel.[164] This was prohibited for peoples from within the land (Deut 20:10–18), because these peoples would teach Israel their religious ways. But the position of the Gibeonites suggests that this was not a problem they posed, and since Israel's oath had considered them as if they were from outside the land, the leaders suggested that they be treated in this way.

9:22–27. Where the previous conversation was between the people of Israel and their leaders, these verses focus on a conversation between Joshua and the Gibeonites. It addresses the nub of the problem noted in verses 18–21 and so finally resolves the differences between leaders and people. Joshua's question to the Gibeonites focused on their deception of Israel, stressing that as a result they were cursed to servitude,[165] hewing wood and carrying water in perpetuity. Although Joshua largely affirmed the decision of the leaders, he introduced one important shift. The initial decision was that the Gibeonites would do this for the community as a whole, but Joshua initially restricted this to the "house of my God" (v. 23). Since verse 27 includes both groups, however, the more specific focus does not exclude the wider needs of the community. This put the Gibeonites into a position similar to the items taken at Jericho, which

---

[163] So Howard, *Joshua*, 229.

[164] On the wider links between Deuteronomy 29 and Joshua 9, though without accepting the literary development he proposes, see Peter J. Kearney, "The Role of the Gibeonites in the Deuteronomic History," *CBQ* 35 (1973): 1–8.

[165] In Joshua, only a potential rebuilder of Jericho (6:26) and the Gibeonites are cursed.

were placed into Yahweh's treasury (6:20): the Gibeonites were given over to God, though of course not destroyed.[166] At this point, there is no "house of God," if by that one means a temple, but the phrase here probably refers to the tent of meeting and so anticipates its establishment in Shiloh (18:1).

The Gibeonites' response shows similarities to the opening of Rahab's confession in 2:9 in its stress on what they already knew and their resultant fear, but it goes beyond in some ways. It is also notable that whereas Joshua had described servitude as a curse, it is here a title that they continued to use for themselves. It might be a curse, but it was obviously better than the alternative. They made known that their decision was not based on rumor but rather on the fact that they had received clear communication of what God had commanded Israel through Moses, specifically that he was giving Israel the whole land and they were to destroy all its inhabitants. This statement most closely matches Deuteronomy 7:24, though it ignores the fact that Deuteronomy more commonly refers to God destroying the inhabitants of the land or to threatening Israel with destruction if they turned from him. Thus, however this information was communicated to the Gibeonites, it was true but only partially so. Nonetheless, because of this information and the great fear that it generated, they acted as they had. But they also knew that, since their deception had been discovered, they were in Joshua's power. So they asked him to do what he determined to be good and right (see csb note)—that is, they asked him to act not only for what was pleasing to him but also what he considered to be just. The Gibeonites thus recognized that there was a standard of justice in Israel that was able to look beyond their deception to their recognition of God's authority.

In response to this, Joshua affirmed the earlier decision of the leaders and in so doing delivered the Gibeonites from the rest of the Israelites who wished to kill them. But whereas the earlier conversation between leaders and people had offered a pragmatic resolution (admittedly shaped by the conviction that they could not revoke their oath), the focus now was on doing what was just. There was no law that addressed this particular situation, so instead Joshua weighed the evidence and determined what was just in a situation in which no decision was wholly right. Justice

---

[166] Similarly, J. Gordon McConville and Stephen N. Williams, *Joshua* (Grand Rapids: Eerdmans, 2010), 49.

was served by assigning them to a state of perpetual servitude and treating them as a people from outside the land as the oath expected, but at the same time by focusing their servitude at the Lord's altar and thus devoting them to God as much as possible, a solution still in effect when this narrative was written. It was a compromise, as indeed are all situations of ethical conflict, but one that attempted to hold in balance both what God had said and the oath that had been sworn. At this point, there is no indication of which place God would choose (an allusion to Deut 12:5 and an anticipation of Josh 18:1), but this allowed for a workable outcome. As with the oath sworn to Rahab, we do not know yet if God would accept Joshua's decision. Only at 11:19–20 will the reader know that God has approved the decision, and this in turn prepares us for the fact that the Gibeonites become an important part of the life of Israel, both as a distinctively recognized people (e.g., 2 Sam 21:1–14) and as a people who are an integral part of Israel's life (Neh 3:7). Once again, a group of foreigners would become an important part of Israel.

Bridge

The story of the Gibeonites is difficult because it describes a situation in which earlier choices meant there was no longer a simple and obvious answer. This is a world that closely matches the one in which we live today. Taking this further, the story uses this setting to explore further the nature of the people of God, complicating the already-complex picture that has emerged in the previous chapters. One might describe the decision-making processes as the presenting problem, with the nature of God's people as the deeper theological problem. However, we cannot separate one from the other, and only through understanding one can we understand the other. This means that although this chapter is not principally written to discuss Israel's decision making, we need to understand this in order to explore the deeper issue.

Unquestionably, the narrator sees the processes that led to Israel making a treaty with the Gibeonites as deeply flawed, though this is mitigated somewhat by the deceptive acts of the Gibeonites. But in the simple statement of verse 14 and its note that Israel had failed to seek God's counsel on this matter, it is clearly implied that Israel could have avoided making an otherwise prohibited treaty. Since the book seldom makes direct comments on the actions of its participants, a note like this should be allowed its full force. Israel's prayerlessness, its failure to use those things (like the Urim and Thummim) that God had given for discerning his will, stands condemned. In this, the book is consistent with the rest of Scripture, which encourages us to be prayerful in discerning God's purposes for us. Note, for example, the way in which Paul prays for the Colossian believers (Col 1:9–12) and also encourages the Roman Christians to discern God's purposes through the transformation of their minds (Rom 12:2). Consistently, Scripture urges us to know what God desires through prayer and the giving over of ourselves to him, something Israel signally failed to do in establishing their treaty with the Gibeonites.

Once their decision was made, however, they had to live with it, discerning what was possible in light of other parts of the law. Obviously, there was no law that began, "If you make a foolish treaty, then insert space..." But it was possible to work through various parts of the law to determine options that were just (whereas believers today have access to the whole Bible), which is why the leaders generally, and Joshua in particular, prevented the rest of the Israelites from killing the Gibeonites. There would be no benefit in adding sin to sin by breaking an oath, even when the basis on which that oath was sworn was flawed. Believers have to live with the consequences of their decisions, and those consequences need to be worked out in light of other parts of Scripture. The difficulty is that we cannot know if God will accept these decisions—but that in fact mirrors the situation here. We will not know for another two chapters that God affirmed Joshua's decision. We can only know at this stage that Joshua sought to do what was good and just, behavior that should mark the people of God.

Although the processes that led to the decision were deeply flawed, the result was the integration of the Gibeonites into Israel and God's people.[167] This process goes beyond the situation of Rahab who effectively confessed faith in Yahweh, or Achan who effectively rejected it. On the basis of partial information, the Gibeonites concluded that accepting Israel's God was their only means of survival; therefore, they had to find a way of circumventing the command for their destruction. Rahab's precedent shows that there was a better way, but since the Gibeonites were operating on partial information they would not necessarily have been aware of this option.

---

[167] On this, see especially William Ford, "What about the Gibeonites?," *TynBull* 66 (2015): 197–216, and his exploration of the possibilities for the Canaanite peoples in Joshua.

Perhaps it's best to understand this through two of Jesus' statements. In Luke 11:23 he declared, "Anyone who is not with me is against me." This is what we might classify as the strong position on discipleship, looking for commitment such as Rahab offered. But in Mark 9:40 Jesus said, "Whoever is not against us is for us." We can classify this as the weak position on discipleship, and it is the model demonstrated by the Gibeonites. They did not wish to oppose Israel, and thus the purposes of God. So they could be considered "for Israel," although their commitment was expressed through deception.

On the whole, Scripture favors the stronger position on discipleship, which is why it has been emphasized in Christian witness (most evidently in conversionist models of evangelism, typified by figures such as D. L. Moody or Billy Graham). But the weaker pattern is also present. Even if we want to encourage the stronger model as preferential, there needs to be scope for the weaker model, especially if it ultimately leads to a fuller incorporation into the purposes of God. Such incorporation seems to have occurred with the Gibeonites. Note, for example, the curious story of the famine in 2 Samuel 21:1–14, which was triggered by Saul's attempt to subvert this treaty, or the fact that Gibeon (which will be allocated to Benjamin in 18:25) would become the site of an important shrine where God appeared to Solomon (1 Kgs 3:4) before the construction of the temple. By the time of Nehemiah, the men of Gibeon were as committed to the rebuilding of the wall as any (Neh 3:7).[168] What started as a simple desire to survive resulted in a committed group of people expressing the stronger position of discipleship, and so Israel became a people even more mixed than before. It is important to remember that, at the end of this chapter, we do not yet know that God approved of this decision (for which we need 11:19–20), but it seems that God was open to a range of ways in which people might come to faithful discipleship when they did not pose a threat to Israel's faith, which was the basis on which destruction was required in Deuteronomy 7 and 20. In a somewhat unexpected way, therefore, the promise that all the clans of the earth would find blessing in Abraham (Gen 12:3) continued to be worked out here. Perhaps, though, this is no more surprising than the grafting of

---

[168] Neh 7:25 mentions Gibeonites among those returning from exile, but this is textually uncertain because the parallel in Ezra 2:20 has "Gibbar's descendants."

Gentiles into the promises of God (Rom 11:17–19), which is why the body of Christ is always so diverse.[169]

E. The Campaign in the South (10:1–43)

[1] Now King Adoni-zedek of Jerusalem heard that Joshua had captured Ai and completely destroyed it, treating Ai and its king as he had Jericho and its king, and that the inhabitants of Gibeon had made peace with Israel and were living among them. [2] So Adoni-zedek and his people were greatly alarmed because Gibeon was a large city like one of the royal cities; it was larger than Ai, and all its men were warriors. [3] Therefore King Adoni-zedek of Jerusalem sent word to King Hoham of Hebron, King Piram of Jarmuth, King Japhia of Lachish, and King Debir of Eglon, saying, [4] "Come up and help me. We will attack Gibeon, because they have made peace with Joshua and the Israelites." [5] So the five Amorite kings—the kings of Jerusalem, Hebron, Jarmuth, Lachish, and Eglon—joined forces, advanced with all their armies, besieged Gibeon, and fought against it.

[6] Then the men of Gibeon sent word to Joshua in the camp at Gilgal: "Don't give up on your servants. Come quickly and save us! Help us, for all the Amorite kings living in the hill country have joined forces against us." [7] So Joshua and all his troops, including all his best soldiers, came from Gilgal.

[8] The Lord said to Joshua, "Do not be afraid of them, for I have handed them over to you. Not one of them will be able to stand against you."

[9] So Joshua caught them by surprise, after marching all night from Gilgal. [10] The Lord threw them into confusion before Israel. He defeated them in a great slaughter at Gibeon, chased them through the ascent of Beth-horon, and struck them down as far as Azekah and Makkedah. [11] As they fled before Israel, the Lord threw large hailstones on them from the sky along the descent of Beth-horon all the way to Azekah, and they died. More of them died from the hail than the Israelites killed with the sword.

[12] On the day the Lord gave the Amorites over to the Israelites, Joshua spoke to the Lord in the presence of Israel:

"Sun, stand still over Gibeon,
and moon, over the Valley of Aijalon."
[13] And the sun stood still
and the moon stopped
until the nation took vengeance on its enemies.
Isn't this written in the Book of Jashar?
So the sun stopped

---

[169] Cf. Dallaire, "Joshua," 924.

in the middle of the sky
and delayed its setting
almost a full day.

¹⁴ There has been no day like it before or since, when the Lᴏʀᴅ listened to a man, because the Lᴏʀᴅ fought for Israel. ¹⁵ Then Joshua and all Israel with him returned to the camp at Gilgal.

¹⁶ Now the five defeated kings had fled and hidden in the cave at Makkedah. ¹⁷ It was reported to Joshua, "The five kings have been found; they are hiding in the cave at Makkedah."

¹⁸ Joshua said, "Roll large stones against the mouth of the cave, and station men by it to guard the kings. ¹⁹ But as for the rest of you, don't stay there. Pursue your enemies and attack them from behind. Don't let them enter their cities, for the Lᴏʀᴅ your God has handed them over to you." ²⁰ So Joshua and the Israelites finished inflicting a terrible slaughter on them until they were destroyed, although a few survivors ran away to the fortified cities. ²¹ The people returned safely to Joshua in the camp at Makkedah. And no one dared to threaten the Israelites.

²² Then Joshua said, "Open the mouth of the cave, and bring those five kings to me out of there." ²³ That is what they did. They brought the five kings of Jerusalem, Hebron, Jarmuth, Lachish, and Eglon to Joshua out of the cave. ²⁴ When they had brought the kings to him, Joshua summoned all the men of Israel and said to the military commanders who had accompanied him, "Come here and put your feet on the necks of these kings." So the commanders came forward and put their feet on their necks. ²⁵ Joshua said to them, "Do not be afraid or discouraged. Be strong and courageous, for the Lᴏʀᴅ will do this to all the enemies you fight."

²⁶ After this, Joshua struck them down and executed them. He hung their bodies on five trees and they were there until evening. ²⁷ At sunset Joshua commanded that they be taken down from the trees and thrown into the cave where they had hidden. Then large stones were placed against the mouth of the cave, and the stones are still there today.

²⁸ On that day Joshua captured Makkedah and struck it down with the sword, including its king. He completely destroyed it and everyone in it, leaving no survivors. So he treated the king of Makkedah as he had the king of Jericho.

²⁹ Joshua and all Israel with him crossed from Makkedah to Libnah and fought against Libnah. ³⁰ The Lᴏʀᴅ also handed it and its king over to Israel. He struck it down, putting everyone in it to the sword, and left no survivors in it. He treated Libnah's king as he had the king of Jericho.

³¹ From Libnah, Joshua and all Israel with him crossed to Lachish. They laid siege to it and attacked it. ³² The Lᴏʀᴅ handed Lachish over to Israel, and Joshua captured it on the second day. He struck it down, putting everyone in it to the sword, just as he had done to Libnah. ³³ At

that time King Horam of Gezer went to help Lachish, but Joshua struck him down along with his people, leaving no survivors.

[34] Then Joshua crossed from Lachish to Eglon and all Israel with him. They laid siege to it and attacked it. [35] On that day they captured it and struck it down, putting everyone in it to the sword. He completely destroyed it that day, just as he had done to Lachish.

[36] Next, Joshua and all Israel with him went up from Eglon to Hebron and attacked it. [37] They captured it and struck down its king, all its villages, and everyone in it with the sword. He left no survivors, just as he had done at Eglon. He completely destroyed Hebron and everyone in it.

[38] Finally, Joshua turned toward Debir and attacked it. And all Israel was with him. [39] He captured it—its king and all its villages. They struck them down with the sword and completely destroyed everyone in it, leaving no survivors. He treated Debir and its king as he had treated Hebron and as he had treated Libnah and its king.

[40] So Joshua conquered the whole region—the hill country, the Negev, the Judean foothills, and the slopes—with all their kings, leaving no survivors. He completely destroyed every living being, as the LORD, the God of Israel, had commanded. [41] Joshua conquered everyone from Kadesh-barnea to Gaza, and all the land of Goshen as far as Gibeon. [42] Joshua captured all these kings and their land in one campaign, because the LORD, the God of Israel, fought for Israel. [43] Then Joshua returned with all Israel to the camp at Gilgal.

Context

The treaty with the Gibeonite cities produced an immediate response from the Amorite population to the south of the land, as five kings from that region allied themselves against Israel. The chapter's opening verses provide an immediate parallel to 9:1–2, except that this time we are told it was Adoni-zedek, the king of Jerusalem, who had heard about events at Ai and Jericho. The pressing issue for him was not just Israel's initial military successes in the land, since neither Jericho nor Ai was a particularly significant site militarily. Important as these sites were for Israel, of more concern for Adoni-zedek was the treaty made by the Gibeonites, because Gibeon was a large city that was apparently also well known for the quality of its soldiers. In addition, Gibeon's location meant that it controlled a significant point of access to the coastal plain and therefore important trade routes. Israel's peace with Gibeon was thus a significant break within the defenses of the Canaanite population.[170] Although Israel's treaty with Gibeon meant some cities no longer required warfare to be taken, it was also a trigger for more immediate conflict. Indeed, where previously Israel had been able to identify cities it wanted to attack, now it would be called to defend its treaty partner when attacked. There is also a pattern that runs across the whole of chapters 9–12, which show a gradual increase in the level of threat Israel experienced. Whereas previously only one city at a time had resisted, now five cities would combine to attack, and a much larger coalition in the north would oppose Israel directly in chapter 11.

All of this raises questions about the treaty with Gibeon. Had Israel moved out of the relationship it should have had with God? The narrator was careful not to comment on the appropriateness of the treaty in chapter 9 (only on the means by which it was brought about), and will not finally resolve the issue until 11:19–20. However, by carefully weaving a number of references to God's speech to Joshua from 1:1–9 throughout this chapter, the author provides several hints that the promises God had made remain valid. This is validated in the capture of a range of cities in the south and the summary statement in 10:40–43. The importance of references to chapter 1 can be seen in these important allusions:

1. 10:6—the Gibeonite call to Joshua not to "give up" on them picks up on God's promise not to "leave" Joshua in 1:5, two of only three occurrences of the verb רפה ("leave alone") in the book.[171]
2. 10:8—God's comment reaffirms the promise of 1:5 (though with a change of verb), while the warning against fear refers to 1:9.
3. 10:10–12—God's actions demonstrated the promise of divine presence in 1:9.
4. 10:19—Joshua's statement that God had given these kings over to Israel depends on the promise of 1:2.
5. 10:25—Joshua's warning against fear echoes God's words to him in 1:6.
6. 10:40—the summary statement shows that Joshua had done everything God commanded, as specified by 1:7.

---

[170] On the politics involved, see Baruch Halpern, "Gibeon: Israelite Diplomacy in the Conquest Era," *CBQ* 37 (1935): 303–16.

[171] The other reference is 18:3, where Joshua complains about the people failing to go and possess the land.

That Gibeon is central to all this is apparent from the fact that it was the trigger for the coalition of southern kings in verse 2 and also the pivot point of Israel's southern campaign in verse 41, effectively forming an inclusio for the whole chapter. And, of course, at Gibeon God fought in a most remarkable way for Israel (10:12–14). Although God did not explicitly affirm the treaty, it becomes apparent that the relationship with the Gibeonites is one that God implicitly affirmed, and that the promises made to Israel would not be troubled by this any more than the oath sworn to Rahab.

This model of gradual acceptance of the inclusion of the Gibeonites then stands in intentional tension with the destruction of so many cities and their inhabitants, especially in the listing of the six cities and their inhabitants that are destroyed (along with others according to v. 40). The verb חרם ("destroy completely") occurs fourteen times in the book, with six occurrences in this chapter alone, and another four in the next chapter, which closely mirrors it, though not after that. There are other terms for military violence throughout the chapter; נכה (traditionally "to smite" but translated in various ways) occurs fourteen times, while, apart from the note about survivors in 10:20, six times we are told Joshua left no survivor. Although much of Joshua does not appear to reflect the popular stereotype of the book as one filled with violence, on first reading it might seem that this chapter does. But without denying the presence of violence—which would seem pointless given the description of the defeat of kings and the capture of cities—there are several points that need to be noted and that suggest at least a limitation of violence, because the text uses idioms that are more limited in focus than a literal translation of the Hebrew might suggest.

First, we cannot miss the contrast intended in verses 19–20. Here we are told both that Joshua completely destroyed the enemies (using the verb תמם rather than חרם), but also that there were survivors. If intended literally, these statements cannot both be true. If everyone was killed, no one survived. But the text has no problem leaving these statements together. If so, then we need to reckon with the possibility that the text uses an idiom that describes a complete victory, but not one that requires the actual destruction of everyone. In other words, hyperbolic language is used to stress the completeness of the victory, not the actual casualty figures (see more in the comment below).

This in turn makes sense of the claims of destruction in verses 28–39. Hebron, we are told, was completely destroyed with no survivors (10:36–37). But after it was allotted to Caleb (14:13–15), he still needed to expel the inhabitants and claim the town (15:13–14). If the town was destroyed and left without inhabitant, how can this be true? Again, the answer lies in the use of hyperbolic language as part of an established idiom that stressed the completeness of the victory at Hebron, though in this case we might note that only those actually in the city when it was captured were destroyed. One thing that has remained true through much of history is that large proportions of a local population tend to leave rather than stay for a battle, returning later once the troops have gone. Israel does not claim to have held these cities, only to have captured them. The most likely conclusion from this is therefore that Israel did indeed destroy those who resisted them (allowing for some hyperbole), but that large portions of the population were neither attacked nor destroyed. Violence is still prevalent in the chapter, but it comes out of a defensive posture adopted by Israel in assisting an ally and then only fighting those who continued to resist. Rahab and Gibeon have already demonstrated a different path, and likely many others followed them so that the claims of this chapter are thus quite narrow in focus. Nevertheless, all this continues to demonstrate that God's promises were being made good to Israel.

Exegesis

10:1–2. The opening line closely matches both 5:1 and 9:1 (see comment on 9:1). But though the two earlier references spoke of "all the kings," this time we are told of a specific king, Adoni-zedek of Jerusalem.[172] The news of Ai's capture and destruction (albeit because it was the same as what had happened at Jericho), along with the peace established with the inhabitants of Gibeon, triggered his response of great fear.[173] Although it was not mentioned in the previous chapter, we now learn that Gibeon

---

[172] Boling, *Joshua*, 278, notes that this is the first time the name Jerusalem occurs in the Bible, though the city has been mentioned previously as Salem in Gen 14:18.

[173] The csb here follows an interpretive reading. The mt has, "They were greatly alarmed," with the subject uncertain. One manuscript, along with Syriac and Vulgate, offer the more expected singular, "He was greatly afraid." But the prevalence of the plural in the textual tradition suggests it is original, and since the king could stand for his people, then understanding it to refer to Adoni-zedek and his people is plausible. The fate of Jericho's king was not mentioned in Joshua 6 but can be implied from the story.

was a large city, compared to a royal city, and that its men were noted as warriors. The comparison to a royal city says nothing directly about whether Gibeon had a king. Rather, it is meant to point to the larger cities whose kings held sway over lesser cities (and their kings) since the Canaanite political model tended to work in a hierarchy of kings.[174] Jerusalem was apparently also a significant center since its king Adoni-zedek was able to summon various kings to serve his purposes, though at this time Jerusalem did not have the significance it would later achieve, which is perhaps why a coalition of kings was needed.[175] Although this will become the first structured resistance to Israel (one anticipated by 9:1–2), his experience of fear is consistent with the earlier representations of the Canaanite communities, reaching back to Rahab (2:9), through the narrative comment of 5:1 and the confession of the Gibeonites in 9:24.

10:3–5. Adoni-zedek's response to Israel was to summon four other kings to bring their forces and help him attack Gibeon. A common feature of treaty relationships of the time was that kings lower in the hierarchy were expected to provide military help to those above them, though kings might also work for mutual benefit without one being greater than the other.

These kings are all described as Amorites, as opposed to the Gibeonites who were Hivites, a factor that could point to divisions among the Canaanite population. However, since "Amorite" can also be a general term for the population west of the Jordan (as in 5:1), care should be taken not to press this point too far. Howard thinks there is ethnic specificity here, though he accepts that strictly the term would apply to residents of the southern hill country, and only Jerusalem and Hebron fit this description.[176]

Hebron at this time lay a little to the west of the modern city of the same name, while the other towns were all in the foothills (the Shephelah). Somewhat confusingly, Debir is the name of the king of Eglon and also the name of a town (captured in 10:38), though in Judges 3 there is also a king called Eglon, while 15:39 also mentions the town of Eglon, situating

---

[174] On balance, preference should probably be given to understanding the Gibeonites as not having a king since comparing the city to a royal city would be unnecessary if it had a king.

[175] See the helpful excursus about Jerusalem in Harstad, *Joshua*, 443–48.

[176] Howard, *Joshua*, 235.

it in the region of Lachish.[177] The striking thing about this alliance is that Adoni-zedek called them to attack Gibeon, not Israel. One might think an attack on Israel would have made more sense. But the assault on Gibeon might have been intended as a lesson to other cities not to ally themselves with Israel while also attempting to control the routes from the central highlands to the coast. This might also be a manifestation of the fear of Israel's God indicated by God's opening speech to Joshua (1:5), a further affirmation of the fact that no one would be able to resist them.[178]

10:6–7. In response to Adoni-zedek, the besieged Gibeonites sent to Joshua and the Israelites in their camp at Gilgal.[179] Their request, that Joshua "not give up" on them, echoes God's word to Joshua in 10:6, while their self-designation as "servants" is consistent with their presentation in chapter 9. Although the terms of the treaty from the previous chapter are never laid out,[180] it now becomes clear that the peace established between them also meant military responsibility toward one another as was normally expected of the superior power in a treaty. Although the Gibeonites were noted as warriors, they were clearly outnumbered and urgently needed Joshua to save them from the alliance of the five Amorite kings.[181] Their plea, "Help us," matches the earlier one of Adoni-zedek to his allies. The request to Joshua thus conforms to the normal political patterns of the age, but it also provides Joshua with an intriguing possibility. Israel had been tricked into swearing not to destroy Gibeon. Might they leave them to be destroyed by the Amorite coalition? They would thus not break their oath (at least, as it is recorded for us) because they would

---

[177] Alternatively, the LXX has Debir as king of Adullam, thus keeping Debir as a personal name and resolving the issue of Eglon, but it is difficult to see how this could have arisen as a copying issue. James Barr, "Mythical Monarch Unmasked? Mysterious Doings of Debir King of Eglon," *JSOT* 48 (1990): 55–68, takes this as a starting point, along with its oddity as a personal name, for denying the existence of Debir as a king. But Richard S. Hess, "Non-Israelite Personal Names in the Book of Joshua," *CBQ* 58 (1996): 205–14 (especially 206–8 for this passage), has shown the reliability of names in the book as a whole, making Barr's proposal less likely.

[178] Firth, *The Message of Joshua*, 121.

[179] This is likely to be the same location mentioned in 9:6 (see comment there) rather than the site by the Jordan mentioned in chapters 4–5.

[180] Baruch Margalit, "The Day the Sun Did Not Stand Still: A New Look at Joshua X 8–15," *VT* 42 (1992): 470, argues that it did not include military cooperation, but this fails to see a gap that had been deliberately left in the previous chapter that is only being filled now.

[181] As Mitchell, *Together in the Land*, 86, notes, their claim that they were being attacked by "all the Amorite kings" exaggerates the threat. But as we shall note (see on vv. 19–20) such hyperbolic language is typical of the chapter.

not themselves have destroyed them, and in the process they would have removed another Canaanite enclave. Whether or not this was considered is not mentioned. Instead, we are simply told that Joshua acted in terms of the treaty and left Gilgal for Gibeon, taking not only all the soldiers but including the best troops. Regardless of how the Gibeonite treaty had been formed, Joshua would honor it.

10:8. God was silent throughout chapter 9, leaving open the issue of whether he approved the Gibeonite treaty. This is his first speech since 8:18, but by evoking themes from earlier in the book it both affirms the agreement with Gibeon and also reassures Joshua that he would grant success against these kings. Telling Joshua not to be afraid of these kings replicates his earlier speech concerning Ai after dealing with Achan (8:1). Stating that they had been given over to Joshua closely resembles the statement about Jericho in 6:2. Assuring Joshua that they would not be able to stand against him echoes 1:5. God's speech thus brings together earlier promises that Joshua knew had been fulfilled to assure him of the certainty of success against these kings. This in turn shows that the agreement with Gibeon was not a sin that would impede Israel's progress, unlike Achan's decision to take from the devoted items (7:1).

10:9–11. Assurance that God was granting victory still required Joshua to advance against the kings, and he did so after a night march from Gilgal that caught them by surprise. However, although Israel participated in the victory through sound military tactics, it was still God who won the battle. This is made clear by the statement of verse 10 that God threw the kings into confusion before Israel.

The Hebrew of verse 10 is actually ambiguous about who then struck the kings and their forces, since the verbs וַיַּכֵּם ("and he struck") and וַיִּרְדְּפֵם could have either God or Joshua as subject. The csb treats God as the subject, whereas the nrsv understands it as Israel who struck them because of God confusing them. That verse 11 assumes the kings and their forces were fleeing before Israel suggests Israel is the subject, but the introduction of God as the subject of the first verb in verse 10 supports the csb. Perhaps a final resolution of this is unnecessary, since both are true—Israel's forces wielded their weapons and also pursued, but it was God who struck and pursued them through Israel.[182]

---

[182] Hence Hall, *Conquering Character*, 166–67, argues that the verbs are probably multivalent, allowing both possibilities.

This combination of human and divine action is made explicit in the comment in verse 42. However, that the victory was God's is made clear by the observation that more died from the hail God had sent than the Israelites killed in battle.[183] The totality of the victory is indicated by the fact that the pursuit of the defeated forces was about eight miles south-west of Gibeon, with Azekah and the probable site for Makkedah both on the Shephelah, at the western end of the Valley of Elah. This was a strategic site since it controlled a point of access between the coastal plain and the highlands. It would later be the site of David's famed confrontation with Goliath (1 Sam 17:1-2) when the Philistines sought to exploit it to attack Saul's nascent kingdom. But for Israel under Joshua, it was a marker of the extent of the victory God had won for them.

10:12-15. At 10:16 the narrative will return to the Amorite kings at Makkedah, but first there is an important pause in order to reflect on the nature of the victory that has been won—and in particular to marvel at how God fought on Israel's behalf. This reflection is achieved by integrating an ancient poem uttered by Joshua and a direct comment by the narrator. The opening "then" (אָז) marks an observation that stands outside the main flow of the narrative apart from noting that it was spoken on the day God gave the victory.[184] However, these verses bristle with interpretive difficulty,[185] starting with the issue of the extent of the poem.

There is at least general agreement that 12b-13a is poetry, and that the statement about the Book of Jashar is a note that is not poetic (13b). But opinion is divided over whether the balance of verse 13 is poetry (e.g., csb) or prose (e.g., esv). The issue is not simply a matter of deciding what text is poetry and what prose, because it is related to the question of what was in the Book of Jashar. If the poem ends at verse 13a, then 12b-13a is the citation of the older source, but if 13c is poetry then it could be the citation from the Book of Jashar, with 12b-13a possibly another

---

[183] Significant hail is a noted meteorological feature for this area; see Pitkänen, *Joshua*, 224 for details.

[184] Margalit, "The Day the Sun Did Not Stand Still," 477-78, seeks to resolve the tensions here on source-critical grounds. However, he does not allow for the possibility that Joshua is citing a preexistent source. This is crucial to seeing how the text works in its current form.

[185] In addition to the matters discussed above, there are also significant variants between the MT and LXX. But with Harstad, *Joshua*, 417, it seems best to regard the MT as superior as the shorter text. For a defense of the priority of the LXX, see Boling, *Joshua*, 274-76.

ancient poem but not one from the Book of Jashar. Howard notes that the term used to introduce the reference to the Book of Jashar also occurs to provide references to the state annals in 1–2 Kings, and since no one supposes that we have a direct citation there, he wonders whether we have one here.[186] But the use of poetry here is distinctive, especially as the other reference to the Book of Jashar also includes a poem (2 Sam 1:17–27), and this makes it more likely that we have a citation here. Since 12b–13a makes clear use of parallelism, it can be recognized as poetry. In addition, the verb from the first line of 12b is elided in the second line, another typical poetic feature. Furthermore, the staccato beat of 13a is also clearly poetic, with the chiastic interchange between sun and moon and the two different verbs for standing still, followed by the note that this continued until the nation avenged itself on its enemies. By contrast, 13c is not strongly marked with poetic features, focusing only on the sun stopping and using the verb previously employed for the moon. As such, it seems best to understand the citation from the Book of Jashar (v. 13b) as referring to verses 12b–13a, so that the note about the book thus follows the quote before additional comment on its significance is provided in verses 13c–15.

If Joshua spoke this to God, we then have the additional problem that he did not address God in the poem. Rather, the sun and the moon are directly addressed. This problem has been resolved in a number of ways. The least satisfactory is to assume that we have a range of traditions that have been brought together in a way that is not resolved.[187] Although the Valley of Aijalon has not been mentioned previously, it should not be taken as a sign of confusion.

An alternative is to see a shift in the identity of the speaker in verse 12, so that we have an initial utterance by Joshua on the day of the victory, but without any speech reported, so that it is God who speaks in the presence of Israel.[188] Grammatically, this is not impossible, but it is awkward, and we would more commonly consider the subject of the first verb to continue into the second rather than its indirect object becoming the subject of the next. In any case, it was spoken "in the presence of Israel," which would be odd if God was the speaker.[189] It is not likely that this

---

[186] Howard, *Joshua*, 240.

[187] E.g., Nelson, *Joshua*, 142.

[188] E.g., Howard, *Joshua*, 240.

[189] Hall, *Conquering Character*, 173.

option would be considered if it were not believed that God is one who can properly speak to the sun and moon.

A simpler solution may be at hand, which is to assume that the old poem existed before Joshua, and he therefore recited it to God. In the poem, sun and moon are addressed, but by quoting it to God, it effectively becomes a request to God to enable these things to happen. Evidence for this can be seen in the reference to the Valley of Aijalon in the poem, somewhere not mentioned previously in the chapter (though its mention here is important for understanding the meaning of the citation in context). The connection to Gibeon makes this an appropriate text to recite. Whatever the poem originally meant is difficult to say with any certainty, because we seem only to have a fragment of it and its meaning here is shaped by Joshua's use of it, though it could refer to another victory in the region (not necessarily Israelite[190]). This does not mean that the Book of Jashar already existed because the poem could subsequently have been placed in that collection, and indeed the inclusion of the poem from 2 Sam 1:17–27 would indicate that the book was collected after the time of David. But if the book is a collection of old poems (and this is only a postulation based on limited information), then the inclusion of poems from various sources into it is certainly possible.

None of this addresses the question of what the poem, and its explanation, means, but it does prepare us to determine this. Given the range of options, brevity is important, so only the figurative interpretation will be argued—the positive evidence for which serves to refute the alternative views.[191] A key fact to note is that the Valley of Aijalon is west of Gibeon, so the poem assumes the sun is in the east and the moon in the west—that is, it must be morning. Joshua's citation of this poetic fragment would suggest this is the time of his recitation of it as well. Views that argue for an extension of the day miss the fact that at this point Joshua had no knowledge of any need for the day to be lengthened. Although the verb דמם (csb, "stop") used for the sun can have a range of meanings (including "be silent" or "cease"), its use in parallel with עמד (and it is this verb that v. 14 affirms happened), which means "to stand," indicates a similar meaning should be applied here. But עמד can also mean "take

---

[190] Both sun and moon were commonly regarded as deities, so if the poem is pre-Israelite it could well have been an invocation of some sort. But Joshua's use of it here means that such views are subverted as Yahweh is seen to take on all aspects of deity.

[191] Howard, *Joshua*, 241–45, helpfully summarizes the options.

one's stand" or "take position" (e.g., Num 22:24, 26) and thus mean "prepare for battle." Such a meaning is appropriate here, because the citation comes at a point when Joshua was preparing for battle. Other passages in the Old Testament refer to cosmic forces participating in battles (e.g., Hab 3:11, another ancient poem and one that seems to know this text) but use such language figuratively. If this is correct, then the text would seem to describe Joshua citing to Yahweh an old poem about a victory in the region of Gibeon, effectively making it a prayer that cosmic forces fight for Israel until they avenge themselves on their enemies.

The reference to the Book of Jashar in verse 13b closes this off, and 13c then reports that cosmic forces did indeed participate in the victory, though it notably refrains from any mention of Israel avenging themselves on their enemies. Although the csb translates the last part of this victory report by saying the sun "delayed its setting almost a full day," it is probably better to translate this as it "did not hasten to set about a whole day." This is more consistent with the regular use of the verb אוץ as meaning "to hasten" (e.g., Prov 19:2) and would mean that nothing caused premature darkness, even though there was clearly a storm (note the hailstone in v. 11), which one might otherwise have expected to reduce the light earlier. It is important to stress that it is not impossible for God to have delayed sunset if he wished.[192] However, in light of the points noted above, it seems more likely that the text is claiming that God brought cosmic forces into the battle but not making a claim about some variant to the length of any day.

One important additional point: Although Joshua's citation of the poem assumed that Israel would avenge themselves on their enemies (with God's help), this is the part of his request that was not granted. Rather, the victory was God's. God did indeed listen to his request, and was truly unique in the attention he gave to it. But the text is clear that it was God who defeated this coalition of kings because he fought for Israel. Joshua's prayer was audacious, and God honored its intent—indeed, he is said to have obeyed Joshua. Such a response to a human voice is not unique, as there are four other times when God responded like this (Gen 30:6, Num 21:3, Judg 13:9, 1 Kgs 17:22), though the text stresses the

---

[192] For a carefully argued example of this view, see Harstad, *Joshua*, 417–24. However, this interpretation means that we do not need more naturalistic solutions (such as an eclipse). Though for this view, see Jan Heller, "Die schweigende Sonne," *Communio Viatorum* 9 (1966): 73–78.

uniqueness of this event, perhaps because of its miraculous nature.[193] But just as Joshua had to work out what obedience meant, so also God ensured that even when he obeyed a human, he did so on his terms, so that he was the one who won the battle. God obeyed Joshua, but only in a way that demonstrated his free choice. God was not under compulsion.

Finally, note that verse 15 fits awkwardly into the context if we understand the events of the chapter to have been reported entirely in chronological sequence—indeed, its content is repeated in verse 43. Given that Joshua was in the region of Makkedah, it would be odd for him to return to Gilgal only for him to return to Makkedah in verse 16. This could be a textual error since it does not occur in the LXX. However, the LXX lacks verse 43, so this evidence needs to be used carefully since one could well imagine a translator (or the editor of the source text) deciding to omit both because of their difficulty. Perhaps slightly more probable is that this statement anticipates the end of the chapter, preparing readers for the fact that although a number of subsequent victories will be described, they all need to be seen in the same framework as verses 12–14. It is God who won these victories, even if Joshua was involved.[194] Taken this way, it also prepares us for the possibility that other parts of the chapter will be presented with overlapping chronology.

10:16–21. Having paused to marvel at how God had fought for Israel, the narrative returns to Makkedah, the point to which the Canaanite coalition had been pursued in verse 10, resuming the battle report that was left aside at verse 11. The focus here is on the kings, a typical feature of the book, which reaches its climax in the list of defeated kings in chapter 12. The kings had hidden themselves in a cave at Makkedah. Since it is always "the cave," it was apparently a well-known location even if it cannot be identified now. The kings were evidently not good at hiding since their whereabouts were reported to Joshua.[195]

---

[193] Cf. Hall, *Conquering Character*, 174–75.

[194] Although he is more concerned to trace the chapter's development, Peter Weimar, "Die Jahwekriegserzälungen in Exodus 14, Josua 10, Richter 1 und 1 Samuel 7," *Biblica* 57 (1976): 51, regards these verses as old structural brackets. Weimar's proposed development of the text is too complex to be persuasive, but his suggestion that it has its origin in the time of David (pp. 61–62) may well be right, though Butler, *Joshua 1-12*, 467, prefers the time of Solomon.

[195] K. Lawson Younger Jr., *Ancient Conquest Accounts: A Study in Ancient Near Eastern and Biblical History Writing* (Sheffield: JSOT Press, 1990), 220–22, notes that this is a stereotypical element in these accounts, though this does not require Rösel's conclusion (*Joshua*, 163) that it is therefore not historical since the frequency of the motif reflects the suitability of

Since the Canaanite forces were not yet fully defeated, Joshua chose not to be distracted by the kings, ordering simply that the entrance to the cave be blocked with large stones and that some men be appointed to guard them (v. 18). He then ordered the troops to continue the pursuit of their enemies (v. 19). When ordering continued attack, he used the unusual verb זנב (csb "attack them from behind"). The verb occurs elsewhere only in Deut 25:18, describing how Amalek had attacked Israel. The related noun refers to an animal's tail (e.g., Exod 4:4), and use of the verb may allude to that here. It would appear to be a technical term for continuing an attack on a retreating enemy, pressing home an advantage. What mattered most was that Israel was not to allow them to enter their cities because God had already granted the Israelites victory, though this did not mean they would not have to fight. It is notable that in verses 28–43 the focus is on the cities that Israel would capture rather than the countryside, perhaps because cities were associated with the model of Canaanite royal power that Israel was rejecting.

Joshua and all Israel inflicted a terrible slaughter on these Canaanite forces until they were destroyed (v. 20a). The language appears to indicate there were no survivors, except we are told that the survivors fled to fortified cities (v. 20b). Although the csb has "a few survivors" this is interpretative, and we might better render הַשְּׂרִידִים as "the remnant" (so esv), a number that is unspecified. The number might well be few, and a remnant is always a portion of a larger unit, but its use here is partly determined by the use of the cognate verb שׂרד ("to flee"). In any case, an obvious contrast exists between the declaration that Joshua and Israel had completely destroyed them (תמם) and the presence of this remnant that fled to fortified sites. Although some feel this is a contradiction introduced because there are continued battles in the rest of the chapter,[196] a more likely reading is that the narrator recognizes the language of complete destruction as an example of hyperbole. In particular, it is an idiom that describes a major victory in terms of total destruction, meaning there was a comprehensive win and not necessarily that all were destroyed.

---

caves for hiding. The more important parallel is that the folly of defeated kings thinking they could hide is effectively mocked.

[196] E.g., Rösel, *Joshua*, 173.

Lawson Younger has demonstrated that the use of such language was standard practice in the ancient Near East, and that this can also be seen in Joshua 9–12.[197] In other words, it is not simply the case that ancient texts routinely used such hyperbole, but that the biblical text does so and that those brought up on it would be familiar with this literary convention. That this chapter employs hyperbole can be seen in verse 29, which refers to "all Israel" when it is clear in context that what is meant (at most) is the whole fighting force. The literary convention does not require this to be explained (otherwise, it would not be a convention), but modern readers who are unaware of it will often literalize an idiom.

A (somewhat trivial) modern analogy might be drawn from the way fans describe the result of a football match where one side has won fairly comprehensively, claiming, "We completely destroyed them." Hearers familiar with the convention know that, if taken in a literalistic manner, the statement is actually false. First, the use of "we" claims a status that exceeds reality. The speaker was not part of the team that won, but through the idiom he identifies with them. Second, the same team that lost one week can come back and play another game the next week. They have not been completely destroyed. The nature of the idiom is such that no one familiar with the convention needs this to be explained. But someone from another culture and language group may well find this language problematic, because they are unable to recognize that the idiom fits into a literary convention.

There is therefore no need to see any contradiction between the two halves of verse 20.[198] Rather, we see here the clearest indicator in Joshua of the fact that, in describing Israel's victories in the land, a literary convention has been employed. This fact in turn can guide us as we read the remaining battle reports in this chapter, and further explains the fact that although Joshua will be said to have completely destroyed various cities, some of them clearly remain later in the book (e.g., compare 10:37 with 14:12–13, where Caleb sees Hebron as an occupied city needing to be captured). Having followed Joshua's order, the people were then able to return to Joshua at the camp at Makkedah, secure from any threat.

---

[197] Younger, *Ancient Conquest Accounts*. For the material in Joshua, see 197–237. See also Paul Copan and Matthew Flanagan, *Did God Really Command Genocide? Coming to Terms with the Justice of God* (Grand Rapids: Baker Academic, 2014), 84–93.

[198] Indeed, once this feature is recognized, then the variations between the city lists here and Judges 1 can largely be resolved.

Israel's victory was complete, but there are survivors, a problem that will need to be addressed in verses 28-43.

10:22-25. With everyone back at Makkedah, Joshua could then address the problem of the five kings who had been captured. As the kings are brought out of the cave, they are listed in the same order as verse 3, except this time only in terms of their city rather than including their names. Joshua summoned the leaders of the military who had gone with him to place their feet on the necks of these kings. This is clearly a sign of the totality of Israel's victory, perhaps providing a concrete example of language that elsewhere is metaphoric in the Old Testament, though the idea of kings being prostrated before their captors is widespread in the ancient Near East. For example, the prayer in Psalm 72:9 asks that the king's enemies "lick the dust." Within the psalm, it is one of several images reflecting the reign of Israel's king over the nations, but here these five kings were physically placed in this position, pointing to the reality of their defeat.

For Joshua, there is a more immediate lesson that he wanted his leaders to recognize. The defeat of these kings provided further evidence that God would continue to defeat Israel's enemies. This reassurance was apparently needed: when they had placed their feet on the kings' necks, Joshua told them not to be afraid or discouraged but to be strong and courageous. Although they are in the reverse order, his words to the leaders echo God's words to him in 1:6, 9. In making these kings an object lesson for the leaders, Joshua was also able to share elements of his leadership role, encouraging them to see God at work just as God had encouraged him. As God had defeated these kings, so he would continue to act as Israel encountered other enemies.

10:26-27. With the reassurance of future victories given, Joshua proceeded to execute the kings and to hang their bodies on five stakes (see CSB note), leaving them there until evening. The punishment and removal of the bodies from the stakes in the evening clearly alludes to Deuteronomy 21:22-23. If so, Joshua had judged the kings to be guilty of a crime that merited the death penalty. The law stipulates that anyone guilty of a capital crime whose body was placed on a stake must be brought down and not left overnight but rather buried, because anyone hung on a tree is under God's curse. Moreover, failing to bury the body would defile the land. The execution of the kings was not therefore an application of the ban but rather a judicial decision against them, presumably because of the nature of their attack against Israel. It should be noted that the law in Deuteronomy does not legislate for the punishment of exposing the bodies of the executed but rather seeks to put a limit on an existing practice, ensuring that even those guilty of capital offenses were respected in their death. In burying the bodies of the kings in the cave where they were found, Joshua was thus scrupulous in following the law and respecting the bodies of Israel's enemies, following the same practice he had in dealing with the king of Ai in 8:29. There, the cairn constructed from the stones was the king's tomb, whereas here the stones were placed at the entrance of the cave. In both cases, the narrator notes that the stones were present at the time of writing. Moreover, reference to the sunset brings to a close the day, and especially the special place of the sun (10:12–15).

10:28. After the kings' execution, we follow Joshua on a journey from the area around Jerusalem down to the far south at Hebron.[199] This journey was a continuation of the battles initiated in 10:1–5 with a focus on those cities. Note that the cities of three of the five kings will have to be taken. Only Jerusalem (whose continued resistance will be noted in 15:63) and Jarmuth are not included in the battle reports here, though both would have been weakened through the death of their king. Jerusalem would not be captured until the time of David (2 Sam 5:7–8); Jarmuth is noted as belonging to Judah in 15:35. Another Jarmuth is mentioned in 21:29, but it is located in Issachar and, thus, too far north for this site. The narrative through to the end of verse 39 follows a logical route into the south, commencing at Makkedah in the Shephelah (csb usually renders this "foothills" but it is more likely a proper noun), where the pursuit of the southern coalition of Canaanite kingdoms had ended.

Much is summarized here. Clearly the concern of this report (and those through to v. 39) is not to provide the sort of detail that has been given so far, but rather to sketch quickly the process by which the southern highlands came under Israel's control. There is no battle report—just the outcome, which is that Makkedah was captured, its king executed, and the city and its inhabitants put under the ban. All this apparently happened on the same day as the pursuit, though "on that day" can be less specific and simply mean "at that time." Certain key elements emerge

---

[199] For a brief summary of the archaeology of each site, see David Merling Sr., *The Book of Joshua: Its Theme and Role in Archaeological Discussions* (Berrien Springs, MI: Andrews University Press, 1997), 123–38.

that recur in the next five reports,[200] though there are small variations between the six cities listed.

Note that, importantly, Joshua destroyed the city, its king, and its inhabitants—not the region. This suggests that it was the cities as fortified areas and royal centers—rendering Israel's occupation of the land insecure—that were of particular importance. Israel was not to model itself on Canaanite practice and thus to find their own security in cities. That they did not destroy the villages indicates this was most likely the goal, since only the city was fortified. So, destruction of the cities represented both a defensive military goal—preventing attacks from within territory Israel controlled—and a positive theological goal of encouraging Israel not to depend on fortifications. The leaving of no survivors was therefore limited to the city itself and, thus, to the combatants who continued to resist Israel. In practice, most non-combatants would have fled before Israel arrived, so those killed were those who actively resisted Israel. The policy of treating the kings on the model of Jericho is repeated in the remaining towns where the king still survived, indicating that the king was the one specifically under the ban and revealing God's opposition to the power model that dominated Canaan.[201]

10:29–30. From Makkedah, Joshua and Israel went to Libnah. Again, its exact location is uncertain, but its listing in Judah's allocation (15:42) indicates a site on the Shephelah somewhere south of Makkedah, probably toward the next site, Lachish. This Libnah is to be distinguished from the place mentioned in Num 33:20–21, which is somewhere in the wilderness. It would also be allocated to the Levites (Josh 21:13). The report here is brief, noting only that God handed Libnah over to Israel, they left no survivors in the city, and the king was placed under the ban.

10:31–33. From Libnah, Joshua crossed over to Lachish, where the Shephelah meets the coastal plain about thirty miles southwest of Jerusalem. It would later be a major city. Although at the time of Joshua it was not massively fortified, he was apparently required to besiege it. In the Late Bronze Age, a destruction layer is evident that some have associated with Joshua, but since the text does not claim Joshua destroyed

---

[200] Note the tabulation of linguistic parallels in Robert David, "Jos 10:28–39, témoin d'une conquête de la Palestine par le sud," *Science et Esprit* 42 (1990), 212–14; and the list of standard elements in Hall, *Conquering Character*, 179–80.

[201] Cf. Jerome F. D. Creach, *Violence in Scripture* (Louisville: Westminster John Knox, 2013), 123–24.

the city there is no reason to look for a destruction layer.[202] Regardless of the city's fortifications, it was captured quickly, falling on the second day.

Again, there is no claim of Israelite military prowess. Rather, Lachish too was given into Israel's control by God. The city was attacked and no survivors left, following the pattern of Libnah. Since Lachish's king had been executed at Makkedah, he is not mentioned. Lachish received assistance from another Canaanite king, Horam from Gezer, which is north of Makkedah. This would suggest that Horam had pursued Israel, catching them at Lachish because of the small delay in capturing the city; however, it is also possible that the two battles are brought together here because of their shared focus on Lachish and that they were actually separated in time. Either way, Horam may have owed fealty to Lachish since he came to its aid. Once again a Canaanite king was defeated in battle with no survivors.

10:34–35. From Lachish, Joshua passed over to Eglon, another uncertain site. Its inclusion in Judah's cities (15:39) indicates that it too was in the Shephelah, perhaps in the region of Lachish. Its king, Debir, was among those executed at Makkedah (10:22–27). As with Lachish, the city was besieged but fell the same day. Eglon was placed under the ban, apparently following the pattern of Lachish (though this is not mentioned in its account), and again there were no survivors in the city.

10:36–37. From Eglon, Joshua went back inland to Hebron. Since this involved a return to the highlands, there is a change in the verb that has introduced each movement. Rather than crossing over (עבר), Joshua "went up" (עלה) to Hebron, a prominent site throughout biblical history. It is generally identified with Tel-Hebron, a site about eighteen miles south of Jerusalem.

Once Israel captured the city, its king too was executed. Yet, contrary to his dealings with the other cities, Joshua not only placed Hebron under the ban and left no survivors in the city itself, but he also followed this policy for its "villages" (csb). However, עיר is not the usual term for a village and is more commonly rendered "city." In general, it means a walled center (i.e., a defensible site). Therefore, rather than a determination to destroy villages, Joshua's change of policy here (and at Debir) appears to be consistent with the regular goal of not permitting defensible sites to remain.

---

[202] Cf. Hawkins, *How Israel Became a People*, 31.

Placing the city under the ban cannot, however, have meant leaving it totally destroyed, because less than five years later it would be assigned to Joshua and was by then already a city that needed to be captured (14:6–14). Although placing a city under the ban (חרם) meant it was given to God, in the case of Hebron this cannot have made it uninhabitable. Again, the language needs to be read carefully as a claim of a comprehensive victory granted by God rather than a statement of destruction. Since Hebron's defeat is patterned on that of Eglon, and Eglon's on Lachish, then the same must be true of these sites too. No king is mentioned because Hebron's king was one of the five executed at Makkedah.

10:38–39. From Hebron, Joshua "turned" (שׁוב) to head to Debir. An exact identification of the site is somewhat problematic because a Debir is mentioned in both 15:7 and 15:49 as part of Judah's allotment, and it is not clear that these two sites are the same. Another Debir is listed in 13:26 as part of Gad's land in Gilead,[203] showing that this was a common toponym. The Debir mentioned in 15:49 was previously called Kiriath-sannah, while 15:15 (cf. Judg 1:11) says Debir was formerly called Kiriath-sepher. The site mentioned in 15:15 (also Judg 1:11) is also in the vicinity of Hebron, making it likely that it is the same site mentioned here. If so, then the site in 15:49 may be another town in the hill country. Although several sites have been proposed, conclusive evidence in favor of them is lacking, and the best we can do is suggest that the Debir mentioned here is to the south of Hebron. Of places bearing this name the most likely match is that of 15:7, but its distance from the Valley of Achor means this can only be tentative.

Again, the report of Joshua's activities is kept to the bare minimum, noting that he captured the city and its king along with its "villages" (csb; but see note on v. 37 above). Once again, the city and the other defensible sites were placed under the ban along with those in them, with no one permitted to flee. As noted above, this most likely refers only to the combatants who actively resisted Israel. The destruction of the town and its fortified sites means that Hebron is the appropriate point of comparison for Debir. However, the absence of a king at Hebron makes this comparison only partially valid, so the execution of the king can be compared to Libnah, the last site that had a living king when attacked by Joshua.

---

[203] The csb note indicates the possibility that this should be Lo Debar, a conjecture based on a variant found in the lxx.

As with Hebron, whatever is meant by placing the city under the ban, it was not destroyed and made uninhabitable or even indefensible, since in 15:15–19 it still needed to be captured by Othniel. Rather, the emphasis seems to be that, in giving these sites over to God, Israel was to learn not to find their security in fortifications.

10:40–43. These verses now summarize the chapter as a whole, though with a particular emphasis on verses 28–39 with their record of the locations captured by Israel. As noted above (see on 10:19–20), the language in the preceding verses followed a stock idiom in which hyperbolic terms are used to describe a comprehensive victory, and we therefore need to read the concluding summary in the same light. Indeed, the claim that Joshua conquered the whole "land" (אֶרֶץ) is an example of this, and it is properly translated by CSB as "region."

The particular areas of the land captured are then listed as the hill country (which can mean only the southern hill country, since nowhere north has yet been taken), the Negev (the wilderness to the south of the territory that would be assigned to Judah), the Shephelah (foothills), and slopes (perhaps the area running down to the Dead Sea). Of course, when we trace Joshua's route on a map to the extent that it is possible, it is clear that only a relatively small part of this territory had been captured. Since we later read of the need to occupy the same sites, it cannot mean that these sites were controlled and occupied by Israel. Rather, the claim here is in fact more limited (as will be confirmed in 13:1–7), which is that Israel had won comprehensive victories at these sites. This in turn prepares us for the wider claim in verse 42 of victories across the south, from Kadesh-barnea in the Negev to Gaza near the coast, though this could be traced back to the north as far as Gibeon, the site from which the battles in the chapter began. The Goshen mentioned here is not the region where Israel had lived in Egypt (Gen 45:10) but a region in the south near a town of the same name (Josh 15:51). These four points thus serve as boundary markers for the territory actually captured.[204] By this point, therefore, Israel had won victories across the south, including some not noted here, but this is not the same as claiming all this territory was under their control. However, Joshua did have a consistently applied policy (seen across the

---

[204] See T. A. Clarke, "Complete v. Incomplete Conquest: A Re-examination of Three Passages in Joshua," *TynBul* 61 (2010): 91–96.

accounts of vv. 28–39) of executing the kings of the region and placing all who lived in the cities under the ban.

Such actions simultaneously opposed the political model of the Canaanite cities and indicated a refusal to develop trust in their fortifications. Placing them under the ban meant learning to trust God for security, not the outward symbols in which the Canaanite population put their trust. This was what God commanded (Deut 7:1–5), and it was required so that all could see that Israel belonged to God. Not trusting in kings or fortifications was contrary to normal practice in the ancient world. And just as Joshua did what God had commanded, so also God fulfilled his promise to Joshua (1:3–5), giving the southern territory to him in a single campaign.[205] Joshua then returned to Gilgal (where the Israelites were in 10:7), repeating the information of verse 15.[206] The return to Gilgal means that the sites defeated are neither occupied nor possessed, which prepares for the statement in 13:1–7.

Bridge

Because of this chapter's use of idioms rooted in ancient culture, we need to read it carefully today. Moreover, the themes are important for contemporary reflection and integration into the life of the church. But just as the chapter requires careful reading, so we must also take care in understanding its significance today.

The chapter begins with Israel in an ambiguous position, having made a covenant with Gibeon, one of the Canaanite peoples with whom they were not to covenant. At this point, the narrator has deliberately withheld information about why the Gibeonites acted as they did, as this will only be revealed in 11:19–20, which summarizes events and provides a framework for understanding chapters 1–12. Preachers working through this text sequentially should be aware of this, though they should probably defer direct mention of it until they reach chapter 11. Doing so respects the text's withholding of interpretative information until a later point and forces readers to wrestle more closely with the details. Moreover, only then do we recognize the challenge that the attack by the southern

---

[205] Admittedly, time has been telescoped in vv. 28–39, because no time is allotted to the journey between each city, nor to the process of completing its destruction where reported, but that does not change the fact that this could be achieved in a single campaign.

[206] As with v. 15, this verse is missing in the LXX, but here it is more likely original since it provides an inclusio with the earlier reference to Gilgal.

kings provided for Israel. Would they see it as a convenient means of avoiding a covenant they should not have made with Gibeon, or would they honor the covenant?

The Old Testament knows how easy it is to play this sort of game. We need only note the ways in which Israel sought to avoid the implications of vows it made to remedy a problem of its own making in Judges 21. No doubt things like this led Qoheleth to warn against making hasty vows (Eccl 5:4–6). The temptation for Israel was acute, because up to that point there was no indication that God approved of their covenant with Gibeon. But Israel kept its promise, and in response God demonstrated his commitment to Israel. At this point we do not know *why* God accepted this arrangement. Yet not only did he do so, but he also fought for Israel in a manner without parallel in the Old Testament in response to Joshua's prayer. Indeed, a constant theme of the chapter is that God is faithful to Israel as they are faithful both to their promise to the Gibeonites and to God's commands. Nevertheless, Israel knew none of this when the chapter began. Instead, we have a report of the process by which they discovered the faithfulness of God as they too were faithful.

Scripture is generally clear that promises made should be kept. Psalm 15:4 recognizes that those who keep their word no matter the cost are approved by God. Jesus said that Christians should lead lives of such transparent honesty that there should be no need for an oath (Matt 5:33–37). But what of promises that should not be made to begin with? Are we required to keep them? When Jephthah vowed to sacrifice whatever came out to greet him if God granted him victory over the Ammonites (Judg 11:30–31), should he have sacrificed his daughter, given the prohibition on human sacrifice in the Old Testament? That text makes no direct comment on the issue, leaving readers to wrestle with the question, though Proverbs 20:25 seems to indicate that rash vows could be reconsidered. Certainly, Numbers 30 recognizes that some rash vows might be overruled by those who are more mature. We need to bear all of this in mind when assessing Israel's position. Perhaps the general perspective is that a promise should be fulfilled without clear evidence from God that it should not be. God's fighting for Israel in so spectacular a way in Joshua 10 is a clear affirmation of the validity of the promise. God thus continues to show himself as the promise-keeping God even as Israel's attempts to live out its covenant life raise questions about whether it can continue to receive those promises.

Alongside this, we should also note the emphasis in the battle reports that Israel was to execute the Canaanite kings and destroy the fortified sites. Such a policy would seem almost counterintuitive to many. On the one hand, kingship was an accepted norm of the ancient world, and even Israel would eventually request a king (1 Sam 8:1–5), something the Torah, on which Joshua was to meditate, permitted (Deut 17:14–20). On the other hand, the insecurity of unfortified dwellings was well known. Together, their removal meant Israel had neither centralized government for each region nor the defenses to protect them. However, Joshua's words of encouragement to the leaders (Josh 10:25) provide the key to understanding this. Israel was not to secure its future along the Canaanite pattern—nor indeed on the standard patterns of the ancient Near East. Rather, they were to trust in God to overcome their enemies. This was not a blank check Israel could cash at any time, because it assumed Israel was living as God intended. Nevertheless, it was a key pattern for them. Security was found in God alone.

This pattern recurs at numerous points in the Bible. Psalms 146–147 reject trust in human leadership, insisting instead that God "values those who fear him" (Ps 147:11). Such a counterintuitive notion informs the Beatitudes (Matt 5:3–10) and Jesus' resistance to the use of violence (Matt 5:38–48). Since the church today is not tied to any particular location—the land promise being specific to Israel's place in God's purposes—we recognize that we too are called to trust in God's promises alone and not the forms of security (such as wealth) that our society typically values. Our security is not defined by visible patterns but by the presence of the invisible God. For an Israel that always knew itself to be a weak, minor power, this was good news. And it continues to be good news today.

F. The Campaign in the North and Summary List of Kings (11:1–12:24)

11 ¹When King Jabin of Hazor heard this news, he sent a message to: King Jobab of Madon, the kings of Shimron and Achshaph, ² and the kings of the north in the hill country, the Arabah south of Chinnereth, the Judean foothills, and the Slopes of Dor to the west, ³ the Canaanites in the east and west, the Amorites, Hethites, Perizzites, and Jebusites in the hill country, and the Hivites at the foot of Hermon in the land of Mizpah. ⁴ They went out with all their armies—a multitude as numerous as the sand on the seashore—along with a vast number of horses and

chariots. [5] All these kings joined forces; they came and camped together at the Waters of Merom to attack Israel.

[6] The Lord said to Joshua, "Do not be afraid of them, for at this time tomorrow I will cause all of them to be killed before Israel. You are to hamstring their horses and burn their chariots." [7] So Joshua and all his troops surprised them at the Waters of Merom and attacked them. [8] The Lord handed them over to Israel, and they struck them down, pursuing them as far as greater Sidon and Misrephoth-maim, and to the east as far as the Valley of Mizpeh. They struck them down, leaving no survivors. [9] Joshua treated them as the Lord had told him; he hamstrung their horses and burned their chariots.

[10] At that time Joshua turned back, captured Hazor, and struck down its king with the sword, because Hazor had formerly been the leader of all these kingdoms. [11] They struck down everyone in it with the sword, completely destroying them; he left no one alive. Then he burned Hazor.

[12] Joshua captured all these kings and their cities and struck them down with the sword. He completely destroyed them, as Moses the Lord's servant had commanded. [13] However, Israel did not burn any of the cities that stood on their mounds except Hazor, which Joshua burned. [14] The Israelites plundered all the spoils and cattle of these cities for themselves. But they struck down every person with the sword until they had annihilated them, leaving no one alive. [15] Just as the Lord had commanded his servant Moses, Moses commanded Joshua. That is what Joshua did, leaving nothing undone of all that the Lord had commanded Moses.

[16] So Joshua took all this land—the hill country, all the Negev, all the land of Goshen, the foothills, the Arabah, and the hill country of Israel with its foothills— [17] from Mount Halak, which ascends to Seir, as far as Baal-gad in the Valley of Lebanon at the foot of Mount Hermon. He captured all their kings and struck them down, putting them to death. [18] Joshua waged war with all these kings for a long time. [19] No city made peace with the Israelites except the Hivites who inhabited Gibeon; all of them were taken in battle. [20] For it was the Lord's intention to harden their hearts, so that they would engage Israel in battle, be completely destroyed without mercy, and be annihilated, just as the Lord had commanded Moses.

[21] At that time Joshua proceeded to exterminate the Anakim from the hill country—Hebron, Debir, Anab—all the hill country of Judah and of Israel. Joshua completely destroyed them with their cities. [22] No Anakim were left in the land of the Israelites, except for some remaining in Gaza, Gath, and Ashdod.

[23] So Joshua took the entire land, in keeping with all that the Lord had told Moses. Joshua then gave it as an inheritance to Israel according to their tribal allotments. After this, the land had rest from war.

12 ¹ The Israelites struck down the following kings of the land and took possession of their land beyond the Jordan to the east and from the Arnon River to Mount Hermon, including all the Arabah eastward:

² King Sihon of the Amorites lived in Heshbon. He ruled from Aroer on the rim of the Arnon River, along the middle of the valley, and half of Gilead up to the Jabbok River (the border of the Ammonites), ³ the Arabah east of the Sea of Chinnereth to the Sea of Arabah (that is, the Dead Sea), eastward through Beth-jeshimoth and southward below the slopes of Pisgah.

⁴ King Og of Bashan, of the remnant of the Rephaim, lived in Ashtaroth and Edrei. ⁵ He ruled over Mount Hermon, Salecah, all Bashan up to the Geshurite and Maacathite border, and half of Gilead to the border of King Sihon of Heshbon. ⁶ Moses the LORD's servant and the Israelites struck them down. And Moses the LORD's servant gave their land as an inheritance to the Reubenites, Gadites, and half the tribe of Manasseh.

⁷ Joshua and the Israelites struck down the following kings of the land beyond the Jordan to the west, from Baal-gad in the Valley of Lebanon to Mount Halak, which ascends toward Seir (Joshua gave their land as an inheritance to the tribes of Israel according to their allotments: ⁸ the hill country, the Judean foothills, the Arabah, the slopes, the wilderness, and the Negev—the lands of the Hethites, Amorites, Canaanites, Perizzites, Hivites, and Jebusites):

⁹ the king of Jericho	one
the king of Ai, which is next to Bethel	one
¹⁰ the king of Jerusalem	one
the king of Hebron	one
¹¹ the king of Jarmuth	one
the king of Lachish	one
¹² the king of Eglon	one
the king of Gezer	one
¹³ the king of Debir	one
the king of Geder	one
¹⁴ the king of Hormah	one
the king of Arad	one
¹⁵ the king of Libnah	one
the king of Adullam	one
¹⁶ the king of Makkedah	one
the king of Bethel	one
¹⁷ the king of Tappuah	one
the king of Hepher	one
¹⁸ the king of Aphek	one
the king of Lasharon	one
¹⁹ the king of Madon	one
the king of Hazor	one
²⁰ the king of Shimron-meron	one

the king of Achshaph	one
21 the king of Taanach	one
the king of Megiddo	one
22 the king of Kedesh	one
the king of Jokneam in Carmel	one
23 the king of Dor in Naphath-dor	one
the king of Goiim in Gilgal	one
24 the king of Tirzah	one
the total number of all kings:	thirty-one.

Context

Following the campaign in the far south, the narrative now moves to the far north, from the borders of the Negev in the south to the region above the Sea of Galilee (here called Chinnereth) in the north. Although this represents a journey of more than one hundred miles, the narrative is not concerned to detail events in between. Accordingly, we are given no indication of events in the central highlands and how Israel came to the north. At no point in the book does Israel enter the coastal plain. Perhaps more than anything else, these omissions (which would have been immediately apparent to ancient readers) make clear that the book offers only a summary of key events in Israel's entry into the land. It is not a comprehensive history because its key theological themes of God's faithfulness and human obedience do not require this.[207] In addition, this prepares for the declaration in 13:1 that "a great deal of the land remains to be possessed." As we will note, possession requires more than simply defeating the current inhabitants even if this is a necessary prerequisite.

Although the narrative has moved to the north, it is immediately apparent that chapters 10 and 11 closely parallel each other,[208] demonstrating the similarities in how these regions were first captured. We can observe this in the close structural similarities between them so that these chapters form a diptych, each panel highlighting particular elements about the capture of the land. Setting out the key parallels in tabular form helps highlight this:

---

[207] See further §1 ("Faithfulness and Obedience"), §4 ("Land as God's Gift"), and §8 ("The Promise of God").

[208] Nelson, *Joshua*, 151, calls chapter 11 a "literary mirror" of chapter 10, though of course this point is not to be pushed such that we ignore the crucial differences between them. On points of escalation in chapter 11, see Hall, *Conquering Character*, 185.

southern alliance (10:1–5)	northern alliance (11:1–5)
divine reassurance (10:8)	divine reassurance (11:6)
victory employing surprise (10:9–11)	victory employing surprise (11:7–9)
execution of kings / destruction of cities (10:16–39)	execution of kings / destruction of cities (11:10–15)
conquest summary (10:40–43)	conquest summaries (11:16–23)

Although there are obvious differences, the two chapters are otherwise very close in structure. The summaries in chapter 11 are more complex than the summary in 10:40–43 because they bring together all the events since 5:13. Conversely, the city destruction report here is considerably shorter and annalistic rather than driven by plot.[209] But both chapters 10 and 11 prepare for the listing of territory and (especially) kings in chapter 12, since these function to complete the summaries begun in chapter 11 while also developing themes from preceding chapters. So although the material in chapter 12 is clearly different from the content in chapters 10 and 11, it needs to be read in conjunction with them so that their summary function is properly understood.

The close parallels serve to highlight the similarities but are also a mechanism for highlighting what is distinctive in each chapter. First, chapter 11 has no parallel to 10:6–9, the Gibeonites' request for help, because in chapter 11 the northern alliance sets itself directly against Israel. So, this time there is no question of whether God would support Israel in the battle. Second, there is no parallel to 10:12–15, Joshua's prayer and God's response. More than anything else, this highlights the key difference between these two otherwise closely similar chapters. In Joshua 10, victory occurs principally through God's miraculous intervention. By contrast, in Joshua 11 victory comes through Israel's obedience to God, a point particularly stressed in 11:15. Both, of course, are mechanisms for emphasizing that the victory is God's, but the means by which the victory is achieved are very different.

Taken together, these two chapters reflect on the initial victory at Jericho with its focus on the combination of obedience and the miraculous, showing that each might be the dominant motif at any given point. Nevertheless, the relative dominance of one compared to the other does

---

[209] Cf. Butler, *Joshua 1–12*, 504.

not reduce the reality of God's involvement. God's victory can be miraculous (Josh 10), an outcome of the obedience of God's people (Josh 11), or a combination of both (Josh 6).

Exegesis

11:1–3. Verse 1 is obviously parallel to 10:1, with both verses reflecting 5:1 and 9:1–2 (see comment there). In this case, the concern is with the news heard by Jabin, king of Hazor. Exactly what he heard is unstated: the parallel with 9:1–2 (the listing of which would have included Jabin since the region described there covers the whole land) suggests that the primary reference is probably to the destruction of Jericho and Ai,[210] but it could possibly include the events narrated in chapter 10.[211] The previous passages have mentioned the fear this caused among the Canaanite kings. Although that feature is omitted here, we are probably to infer it on the basis of 9:1–2. In any case, Jabin's actions are similar to those of Adoni-zedek, who formed an alliance with local kings to oppose Israel. As in the previous chapter, although Israel had entered Canaanite territory, it was the Canaanites who attacked so that Israel fought a defensive campaign. Adoni-zedek's forces had represented a significant obstacle for Israel, but they were much smaller than those that Jabin would raise.

In part, this is because Hazor was a particularly large city, far more significant than Jerusalem at that time. The text itself makes this clear, noting the massive size of the forces the city could raise (11:4),[212] while also noting that Hazor had been head of these kingdoms (11:10). The city itself was highly significant because its location (Tell el-Qadeh, a little over ten miles north of the Sea of Galilee) at major crossroads gave it both commercial and military importance. Although the city had probably declined a little in importance by Joshua's time, it still dominated the region. The total area covered by the city and its surroundings could still have been close to two hundred acres, with a potential population of

---

[210] See also Hall, *Conquering Character*, 185.

[211] Rösel, *Joshua*, 186, claims the events described here could not have happened because Joshua is based in Gilgal, well to the south. But this assumption is unnecessary and fails to recognize the ways in which chapters 10 and 11 are parallel accounts, not necessarily events that happened immediately after one another.

[212] As Dallaire, "Joshua," 938, notes, this continues the pattern where each stage of Israel's entry to the land faces a larger opposing force than before.

about 30,000.[213] That such a major city saw the need to respond to Israel's presence demonstrates the extent to which their arrival was changing the makeup of the land.

Hazor's king is called Jabin, a name that recurs in Judges 4:2, referring to a "king of Canaan" who reigned in Hazor. The relationship between these kings is complex, but it seems likely that "Jabin" is a hereditary title since it means "one who is insightful."[214] The report of Hazor's destruction here makes it likely that Hazor represents the region where Jabin was based rather than his home city, since the title "king of Canaan" suggests that, contrary to the normal Canaanite pattern, he was not associated with a particular city. This makes it unlikely that there has been any confusion between these two kings.[215]

Jabin organized a major alliance of various kings, only one of whom is named. The list of the alliance is arranged from the most specific to the most general, moving from a named king and town to named towns and then to regions and finally people groups. Unfortunately, not all of these sites can be identified.[216] Madon's king Jobab is named, but we cannot be certain where the town was, though it would presumably be in the region of the Sea of Galilee, perhaps a little south of the Waters of Merom. Several figures in the Bible bear the name Jobab, yet this particular figure is not mentioned again. The kings of Shimron and Achshaph are not named. Shimron would be allocated to Zebulun (see on 19:15) and Achshaph to Asher (see on 19:25), so both were in the far north. These locations indicate that Hazor was able to exert influence across a large sweep of the north, from the Jordan Valley to the Mediterranean coast.

After these specific place names, the listing becomes more general in verse 2, perhaps indicating that the compiler of this chapter was from the south and thus unwilling to guess at details of unfamiliar geography. The kings of the north are presumably those above the Sea of Galilee. This is because the Arabah, though it more commonly refers to the region of the Jordan Valley around the Dead Sea, more strictly describes the whole of the valley from south of the Sea of Galilee to the Dead Sea. Given the

---

[213] See Hawkins, *How Israel Became a People*, 111–17.

[214] Similarly, Howard, *Joshua*, 265; Woudstra, *Joshua*, 187–88.

[215] As suggested by, e.g., Rösel, *Joshua*, 182.

[216] For a helpful overview, see Merling, *Joshua*, 139–145. The LXX presents different spellings of the place names and therefore potentially different identifications. But with Rösel, *Joshua*, 183, preference should be given to the MT.

other locations, it is likely that only the northern area is meant—the area immediately south of the sea. Thus, the regions north and south of the sea were summoned. This makes it more likely that we should follow the CSB note and read "the Shephelah" as a proper noun rather than the sense of "Judean foothills." Here it would refer to the lower hills of western Galilee as one travels toward the coast in the area later assigned to Issachar, Zebulun, and Asher, with the Slopes of Dor as the westernmost boundary since they lie on the Mediterranean coast. So, having first described the areas north and south of the sea, we then have an extensive sweep of territory west of Hazor.

The alliance included six of the indigenous groups (only the Girgashites are unmentioned): the Canaanites in the east and west (presumably with reference to Hazor); the Amorites, Hittites, Perizzites and Jebusites in the hill country (the mountainous region around the sea); and the Hivites in the far north at Mizpah. Although several places are called "Mizpah,"[217] this one is said to have been at the foot of Hermon, and so about thirty miles northeast of Hazor. Therefore, the alliance effectively covered the whole of the north of the land, more or less everywhere north of the Jezreel Valley, and represented a massive challenge to Israel's presence in the land.

11:4–5. The challenge these forces posed is summed up in military terms. The kings and their armies formed a multitude, described by the proverbial expression "as numerous as the sand on the seashore" (v. 4).[218] This included not only soldiers but also a vast number of horses and chariots. Such equipment indicates that at least some of these forces were professional soldiers rather than a citizen militia, which was most likely what Israel had encountered to this point.

Such forces were enough to generate fear. Indeed, in 17:16 the Joseph tribes would complain that the iron chariots of Canaanite groups were preventing them from claiming their land. The observation in Psalm 20:7 that "some trust in chariots" (ESV) is contrasted with trust in Yahweh, a declaration of faith that matters precisely because of how easy it was to trust in the military power that chariots suggested.[219] Similarly, Psalm

---

[217] The name means "watchtower," and so naturally leant itself to being the name of a good lookout.

[218] For this as a positive image, cf. Gen 22:17; 32:12; 41:49. In Judg 7:12, it is used to describe the Midianite army that Gideon would attack.

[219] See the photograph of a replica chariot of this period in Harstad, *Joshua*, 454.

147:10 stresses that God is not "impressed by the strength of a horse" because the power of horses was obvious to this society and, thus, was a seductive temptation. The background provided by these verses makes clear that Israel could easily have been overawed by the power of this force assembled by Jabin. But this is multiplied by the sheer size of his army. In short, the opening verses have outlined a situation in which Israel is faced by an enemy that was overwhelmingly huge, representative of a united Canaanite opposition, and equipped with the latest and most potent military technology.

These forces were not simply gathered; they had camped at the Waters of Merom, a wadi that flows into the northwest side of the Sea of Galilee. This indicates the possibility that Jabin's forces had chosen the ground that suited them for battle, allowing them to operate on the valley floor where chariots and horses could move with freedom not possible on the surrounding mountains.[220] This therefore sets another contrast with chapter 10, in which Israel chose the battle sites, picking off cities largely without interference. Here, the site had already been claimed by the massed Canaanite forces.

Howard points out that reference to so much military equipment, and in particular horses, stands in contrast with the stipulation in Deuteronomy 17:16 that future Israelite kings should not accumulate horses, perhaps providing an important textual background hinting that such a force might not succeed.[221] Likewise, the memory of the defeat of Pharaoh's horsemen and chariots (Exod 14:21–31) could have provided some encouragement in the face of this foe. However, the way the narrator describes this situation, it was probably something only recognized with hindsight. At the end of this presentation, we are left simply to wonder at the might of the force Jabin assembled.

11:6. In light of the careful way in which the size of Jabin's forces has been laid out, we can well understand the need for God to tell Joshua not to be afraid. Arraying a force like this was intended to generate fear simply by its size (as some military parades are intended to do today).

---

[220] Alternatively, the chariots could have been disassembled for transport (see John Gray, *Joshua, Judges, Ruth*, [Grand Rapids: Eerdmans, 1986], 115). In the absence of a clearer location, this cannot be resolved, but since the portrayal of Jabin's forces is intended to suggest their overwhelming power, preference should be given to the option that he has chosen a site that would suit him.

[221] Howard, *Joshua*, 267.

So, although warnings against fear were often spoken to those facing overwhelming opponents (in Gideon's case this was achieved by letting him overhear a dream report in the Midianite camp, Judg 7:9–14), God needed to say this to Joshua precisely because fear was a natural response. But God did not simply tell Joshua to banish his fear; he explained why fear was unnecessary. By the same time the following day, he would have given the Canaanite forces to be killed by Israel. God did not say how this would happen, but the fact that he would do so made fear unnecessary. No further explanation was needed because Joshua had already experienced God fighting on Israel's behalf. He was not being asked to trust without evidence, even if it still required an act of faith in God to honor his commitment.

The focus is instead on what Joshua was to do in response to this coming defeat of Jabin's forces. God's directives focus specifically on the issues that would have generated fear. Both "their horses" and "their chariots" stand at the head of their respective clauses, making them the point of focus. Hamstringing their horses, an act replicated elsewhere only by David in 2 Samuel 8:4, would have rendered them unable to run and, thus, unfit for military activity (but probably fit for agricultural activity). Chariots, however, would have no civil function and were to be burned. This is closely aligned with the destruction of cities (rather than open country) in the previous chapter, since these were a source of military strength, used to control the local population. Thus, Israel was told from the outset that they were not to align themselves with the models of power that previously dominated Canaan.

Walter Brueggemann has argued that this treatment of the horses and chariots is the only normative element in the chapter for modern readers, essentially seeing this as an element that can be retrieved today.[222] Although there is much to be said for recognizing the importance of this, and it is clear that the book of Joshua is opposed to the sort agglomeration of power that typified Canaanite city-states, this seems too narrow a reading of the text, especially because of the ways in which it emphasizes the importance of reflective obedience to God. Nevertheless, Brueggemann has highlighted an important element of the book's theology that might otherwise be missed.

---

[222] Walter Brueggemann, *Divine Presence amid Violence: Contextualizing the Book of Joshua* (Milton Keynes: Paternoster, 2009), 33–41.

11:7–9. The assurance of victory did not mean that Israel had no involvement in it. On the contrary, just as in 10:9 Joshua launched a surprise raid on the enemy forces. Once again, the promises of God do not preclude wise actions. In chapter 10 this involved a night march, but as is typical of this chapter such details are omitted. The text reports that Joshua took his military force and surprised them at the Waters of Merom. This may have been the site Jabin had decided would best suit his army, but true to his word, God defeated them. Although Israel struck down the Canaanites (v. 8), it does not change the fact that God won the victory. As such, the statement in verse 8 closely parallels that of 10:9, and once again resulted in Israel pursuing the fleeing Canaanite forces.

The pursuit is described in terms of both west and east, though the whole area was north of the battle site. To the west, the pursuit went as far as the coast, with Misrephoth-maim about fifteen miles south of Tyre in the territory that would be allotted to Asher, while "greater Sidon" is presumably the Phoenician city normally known simply as Sidon about twenty-five miles north of Tyre. Reaching Sidon from the Waters of Merom involves a journey of more than one hundred miles, and even Misrephoth-maim would be about sixty miles from the battle site. The group that pursued to the east reached "Mizpeh," presumably the "Mizpah" of verse 3, a journey of over eighty miles from the battle site. This is a massive area, and must be the points reached by the final remnants of the fleeing forces rather than the area that was covered by the whole of the Israelite forces. If so, as is typical of the book, the statement that they left no survivors would refer to those who continued to resist rather than indicate that everyone in the area was killed.

In any case, the greater emphasis here is on Joshua's obedience to God's command in verse 6. He did indeed hamstring the horses and burn the chariots (v. 9). Israel had thus defeated a massive foe because of God's actions for them. They had been shown that the typical power structures of their day could not overcome God's power. They were also to remove this military equipment and the corresponding temptation to trust in such things. Israel was to model a different type of society. Joshua's obedience to all God had commanded was thus a leading example of this alternative—not conforming to the power structures of the time but committing to obey God.

11:10–11. With the combined Canaanite forces defeated, Joshua could return to Hazor. This was the major city of the region that had controlled the other northern kingdoms. The fact that those who continued to resist were executed indicates that the city did not simply surrender. Following the pattern of the southern campaign, Joshua executed its king (see 10:22–25). If this was Jabin and not his successor, then this is further evidence that the language of verse 8 employs a hyperbolic idiom (see on 10:20)—the language of "no survivors" once again used to indicate a total victory rather than that everyone was killed. The execution of the king is a specific action falling outside of the idiom, which is why the king can be identified. But the balance of verse 11 (other than the burning of the city) needs to be interpreted along similar lines so that those who are struck down and devoted to destruction are those who continued to resist, following the pattern we observed in 10:28–39. The burning of the city stands outside of the pattern, since otherwise only Jericho and Ai are said to have been burned. Nonetheless, destruction of the city is consistent with the pattern of the previous chapter since it involved rendering the city incapable of being used by Israel as a major military and political center.[223]

11:12–14. Hazor was singled out because of its prominence, but the rejection of cities as sites that could attract an agglomeration of power continues from the previous chapter. Exactly how many cities were involved is unclear because only three cities apart from Hazor are named: Madon, Shimron, and Achshaph (v. 1). But since verse 2 specifies kings from a wide area, we have to assume that the cities and kings mentioned in verse 12 are a shorthand summary for the principal towns of the north that could be captured because of the fall of Hazor.

The executions and devotions to destruction mentioned in verse 12 could possibly refer only to the kings and not the cities since the suffix rendered "them" on the verb "struck down" (נכה) is masculine, agreeing with "kings" ("city" in Hebrew is a feminine noun). However, other suffixes clearly referring to the cities are also masculine (and it is not uncommon that plural suffixes referring to feminine nouns revert to the

---

[223] Hazor's destruction can be compared with the archaeological record of the city, though the destruction can be matched to either a fifteenth- or thirteenth-century conquest. For a defense of a fifteenth-century interpretation, see Douglas Petrovich, "The Dating of Hazor's Destruction in Joshua 11 by Way of Biblical, Archaeological and Epigraphical Evidence," *JETS* 51.3 (2008): 489–512. For the thirteenth century, see Hawkins, *How Israel Became A People*, 111–17.

more common masculine[224]). Thus, it is more likely that the cities as well as their kings were devoted to destruction (חרם). But as noted previously (see comments on 10:19, 36–37), this needs to be read as an idiom claiming complete victory and not be over-literalized since the text itself does not do this. The same is true of the claim of annihilation (שמד) in verse 14.

Joshua's obedience to what had previously been commanded is a key motif that will be developed as the chapter progresses (cf. vv. 12, 15, 23), so its introduction in verse 12 is significant. His obedience has already been indicated in verse 9, but now we are told that it reaches back to the command of Moses (described again as Yahweh's servant). The obvious points of reference are Deuteronomy 7:1–6, where the ban (or devotion to destruction, חרם) is commanded, and Deuteronomy 20:16–18, where the command is developed in relation to the cities of the land. In particular, that command stresses the importance of devoting the population to destruction so that "they won't teach you to do all the detestable things they do for their gods" (Deut 20:18). The cities themselves did not need to be destroyed, but the people were to be placed under the ban. This Joshua did, save for Hazor, which (along with Jericho and Ai) was treated as a special case and burned. The other cities, recognizable because they were on mounds, were not burned but plundered—something consistent with Deuteronomy 20:16–18.

The claim that no one was left alive (more literally, "there was none drawing breath") both in verse 14 and in verse 11 thus indicates that God gave Israel a total victory and that all who continued to resist were killed—not that Israel physically sought out and killed everyone in the area. This is clear from the fact that God's speech to Joshua in 13:5–6 indicates this region was still possessed by the local people who needed to be driven out. Accordingly, the claim in verse 14 needs to be read in that light. Once more we observe that this language of total victory employs an idiom that was understood at the time and that must not be over-literalized. Israel had defeated the northern coalition and thus controlled the north, but significant challenges remained.

11:15. This verse provides an important summary of events to this point in the book. Although it initially refers to the victories in the north, it is actually an extension of the observation in 10:40–43, which emphasized that God had fought for Israel because of their obedience. In

---

[224] *GKC* §144a.

particular, Joshua is said to have left "nothing undone of all that the LORD had commanded Moses." Not all commentators are convinced that this comment is true. Daniel Hawk, for example, finds this observation "problematic."[225] After all, if Deuteronomy 7 and 20 require total destruction of the Canaanite population and prohibit any covenant with them, are not the agreement with Rahab (chapter 2) and the covenant with Gibeon (chapter 9) acts of disobedience? Can we really say that Joshua obeyed everything?

In light of the above observations, two comments need to be made. First, as noted, the language of battle frequently employs hyperbole. There is good reason to think this is also true in Deuteronomy, where the commands to destroy function primarily as a means of stressing the importance of giving Yahweh undivided loyalty.[226] In particular, Deuteronomy 7:1–6 places the Canaanite population under the ban and then directs Israel not to intermarry with them. If the law was meant as Hawk interprets it, there could be no one to marry since all would have been destroyed. So we must recognize the presence of the idiom in Deuteronomy, though perhaps we see this most clearly only when we have read Joshua's exploration of this issue.

Second, once we observe this feature in the commandment, we can also appreciate the need to apply the commandment in a discerning manner and see that it needs to be worked out in terms of someone's response to Yahweh.[227] Rahab had clearly committed herself to Yahweh; therefore, she is precisely *not* the sort of person against whom Deuteronomy 20:18 had warned. Ethnicity could not be the basis for destroying her since she was showing the sort of absolute commitment to God that the law demanded. Achan, though an Israelite, stands as the absolute contrast to this, since he acted like a Canaanite and was treated as such. The case of the Gibeonites is more complex (and receives further comment in vv. 19–20), but they had no desire to stand in the way of what God was doing in giving Israel the land.

All of this points to the importance of Joshua continually reflecting on God's instruction (1:8), because only by doing so could he understand

---

[225] Hawk, *Joshua*, 172.

[226] On this, see especially R. W. L. Moberly, *Old Testament Theology: Reading the Hebrew Bible as Christian Scripture* (Grand Rapids: Baker Academic, 2013), 53–71.

[227] See David G. Firth, "Models of Inclusion and Exclusion in Joshua," in *Interreligious Relations*, ed. Hallvard Hagelia and Markus Zehnder (London: T&T Clark, 2017), 71–88.

the challenges involved in applying it. Since his life was shaped by this, he was able to obey fully, though his obedience is best understood as a "dynamic conversation" with what God had commanded through Moses that made sense of it in Joshua's setting.[228] Nothing was left undone of all that God had commanded through Moses.[229]

11:16–17. Verse 16 provides an important summary statement, tying together the campaigns in the north and south with the earlier action in the central highlands. The balance of this chapter (and chapter 12) is then given over to a series of summaries that reflect on the whole book to this point.

The initial focus of the summary is on the land that was taken, seemingly moving from south to north. This is not entirely clear since, although the Negev typically refers to the wilderness to the south of Judah, and thus south of Hebron, the word also occurs in verse 2 where it refers to the area south of the Sea of Galilee (Chinnereth), and thus in the north of the land. The difficulty is that the word can function as a proper noun, and thus describe the southern wilderness, or be used as one of several terms that can mean "south." This is because Hebrew does not have technical terms for the cardinal points of the compass but recognizes them either by the dominant geographical feature of the area or by someone orienting themselves to the sunrise. As a result, the cardinal points are described relative to that person (in which case, "south" is also "right hand").

Similarly, the "foothills" can be either a common noun or a proper noun (Shephelah), specifically naming the slopes running down from Judah toward the coast. "Arabah" could also be a proper noun, typically describing the Jordan Valley (more commonly the area toward the Dead Sea, though in verse 2 it was the area immediately south of Chinnereth), or a common noun meaning "steppe." Since two lots of foothills are mentioned, care needs to be taken in understanding what is claimed.

Moreover, use of "Goshen" as a point of reference is unclear since, apart from 10:41 and 15:51, which mention a town in the Judean hills by that name (making clear it is not the Goshen in Egypt in Gen 46:34), the location is unknown. However, if we recognize that this is a town in Judah, then it would seem to clarify that the description is covering the land

---

[228] Matties, *Joshua*, 254.

[229] As Hall, *Conquering Character*, 197, notes, this is a point where Joshua exceeds Moses, whose failure to obey fully in Num 20:8–12 was the reason he could not enter the land.

from south to north by regions in verse 16. This means that the words function as proper nouns (though the second mention of the foothills would be as a common noun), and then by specific points of reference in verse 17, with Mount Halak on the ascent to Seir in Edom south of the Dead Sea and Baal-gad in the Valley of Lebanon beneath Mouth Hermon in the far north, possibly near the headwaters of the Jordan. However, what this description carefully avoids is any mention of the coastal plain, since at no point has Joshua entered that area and it will represent a particular point of challenge going forward. Likewise, Galilee is excluded. Both it and the coastal plain are noted in 13:1–7 as territory to be possessed. All of this area had been captured, and its kings executed, though as the rest of the book will make clear, capture and control are not the same thing.

11:18–20. The geographical description of the campaign is then matched by a chronological one, which notes that waging war with "all these kings" was a drawn-out process (v. 18). As a summary of the book to this point, the kings here would be more than just those mentioned in the earlier part of the chapter. That the war was with the kings again emphasizes the point that Israel was opposed to the social structure that characterized the Canaanite city-states more than to the people themselves. Rahab, after all, demonstrates the possibility that existed for the indigenous populations. In addition, if 10:2 indicates that Gibeon had no king (though the text does not require this), then it also prepares for Gibeon's exclusion from this pattern of war with kings in verse 19.[230]

The note that the campaign had been prolonged might surprise readers in that the book has so far described campaigns that appear to have been fought relatively quickly. However, it is also clear that large parts of the story have been telescoped. For example, nothing is said of events between the conclusion of the campaign in the far south at the end of chapter 10 and how Israel then moved to the far north at the start of chapter 11. To give only one example, we can note that chapter 24 records Joshua assembling the nation at Shechem (an important city in the central highlands). Clearly, the city was under Israelite control, but nothing in the narrative tells us how this happened or describes any campaign in the region. Perhaps more importantly for the narrator, the statement in verse 18 is also consistent with Deuteronomy 7:22, where God promises

---

[230] The exception of the Gibeonites is absent from the LXX of 11:19, but its presence in the other textual traditions supports the MT.

only to drive out the nations "little by little" before Israel rather than all at once. Given the importance of Deuteronomy 7 for the book of Joshua, it is not surprising that there is a link back to it here.

The more important point, though, is that in the context of Joshua's obedience to God we also see God's faithfulness to his promises. This is because, although it is possible to assess history from the perspective of divine action, it can also be interpreted from the perspective of human decisions. Both of those elements are held together here. So, another way of thinking about the reason why the campaign took so long is to note that none of the Canaanite cities took the option of making peace with Israel. At one level this is simply a statement of historical reality, but it does indicate that this possibility existed. Even though they carried it out in an irregular way, the example of the Gibeonites confirms this.

Matched with this is the fact that (apart from Gibeon) all these peoples confronted Israel in battle. The reason is that they stood under God's judgment, and he determined to judge them through Israel. The statement that he chose to "harden their hearts" (v. 20) evokes the experience of Pharaoh in Exodus.[231] There, the verb "to harden" (חזק)[232] is used to describe Pharaoh's own decision (Exod 7:13), God's action against Pharaoh (Exod 9:12), and instances in which it is unclear who has done the hardening (MT Exod 8:15 [ET 8:19]). In the plague narrative, Pharaoh's hardened heart contributes to the goals of Yahweh's name being proclaimed in all the earth (Exod 9:18) and Israel knowing Yahweh (Exod 10:2).[233] The motifs of ensuring that all the earth may know about God's might and that he might be feared have already emerged in Joshua 4:24, which draws together both goals from the exodus. This occurs at the point when Israel crosses the Jordan and symbolically concludes the exodus. So repetition of the exodus motif in verse 20 also prepares for the conclusion of a section of the book while indicating that the whole of the occupation of the land continues as the fulfillment of God's promise of the land to Abraham (Gen 12:7). This promise was itself the foundation for the exodus (Exod 6:8).

---

[231] For this motif in the accounts concerning Sihon, see comments on 12:1–6.

[232] Not all instances of Pharaoh's hard heart use this verb. The verbs כבד and קשה are also used with the sense of "harden."

[233] On the importance of these passages for understanding the plagues narrative, see William A. Ford, *God, Pharaoh and Moses: Examining the Lord's Actions in the Exodus Plagues Narrative* (Milton Keynes: Paternoster, 2006), especially 30–124.

Gibeon, noted here as a Hivite center, stands as the exception to the other cities in that it made peace, but this was because God had not hardened their hearts, unlike the others.[234] Nothing in chapter 9 prepares us for this fact, but this note closes the loop on why the Gibeonites were the enduring exception to all the other towns in the land. God had intended that they should not confront Israel in battle. The destruction of the Canaanite kings was thus something decided by God, achieved through their attacking Israel and precipitating their own downfall. This reality also explains the fact that both chapters 10 and 11 essentially show Israel acting to defend themselves against these kings, perhaps reminding later readers that they could not themselves bring about the circumstances where a people could be destroyed. Only God could do that.

11:21–22. Verse 21 mentions the Anakim, a group not normally listed among the Canaanites. These were the descendants of Anak (Num 13:22), known for their great height (Deut 9:2). The presence of Anakim had particularly concerned those who initially spied out the land, leading all but Joshua and Caleb to be barred from entering (Num 13:21–33). They were thus an unresolved issue from Israel's past, which Joshua addressed.

The statement that Joshua did this "at that time" should probably be taken only in the general sense of the conquest battles as a whole, and not in reference to the specific events in the north recounted earlier in this chapter. This is because all of the sites mentioned here (Hebron, Debir, and Anab) are in the Judean hills, and thus far from the Waters of Merom, though reference to the hill country of Israel suggests some were more widely scattered. Battles with Hebron and Debir are recounted in the midst of the southern campaign (Josh 10:36–39), while Anak is also in the Judean hills (15:50). The destruction of the Anakim may also be understood to have taken some time since they were still an issue when Hebron was allocated to Caleb. But the record of their destruction is important because it demonstrates that Joshua and Caleb's confidence concerning them was well-placed.

Once again, the statement of their being completely destroyed must be understood as a claim of total victory since verse 22 indicates that some

---

[234] This renders unlikely the argument of Jacob L. Wright, "Rahab's Valor and the Gibeonites Cowardice," in *Worship, Women and War: Essays in Honor of Susan Niditch*, ed. John J. Collins, T. M. Lemos, Saul M. Olyan (Providence: Brown University, 2015), 199, that the Gibeonites' act of "pusillanimous duplicity" was an act of cowardice and so part of a temple-based polemic against Gibeon.

continued to live in Gaza, Gath, and Ashdod—towns on the coastal plain
not included in the territory taken by Israel (see vv. 16–17). These would
all become Philistine centers. Some may well have fled there. Perhaps the
more important element is that this locates these tall figures in the area
where David and his men will later encounter Philistine giants (2 Sam
21:15–22) as part of the process by which David would complete the occupation of the land.

11:23. A closing note summarizes the book thus far. Joshua had taken
"the entire land" and given it as an inheritance by tribal allotments, after
which "the land had rest from war." Each of these statements needs to
be read carefully. The "entire land" taken by Joshua refers only to the
territory west of the Jordan since the area east of the Jordan was taken by
Moses. Beyond this, the chapter has already provided certain exclusions
relative to the boundaries promised in Gen 15:18–21, notably the coastal
plain. So, the "entire land" is shorthand for the areas described to this
point. The importance of this will soon become clear in 13:1 when God
tells Joshua that much of the land remained to be possessed, demonstrating that defeating the land's inhabitants and possessing it are not
the same thing since the former can be temporary.[235] Moreover, Joshua
did this in accordance with all God had said to Moses, again affirming the
importance of Joshua's obedience. The first half of the verse thus provides
a neat summary of all that has happened and the key theological grid
(obedience) through which to read the story.

The next two statements, that Joshua assigned the land and that the
land had rest, are past events from the point of view of the narrator,
but are still future within the narrative. Since the allocation of the land
as an inheritance by tribal allotments will dominate the second half of
the book, this statement is both a summary of what Joshua did and an
anticipation of what is about to be recounted. The statement about the
land having rest from war thematically echoes Joshua's statement to the
eastern tribes in 1:13–15. But by using a different term for "rest" (שקט),
it has the more important function of anticipating 14:15 (the only other
place in the book this term occurs) where the land has rest through Caleb,
meaning that rest is given through the faithfulness of the two surviving
spies from Numbers 13. This term for "rest" is an important one in Judges
(3:11, 30; 5:31; 8:28; 18:7, 27), where it is always temporary. If this sense

---

[235] Cf. Younger, *Conquest Accounts*, 244.

is present here, it may be one reason why Heb 4:1–11 (via Ps 95) stresses that final rest was not given through Joshua.[236] Nevertheless, even within a series of battle accounts, the clear implication is that obedience to God is foundational to the experience of rest, of which the absence of battle is a clear initial marker.[237]

12:1–6. The summaries of events that marked 11:16–23 are now expanded to consider the kings who were defeated and whose land was possessed by Israel.[238] These kings serve as representatives of the land and symbolize the Canaanite social structure Israel rejected. This is divided into two main groups: the kings east of the Jordan in verses 1–6 and those west of the Jordan in verses 7–24. A more significant distinction between the two groups is found in how their land is described. The kings east of the Jordan are both struck down by Israel and have their land possessed, enabling Moses to allocate it as an inheritance to Reuben, Gad, and the half-tribe of Manasseh. The kings west of the Jordan are struck down but nothing is said about possession or allocation of their land. This is because chapter 12, like 11:23, has the important function of closing off the account of how the land was taken while also preparing for the allocation. In doing so, it is important to focus on all Israel as something that existed on both sides of the Jordan. This unity was vital to 1:12–18, so this listing of the kings and land allocation of the eastern tribes reaffirms the importance of this theme. The language of "possession" (ירש) also echoes 1:15, which had already noted the possession held by the eastern tribes while insisting that they could only enjoy it once the western tribes had theirs. Because possession for the western tribes will dominate chapters 13–21, we cannot have the narrative of the return of the eastern tribes until that is complete. All of this indicates how carefully this list is integrated into the narrative, even if it is something that modern readers are often tempted to skip over fairly quickly.

Verse 1 describes the land the Israelites had taken east of the Jordan Valley (the Arabah) as stretching from the Arnon (a wadi that flows into the Dead Sea at about the midpoint of its length), along the Jordan River, to its headwaters in the region of Mount Hermon. For the most part, this territory stays fairly close to the Jordan but is here described only in

---

[236] See further §7 ("Rest").

[237] Earl, *Reading Joshua as Christian Scripture*, 170.

[238] Younger, *Conquest Narratives*, 230–32, demonstrates that the inclusion of lists such as this is a standard element in ancient conquest texts.

general terms. Given that this chapter is otherwise more interested in the kings who were defeated, it is not surprising that attention is given to Sihon and Og.

The defeat of Sihon is recounted in Numbers 21:21–30 and Deuteronomy 2:26–37. The details from those accounts are passed over here, though the motif of the hardening of the king's heart in Deuteronomy 2:30 so that he attacked Israel and thus brought about his own demise was echoed in the summary of Canaanite kings in 11:20. Rather, the concern is with his land. His capital was Heshbon, a town just north of the Dead Sea and about sixteen miles east of the Jordan, though the territory he ruled went from Aroer (just above the Arnon) to the Jabbok, a wadi that runs into the Jordan about twenty-five miles north of the Dead Sea. From this point north, Ammon was recognized as occupying territory further to the east, but Sihon's territory still covered the east side of the Jordan Valley up to the Sea of Galilee (Chinnereth) as its northernmost extent, while Beth-jeshimoth on the north of the Dead Sea and down its eastern shore was also his territory. Mention of the slopes of Pisgah, a little east of Beth-jeshimoth, is important because Moses had died there (Deut 34), and it was thus close to the point where the book of Joshua had begun. Sihon is of pivotal importance because his territory was so extensive, indicating that he, like Jabin (Josh 11:1–15), would have been head of numerous other kings.

King Og was killed after Sihon (Num 21:31–35; Deut 3:1–11). Like Sihon and the Canaanite kings, he died because of his decision to attack Israel. Deuteronomy 3:4–5 notes that he had sixty fortified cities, suggesting that he too was head of a group of kings. Of more importance here is the fact that he was a descendant of the Rephaim, a people who included the Anakim (see on 11:22). The Rephaim were known for their size (note the size of Og's bed in Deut 3:11), and so represented a significant challenge. However the interest here is in Og's territory that the eastern tribes had come to possess. Ashtaroth, where he lived, is in the Golan Heights, about twenty-five miles east of the Sea of Galilee, while Edrei is about fifteen miles southeast of there. His rule over Bashan went north from there to Mount Hermon. This is traced to Salecah, a site that cannot be identified with certainty but that (along with Edrei) marks the eastern boundary of Bashan (Deut 3:10). Geshur was a region east of the Sea of Galilee (and distinct from the Geshur mentioned in 13:2), and Maakah was northeast of the sea. Both of these regions would be important during the reign of David: Absalom's mother was from Maakah (2 Sam 3:5), and Absalom would later flee to Geshur (2 Sam 13:37–38). These represented the northernmost points of Og's rule, while he shared the rule of Gilead with Sihon.

The territory controlled by these kings was thus extensive and represented a considerable extension on the boundaries promised west of the Jordan. This was the territory that Moses had taken and allocated as a possession to the eastern tribes. The description of Moses as the Lord's servant is typical of the book, a phrase used of him fourteen times. But this is the only verse in which the designation occurs twice, stressing the importance of him allocating this territory as an inheritance to the eastern tribes in Numbers 32. Moreover, this title is used three times in Joshua 1, ensuring that this chapter provides a summary of everything in the book to this point by reaching to the first chapter for the frame needed to understand it.

12:7–24. The balance of the chapter lists the kings defeated by Joshua, not all of whom have been previously mentioned. As such, the listing fills out gaps in the narrative, demonstrating that what has been recounted is only a summary of those events deemed most theologically important. The area to the west is largely a mirror of that described east of the Jordan. The northernmost boundary is Baal-gad, a town in the Valley of Lebanon mentioned in 11:17. Mount Halak is in the far south, below the Dead Sea, and also provided the boundary in 11:17. After mention of these boundaries, a digression in verses 7b–8 notes that Joshua gave the land of the kings to the Israelite tribes by their divisions, again anticipating the allotment account in Joshua 13–21. Mention of this point is important because it enables the narrator to parallel Joshua with Moses in verse 6, preparing for Joshua to receive the title of the Lord's servant in 24:29. It is notable that again the territory that Joshua would allot is defined so that it follows the highlands and foothills from south to north along the Jordan Valley. Rather than the Negev alone belonging to the Canaanite nations (six of whom are listed, omitting the Girgashites), it is probably better to understand the whole land as having previously belonged to them (csb rather than hcsb).[239]

---

[239] hcsb's rendering "Negev of the Hittites" takes Negev as a construct noun, but since it is in pause the accentuation of the mt indicates that we should not read it as a construct. The csb is thus an improvement at this point.

The list of kings follows a standard pattern, in which each king is identified by his city followed by the number "one" before the closing verse of the chapter provides the total of thirty-one kings.[240] A system of adding up totals is also used in 15:20–63, where totals for regions are given before their listing. There is a well-established tradition in Masoretic manuscripts of laying this out in columns, a pattern repeated elsewhere only for the listing of Haman's sons (Esth 9:7–10), though the reason for using these columns is unknown.

The kings themselves are listed in a pattern that broadly conforms to the narrative of the book (entry to the land, the south, and then the north), though diverging at certain points. Thus, the list is probably from a source distinct from the various battle accounts, but its variants were not such that they needed to be brought into exact alignment. The first two kings (v. 9) are those of Jericho and Ai, conforming to the events of chapters 6–8. In verses 10–12a the kings who formed an alliance against Israel in 10:1–5 are named (Jerusalem, Hebron, Jarmuth, Lachish, Eglon, Gezer), with their order here conforming to their listing there. Verses 12b–16a list kings defeated in the balance of the account in chapter 10 but with variances in order and additional kings mentioned, as can be seen in the following table:

Joshua 12:12b–16a Sequence	Joshua 10 Sequence
Debir	Makkedah
Geder	Libnah
Hormah	Debir
Arad	
Libnah	
Adullam	
Makkedah	

---

[240] The LXX has twenty-nine kings because it divides the text differently. Both the LXX and MT are internally consistent. The LXX does not have a king for Bethel and treats Lasharon as a geographical marker. The absence of a king for Bethel is perhaps because no king is mentioned in chapters 7–8, so it probably represents an exegetical correction but an unnecessary one since nothing there precludes a king. "Lasharon" is more difficult, and at that point the LXX may well be correct, in which case it should be thirty kings. But given the possibility that LXX has made one exegetical correction, it may have done the same here, in which case preference should be given to the MT.

On Makkedah, Libnah, and Debir, see comments on Joshua 10:28, 29, 38. Of the other sites, Geder and Hormah would both be allocated to Judah (15:30, 58) and are in the same area as that described in Joshua 10. Geder and Arad are not mentioned elsewhere in the book, though Adullam is also allotted to Judah (15:35), suggesting that Geder and Arad are in this area as well. After this, the list moves north into the central highlands in verses 16b–17. Bethel has been used as a reference point before (e.g., 8:9), but no account of its capture has been given. According to 16:1 it lies on the boundary of the Joseph allocation. There are two possible sites named Tappuah in 15:34 and 16:8, but there are textual difficulties at 15:34 that make this less certain. In any case, the Tappuah mentioned in 16:8 (also 17:8) is a border town between Ephraim and Manasseh, making this the more likely reference. Hepher is elsewhere used as a clan name within Manasseh (17:2, 3), though allotments were made to the clans. Since Hepher is a name that would have applied only after Israel had settled in the land, the name here must be one that was current when the list was compiled. This section hints at accounts of the capture of the central highlands that have not been included in the book.

In verses 18–20, the list moves into the far north. Aphek would be allocated to Asher (19:30). If Lasharon is correct (it could be "to the Sharon" and thus a region near the coast), it is presumably in the same area, but it is not mentioned again. We then have the three kings at the heart of the northern alliance in 11:1. Madon was one of the cities aligned with Hazor, and Shimron-meron is presumably a fuller name for Shimron from 11:1. Achsaph completes the alliance. The only variation from their narrative order in Joshua 11 is the placement of Hazor second, even though it was the most prominent city. This perhaps reflects its decline in status by the time the list was compiled.

Verses 21–24a complete the list of northern kings before the total is given in verse 24b. None of these kings are mentioned elsewhere in the book. Both Taanach and Megiddo are in the Jezreel Valley. This would seem to associate them with Asher and Issachar, but 17:11 indicates they were associated with Manasseh. In 21:25 Taanach is included in the Levitical cities. The Kedesh mentioned here is probably that allotted to Naphtali (19:37) rather than the one in Judah (15:23). If so, it would become both a Levitical city (21:32) and a city of refuge (20:7). Jokneam, located near Carmel, would be allotted to Zebulun (19:11). Naphoth-dor was mentioned as a region in 11:2 (though there rendered as "Slopes of Dor"), but the city itself has not been mentioned. One can presume its capture is included in 11:1-9. The town is possibly mentioned in 17:11 (though the spelling is different). If so, it is associated with Taanach and Megiddo, though its location on the coast would make it a significant port. The location of Goiim is uncertain. If we follow the MT, it is in Gilgal and thus most likely in the area where Israel first entered the land. But the LXX places it in Galilee, a small change in Hebrew (so CSB note), and this is slightly more likely given the location of the town among other northern cities. If so, it would be the town mentioned in Isaiah 9:1 and may also be associated with Sisera (Judg 4:2). Tirzah is also the name of one of the daughters of Zelophehad (Josh 17:3), and is a town in Manasseh just west of the Jordan. As with Hepher, this would be an example of the use of a name that was subsequently applied, showing that the list was updated from time to time. That some of the place names later in the list (Jokneam, Dor) have some additional guidance as to their location, while the geographical association of the last two cities (Goiim and Tirzah) is less closely aligned geographically to those around, it may also point to evidence of the technique of periodic updating to assist later readers.

Bridge

Many modern readers will find Joshua 12 dreadfully dull. Given that some of these cities are not mentioned elsewhere in the book and that many occur only in the allocations to the tribes, readers may fail to see this chapter as the great summary of events that it is. Chapter 12 is a key bridge within the book, simultaneously looking back to the victories God won for Israel and anticipating the allotment of the land to come. Beyond this, by aligning these events under Joshua's leadership (12:7-24) with those under Moses' (12:1-6), it places the events into the larger story of God's saving purpose through Israel. The story is still incomplete: Although Moses had allotted the land east of the Jordan, the land west of the river had not been, reminding readers of the ongoing nature of God's saving purpose. But the summary nature of this chapter does not stand alone. Instead, it emerges from the summary statements in 11:16 stressing the importance of Israel's obedience in taking the land, a motif that in turn emerges from the defeat of the northern alliance in 11:1-15 (the motif of obedience is particularly stressed in verses 12 and 15). Israel's obedience is matched by Canaanite obduracy, albeit a hard-heartedness determined by God for all but the Gibeonites. In this way, Joshua 11–12 is closely knit and reflects on the narrative as a whole.

In providing this summary, the chapter asks us first to reflect on the nature of obedience.[241] The insistence that Joshua obeyed everything God had commanded through Moses gives us a frame of reference for understanding Israel's successes, a frame that is a development of events at Jericho. This time, however, there are no obvious miracles—only that the Israelites were able to defeat a massive foe because they obeyed God. Their obedience includes both the immediate command to hamstring the horses and burn the chariots (11:9) and also what God had earlier commanded. But as noted above, this obedience is complex because the commands of God given through Moses do not address every possible eventuality, and Joshua needed to decide on the means by which the commands should be obeyed. This is why his life needed to be shaped by reflection on God's instruction (1:7–8). Only by such reflection could he work out how God's instructions were to be obeyed, including decisions about why Canaanites like Rahab were not devoted to destruction.

Such a pattern is not unique to Joshua. In Psalm 1 we see the theme of meditation on God's instruction broadened to include all worshipers; this reflection helps the worshiper to understand the significance of various psalms and the life of faith. Trust in God does not remove all challenges or ethical dilemmas, but the pattern in both Joshua and Psalms is that those who spend their lives reflecting on what God has said and seek to live in obedience to it flourish and have the key mechanism to address these challenges. Thus, obedience is not mechanical. It is often about a life shaped around God's principles rather than a simple case of "God said it, we do it," since that is only the starting point of obedience.

This is something Jesus particularly recognizes in the Farewell Discourse (John 14–17). In John 14:15–18, he says those who love him will keep his commandments, but then he immediately goes on to speak of the promise of the Spirit, the one through whom Jesus continues to teach believers. This becomes clear in John 15:9–17 where he commands disciples to love one another, recognizing in that discussion that love involves complex decisions, while in his later teaching about the Spirit he also says the Spirit will guide believers into all the truth (John 16:13). Believers need to obey Jesus, and they need the help of the Spirit—both to

---

[241] See further discussion in §1 ("Faithfulness and Obedience").

remind them of Jesus' teaching and also to lead them to work out how it applies. If the reference to Joshua having a "spirit of wisdom" (Deut 34:9) is intended to refer to God's Spirit, then it may well hint that we are to interpret his ability to understand the shape of obedience as an early example of what Jesus explained.

Alongside this larger issue of obedience, these chapters also focus on the need for Israel to reject Canaanite models of power. Popular discussion of the Canaanites often treats them in broad brushstrokes, usually as sexually degenerate. This may have been true of some, but the Bible as a whole does not present them this way. The more consistent pattern within Joshua is to reject the trappings of power that marked Canaanite politics. The key elements that kept the local population under the kings' control were fortified cities and a significant military, for which horses and chariots were necessary. These in particular are what Joshua rejected, building on the pattern of the previous chapter. This is also why the listing in chapter 12 focuses on kings—the ones who kept the local population down. Israel was not to be a society given to hierarchy in which some were to prosper through taking from others, and the destruction of these Canaanite symbols of power particularly points to this.

This pattern is something typical of the Old Testament. Isaiah's rejection of the king of Babylon (Isa 13:1–14:22) and Ezekiel's exposé of the king of Tyre (Ezek 26:1–28:19) embody a similar attitude, while the fall of Babylon in Revelation draws these themes together into God's eschatological purpose for his people through the pattern of the fall of Rome. Babylon, Tyre, and Rome (among others) all sought to empower and enrich themselves through the impoverishment of others. The Canaanite towns had also done this. But their model is rejected in Joshua, and it continues to be rejected throughout the Bible. Although there is no one model throughout the Bible by which the people of God are to structure themselves, it can never be built on a pattern of perpetuating inequity through unfair power structures. As here, that stands under God's judgment.[242]

---

[242] See further §6 ("Power and Government").

III. Allotting the Land (13:1–21:45)

A. Preparations for Distributing the Land (13:1–14:15)

13 ¹ Joshua was now old, advanced in age, and the Lᴏʀᴅ said to him, "You have become old, advanced in age, but a great deal of the land remains to be possessed. ² This is the land that remains:

> All the districts of the Philistines and the Geshurites:
> ³ from the Shihor east of Egypt to the border of Ekron
> on the north (considered to be Canaanite territory)—the
> five Philistine rulers of Gaza, Ashdod, Ashkelon, Gath, and
> Ekron, as well as the Avvites ⁴ in the south; all the land of
> the Canaanites, from Arah of the Sidonians to Aphek and
> as far as the border of the Amorites; ⁵ the land of the Geb-
> alites; and all Lebanon east from Baal-gad below Mount
> Hermon to the entrance of Hamath— ⁶ all the inhabitants
> of the hill country from Lebanon to Misrephoth-maim,
> all the Sidonians.

I will drive them out before the Israelites, only distribute the land as an inheritance for Israel, as I have commanded you. ⁷ Therefore, divide this land as an inheritance to the nine tribes and half the tribe of Manasseh."

⁸ With the other half of the tribe of Manasseh, the Reubenites and Gadites had received the inheritance Moses gave them beyond the Jordan to the east, just as Moses the Lᴏʀᴅ's servant had given them:

> ⁹ From Aroer on the rim of the Arnon Valley, along with
> the city in the middle of the valley, all the Medeba pla-
> teau as far as Dibon, ¹⁰ and all the cities of King Sihon
> of the Amorites, who reigned in Heshbon, to the border
> of the Ammonites; ¹¹ also Gilead and the territory of the
> Geshurites and Maacathites, all Mount Hermon, and all
> Bashan to Salecah— ¹² the whole kingdom of Og in Bashan,
> who reigned in Ashtaroth and Edrei; he was one of the
> remaining Rephaim.

Moses struck them down and drove them out, ¹³ but the Israelites did not drive out the Geshurites and Maacathites. So Geshur and Maacath still live in Israel today.

¹⁴ He did not, however, give any inheritance to the tribe of Levi. This was their inheritance, just as he had promised: the food offerings made to the Lᴏʀᴅ, the God of Israel.

¹⁵ To the tribe of Reuben's descendants by their clans, Moses gave ¹⁶ this as their territory:

> From Aroer on the rim of the Arnon Valley, along with the
> city in the middle of the valley, the whole plateau as far as
> Medeba, ¹⁷ with Heshbon and all its cities on the plateau—
> Dibon, Bamoth-baal, Beth-baal-meon, ¹⁸ Jahaz, Kedemoth,

Mephaath, [19] Kiriathaim, Sibmah, Zereth-shahar on the
hill in the valley, [20] Beth-peor, the slopes of Pisgah, and
Beth-jeshimoth— [21] all the cities of the plateau, and all the
kingdom of King Sihon of the Amorites, who reigned in
Heshbon. Moses had killed him and the chiefs of Midian—
Evi, Rekem, Zur, Hur, and Reba—the princes of Sihon who
lived in the land. [22] Along with those the Israelites put to
death, they also killed the diviner, Balaam son of Beor,
with the sword.

[23] The border of the Reubenites was the Jordan and its plain. This
was the inheritance of the Reubenites by their clans, with the cities
and their settlements.

[24] To the tribe of the Gadites by their clans, Moses gave [25] this as
their territory:

Jazer and all the cities of Gilead, and half the land of the
Ammonites to Aroer, near Rabbah; [26] from Heshbon to
Ramath-mizpeh and Betonim, and from Mahanaim to the
border of Debir; [27] in the valley: Beth-haram, Beth-nimrah,
Succoth, and Zaphon—the rest of the kingdom of King
Sihon of Heshbon. Their land also included the Jordan and
its territory as far as the edge of the Sea of Chinnereth on
the east side of the Jordan.

[28] This was the inheritance of the Gadites by their clans, with the
cities and their settlements.

[29] And to half the tribe of Manasseh (that is, to half the tribe of
Manasseh's descendants by their clans) Moses gave [30] this as their territory:

From Mahanaim through all Bashan—all the kingdom
of King Og of Bashan, including all of Jair's Villages that
are in Bashan—sixty cities. [31] But half of Gilead, and Og's
royal cities in Bashan—Ashtaroth and Edrei—are for the
descendants of Machir son of Manasseh (that is, half the
descendants of Machir by their clans).

[32] These were the portions Moses gave them on the plains of Moab
beyond the Jordan east of Jericho. [33] But Moses did not give a portion
to the tribe of Levi. The Lord, the God of Israel, was their inheritance,
just as he had promised them.

14 [1] The Israelites received these portions that the priest Eleazar,
Joshua son of Nun, and the family heads of the Israelite tribes gave
them in the land of Canaan. [2] Their inheritance was by lot as the Lord
commanded through Moses for the nine and a half tribes, [3] because
Moses had given the inheritance to the two and a half tribes beyond
the Jordan. But he gave no inheritance among them to the Levites. [4] The
descendants of Joseph became two tribes, Manasseh and Ephraim. No
portion of the land was given to the Levites except cities to live in, along

with pasturelands for their cattle and livestock. ⁵ So the Israelites did as the Lord commanded Moses, and they divided the land.

⁶ The descendants of Judah approached Joshua at Gilgal, and Caleb son of Jephunneh the Kenizzite said to him, "You know what the Lord promised Moses the man of God at Kadesh-barnea about you and me. ⁷ I was forty years old when Moses the Lord's servant sent me from Kadesh-barnea to scout the land, and I brought back an honest report. ⁸ My brothers who went with me caused the people to lose heart, but I followed the Lord my God completely. ⁹ On that day Moses swore to me, 'The land where you have set foot will be an inheritance for you and your descendants forever, because you have followed the Lord my God completely.'

¹⁰ "As you see, the Lord has kept me alive these forty-five years as he promised, since the Lord spoke this word to Moses while Israel was journeying in the wilderness. Here I am today, eighty-five years old. ¹¹ I am still as strong today as I was the day Moses sent me out. My strength for battle and for daily tasks is now as it was then. ¹² Now give me this hill country the Lord promised me on that day, because you heard then that the Anakim are there, as well as large fortified cities. Perhaps the Lord will be with me and I will drive them out as the Lord promised."

¹³ Then Joshua blessed Caleb son of Jephunneh and gave him Hebron as an inheritance. ¹⁴ Therefore, Hebron still belongs to Caleb son of Jephunneh the Kenizzite as an inheritance today because he followed the Lord, the God of Israel, completely. ¹⁵ Hebron's name used to be Kiriath-arba; Arba was the greatest man among the Anakim. After this, the land had rest from war.

Context

At this point we enter a major new section of the book, albeit one that was anticipated by the statement in 11:23 that Joshua gave the land as an inheritance to the tribes according to their allotments. Since that verse serves as a summary of chapters 1–11 and as an overview of what follows, it naturally cannot cover everything that follows in this section, but it clearly emphasizes that taking the land west of the Jordan was not an end in itself. Israel was to live in the land God was giving them. For this to come about, the tribes needed to receive their inheritance. The anticipatory nature of that verse is clear when one notes that its first half looked back on Joshua taking the land, something that had been narrated to that point. But the allotment had not happened and so becomes the primary focus of Joshua 13–21.

The possibility of this allotment is further confirmed by the listing of kings defeated in the land in 12:7–24, a listing that geographically exceeded the territory whose conquest has been narrated and so showed that the land could be allotted. Alongside this, 12:1–6 returned to the land east of the Jordan that Moses had already allotted to Reuben, Gad, and the half-tribe of Manasseh. Joshua's role in allotting the land is thus continuing the work Moses had begun except that he was giving the land that had actually been promised to Abraham west of the Jordan. Thus, the text makes the crucial point that God had the right to distribute the land, something that overrode existing political structures.[243]

The whole of chapters 13–21 are carefully structured, with a particular focus on the root חלק (csb "divide").[244] After the opening address to Joshua (Josh 13:1–7), chapters 13 and 14 address issues left over from the book of Numbers, the pentateuchal text that is the primary point of reference for these chapters. The main concern in chapter 13 is clarifying the allotments east of the Jordan, leading to the observation that Moses had given no inheritance to Levi (13:14, 33). This issue will be addressed in Joshua 20–21, since the Levites' allotment uniquely was on both sides of the Jordan, so that their position bookends the whole of the allotment as well as that of the eastern tribes. Joshua 14:1–15 and 19:49–51 focus on the allotments given to Caleb and Joshua, the two surviving spies. Following this, 15:1–19:48 considers the allotments to the western tribes, with those of Judah (15:1–63) and Joseph (divided into the territories of Ephraim and west Manasseh, 16:1–17:18) prominent, indicating that these were the dominant tribes. At the heart of this section is the report of the assembly at Shiloh and the setting up of the tent of meeting (18:1–10) before the report of the allotment to the remaining tribes (18:11–19:48).

After God's introductory speech (13:1–7), and recognizing that 21:43–45 summarize more than just Joshua 13–21, a broadly chiastic structure can thus be traced:

---

[243] Jerome F. D. Creach, "Joshua 13–21 and the Politics of Land Division," *Interpretation* 66 (2012): 154.

[244] Following Koorevaar, *De Opbouw van het Boek Jozua*, 118, 120. The orderly nature of these chapters thus argues against various scholarly proposals that see them as coming through diverse sources and redactions. For a helpful summary of these, see Trent C. Butler, *Joshua 13–24* (Grand Rapids: Zondervan, 2014), 37–42. This does not preclude the use of sources with updating at various points, and the whole of these chapters is clearly written looking back to the time of Joshua, but it does mean we need to consider their coherence as a crucial element in their interpretation. Where the accounts in chapters 1–12 probably go back largely to oral traditions, the tradents behind these chapters are almost certainly literary.

A   East Jordan Inheritance (13:8–33)
   B   Caleb's Allocation (14:1–15)
      C   Judah and Joseph's Inheritance (15:1–17:18)
         D   The Tent of Meeting at Shiloh (18:1–10)
      C' The Remaining Tribes' Inheritance (18:11–19:48)
   B' Joshua's Allocation (19:49–51)
A' Levi's Inheritance (20:1–21:42)[245]

The importance of this structure will be particularly noted in the treatment of 18:1–10, but we can here note that it demonstrates the importance of the tent of meeting at Shiloh as the pivotal passage for this section, if not for the book as a whole. The Israelites not only needed to take the land (Josh 1–12), they also needed to allot the land (Josh 13–21). The land made sense for them only when it was a land where the worship of Yahweh was central. Setting up the tent demonstrated this, and from there it was possible to allot even the land that had not yet been taken.

But we cannot so stress the raising of the tent that the extensive tribal lists simply become a supporting structure for it. Israel could only be a worshiping community when it lived securely in its land, and that security included each part of the nation, down to the tribe and clan, knowing where it could farm and had military responsibility. From the outset, there was a need to know where everyone belonged, which suggests that lists such as these do reach back to the time of Joshua.[246] Indeed, given that Israel only possessed the land described here for a very short period, it makes most sense to date the origins of these lists to the time the Bible sets them.

This is, however, not the only structural element that holds these chapters together. Nelson has pointed to five "land grant" narratives that look back to promises made in the wilderness period and are to be resolved at this point.[247] According to Nelson, these narratives occur at 14:6–15; 15:18–19; 17:3–6, 14–18; and 21:1–3, though the account in 17:14–18 only fits the pattern partially in that there is no wilderness promise claimed there. One might also add Joshua's own allocation (19:49–51), though it

---

[245] Adapted from Koorevaar, *De Opbouw*, 229.

[246] To place the various lists here in their context and so appreciate how they might have functioned within early Israel, see Richard S. Hess, "A Typology of West-Semitic Place Name Lists with Special Reference to Joshua 13–21," *The Biblical Archaeologist* 59 (1996): 160–70.

[247] R. D. Nelson, *Joshua*, 177.

is a report rather than a narrative. If we make these modifications to his list using the existence of a promise from the wilderness period as the key feature, then we have three accounts before the setting up of the tent at Shiloh and two afterward. But since the first two are concerned with Caleb, it is better to recognize that there are two promises resolved before Shiloh, and two resolved after Shiloh, again showing the importance of this particular text for the whole of this section of the book.

The transition introduced at 13:1 is also linked to 1:1 since both passages include a comment by the narrator that is then affirmed in a speech by God to Joshua. Joshua 13:1 will also be alluded to in 23:1. Both 1:1–9 and 13:1–7 represent key initiatives taken by God and so function to introduce the narrative plot for the balance of the section, indicating what Joshua is to do in what follows. Although Koorevaar argues that 5:13–6:5 represents an equivalent initiative,[248] it is better to see this as introducing a particular stage in Israel's entry to the land in that God's commands concerning Jericho are not iterative, whereas those in 1:1–9 and 13:1–7 are. So, although the Passover account in 5:10–12 does represent the conclusion to Israel's entry into the land, it is a conclusion that marks a significant change, but for the structure of the book it is not as significant as 13:1 because of the clear link to 1:1. At the other end of this section, 21:43–45 also links to 23:14–16, so that the beginning and end of Joshua 13–21 are joined to the beginning and end of Joshua 23, a factor that marks out chapter 24 as being of particular importance for the book as a coda that reflects on how the book's themes can be taken forward.

Although the chiastic structure above shows the distinctions that exist between Joshua 13 and 14 in the overall structure of this section, there is still good reason for treating them together. Most importantly, although Joshua is told to begin dividing the land as the inheritance for the west-of-Jordan tribes, the actual division does not begin until 15:1. These chapters are thus preparatory for this process, tying this allocation to that of the east-of-Jordan tribes, while also (narratively) delaying the account of the division. The means of achieving the delay varies. Joshua 13 focuses on the east-of-Jordan tribes while Joshua 14 addresses the issue of Caleb's allocation, but what unites them is their focus on events recounted in Numbers. Beyond this, the focus on the eastern tribes in Joshua 13 provides a further link to Joshua 1 and its insistence that taking the land

---

[248] Koorevaar, *De Opbouw*, 227.

required all Israel to work together. The theme of the unity of Israel will be taken up again in Joshua 22, the beginning of the next section, so that each major section begins with this theme. But we cannot, therefore, see Joshua 14 as simply something added to this, because just as Joshua 1–2 provided a double introduction to the book, so Joshua 13–14 provide a double introduction to the land allocation. Joshua 1 focused on the unity of Israel, while Joshua 2 raised the question of foreigners through Rahab.[249] Here, Caleb's foreignness—his description as "the Kenizzite" (14:6, 14)— stresses his Edomite background. Hence, the account of the division of the land begins by stressing the same two themes that were central to the initial entry to the land.

Exegesis

13:1. Just as 1:1 began by noting Moses' death and then reporting that God began his speech by telling Joshua this, so 13:1 commences by noting Joshua's advanced age (to which we return in 23:1) and reporting this as the point from which God's directions to Joshua began. Although this might seem repetitive to modern readers, we should bear in mind that repetition was one of the key techniques available to ancient writers to emphasize important points.[250] Here, that repetition emphasizes the urgency of the point made in the second half of God's speech: much of the land remained to be possessed.

This is consistent with the summary of the land taken in 11:16–17, which focused on the highlands rather than the coast. Likewise, although the listing of kings in 12:9–24 filled in some of the gaps in the previous narratives, it too is focused on the highlands rather than the coast. So, although Israel had successfully taken much of the land under Joshua, the task of putting the people into possession of the whole land outlined in 1:6 was still only partially complete. The verb translated "possess" in 1:6 (*hiphil* נחל)[251] is different from the one used in 13:1 (ירש), but this verb was also prominent in Joshua's speech to the eastern tribes (1:11, 15) and will be particularly important throughout Joshua 13–21, occurring fifteen times in these chapters. The verb נחל is also important in these chapters,

---

[249] See further §2 ("The Identity of the People of God").

[250] See Meir Sternberg, *The Poetics of Biblical Narrative: Ideological Literature and the Drama of Reading* (Bloomington: Indiana University Press, 1987), 365–440.

[251] We might, over-literally, translate this as "cause to inherit." By contrast, ירש has the sense of "possess" or "dispossess" depending on context.

occurring seven times, showing that there is a considerable overlap in meaning between these words. The key distinction is that land can only be occupied as an inheritance once it has been possessed. Notably, only land that had already been possessed by Israel would be allocated as an inheritance (נחל) throughout chapters 13–21. Possession (ירש) was the necessary first step. Though the inheritance could be allotted before possession, the fact that much remained to be possessed meant Joshua's advanced age represented a significant issue for Israel.

13:2–6a. These verses outline the regions remaining to be possessed. Although the territories listed here and in 11:16–17 are described in fairly general terms, nevertheless it is possible to see how they fit together, rather as if someone had taken a map of the land and made it into a two-piece jigsaw puzzle.

The territory here focuses especially on the coastal plain that had been occupied by the Philistines. In addition, some Geshurites are mentioned, though they are to be distinguished from another group of Geshurites in 13:11, 13. The latter group was in the region of the Sea of Galilee (cf. 12:5), whereas this southern group was located in the south of Israel and would be among the groups David would later raid from Philistine territory (1 Sam 27:8). Presumably, there was some link between these groups, but as the only other mention of them in the Old Testament is in Deuteronomy 3:14 (referring to the northern group) we do not know what this was. The territory covered by the Geshurites and Philistines ran from the Shihor, which is generally considered to be a stream that ran into the Wadi el-Arish, forming the eastern border with Egypt. The area from the Egyptian border and along the coastal plain to Ekron, the northernmost of the Philistine cities, was still reckoned as Canaanite and thus part of the land promised to Israel (though the Philistines are never considered Canaanite).

The Philistines were to remain a significant problem for Israel, and although Judges 1:34–36 only mentions the Amorites as preventing the tribe of Dan from claiming its allotted territory, the Samson stories (Judg 13–16) make clear that the Philistines were a significant factor. David would later flee from Saul to the Philistines and reside among them prior to his accession (1 Sam 27–2 Sam 1), though he did ultimately defeat them (2 Sam 5:17–25).

The origins of the Philistines are uncertain,[252] though Amos 9:7 seems to associate them with Crete, something that is consistent with the archaeological record of the coastal plain in the Late Bronze and Early Iron ages. If so, then it is possible that the Philistines mentioned in Genesis 26 are so called because they occupied the Philistine territory. It is also possible that the Philistines were a people who absorbed many different cultural features over time. However, they were clearly regarded as a people with distinctive customs, since verse 3 notes their five cities (the three coastal cities first, then the two inland) and that each had a "ruler" (סֶרֶן), a term used only for the Philistine cities and seems to be a loanword from their language (though its etymology is uncertain). This clearly distinguishes them from the Canaanites, as does the fact that their rulers seem to have worked cooperatively rather than under the hierarchical system that typified Canaanite polity.

Within this area, the Avvim (csb "Avvites") are also mentioned. These people are referred to in Deut 2:23 as having lived in the region of Gaza, the southernmost Philistine city, and having been destroyed by invaders. A city is also mentioned for them in Joshua 18:23 within the territory of Benjamin. If these groups are connected, then presumably a remnant of the coastal group moved to the lower highlands. However, if csb is correct in connecting the opening word of verse 4 with them ("in the south"), then those in the region of Gaza are probably meant here, but this is uncertain.[253] Perhaps the most important point is that the Philistines, Geshurites, and Avvim appear to be regarded as ethnically separate from the Canaanites (and so to be treated differently as a people), but the land where they dwelled was still within the boundaries promised to Israel.

This distinction in ethnicity seems to control the comments in verses 4–6a as the description moves along the coast from the Philistine region in the south to Sidonian-controlled territory in the north. Reference to Mearah (csb "from Arah") is obscure, as this is the only time where a

---

[252] See the excursus in Butler, *Joshua 13–24*, 72–79.

[253] The csb here goes against the accentuation of the mt, which connects this word (מִתֵּימָן) with the words that follow (cf. esv). Accentuation, like vowel points, is an addition to the consonantal text and so not definitive, but it is usually a good guide as it represents what the Masoretes regarded as the received pronunciation of the text. The syntax of vv. 2–6a is choppy, so it is difficult to make a strong case either in support of the accentuation or for rejecting it. See also Harstad, *Joshua*, 498.

word that usually means "cave" is used as a proper noun.[254] Most likely, it refers to a site north of the Philistine cities on the coastal plain. Aphek is probably not the town east of modern-day Tel Aviv that the Philistines later used as a mustering point for attacking Israel because of its strategic access to the highlands (1 Sam 4:1; 29:1), but rather a town that would be allotted to Asher (Josh 19:30) and thus somewhere that would be thought of as marking the boundaries of Sidon's influence. Reference to the Amorites would thus be a general designation for residents of the far north. The Gebalites are residents of the Phoenician city of Byblos (north of Sidon). "Lebanon" refers roughly to the south of modern Lebanon in the mountains. Baal-gad is in the foothills of the Hermon range and so a little further inland. Lebo Hamath (csb "entrance of Hamath") is the traditional northernmost point of Israel and is probably located in the northern Baqaa Valley. The final reference to Misrephoth-maim moves back to the coast, about fifteen miles south of Tyre.

In summary, the territory to be taken is the coastal plain in the south and the north since the victories recounted in 11:1–15 had taken Israel to the coast along the Carmel spur, which more or less separates the coastal areas mentioned here. There was thus a great deal of land remaining to be possessed.

13:6b–7. Although the territory is extensive, Israel already had evidence from events so far that God would give it to them. However, God indicated that he would personally drive out the inhabitants of the land before Israel. When this would happen was not indicated, and it is clear in the case of the tribes whose allotments are described in 18:11–19:48 that they were allotting land not yet possessed. In response to this, Joshua was to allot the land as an inheritance in accordance with God's command. Joshua's obedience is a well-established motif in the book, so this is not a surprise, but once again he would need to work out how to go about this (e.g., 18:2–7). However, Israel's inheritance could be allotted in advance of possession precisely because it was God's to give, and so Joshua was directed to divide (*piel* חלק) the land as an inheritance for the western tribes, the nine tribes that had not yet received an allotment plus the western half of Manasseh.

---

[254] The lxx has Γάζης (Gaza). Although this is a simple consonantal change (assuming מעזה for the mt מערה, with the initial מ treated as the preposition "from"; something made explicit in some mss), it looks suspiciously like a correction to a difficult text.

13:8–13. Although we might expect the narrative to move immediately to the allocation of the land west of the Jordan, we return instead to the allotment east of the Jordan. A further delay of the allotment is introduced in 14:1–5, a factor that holds these two chapters together. So, the narrator provides a summary of the territory taken by Reuben, Gad, and the eastern half of Manasseh before providing a more detailed summary for each tribe. Again, the text notes that this territory was given by Moses, with verse 8 closely matching 12:6. The summary in these verses is similar to that in 12:1–5, again moving through the territory of Sihon and the territory of Og (for details on sites mentioned in both, see comments on 12:1–5). Medeba would later be a Moabite city but was taken by Israel in Num 21:30, where it is also associated with Dibon. Both were allotted to Reuben (Josh 13:16–17).

Once again, it is noted in verse 13 that the Geshurites and Maacathites (see on 12:5) were not driven out but continued to live within Israel. The continued presence of Canaanites within Israel could seem problematic (e.g., 15:63), but the fact that neither of these groups were included in the Canaanite nations suggests their continued existence was a problem only in that Israel could not gain full control of the land, though their territory appears to have been regarded as something Israel could in theory possess.[255] Since these kingdoms had both largely disappeared by the middle of the ninth century, this indicates that this note comes from relatively early in Israel's history.

13:14. At this point, the Levites are introduced. They, along with Manasseh, were the only tribe that would receive territory on both sides of the Jordan—cities, in the case of the Levites. Their primary inheritance was not land but rather the offerings presented to God in worship. This is consistent with God's earlier promises to them in Deut 18:1. It is of more importance for this chapter, and the whole of Joshua 13–21, that reference to Levi here is a bookend to both the eastern allocation (cf. 13:33) and also to the allocation across the whole of Israel (Josh 20–21).

13:15–23. The text describes how the eastern allotments were broken up by tribe, with the tribe of Reuben listed first. Description of their territory is more complete than for the other two eastern tribes, perhaps

---

[255] Cf. B. Mazar, "Geshur and Maacah," *JBL* 80 (1961): 17–18. Since neither appears to have been a kingdom, they (perhaps like the Gibeonites) appear to have been regarded as less of a threat than other Canaanites.

indicating that the compiler of this section had greater knowledge of Israel's southern geography. In this respect, the eastern allocation is similar to the western allocation, where Judah's territory is described in much more detail than any of the others. A key element introduced here is that the inheritance is given according to "their clans" (מִשְׁפְּחָה). Up to this point, reference to "clans" as a significant division of the tribes has been made only in the stories of Rahab and Achan (6:23; 7:14, 17), but from this point on it will be used as a reference point for each tribal allotment (13:24, 29; 15:1; 16:5; 17:2; 18:11; 19:1, 10, 17, 24, 32, 40).

With the exception of western Manasseh, a second statement about the clans closes off the allocation of the western tribes too, though in the case of Judah the details of the allotment have been expanded with additional information (15:13–63). The exact distinctions between the various levels of family in Israel are not always clear, but it is likely that the clan was a collection of households that lived in a particular area, perhaps in a village or group of related villages. The point is that, although the land was allotted by tribes, each tribe's allocation could be seen in more local terms and each clan could recognize its particular place within the larger tribal inheritance. Israel's association with the land was not just the land as a whole, not even the tribal allotments, but came down to a much more local sense of place.

All of the toponyms in verses 15–16a (up to Dibon) repeat places named in verses 8–13, largely because Reuben's inheritance covers the southern boundaries of the eastern tribal allotments with the Wadi Arnon as the southern boundary and Heshbon as the northern. Verses 16b–20 then move through Reubenite territory, identifying various towns that belonged to them. Not all of these can be identified, making it difficult to track the exact route described, but it appears to be in a semicircle that runs clockwise from just above the northernmost point of the Dead Sea down to where the Arnon enters it, about halfway along.

Bamoth-baal is where Balaam had been taken to curse Israel (Num 24:1). Apart from its being in the hills east of the Dead Sea, it is not possible to be more specific. Beth-baal-meon is about ten miles east of the Dead Sea, about five miles south of where the Jordan enters it.

Jahaz (where Sihon had been defeated, according to Num 21:23–26),[256] Kedemoth, and Mepaath (along with Bezer, a town not mentioned here but noted in Josh 20:8) are all towns allotted to the Levites (21:36), but their locations are not agreed.

Kiriathaim is probably a few miles northwest of Beth-baal-meon, about seven miles east of the Dead Sea. Sibmah may be about five miles east of Heshbon, just north of Mount Pisgah and so in the north of Reuben's territory, while Zereth-shahar is farther south, on the Dead Sea coast about twelve miles south of Beth-jeshimoth at almost the northernmost point of the Dead Sea.

Beth-peor is probably a little north of Sibmah. On the slopes of Pisgah was where Israel sinned by worshiping Baal of Peor (Num 25:1–9) and where Moses had seen Jericho before his death (Deut 34:1–8). The territory allotted to Reuben was the Heshbon tableland, the hills east of the Dead Sea, the area previously controlled by Sihon (Num 21:21–30; Deut 2:26–37), and also the area where Moses had led Israel to victory over the five kings of Midian (Num 31:1–12; the five Midianite kings are also listed in Num 31:8). That passage also reports that Israel had killed Balaam, so the allusion to those events is continued here by noting Balaam's death.[257] As an eastern tribe, Reuben had the Jordan as a natural boundary, though in truth their territory only continued a few miles north of the Dead Sea along the river.

13:24–28. Gad's inheritance was immediately north of Reuben, occupying land that hugged the east bank of the Jordan to the north of the Dead Sea and moving eastward into the territory of the Ammonites. The description here is less comprehensive than that of Reuben, though it still notes that the land was allotted by clans.

As with Reuben, the locations are not all known, making it difficult to trace the exact boundaries. The first place mentioned, Jazer, is a case in point since its location is unknown, and the word translated "territory"

---

[256] In Joshua 21:36, csb spells the place name as Jahzeh, but the same place is meant. The spelling in 21:36 is a more accurate transliteration of the Hebrew, but the Hebrew spelling is the same in the two passages.

[257] Balaam is here called a "diviner" (הַקֹּסֵם), a term that confirms his negative portrayal. This label is not used of him previously, but it does evoke allusions to Num 22:7 and 23:23, where the root occurs within the Balaam narrative. Although Balaam's prophecies in Numbers 22–24 are positive toward Israel, designating him as a "diviner" shows that he is not to be regarded positively, since his basic practice is contrary to what God requires of his people.

(גְּבוּל) might also be "border." Perhaps it represented a border point to the east, whereas the towns of Gilead here are those of the hills east of the Jordan. The designation "Gilead" can cover territory on either side of the River Jabbok, though the area north of there can also be known as "Bashan." Here it appears to be the area south of the Jabbok that is intended, since eastern Manasseh's territory covers the northern part of Gilead. The better-known Aroer is just north of the Arnon and forms part of Reuben's territory (v. 16). Another town with this name is to the south of Beersheba (1 Sam 30:28). The Aroer mentioned here features in the Jephthah story (Judg 11:33), but apart from being east of the principal Ammonite town of Rabbah (itself about twenty-five miles east of the Jordan) is otherwise unknown. This is the only place where Israel is said to occupy Ammonite territory, something that Deuteronomy 2:19 might seem to preclude. Barring some form of textual emendation here,[258] it is perhaps better to read that text as referring only to the eastern part of the region then controlled by Ammon, in which case these two passages cohere with one another.[259]

Heshbon seems to have been a border town with Reuben, which was variously claimed by both tribes. Reuben had initially rebuilt it (Num 32:37), but here it appears to belong to Gad. By contrast, Gad had rebuilt Dibon (Num 32:34), but it here appears in the territory of Reuben. The boundaries between these tribes were thus rather fluid. In the case of Dibon, it would more naturally fit the territory of Reuben. Heshbon would later be allotted to the Levites (Josh 21:39). Ramath-mizpeh is not mentioned elsewhere in the Old Testament, but toponyms including "Ramath" (meaning "heights") and "Mizpeh" (meaning "lookout") are common and suggest that it had a commanding view. Perhaps it looked out over the Jordan Valley since the next place mentioned, Betonim, is thought to be in the south of Gilead overlooking the valley. These three towns may have been the southern border of Gad at one point. Mahanaim, where Jacob had his strange wrestling match (Gen 32:22–32) on the River Jabbok, is then on their northern boundary, where Debir is also likely to be found. Unfortunately, neither this reference nor 2 Samuel 9:4–5 or 17:27 provide

---

[258] As, e.g., proposed by B. Oded, "A Note on Joshua XIII 25," *VT* 21 (1971): 239–41.
[259] Similarly Woudstra, *The Book of Joshua*, 221.

more clarity on its location,[260] though it needs to be distinguished from the better-known site in Judah (Josh 15:49).

The towns in verse 27 are all in the Jordan Valley and appear to be listed from south to north, though the location of Beth-haram (probably Beth-haran in Num 32:36) is uncertain. Gad's territory covered the portion of Sihon's territory that had not been allotted to Reuben. Although most of it seems to have run as far north as the region of the Jabbok, Gad apparently also held the valley floor as far as the lower reaches of the Sea of Galilee (called Chinnereth).

13:29–31. Gad's territory was less clearly defined than Reuben's, and the allotment of the eastern part of Manasseh is less clear again, defined in only general terms. "Half the tribe of Manasseh" here means that it is the half of the tribe who lived east of the Jordan whose allotment is described. Again, Moses is said to have given them their inheritance according to their clans.

Mahanaim, on the Jabbok, was the southern point of their territory, forming a border with Gad (13:26). Manasseh's territory extended north from there into Bashan, the region of Gilead north of the Jabbok. This was the kingdom of Og (13:11–12), reaching up to the villages of Jair (or Havvoth-jair), which was a region running east of the Jordan from just south of the Sea of Galilee and so part of Bashan.

Manasseh's eastern boundary ran along the hills northeast of the Jabbok in the northern half of Gilead up to Ashtaroth, a town about twenty-five miles east of the Sea of Galilee, and included Edrei about fifteen miles to the south as its eastern border (see on 12:4). Although the text routinely speaks of the "half-tribe" of Manasseh, this allotment represented only one main clan in the tribe, that of Manasseh's eldest son Machir (Num 26:29), whereas the other clans were allotted their land west of the Jordan. So, "half-tribe" is a geographic, not numerical, description. However, mention of Machir prepares for the allotment to the western half of the tribe under Joshua (Josh 17:1–13).

13:32–33. Verse 32 functions as a summary of 13:8–31, noting that this is what Moses had done in the past. This passage closes off the report of the inheritance of the eastern tribes. In light of God's directives to Joshua in 13:1–7, we expect that the allotments for the tribes west of the

---

[260] The Samuel references are to Lo Debar (and even in Samuel the spelling varies), but this does appear to be the same site.

Jordan will begin. This, however, is deferred until Joshua 15, as the issue of Caleb's allotment is considered first.

The chapter closes with a note that the Levites received no land since Yahweh was their inheritance, thus forming a link with verse 14 and bracketing the territories received by the eastern tribes.[261] This concluding note therefore functions as a reminder that there were some things Moses could not do because he had died outside the land (Deut 34), and that the allocation of towns for Levi could only occur once Israel was in the land. Joshua would address this issue, though the Levites will not be considered until chapter 21, so that comment on them concludes both Moses' allocation of the land east of the Jordan and Joshua's allocation of the land west of the Jordan. Moreover, Levi would be scattered throughout Israel, stressing the importance of the unity of the nation. Each tribe, and each clan, was allotted its inheritance, but Israel needed to remain a united people.

14:1–3a. The unity of the tribes is then emphasized by the allotment to the western tribes as part of a single but extended process. As 13:8–13 summarized the eastern allocation before focusing on the allotment of each tribe, so these verses summarize the process west of the Jordan. From the perspective of the narrator, all the allotments are past, which is why verse 1 (and 4) describes the giving of the land within Canaan in the past even though the actual narration of this will only begin in chapter 15.

The land east of the Jordan was allotted by Moses, but the land within Canaan was allotted by Eleazar and Joshua. Notably, Eleazar (mentioned for the first time in the book) is named before Joshua, even though Joshua was told to divide the land (13:7). The process also included the heads of the tribes, indicating the collective nature of Israel's leadership in this period, a clear contrast with Moses' distinctive role. The combination of Eleazar, Joshua, and the heads of the families recurs in 19:51, the point at which the division of the land was completed, with the part played by the heads of families paralleling the part played by the officers of the people (1:10–12). That Eleazar and Joshua were the principal figures in this process seems to be indicated by the fact that in 17:4 the daughters of Zelophehad approached them to raise the question of their inheritance.

---

[261] Verse 33 is missing from the LXX. Nelson, *Joshua*, 130, is representative of those who consider its presence in the MT to be an expansion, supporting the shorter reading of the LXX. But the MT is preferable because this opens up the structure of the whole of chapters 13–21, something the LXX apparently missed and so abbreviated the text.

According to verse 2, a further distinctive for the granting of each western tribe's inheritance was that it was accomplished by lot. Casting lots was a common means of determining God's will in the Bible (Prov 16:33), and was used even in the appointment of Matthias (Acts 1:23–26), though the exact process can only be inferred.[262] The process seems to assume that objects indicating a particular option (perhaps a stone or wooden counter) were placed in a container and shaken so that the one that came out represented God's decision (see 18:6; 19:1). Casting lots was a widespread practice in the ancient Near East, so by employing this practice God was working with Israel's established worldview. However, it is clear from Esther 3:7 that God might sovereignly control this practice even among peoples. (In that case, God subtly subverted Haman's attempt to obtain a propitious day for destroying the Jews, giving them time to plan their resistance against his edict.) Here, though, Eleazar and Joshua were following Numbers 25:55–56, where the casting of lots was the means by which the land would be allotted in proportion to the relative needs of each tribe. Just as Joshua 1:7 emphasized Joshua's need to do all that Moses had commanded, and 11:15 stressed his obedience in taking the land, so this passage emphasizes his obedience in allotting it.

14:3b–5. Two exceptional points are now raised. First, the issue of the Levites, which bounded the report of the eastern allocation (13:14, 33), is repeated. This highlights the fact that Moses had not provided their allotment because their inheritance would be on both sides of the Jordan. Since tribal allotments were on the basis of need relative to the land possessed, this could not happen until the western allotments were made. Just as the Levitical allocation had bounded discussion of the tribal allotments, so here it forms an inclusio around the discussion of the Joseph allotment and notes that the Levites would only receive towns and grazing land rather than a designated portion of the land.

Second, since the clan of Machir from Manasseh received land east of the Jordan, the rest of Manasseh needed their land west of the Jordan. But this division of Manasseh also meant that the larger tribe of Joseph was effectively treated as two distinct tribes. This division reaches back to Jacob's blessing of Joseph's sons Manasseh and Ephraim (Gen 48),

---

[262] Anne M. Kitz, "Undivided Inheritance and Lot Casting in the Book of Joshua," *JBL* 119 (2000): 601–18, has drawn on the background of assigning Mesopotamian estates to the heirs to show that the estate was held undivided until it could be allotted on this basis to the heirs. Joshua was effectively the estate administrator, ensuring appropriate division.

although in the blessing of the tribes Jacob continued to treat Joseph as a single tribe (Gen 49:22–26). This ambiguity of their status is also clear in the censuses of the wilderness period, which recognized Joseph as a single tribe but provided separate counts for Manasseh and Ephraim (Num 1:32–35; 26:28–37). That Joseph could still be thought of as one tribe is clear in Joshua 17:14–18, when Ephraim and Manasseh were treated as a single unit. Nevertheless, the practicality of having part of Manasseh on each side of the Jordan meant they were functionally treated as separate tribes, even if in Numbers the stricter definition of them as clans is maintained.

Since this process was carried out by Eleazar, Joshua, and the tribal heads, verse 5 can thus note that the Israelites had done as God commanded through Moses, reflecting the distributed pattern of leadership seen here.

14:6–9. Although 13:1–7 indicated that Joshua was to begin dividing the land, the account was postponed in 13:8–33 to summarize the territory east of the Jordan. The statement that Israel received the territory that Eleazar, Joshua, and the family heads allocated west of the Jordan (4:1) sounds like we will begin to read of the division of the land. But that account is once again deferred for the balance of this chapter, this time to resolve the issue of the inheritance promised to Caleb in the first of the "land grant" narratives (see discussion above under Context).

In this case, Joshua was approached at Gilgal by representatives of the tribe of Judah, though Caleb (who was Judah's spy; see Num 13:6) is immediately marked out as the central figure. Given that several different sites named Gilgal are mentioned in the book, we cannot be certain which is meant here. Perhaps preference should be given to the place just across the Jordan where Israel first entered the land (Josh 4:19). If so, then this first allocation occurs at the place where Israel began to take the land.

Perhaps the more important point is that Caleb is called "son of Jephunneh the Kenizzite" in verse 6 and verse 14, creating an inclusio around the land grant account. Use of the patronym "Jephunneh" is a standard way of referring to Caleb (e.g., Num 13:6), but the designation "Kenizzite" occurs elsewhere only in Numbers 32:12. The verse from Numbers provides key background to this whole passage, since there God indicates that both Joshua and Caleb had remained loyal to God. The phrase translated "remain loyal" in Numbers (where it applies to both Joshua and Caleb) is rendered "followed" in Joshua (14:8–9). Designation of Caleb as a Kenizzite marks him out as someone of foreign, in particular Edomite, descent. The term "Kenizzite" first occurs in Genesis 15:19, where it specifies one of the peoples whom the descendants of Abraham are to displace, seemingly referring to a people resident in the south of Canaan. In Genesis 36:11, 15, and 42, Kenaz is as a descendant of Esau, and this appears to be the particular association intended for Caleb. Evidence for this is also seen in the fact that Othniel, a kinsman of Caleb, is described as a "son of Kenaz" in Joshua 15:19.[263]

Joshua, therefore, accentuates an otherwise relatively minor point about Caleb—that his roots are foreign—while also holding him up for the rest of Israel as the paradigmatic figure in these chapters, a model for what it meant to claim the land Yahweh was giving. Caleb thus becomes a parallel to Rahab, the foreigner who is a paradigmatic figure for the first twelve chapters. A further link between these two is seen in the fact that Caleb charged his fellow spies with having "caused the people to lose heart" (14:8), using the same verb Rahab employed to describe the Canaanites when they heard about Israel (2:9, 11). Since Numbers 32:12 makes clear that Joshua had also completely followed God, he is excluded from this accusation. Furthermore, Joshua was being addressed by Caleb when this charge is made, so that "my brothers" (v. 8) refers to the other ten spies.

What distinguished Caleb among the spies at Kadesh-barnea in Numbers 13–14 was his trust in God's promise. His claim for the land that God had promised him brings that feature to the forefront in Joshua. The original promise to Caleb occurred in the midst of God's announcement of judgment on the rest of the nation, a judgment from which only Caleb and Joshua were excluded (Num 14:20–38). At that point, there was no indication of an oath from Moses that Caleb would receive a particular allocation, only the promise that God would bring him into the land because he had "remained loyal" to him (Num 14:24; cf. Deut 1:36). Caleb's claim here goes beyond that point, asserting that Moses had sworn that

---

[263] Although 1 Chr 4:13 and 15 integrate Caleb into the tribe of Judah, it does not do so in a way that removes the fact that he is still a foreigner. The implications of Caleb's foreignness are explored more thoroughly in my "Joshua 24 and the Welcome of Foreigners," unpublished paper given at the 2016 annual meeting of the Society of Biblical Literature.

the land where he had "set foot"[264] in the region of Hebron would belong to his descendants forever. It is this land that Caleb now claims.

14:10–12. Caleb's speech to Joshua moves from recalling promises made to requesting those promises be kept. The speech is bounded by three occurrences of the phrase "and now" in verses 10 and 12 (וְעַתָּה). Since this does not result in smooth English, csb omits the first, focusing instead on the particle הִנֵּה (usually "behold," but here, "As you see"), and the second, just before his declaration of age. Taken together, these occurrences of "and now" stress the importance of granting Caleb's request.

Tied to this, Caleb three times mentions God's promise (דִּבֶּר): once in verse 10 and twice in verse 12. Furthermore, he twice appeals to Joshua's own experience—what he saw (v. 10) and heard (v. 12). These repetitions stress the urgency of Caleb's request while grounding it in God's prior commitments; Caleb thus becomes a paradigm for all that follows. This is clear from the fact that the land to be granted was still occupied even though it was the site of a previous victory (see on vv. 13–15). This pattern will be repeated in the allocations in 18:11–19:51, where the remaining tribes would need to focus on claiming land not yet fully possessed.

Caleb initially based his claim on the fact that God had kept him alive for forty-five years since he had initially spied out the land, thus fulfilling the promise from Numbers 14:20–38. Given the period of about thirty-eight years after this in which Israel was in the wilderness, Caleb's forty-five years supports Joshua's statement in 11:18 that he had waged war for a long time. Clearly, a further seven years had passed since Israel had entered the land. Even if Caleb was rounding off, we would still have to allow a period of about five years since Israel crossed the Jordan. He had therefore waited a considerable period of time, but one in which he had seen God keep his promise, so that Caleb was still alive to claim his land.

We might suspect Caleb's ability to enjoy the promise to be limited at age eighty-five. However, he was as strong then as he had been when he first scouted the land. Not only had God kept him alive, but he had also kept him fit and active, able to participate in Israel's wars and in normal life activities. Therefore, Caleb could ask for the hill country he had been promised even though it was the site of the Anakim (see on 11:21) who,

---

[264] There is a play on words here. The verb translated "scout" in v. 7 is from the same root as the word "foot" (רגל), so that the area he had scouted was indeed where he had placed his foot. This in turn is tied to the promise to Joshua (1:3) that God would give Israel everywhere the sole of his foot trod.

along with the fortifications of their cities, had so terrified the other spies and the wilderness generation. Those fortifications would not be able to resist Israel, just as Joshua and Caleb had declared, because God would give them the land (Num 14:8).

When Caleb says "perhaps" (אוּלַי) God will be with him to drive out the existing inhabitants, he is not expressing doubt, because he again grounds his statement in the divine promise. Rather, it is an expression of humility, recognizing that only God could drive them out . When "perhaps" is used outside of the context of God's promise (e.g., Num 22:6, 11), a sense of uncertainty is certainly present, but there is no doubt in verse 12 of what God would do. The fulfillment of related promises assured Caleb that God would fulfill this one, too.

14:13–15. In response to Caleb's request, Joshua blessed him and gave him Hebron, a town in the far south of Israel (see comments on 10:3, 36–37) as his inheritance. Although Israel had previously won a victory there, clearly this was not the same as occupying the territory, and it was this that Caleb needed to do. Just as Caleb's foreign status was noted in verse 6, so this status is stressed in verse 14. Hebron would continue to belong to Caleb's clan up to the time this passage was written.[265] The reason for this was his loyalty (see on 14:6–9) to God. Ethnicity was not the defining mark of Israel; rather, the people who continued to live as the people of God were those who were faithful to him.

Claiming this city was no easy task. Hebron used to be called Kiriath-arba—that is, the city of Arba,[266] the greatest of the Anakim. It was the Anakim who had terrified Israel when they first reached the land (Num 13:33), but since Caleb had been wholly loyal to God, he could possess this city and remove even the name of Arba from it. Reference to "rest" in verse 15 balances the comment in 11:23, showing the close links between this account and events summarized there. In this case, the nature of that rest is given a concrete form in Caleb's possession of Hebron.

Bridge

Unlike the first twelve chapters, in which modern readers are more likely to have ethical concerns about the nature of the stories and the warfare

---

[265] On the significance of the phrase "until this day" in Deuteronomy and the Former Prophets as a whole, see Brian Neil Peterson, *The Authors of the Deuteronomistic History: Locating a Tradition in Ancient Israel* (Minneapolis: Fortress, 2014), 81–85.

[266] "Arba" (עַרְבַּע) commonly means "four," but here is understood as a proper noun.

recounted, chapters 13–21 are difficult because most modern readers lack points of contact with the narrative. They have little knowledge of the ancient geography and would therefore be helped through the sensitive use of a map to place these events in time and space. Without that, it is difficult to appreciate just how much land is occupied by the eastern tribes.

Yet these chapters do not exist simply to provide a geographical index to the territory taken by the eastern tribes. Rather, chapters 13–14 (and the whole of Joshua 13–21) have been carefully composed to be read and appreciated because they serve as an introduction to the land allocation and as a deliberate parallel to chapters 1–2. Just as those two chapters introduce the key themes explored in the first twelve chapters of the book—the unity of God's people, reflection on and obedience to God's teaching, and the reality that God's people are those committed to fulfilling his purposes—so chapters 13–14 introduce chapters 13–21 by focusing on exactly the same issues.

The land was not only to be taken but to be allotted according to need, operating down to the level of local villages and not just at the macro-level of the nation. Reflection on and obedience to God's teaching took a particular form in Caleb's claim of the land promised to him, a claim that emerged from his loyalty to God and God's consistency in keeping his promises. And this took place in the larger context of the unity of the nation as a whole, because although God's faithfulness to his promises was consistent and reached down to the level of the individual family, the pairing of chapters 13 and 14 makes clear that this was something that involved the whole nation. God's people were not to be divided by boundaries like the Jordan, and neither were they divided on the basis of ethnicity. It was the whole people, living in faithfulness and trusting God, who experienced the fulfillment of God's promises.[267] That both the eastern tribes and Caleb were able to possess their land fully also stood as a reminder to others that full possession was possible for those who trusted God.[268]

These themes are of particular importance for Joshua but are not restricted to this book. Rather, they have echoes throughout Scripture.[269]

---

[267] See further §1 ("Faithfulness and Obedience"), §2 ("Identity of the People of God"), and §4 ("Land as God's Gift").

[268] See Mitchell, *Together in the Land*, 106.

[269] For other echoes, see Robert Dahlen, "The Savior and the Dog: An Exercise in Hearing," *Word & World* 27 (1997): 269–77, though care needs to be taken with his more homiletical touches when focusing on Caleb's background.

In the New Testament it quickly becomes clear that the people of God are not to be divided on the grounds of ethnicity. The absence of ethnic divisions is apparent on the day of Pentecost when those present were astonished that they heard the apostles speaking in their own languages (Acts 2:7–12). One might claim that all these people were Jewish and that, therefore, issues of ethnicity did not arise. The account of Acts 10 makes clear that there had been divisions between Jew and Gentile. All this was changed through Peter's vision, leading him to report to the church that such divisions did not matter (Acts 11:1–18). This is why Paul could later point out that God had made a people for his name that was not divided (Acts 15:12–17). Indeed, in Christ the things that had previously divided Jew and Gentile were abolished, as all are built into a spiritual temple (Eph 2:11–22). Caleb is a forerunner of this, demonstrating that the relationship with God is what matters.

Moreover, Caleb could claim his land because God had been faithful in keeping his promises—and not in a stingy way. Caleb had reached old age, but God had kept him so that he could truly enjoy the land he was granted. He had received what Paul would describe as the "immeasurable riches of his grace" (Eph 2:7), though of this Caleb was a firstfruits, not yet the fullness. God's faithfulness to his promises is a pivotal theme throughout the Bible.

We are also continually reminded of the need for unity among the people of God. Occasionally, God's people are called to come out and be separate (2 Cor 6:17); however, this means separation from sin, not separation within the church. That is why we are reminded of the importance of keeping the unity of the Spirit (Eph 4:3), because we are one body in Christ. Such unity, such dependence on the promises of God, is never easy. It was not easy for Israel in Joshua's day, and Paul's exhortations in Ephesians make clear that it is not easy today. Joshua 13–14 demonstrates that unity was a challenge for Israel; it remains a challenge for contemporary believers. Similarly, as Earl points out,[270] Caleb functions as someone who boldly claims God's promises, serving as a model for both outsiders like the Syro-Phoenician woman (Matt 15:21–28) and insiders as they approach God in Christ and ask for his grace (Heb 4:16).

---

[270] Earl, *Reading Joshua as Christian Scripture*, 171–72.

B. The Allotment for Judah (15:1–63)

¹ Now the allotment for the tribe of the descendants of Judah by their clans was in the southernmost region, south to the Wilderness of Zin and over to the border of Edom.

> ² Their southern border began at the tip of the Dead Sea on the south bay ³ and went south of the Scorpions' Ascent, proceeded to Zin, ascended to the south of Kadesh-barnea, passed Hezron, ascended to Addar, and turned to Karka. ⁴ It proceeded to Azmon and to the Brook of Egypt and so the border ended at the Mediterranean Sea. This is your southern border.
>
> ⁵ Now the eastern border was along the Dead Sea to the mouth of the Jordan.
>
> The border on the north side was from the bay of the sea at the mouth of the Jordan. ⁶ It ascended to Beth-hoglah, proceeded north of Beth-arabah, and ascended to the Stone of Bohan son of Reuben. ⁷ Then the border ascended to Debir from the Valley of Achor, turning north to the Gilgal that is opposite the Ascent of Adummim, which is south of the ravine. The border proceeded to the Waters of En-shemesh and ended at En-rogel. ⁸ From there the border ascended Ben Hinnom Valley to the southern Jebusite slope (that is, Jerusalem) and ascended to the top of the hill that faces Hinnom Valley on the west, at the northern end of Rephaim Valley. ⁹ From the top of the hill the border curved to the spring of the Waters of Nephtoah, went to the cities of Mount Ephron, and then curved to Baalah (that is, Kiriath-jearim). ¹⁰ The border turned westward from Baalah to Mount Seir, went to the northern slope of Mount Jearim (that is, Chesalon), descended to Beth-shemesh, and proceeded to Timnah. ¹¹ Then the border reached to the slope north of Ekron, curved to Shikkeron, proceeded to Mount Baalah, went to Jabneel, and ended at the Mediterranean Sea.
>
> ¹² Now the western border was the coastline of the Mediterranean Sea.

This was the boundary of the descendants of Judah around their clans.

¹³ He gave Caleb son of Jephunneh the following portion among the descendants of Judah based on the Lord's instruction to Joshua: Kiriath-arba (that is, Hebron; Arba was the father of Anak). ¹⁴ Caleb drove out from there the three sons of Anak: Sheshai, Ahiman, and Talmai, descendants of Anak. ¹⁵ From there he marched against the inhabitants of Debir, which used to be called Kiriath-sepher, ¹⁶ and

Caleb said, "Whoever attacks and captures Kiriath-sepher, I will give my daughter Achsah to him as a wife." [17] So Othniel son of Caleb's brother, Kenaz, captured it, and Caleb gave his daughter Achsah to him as a wife. [18] When she arrived, she persuaded Othniel to ask her father for a field. As she got off her donkey, Caleb asked her, "What can I do for you?" [19] She replied, "Give me a blessing. Since you have given me land in the Negev, give me the springs also." So he gave her the upper and lower springs.

[20] This was the inheritance of the tribe of the descendants of Judah by their clans.

[21] These were the outermost cities of the tribe of the descendants of Judah toward the border of Edom in the Negev: Kabzeel, Eder, Jagur, [22] Kinah, Dimonah, Adadah, [23] Kedesh, Hazor, Ithnan, [24] Ziph, Telem, Bealoth, [25] Hazor-hadattah, Kerioth-hezron (that is, Hazor), [26] Amam, Shema, Moladah, [27] Hazar-gaddah, Heshmon, Beth-pelet, [28] Hazar-shual, Beer-sheba, Biziothiah, [29] Baalah, Iim, Ezem, [30] Eltolad, Chesil, Hormah, [31] Ziklag, Madmannah, Sansannah, [32] Lebaoth, Shilhim, Ain, and Rimmon—twenty-nine cities in all, with their settlements.

[33] In the Judean foothills: Eshtaol, Zorah, Ashnah, [34] Zanoah, En-gannim, Tappuah, Enam, [35] Jarmuth, Adullam, Socoh, Azekah, [36] Shaaraim, Adithaim, Gederah, and Gederothaim—fourteen cities, with their settlements; [37] Zenan, Hadashah, Migdal-gad, [38] Dilan, Mizpeh, Jokthe-el, [39] Lachish, Bozkath, Eglon, [40] Cabbon, Lahmam, Chitlish, [41] Gederoth, Beth-dagon, Naamah, and Makkedah—sixteen cities, with their settlements; [42] Libnah, Ether, Ashan, [43] Iphtah, Ashnah, Nezib, [44] Keilah, Achzib, and Mareshah—nine cities, with their settlements; [45] Ekron, with its surrounding villages and settlements; [46] from Ekron to the sea, all the cities near Ashdod, with their settlements; [47] Ashdod, with its surrounding villages and settlements; Gaza, with its surrounding villages and settlements, to the Brook of Egypt and the coastline of the Mediterranean Sea.

[48] In the hill country: Shamir, Jattir, Socoh, [49] Dannah, Kiriath-sannah (that is, Debir), [50] Anab, Eshtemoh, Anim, [51] Goshen, Holon, and Giloh—eleven cities, with their settlements; [52] Arab, Dumah, Eshan, [53] Janim, Beth-tappuah, Aphekah, [54] Humtah, Kiriath-arba (that is, Hebron), and Zior—nine cities, with their settlements; [55] Maon, Carmel, Ziph, Juttah, [56] Jezreel, Jokdeam, Zanoah, [57] Kain, Gibeah, and Timnah—ten cities, with their settlements; [58] Halhul, Beth-zur, Gedor, [59] Maarath, Beth-anoth, and Eltekon—six cities, with their settlements; [60] Kiriath-baal (that is,

Kiriath-jearim), and Rabbah—two cities, with their settlements.
[61] In the wilderness: Beth-arabah, Middin, Secacah, [62] Nib-
shan, the City of Salt, and En-gedi—six cities, with their
settlements.
[63] But the descendants of Judah could not drive out the Jebusites
who lived in Jerusalem. So the Jebusites still live in Jerusalem among
the descendants of Judah today.

Context

Although 13:7 indicated that Joshua was to divide the land, it is only here
that the process begins. As noted (see Context on Joshua 13:1–14:15) this
was because key theological themes had to be established first, especially
the importance of the unity of the tribes and the consistency of Joshua's
practice with that of Moses. With these points clarified, the allotment
could begin. Since the proportion of the narrative devoted to Judah is
greater than that of the other tribes (especially Joshua 10 with its focus
on the southern conquest), and also given that Caleb's claim (14:6–15)
was within their territory, it is not surprising that Judah's allotment
is described first. A link with the previous chapter is also established
through Achsah's claim for the springs around Hebron (15:13–19), since
this is a clear continuation of Caleb's claim and places Caleb in the role
of Joshua allocating Judah's territory (Num 34:19).

Unlike the other tribal allotments, Judah's is described from two
clearly different perspectives. The first, in verses 1–12, describes the
tribal boundary in which an imaginary line is traced around the region
that is to become Judah. Similar boundary lines are traced for Joseph as
a whole (16:1–3), as well as the constituent tribes of Ephraim (16:5–9)
and west Manasseh (17:7–11) before the establishment of the sanctuary
in Shiloh (18:1–10). After Achsah's land-grant narrative, a city list is then
provided for Judah (15:20–63), providing a second perspective. In Judah's
case, the statement about the tribe's ability to expel the indigenous population occurs at the end of the city list (15:63), whereas the equivalent
statement for the Joseph tribes is included within their boundary lists
(16:10; 17:12–13). The allotments for Judah and the Joseph tribes largely
represent the land taken in Joshua 1–12, which is why God's speech to
Joshua in 13:2 pointed out that much land remained to be taken.

The allotments for the remaining seven tribes in 18:11–19:48 (except
for Benjamin) operate from the perspective of land to be taken and so do

not include a statement on the ability of the tribe to expel the indigenous population, except for Dan in 19:47. This reflects the fact that they moved to the far north rather than settling on the coastal plain in the south. The allotments for these seven tribes are principally described in terms of their boundaries rather than providing a comprehensive listing of cities, other than for Simeon (because it was included in Judah) and Dan (presumably because the territory was already lost). Only Benjamin and Naphtali receive both a boundary and city list, though both are abbreviated in comparison with Judah. In Benjamin's case, this is presumably because its territory represented land already possessed, while Naphtali's lists both represent only a bare outline. We can tabulate the presence of the three key elements of the allotments as follows:

Tribe	Boundary List	City List	Indigenous Population Comment
Judah	X	X	X
Ephraim	X		X
Manasseh	X		X
Benjamin	X	X	
Simeon		X	
Zebulun	X		
Issachar	X		
Asher	X		
Naphtali	X	X	
Dan		X	X

The account of Judah's allotment is the only one to include all possible elements, and its town list is unique in being longer than its border list.[271] As noted, with the exception of Simeon and Dan all the tribes received a boundary list, though there are good reasons why they should vary from the other tribes. The western tribal allotments are all reported differently from those of the eastern tribes. In the case of the latter, the boundary

---

[271] Rösel, *Joshua*, 235. It is possible that there was a city list for Ephraim at 16:9, though it is also possible that it is simply a matter of awkward syntax there and no list existed. See comments on 16:9.

description was provided for the two and a half tribes (13:8–12), with the indigenous population comment placed there (13:13), and their territories then described in a combined boundary and city list. The combined boundary list for these tribes is paralleled by that for the Joseph tribes west of the Jordan (16:1–3), except that these tribes have a much more clearly defined boundary list.

All this points to the importance of Judah for the book of Joshua, since it is the only tribe to include all three elements. Apart from the indigenous population comment (all of which are brief), both the boundary list and the city list for Judah are considerably longer than for the other tribes. This may derive from the fact that Judah was the largest tribe according to the census in Numbers 26 (76,500; Num 26:19–21), though the combined Joseph tribes were actually larger (85,200; Num 26:29–37). But once we allow for the clan of Machir settling east of the Jordan, the western Joseph tribes were probably smaller than Judah. Nevertheless, the literary distinction between the tribes is out of proportion to the tribal populations, and that discrepancy increases when we compare the space given to the tribes after the establishment of the Shiloh sanctuary. At that point, the space given to Benjamin is also out of proportion to its population, though in this case the relative space given to Benjamin is more or less in proportion to its size relative to the Joseph tribes. Indeed, when we recognize that there are probably eleven cities in Judah's city list missing from 15:59 (see comments there), and the majority of cities in the list are not mentioned elsewhere, then it is possible to appreciate the level of attention given to Judah.[272]

Can we identify reasons for this? Given the strong emphasis on the unity of the nation in Joshua 1 and 13–14, a theme that reemerges in Joshua 22, it is unlikely that the attention given to Judah reflects any view of Judah having priority. A more likely reason can be seen when we note the different forms in which the allotments for each tribe are recorded. The presence of indigenous population comments in four of the ten western allotment reports shows clearly that these lists are written from a perspective of looking back on the conquest period from some time later. How much later is unclear. But in the case of Judah, the fact

---

[272] The chapter bristles with text-critical problems, reflecting the difficulties of transcribing a list like this. This is compounded by the difficulties involved in rendering it in other languages (e.g., the LXX). As such, only those variants that have a significant impact on the meaning of the chapter receive comment here.

that Jerusalem was still a Jebusite city (15:63) suggests that this list was compiled prior to David's capture of the city (2 Sam 5:6–10). The comment on Dan (Josh 19:47) reflects the fact that they were unable to take their assigned territory almost from the beginning (though the Samson narrative of Judges 13–16 is set in a period when the attempt was being made). But since it also acknowledges the traditions found in Judges 17–18, though with some degree of independence from them,[273] then it too is probably fairly early. The comments on Ephraim and western Manasseh presume these tribes were still present in the land (note the use of the "to this day" formula in 16:10),[274] meaning that these comments were made prior to the exile of the Northern Kingdom (721 BC), though how much earlier cannot be determined.

These comments demonstrate enough diversity to suggest that the material gathered together in these chapters came from a range of periods and sources. If so, then the most likely reason for the prominence given to Judah is simply that more was recorded there than for other tribes. If the final compilation of the book was carried out in Judah, then this material would have been the most readily available. Importantly, this suggests the compilers of Joshua were faithful in passing on the traditions available to them rather than making tendentious use of them.[275] Hence, for the authors of the book of Joshua it is important to retain the traditions that had been passed down while continuing to stress the importance of unity among the tribes.

Exegesis

15:1–12. Consistent with 14:2 (see comments there), the allotment for the tribe of Judah was given by lot to each clan, which also followed the pattern of the eastern tribes (see comments on 13:15). This passage establishes a general pattern for the boundary lists, using a system of describing an imaginary line that can be traced from point to point to

---

[273] The former name of the city of Dan in Judg 18:27 was Laish, whereas here it is Leshem. These are likely byforms of the one name, but the different forms suggest they were not written down by the same person. The variants in the LXX indicate that the text of Josh 19:47 is problematic. See comments there.

[274] See further the discussion of date and authorship in the introduction.

[275] Such a reading would stand strongly against the sort of approach developed by Rowlett, *Joshua and the Rhetoric of Violence*, especially her fundamental claim (p. 12) that the book was produced as a threat to later generations against resisting established power.

mark out the boundary. Key verbs are used that recur in other boundary lists, such as יצא (usually "went"; e.g., v. 3), עבר (usually "proceeded"; e.g., v. 4), עלה (usually "ascended"; e.g., v. 6), and פנה (usually "turned"; e.g., v. 7). Not only do these terms describe the boundaries, they also help a culture without printed maps to visualize the territory being described. Each verb provides guidance as to the type of journey involved in reaching the next point on the boundary.

Judah's allotment is placed in the south of the country (see map of tribal allotments). The opening statement of verse 1 indicates the general area, while pointing out that the southernmost points stretched from the Wilderness of Zin to the territory of Edom south of the Dead Sea (Num 34:6). Zin is roughly equivalent to Kadesh (Num 33:36); a town there was the point from which the original spies began their work (Num 13:21). The land south of this was wilderness unsuited to permanent settlement.

The boundary list itself traces the borders to the south (vv. 2–4),[276] east (v. 5a), north (vv. 5b–11), and west (v. 12a). Then a summary statement in verse 12b matches verse 1a, creating an inclusio around the whole. The eastern boundary, from the Jordan's entry into the Dead Sea[277] along its western shore, could be described quite simply because the sea provides a natural boundary. Likewise, the western boundary was the Mediterranean coast, limited by the northern and southern boundaries. By contrast, the north and south lacked clearly defined natural boundaries and so required more careful explanation.

The southern boundary could be described more loosely than the northern boundary because of the nature of the land to the south as a region for nomads rather than settled communities. The imaginary line runs from the "south bay" (v. 2)[278] at the southernmost point of the Dead Sea southwest for about fifteen miles to the Ascent of Akrabbim (translated as "Scorpions' Ascent" in csb) continuing down the Arabah to Zin and then below Kadesh-barnea, where Israel had camped in Numbers 13:26. From there the line turns to Hezron, Addar (called Hazzar-addar in Num 34:4), Karka, and Azmon, towns that must be northwest of Kadesh-barnea but cannot be identified. The Brook of Egypt is perhaps the Wadi

---

[276] This draws on the same traditions as Num 34:3–5.

[277] Throughout, the Dead Sea is more literally the Salt Sea, which describes its character, but the more familiar modern label is used in translation.

[278] Lit., "the tongue" (see csb note). Also v. 5. Matching these bays to the form of the Dead Sea now is almost impossible because of the ways its level has varied over time.

el-Arish, a stream that runs through the center of the Sinai Peninsula, though a branch of the Nile that is no longer extant is also possible. The brook is again mentioned in the city list (15:47).

Because the northern boundary represented a densely populated area, it is more tightly defined beginning in verse 5. Similarly beginning at the Dead Sea, the line rises to Beth-hoglah between the Jordan and Jericho, though the town itself was allotted to Benjamin (18:21). The boundary ran north a few miles to Beth-arabah, though again the town was allotted to Benjamin (18:22). The Stone of Bohan served as a boundary marker between Judah and Benjamin (18:17). The patriarch Reuben is not otherwise said to have had a son called Bohan, so another Reuben may be meant here. The Valley of Achor runs down to the Jordan Valley from a few miles west of the Dead Sea, and from here the boundary ran to Debir, though this is likely a different town from the one mentioned in verse 15, which is too far to the south. From there it ran north to Gilgal, the site where Israel entered the land (4:19), opposite the Ascent of Adummim (18:17), a pass that climbed up from the Jordan past Jericho. Both En-shemesh and En-rogel are border towns with springs on the road toward Jerusalem.

From there the border runs to the Ben Hinnom Valley (later famous as Gehenna, Mark 9:43), a valley to the south and west of Jerusalem (18:6).[279] This valley intersects with Rephaim Valley, where David would later defeat the Philistines (2 Sam 5:18, 22; apparently this was a favored location for them, cf. 2 Sam 23:13). Reference to the Jebusites in verse 8 provides evidence that this area was controlled by them when the boundary list was compiled. The line described has passed through only about twenty miles from the Jordan, but from this point the rate of movement accelerates toward the Mediterranean coast.

The curving of the line to the Waters of Nephtoah means the border heads northwest from Jerusalem across the cities of Mount Ephron (location unknown) to Baalah (known also as Kiriath-jearim), which is about ten miles west of Jerusalem. At this point the border with Benjamin ends and follows the boundary with Dan. Since Dan was not in this territory when the list was compiled, it is recorded with considerably less precision. Initially, the border runs southwest through Mount Seir (not to be

---

[279] Verse 7 poses numerous textual difficulties, but (with Nelson, *Joshua*, 183) there is insufficient evidence to change the MT. So CSB is right to follow it.

Used by permission, Holman Bible Publishers, copyright 2019.

confused with the better-known mountain in Edom),[280] though the exact location is uncertain. Given that it is close to Mount Jearim, we presumably have not moved too far from Baalah, but Beth-shemesh is about ten miles southwest of Baalah, with Timnah (see Judg 14:1–2) about five miles further west and Ekron (the northernmost Philistine city) another five miles west and slightly north. The curve heads north a similar distance to Shikkeron before running northwest for about ten miles through Mount Baalah and Jabneel until it reaches the Mediterranean.

15:13–19. This second land-grant narrative (see exposition on Joshua 13:1–14:15) is in reality an extension of Caleb's narrative from 14:6–15 and was probably originally attached to it (perhaps with additional material). This can be seen from the fact that there is no subject for the verb "he gave" in verse 13, with Joshua understood only from the wider context. The passage functions both to link Judah's inheritance to Caleb and also to divide the boundary list from the city list. Caleb's model of trusting faith is continued here. But whereas Caleb's story was paradigmatic for all the tribes, this story is applied only to Judah. A slightly abbreviated version of this narrative (with some differences in wording) appears in Judges 1:11–15, though its function there is slightly different.

Caleb was originally an outsider who was integrated into Judah (evident in his description as a Kenizzite in 14:6, 14). His integration is affirmed by his reception of a portion among the descendants of Judah on the basis of God's instruction to Joshua, though we have no other record of this. Although the town was known as Hebron by the time this report was written, its former name of Kiriath-arba is noted. The name Arba was derived from the father of Anak, making him a prominent figure among the Anakim (see discussion on 14:15). Whereas Caleb's land-grant narrative had shown him expressing the hope that he would be able to drive out the Anakim (14:12), we are told here that he did indeed do this. Mention of Anak's three sons, Sheshai, Ahiman, and Talmai refers back to Numbers 13:22, which noted that they were then resident in Hebron. Caleb's expulsion of them is thus confirmation of his confidence when the spies returned to Kadesh-barnea (Num 13:30) and fulfillment of his hope (Josh 14:12).

---

[280] H. G. T. Mitchell, "Joshua xv. 10," *JBL* 8 (1888): 161–62, proposes an emendation at this point, but this is unnecessary because he fails to realize that the Seir here is not the one in Edom.

Although Caleb had been allotted Hebron, he also headed about ten miles south to Debir. Joshua had defeated this city (10:38–39; 12:13) and the Anakim in the region (11:21), though Israel had not yet taken possession of the city. Like Hebron, Debir had previously been known by another name, Kiriath-sepher, which we might translate as "Book Town" or (with a slight change of vowels) "Scribe Town." In 15:49 the former name of Debir is said to be Kiriath-sannah, but there is good reason to believe that this is a scribal error (see comments there). Since Caleb used the former name (v. 16), this was presumably what the indigenous population called it, with Debir subsequently becoming the city's Israelite name.

Caleb's offer of his daughter Achsah as the bride of whomever struck down and captured the city reflects the very different view of marriage in ancient Israel from modern Western patterns. Marriage was normally something negotiated between parents, with wives and children both understood as subordinate to the head of the household, though this did not reduce them to chattel. They were not property in the sense of something that could be traded, but their rights were limited relative to the head of the household. We should therefore not think that the model of marriage shown here is representative of God's ideal so much as an instance of God working with the cultural values of the time.[281] Achsah was subordinate to her father, and her marriage would need to contribute to the well-being of the whole household. Therefore, it was culturally appropriate for Caleb to offer her in this way. But this offer came with high demands on whomever would marry her precisely because the marriage needed to contribute to the family. In particular, the city had to be struck down and captured. According to 10:38–39, Joshua had captured the city and struck it down, using the same verbs as Caleb uses here though in reverse order. From the larger context, though, it is clear that Joshua's action had led to only a temporary holding of the town, whereas Caleb envisaged something more permanent.

---

[281] On the broader issue of the status of wives and children, see Christopher J. H. Wright, *God's People in God's Land: Family, Land and Property in the Old Testament* (Carlisle: Paternoster, 1990), 181–238. On the specific issue of chattel, which provides an important modification to Wright's view of wives and children as a limited form of property, see T. M. Lemos, "Were Israelite Women Chattel? Shedding New Light on an Old Question," in *Worship, Women and War: Essays in Honor of Susan Niditch*, ed. John J. Collins, T. M. Lemos, and Saul M. Olyan (Providence, RI: Brown University, 2015), 227–41

The narrator is unconcerned with the process by which Debir was secured for Israel. Instead, the focus is on how Achsah continued to demonstrate the same sort of faith that Caleb had demonstrated in claiming Hebron. We are told that Caleb's kinsman Othniel[282] captured (לכד, the verb matching 10:39) the city; therefore, Caleb gave his daughter Achsah to him in marriage. Othniel would later be the first deliverer mentioned in Judges (Judg 3:7–11), but that is of no interest here since the focus is on Achsah's initiative.

Achsah persuaded Othniel to request a field as well as the city,[283] presumably as a place for livestock. In fact, Othniel is so marginalized that we are never told of him making the request. Instead, Achsah dismounted[284] from her donkey, and Caleb enquired what he could do for her. Her request was based on the fact that water becomes scarce this far south[285] in Israel and also on the assumption that Caleb had indeed granted Othniel's request of a field, necessitating water for both people in the town and their livestock. Accordingly, she asked for a blessing: the provision of the springs of water.

The request shows that a father blessing his daughter with material provision in marriage was something that could be expected,[286] though

---

[282] The Hebrew עָתְנִיאֵל בֶּן־קְנַז אֲחִי כָלֵב is ambiguous and, depending on how it is punctuated, could mean either that Othniel was Caleb's younger brother (so Woudstra, *The Book of Joshua*, 241) or nephew (so CSB). Although CSB requires the existence of an otherwise unknown Kenaz who was Caleb's younger brother, it is not improbable that Kenaz would have a son with the same name, and marriage to a cousin is a more likely choice since the alternative would contravene the spirit if not the letter of the laws on sexual relations in Leviticus 18 and 20.

[283] Alternatively, according to Paul G. Mosca, "Who Seduced Whom: A Note on Joshua 15.18; Judges 1.14," *CBQ* 46 (1984): 18–22, Achsah could have persuaded her father, with Othniel effectively absent. Both interpretations are possible, with a marginal preference for the rendering of the CSB because it avoids an otherwise harsh change of subject, though in so compressed a narrative this is not a strong argument.

[284] The verb צנח elsewhere occurs only in the parallel account in Judg 1:14 and also in describing the motion of the tent peg through Sisera's head in Judg 4:21. The exact sense of the verb is uncertain, but some sort of downward motion seems likely, hence the CSB translation, "she got off." The uncertainty of this, though, can be noted from the fact that DCH also considers "implore," "clap hands," "belch," or "pierce through" to be possible alternatives.

[285] The CSB treats נֶגֶב as a proper noun ("the Negev"), but although Debir is close to the Negev it is not really within it. It seems better to understand נֶגֶב as a common noun meaning "south."

[286] Joseph Fleishman, "A Daughter's Demand and a Father's Compliance: The Legal Background to Achsah's Claim and Caleb's Compliance (Josh 15,16–19, Judges 1,12–15)," *ZAW* 118 (2006): 354–73, is therefore correct to argue that Achsah asked for an expanded dowry since she could not inherit from her father given that she had brothers (cf.

there is also a play on words. The word "blessing" (בְּרָכָה) can, with a change of one vowel (to בְּרֵכָה), mean a "pool," reflecting the fact that in such a climate water was seen as a great blessing. Accordingly, Caleb gave her the springs (גֻּלֹּה, a word that can mean either a spring or a pool) above and below the town, ensuring that she not only had a town but also the water necessary to sustain residents and livestock. More importantly, we see Achsah as one who demonstrated the faith that Caleb had shown in making real the promise of the land.

15:20. Although verse 12 had given a summary of the boundaries of Judah's allocation and stressed that the allocation was concerned with the clans within the tribe, the towns that made up that allotment and to which the clans would relate had not been indicated. Because the inheritance of the tribe was not land in general but also the towns within it, the focus for the rest of the chapter is on the towns that made up that inheritance.

Since there is a concern to address the interests of the clans, each of whom would have settled in a particular part of Judah's territory, the area is divided into four main regions that follow a broadly clockwise journey through the territory. Accordingly, verses 21–32 describe the southern region toward Edom, verses 33–47 describe the foothills and coast, verses 48–60 describe the hill country, and verses 61–62 describe the western coast of the Dead Sea. Some of these are further subdivided, with the subdivisions usually marked off by counts, numbering the cities within that district. For example, verses 33–47 can on this basis be divided into verses 33–36, 37–41, 42–44, and 45–47.

The location of many of these towns is unknown, and in many instances nothing more is known about a town than its mention here. Therefore, comment is only made on places that can be identified, are mentioned elsewhere, or where a place here needs to be distinguished from another with the same name. No explanation is given for the counts provided, but they possibly reflect use of the list for administrative purposes. In light of our lack of knowledge, no comment is made on the following towns:

---

1 Chr 2:42–49; 4:15). Moreover, there is broad evidence to indicate that such a dowry, though managed by the husband, would belong to the woman and then be inherited by her children.

Town	Verse
Eder, Jagur	21
Kinah, Dimonah, Adadah	22
Ithnan	23
Telem, Bealoth	24
Hazor-hadattah,[287] Kerioth-hezron	25
Amam, Shema	26
Hazar-gaddah, Heshmon, Beth-pelet	27
Hazar-shual, Biziothiah	28
Iim	29
Chesil	30
Sansannah	31
Lebaoth, Shilhim	32
Adithaim, Gederah, Gederothaim	36
Zenan, Hadashah, Migdal-gad	37
Dilen, Jokthe-el	38
Cabbon, Lahmam, Chitlish	40
Gederoth, Beth-dagon, Naamah	41
Iphtah, Ashnah, Nezib	43
Dannah	49
Anim	50
Janim, Beth-tappuah, Aphekah	53
Humtah, Zior	54
Jokdeam	56
Kain	57
Halhul	58
Maarath, Beth-anoth, Eltekon	59
Culom, Tatam, Sores, Carem, Baither, Manach	59mg[288]
Middin, Secacah	61
Nibshan, City of Salt	62

[287] The element "Hazor" in a place name refers to a settlement, and is thus a common element in toponyms.

[288] "mg" refers to the marginal reading in the CSB.

15:21-32. The first region within Judah covers southern towns, toward the border with Edom, south of the Dead Sea and across the Negev, on the edge of Israel's territory. Kabzeel is perhaps about ten miles south of Debir and was home of Benaiah, one of David's warriors (2 Sam 23:20) who later functioned as Solomon's executioner (1 Kgs 2:25-46).

Kedesh (v. 23) is not the town mentioned in 12:22, nor is Hazor the city central to 11:11-15. Ziph is probably near the Ascent of Akrabbim rather than the town five miles south of Hebron. Moladah (v. 26) is later reassigned to Simeon (19:2). Beer-sheba (v. 28), a site about fifty-five miles southwest of Hebron and known for its well (which will also be allotted to Simeon in 19:2), is often mentioned in the Bible. Disputes about access to the water there (vital in such a dry area) are recorded in the patriarchal narratives (Gen 21:22-34; 26:12-33), and the town also became the proverbial southern boundary of the land in the phrase "Dan to Beersheba" (e.g., Judg 20:1). Baalah (v. 29) is not the town mentioned in Josh 15:9-10 since this town is further south. Hormah, near Beer-sheba, was where Israel was defeated when they attempted to enter the land against God's directive (Num 14:45; cf. Num 21:1-3). David sent spoil taken from the Amalekites there when negotiating support in the Negev (1 Sam 30:30). Ziklag (where the Shephelah meets the coastal plain) is another significant site for David (1 Sam 28:6; 30:30; 2 Sam 1:1-10). Madmannah, probably about fifteen miles east of Ziklag and about twenty miles southeast of Hebron, is mentioned (spelled "Madmenah" in the csb) in an oracle about an Assyrian attack in Isa 10:31. Ain (not the site in Num 34:11) and Rimmon (v. 32) are reassigned to Simeon (Josh 19:7),[289] with Ain also becoming a Levitical city. In all, seven cities from this region are reassigned to Simeon (Moladah, Beer-sheba, Ezem, Eltolad, Hormah, Ain, and Rimmon). As the list is presented in the csb (and this seems probable), there are thirty-six place names, not the twenty-nine claimed. A range of plausible textual corruptions could explain this, none of which can be proved. However, the solution may be the difference between the number of towns mentioned and those that remained with Judah (removing those reassigned to Simeon), since that would leave a total of

---

[289] In Josh 19:7 the mt could be read as Ain-rimmon, joining these to a single town, but given the total of four towns mentioned in the verse it is best to understand them as separate toponyms.

twenty-nine.[290] Alternatively, some of the sites may have been considered too small to be regarded as cities, though we cannot know the criteria used to determine this.

15:33–47. The list moves to the foothills and coast, as noted by the opening comment (v. 33). CSB "Judean foothills" renders שפלה, a term that can also be a proper noun, hence the CSB note, "or *the Shephelah*." The various subsections within this section are divided by the use of counts at verses 36, 41, and 44. Each count is marked by the phrase "with their settlements" to indicate that only the towns have been named. The final subsection (vv. 45–47) deals with three Philistine towns and their settlements, though no count is provided. Nevertheless, it is clear from the new heading in verse 48 that these towns should be included in this section.

Verses 33–36 comprise the first district, the count in verse 36 noting that it covers fourteen towns, probably toward the northern end of the region. As rendered in the CSB, there are fifteen towns. The probable solution to this is reflected in the margin, where either En-gannim and Tappuah or Adullam and Socoh should be merged as a single toponym due to an absent conjunction. There is a disjunctive accent attached to each word, which is why the CSB treats these as separate names, but this perhaps shows that the Masoretes did not know how to divide these towns. However, we lack the evidence to determine which of these options is more likely correct. Of the other towns, Eshtaol and Zorah are later noted in Dan's allotment (19:41), indicating we should see them as border towns. Both are important for the stories of Samson (Judg 13:25; 16:31) and Micah and his idol (Judg 18:2, 8, 11). They are probably in the Valley of Sorek. Another Zanoah is mentioned in verse 56 in the hill country. If En-gannim is correct, then it is not the town in Issachar later allotted to Levi (Josh 19:21; 21:29). If Tappuah is correct, it is not the site in Josh 16:8. Jarmuth is mentioned frequently (10:3, 5, 23; 12:11), but is not the town from Issachar given to Levi (21:29; probably Remeth in 19:21). Adullam (cf. 12:15) was the site of a cave used by David (1 Sam 22:1). Another Socoh is mentioned in Joshua 15:48, but this site is probably the one in the

---

[290] The LXX also gives a total of twenty-nine but has thirty names. Although a shorter text often should be given priority, the difficulty of copying a list such as this means that lines could easily be missed, and the LXX has numerous internal issues as well. Conversely, the longer list in the LXX at v. 59 should be given priority precisely because it is so easy for a copyist to miss a line.

Valley of Elah where David confronted Goliath (1 Sam 17:1, 2). Azekah
(cf. Josh 10:10, 11) is also mentioned in the Goliath story (1 Sam 17:1).
Shaaraim ("Two Gates") is west of Azekah and Socoh, heading toward
Ekron, on the route taken by Israel's forces as they pursued the Philistines
after Goliath's death (1 Sam 17:52).

The second district (vv. 37–41), a further sixteen towns and their
settlements, is south of the first district. Mizpeh ("Watchtower") is a
common place name in the Bible, describing towns built on hills with
a good view of the surrounding territory. Lachish became one of the
most important towns in Judah. It is about thirty miles southwest of
Jerusalem and is probably modern-day Tell el-Duweir. Although allocated to Judah, it only came to prominence in the monarchic period. If
this listing is derived from early material, then it would explain why it is
simply included with other towns of no great significance. Nevertheless,
it provides us with a geographical anchor for this district. Bozkath was
the hometown of Josiah's mother (2 Kgs 22:1). Like Lachish, Eglon is an
important town in the southern campaign (Josh 10:3, 5, 23, 26, 36, 37), as
was Makkedah (10:10, 16, 17, 21, 28, 29; 12:16).

The third district is presented in verses 42–44. As with the second
district, the number of towns and settlements (nine) agrees with the list.
Certainty about the location of most of these towns is impossible, but they
may be further inland than the second district. Libnah, later allotted to
Levi (21:13) is an important town for the southern campaign (10:29, 31, 32,
39; 12:15). Ether and Ashan are later assigned to Simeon (19:7). Keilah, an
important town during David's flight from Saul (1 Sam 23:1–13), is northwest of Hebron. Achzib (not the town in Asher of Josh 19:29; Judg 1:31)
occurs along with Mareshah in Micah's puns on Shephelah place names
(Mic 1:14–15).

The fourth district (vv. 45–47) covers three of the five Philistine cities—
Gath and Ashkelon are omitted. No count is provided, perhaps because at
the time of the compilation of the list these towns were not controlled by
Israel (cf. 13:3), and so there was no need to provide administrative details.
Gath's omission is puzzling given that the Philistine towns were all on
the coastal plain, and it may have formed a boundary point. It is known
in the book (11:22; 13:3), so we should probably assume it has fallen out
of the list, and most probably belongs in verse 46. Ashkelon's absence is
also curious, though it is covered by the fact that both Ashdod and Gaza

are mentioned as it lies directly between.[291] Irrespective of whether or not Gath is included, the Philistine towns are arranged so that the more inland center(s) are mentioned first, then the coastal towns from north to south. If Gath is included, then the inland towns are also arranged from north to south.

Ekron is likely in the Valley of Sorek, about fifteen miles from the coast, and has already been noted as lying on Judah's boundary (15:11) and in 19:43 is also listed in the allocation for Dan, though border towns are often listed with both tribes affected. As the text now stands, the territory from Ekron to the coast and its associated villages and settlements is also covered in the allotment to Judah, covering the area near Ashdod before mentioning Ashdod and its associated localities. Ashdod is almost on the coast about twelve miles west of Ekron. Apart from passing references (11:22; 13:3), it is not mentioned elsewhere in Joshua though it will be an important site in the story of the ark of the covenant (1 Sam 5–6). The last Philistine city mentioned is Gaza, though as noted to reach Gaza from Ashdod requires that one pass through Ashkelon. It too lies on the coast and was listed in the territory taken by Joshua in his southern campaign (Josh 10:41). As the last major settlement before the Egyptian border, it is also used to mark this region. On the Brook of Egypt, see on 15:4.

15:48–60. The third major region is the hill country. This represents the mountainous area inland from the foothills, roughly as far north as the top end of the Dead Sea. If the MT is correct, this region is divided into five districts, each marked off by the provision of a count for the towns included within the district (vv. 51, 54, 56, 59, 60). However, there is good reason to believe that a further district is to be included at the end of verse 59 consisting of eleven cities included in the LXX (cf. CSB note). Given the difficulties of copying a list like this accurately, one can easily imagine a scribe skipping several lines since each district ends with the phrase, "cities with their settlements," and there is no obvious reason for adding these towns to the list. Comment on this sixth district in the

---

[291] R. E. Tappy, "Historical and Geographical Notes on the 'Lowland Districts' of Judah in Joshua xv 33–47," *VT* 58 (2008): 381–403, argues that the omission of Gath and Ekron point to these verses being added to an earlier list at the time of Sennacherib, noting that the omitted towns are also omitted then. Although this is possible, the fact that Gath at least seems to have fallen out suggests that these verses were added to the main list earlier, perhaps close to the tenth century, which he notes as a possible date for the compilation of the main list.

hill country is included with verse 59. These districts run in a roughly south-to-north pattern.

The first district is covered by verses 48–51, the eleven cities listed matching the count given in verse 51. Precision is impossible because of the uncertainty of many locations, but it appears to cover the area in Judah's far south, moving toward the Negev. Shamir will be noted as the home of the judge Tola (Judg 10:1–2). Jattir, twenty-eight miles south of Hebron, is later allocated to Levi (Josh 21:14). It was one of the Negev towns where David sent gifts (1 Sam 30:27). The Socoh mentioned here is not the one in 15:35. Kiriath-sanneh is mentioned as another name for Debir. In 15:15, it is said that its former name was Kiriath-sepher. The name in the LXX suggests it had Kiriath-sepher here too, which could indicate a scribal error in the MT, perhaps where the end of Dannah has accidentally been transposed to the end of the place name.[292] Anab is one of the towns where the Anakim were resident (Josh 11:21). Eshtemoh is probably called Eshtemoa when reassigned to the Levites (21:14). It may lie about fifteen miles south of Hebron. Goshen is probably the site mentioned in Joshua 10:41 and 11:16, not the Israelite settlement in Egypt (Gen 45:10). Holon is allotted to Levi in Josh 21:15. Giloh could be related to the springs given to Achsah (15:19). It would later be noted as the hometown of David's counselor Ahithophel (2 Sam 15:12).

The second district (vv. 52–54), with nine cities (again agreeing with the count) is probably in the vicinity of Hebron. Arab could be the home of one of David's elite fighters (2 Sam 23:35). Although BHS would suggest "Rumah" as the correct spelling of the second town in verse 52, CSB (probably rightly) has "Dumah." Kiriath-arba (also known as Hebron, cf. Josh 14:15) was the most significant town in southern Israel, and is often mentioned in the book (cf. 10:3–5; 14:6–15). It would later become both a city of refuge (20:7) and a Levitical town (21:11).

The third district is covered by verses 55–57. Ten cities are listed, again agreeing with the count. These are near Hebron, but probably east of the towns listed so far. David was near Maon at one point while he was fleeing from Saul (1 Sam 23:24–25). Carmel is not the northern site mentioned

---

[292] See also Harry M. Orlinsky, "The Supposed *Qiryat-Sannah* of Joshua 15.49," *JBL* 58 (1939): 255–61. Orlinsky also raises the possibility that the corruption might have come about through earlier stages of Hebrew orthography. But this merely indicates that there are various ways this corruption might have come about and that we should read Kiriath-sepher here.

in Joshua 12:22 and 19:26, but it is probably mentioned in 1 Samuel 25:2 since there it is associated with Maon. Ziph is not the site mentioned in Joshua 15:24, though it too is in the far south. Juttah would later be allotted to Levi (21:16). Jezreel is not the well-known northern site mentioned in 17:16 and 19:18. Zanoah is to be distinguished from the site in 15:34. A better-known Gibeah was Saul's hometown (1 Sam 10:26, cf. Judg 19), but it was in Benjamin. This Gibeah is also not the site where Eleazar was buried (Josh 24:33); it is otherwise unknown. Timnah was mentioned in 15:10.

The fourth district is covered by verses 58–59. Six cities are listed, again agreeing with the count. Beth-zur is a little north of Hebron and was later fortified by Rehoboam (2 Chr 11:7). Gedor is unlikely to be the site mentioned in 1 Chronicles 12:7 (it is more likely Benjaminite) but is not otherwise known.

As noted above, on the basis of the LXX we should identify a fifth district, recorded in the CSB note on verse 59. This covers eleven towns, probably in the eastern highlands and heading toward the Dead Sea, but north of Hebron and toward Jerusalem. Again, the count agrees with the towns listed. Tekoa is south of Jerusalem and is best known as the hometown of the wise woman employed by Joab to convince David to bring Absalom back from exile (2 Sam 14:1–20) and the hometown of the prophet Amos (Amos 1:1). Ephrathah is an alternative name for Bethlehem (cf. ET Mic 5:2 [MT 5:1]), the town about five miles south of Jerusalem that would gain fame as the birthplace of both David (1 Sam 16:1–13) and Jesus (Matt 2:1; Luke 2:1–7). Peor is not the mountain mentioned in Num 23:28 and is otherwise unknown. Etam was fortified by Rehoboam (2 Chr 11:6), along with Bethlehem and Tekoa, as part of a defensive strategy for Judah. Gallim is obscure but is possibly the home of Paltiel, the man to whom Saul gave Michal when he took her from David (1 Sam 25:44), though an alternative site is mentioned in Isa 10:30 to the north of Jerusalem.

A sixth district containing only two towns is mentioned in verse 60. Kiriath-baal is an alternative name for Kiriath-jearim, a Gibeonite town in 9:17. It marks the end of Judah's territory in 15:9 and 18:14. Rabbah is not the Ammonite site mentioned in 13:25 but is otherwise unknown.

15:61–62. The fourth major region is the wilderness, the area along the western coast of the Dead Sea. Six cities are listed, agreeing with the count. Beth-arabah was part of Judah's border with Benjamin (15:6; cf. 18:22). En-gedi is at about the midpoint of the western shore of the Dead Sea. This was the region where David hid from Saul in a cave (1 Sam 24:1–2).

En-gedi's significance as a source for salt was such that even in Ezekiel's vision of a renewed Dead Sea that was teeming with life, its swamps and marshes are kept to provide salt (Ezek 47:11).

15:63. After the lengthy list, one might be surprised to learn that any towns were missed. But the list has avoided Jerusalem, though it was mentioned as a border point in verse 8. In part, this is because the city is allotted to Benjamin (18:28), though the southern slope was Judah's. A consistent feature of references to Jerusalem is its association with the Jebusites, reflecting the fact that the descendants of Judah were unable to expel them and they continued living there at the time of writing. This might be unexpected after Joshua 1–12, which stressed the defeat of the indigenous population, but nowhere is Jerusalem said to have been captured. This is a deliberate reminder of God's declaration to Joshua that much of the land remained to be taken (13:1).[293]

Jerusalem is also mentioned in Judg 19:10–15, stressing that the city was not then in Israelite hands. This indicates that verse 63 was added to the list no later than the time of David, since he captured the city from the Jebusites (2 Sam 5:6–10), even though Jebusites continued to live there afterward (2 Sam 24:18). In context, the note provides a contrast to the experience of Caleb and also introduces an important theme regarding the inability of the remaining tribes to take the whole land (e.g., Josh 16:10; 17:12–13), culminating in Dan being expelled from their territory (19:47). It becomes the first clear hint at a question that emerges for readers: God gave the land, and Israel could identify the details of that land, but would they take all that God was giving? If verse 63 is intended to make us think of David taking the city, then he stands as an unstated parallel to Caleb, someone who believed God's promises and who therefore remained as a model for subsequent readers.

Bridge

This is undoubtedly a challenging chapter for modern readers. Its focus on geography, often to a micro level, makes it a difficult text. Apart from the short story about Caleb and Achsah, it is predominantly a list of places and towns, one made more difficult by the fact that we do not know anything

---

[293] Butler, *Joshua 13–24*, 122, regards this as a "countertradition," but he claims too much and fails to recognize the ways the book deliberately establishes patterns that are then destabilized within the text.

about many of them. The text also shows some signs of editing over time (e.g., the addition of names used later than the time of Joshua and the editorial comment in verse 63), though this actually indicates that this was an important text for ancient readers and, therefore, needed to be presented in a manner that communicated to later readers. This process of updating was presumably completed when the list was integrated into the book of Joshua, something the closing note suggests happened around the time of David's reign (which might also be supported by the fact that so many of the towns recur in the story of David).

Preachers bold enough to preach on this chapter will need to be aware of these challenges and find ways of visualizing what is presented so modern audiences can grasp it. Nevertheless, it is important to bear in mind that the importance of any passage of Scripture is not measured by how exciting readers find it. That is particularly true here, but preachers and congregations will need some patience if they are to appreciate this.

The chapter has three seemingly disparate sections, but they are woven together to make a whole unit. Central is the reality of God's gift of the land to his people. The chapter is particularly important because unlike the earlier allocations east of the Jordan, Israel was now in the land God had promised to Abraham in Genesis 15:18–21. Indeed, there may be a hint of this promise in the closing note of verse 63 since the Jebusites are the last people mentioned in Genesis 15:21. Up to this point, Israel had been capturing the land (or portions of it), but they had not yet begun to dwell in it. Only by doing so could they truly "possess the city gates of their enemies" as they had been promised (Gen 22:17). The allocation to Judah, as exemplified in the story of Caleb and Achsah, demonstrates this in practice, though the closing note in verse 63 also stresses the importance of this being a continuing experience for Judah. God's promise had been fulfilled but also needed to be fulfilled in the faithfulness of God's people, with the possible allusion to David in verse 63 indicating ways in which that could happen.

The fulfillment of God's promise to Abraham was crucial because of the purpose of the promise—that all peoples might "find blessing through you" (Gen 12:3, csb note). This land was the place where Israel could live as a witness to the nations of both the justice and nearness of God (Deut 4:6–8). Israel was charged with the task of living out what this meant—the land providing the means for doing so. These boundaries recur in Ezekiel 47:19 and 48:28 within an otherwise stylized description of the boundaries of the land for a restored Israel.[294] Given the context in Ezekiel, a hermeneutical process has already begun (one that will be worked out more fully in the New Testament) of not seeing God's people tied to a particular place. It is this same promise to Abraham that is worked out in the gospel (Gal 3:14). Although Christians are not tied to a particular place, we are still challenged to live out the demands of the gospel, something Paul works out in some detail in Galatians 5–6. Likewise, we are encouraged to claim the promises of God and "approach the throne of grace with boldness" (Heb 4:16).[295]

This chapter is concerned with Judah as a whole, but the focus on Caleb and Achsah brings out another important theme, something made explicit in verse 1: The allocation is not just for Judah as a tribe but also for all the clans within the tribe, descendants that in Caleb's case were not necessarily Israelite to begin with. In other words, God's promise works at the macro level of the nation and tribe as a whole; nevertheless, every clan would know that its inheritance was part of this larger pattern. So, although one can trace the whole territory of Judah (vv. 1–12), it is also important to know all the places that would belong to the tribe because each of these localities would be the way that the clans, and within them the individual families, would experience the gift of the land.

The view of Israel as a family is a crucial one within the book—the nation is often called "the children of Israel." It feeds into the understanding of the land as a place where a family dwells, a place where each family would know its portion of the larger inheritance. Family, including those adopted into the nation such as Caleb, is fundamental to Israel's view of itself and its relationship to the promise of God. Each family had its land, and that land was part of the larger promise of God. The promises of God are therefore not remote, belonging only to some elite. Rather, they are experienced in a very concrete way by every family.

This provides an important link between chapter 15 and the larger movement of the Bible. The themes of inheritance and family are vital ones for understanding biblical theology. Israel could indeed understand itself as family since its inheritance came from the promise of God to Abraham, a promise rooted in the fact that he had children who became his family. This ultimately leads to the use of family language

---

[294] See the helpful chart in Harstad, *Joshua*, 533.
[295] Earl, *Reading Joshua*, 175.

for describing the church. Indeed, it is this combination of family and inheritance that drives Paul's argument in Galatians 4:1–7. Moreover, the church is made up of people adopted into a family that was not theirs by birth but rather by faith, precisely what we see in Caleb. Paul also links our status to that of Isaac (Gal 4:28), stressing that we are children of the promise. Seen through the grid of this chapter, we understand how Paul links the promise to Abraham to the initial fulfillment of promise here to a greater fulfillment in Christ. And this greater fulfillment also means that we are family and so have the responsibility of supporting each other as such (Gal 6:1–10).

C. The Allotment for Joseph (16:1–17:18)

16 ¹ The allotment for the descendants of Joseph went from the Jordan at Jericho to the Waters of Jericho on the east, through the wilderness ascending from Jericho into the hill country of Bethel. ² From Bethel it went to Luz and proceeded to the border of the Archites by Ataroth. ³ It then descended westward to the border of the Japhletites as far as the border of Lower Beth-horon, then to Gezer, and ended at the Mediterranean Sea. ⁴ So Ephraim and Manasseh, the sons of Joseph, received their inheritance.

⁵ This was the territory of the descendants of Ephraim by their clans:

> The border of their inheritance went from Ataroth-addar on the east to Upper Beth-horon. ⁶ In the north the border went westward from Michmethath; it turned eastward from Taanath-shiloh and passed it east of Janoah. ⁷ From Janoah it descended to Ataroth and Naarah, and then reached Jericho and went to the Jordan. ⁸ From Tappuah the border went westward along the Brook of Kanah and ended at the Mediterranean Sea.

This was the inheritance of the tribe of the descendants of Ephraim by their clans, together with ⁹ the cities set apart for the descendants of Ephraim within the inheritance of the descendants of Manasseh— all these cities with their settlements. ¹⁰ However, they did not drive out the Canaanites who lived in Gezer. So the Canaanites still live in Ephraim today, but they are forced laborers.

17 ¹ This was the allotment for the tribe of Manasseh as Joseph's firstborn. Gilead and Bashan were given to Machir, the firstborn of Manasseh and the father of Gilead, because he was a man of war. ² So the allotment was for the rest of Manasseh's descendants by their clans, for the sons of Abiezer, Helek, Asriel, Shechem, Hepher, and Shemida. These are the male descendants of Manasseh son of Joseph, by their clans.

³ Now Zelophehad son of Hepher, son of Gilead, son of Machir, son of Manasseh, had no sons, only daughters. These are the names of his daughters: Mahlah, Noah, Hoglah, Milcah, and Tirzah. ⁴ They came before the priest Eleazar, Joshua son of Nun, and the leaders, saying, "The Lord commanded Moses to give us an inheritance among our male relatives." So they gave them an inheritance among their father's brothers, in keeping with the Lord's instruction. ⁵ As a result, ten tracts fell to Manasseh, besides the land of Gilead and Bashan, which are beyond the Jordan, ⁶ because Manasseh's daughters received an inheritance among his sons. The land of Gilead belonged to the rest of Manasseh's sons.

⁷ The border of Manasseh went from Asher to Michmethath near Shechem. It then went southward toward the inhabitants of En-tappuah. ⁸ The region of Tappuah belonged to Manasseh, but Tappuah itself on Manasseh's border belonged to the descendants of Ephraim. ⁹ From there the border descended to the Brook of Kanah; south of the brook, cities belonged to Ephraim among Manasseh's cities. Manasseh's border was on the north side of the brook and ended at the Mediterranean Sea. ¹⁰ Ephraim's territory was to the south and Manasseh's to the north, with the Sea as its border. They reached Asher on the north and Issachar on the east. ¹¹ Within Issachar and Asher, Manasseh had Beth-shean, Ibleam, and the inhabitants of Dor with their surrounding villages; the inhabitants of En-dor, Taanach, and Megiddo—the three cities of Naphath—with their surrounding villages.

¹² The descendants of Manasseh could not possess these cities, because the Canaanites were determined to stay in this land. ¹³ However, when the Israelites grew stronger, they imposed forced labor on the Canaanites but did not drive them out completely.

¹⁴ Joseph's descendants said to Joshua, "Why did you give us only one tribal allotment as an inheritance? We have many people, because the Lord has been blessing us greatly."

¹⁵ "If you have so many people," Joshua replied to them, "go to the forest and clear an area for yourselves there in the land of the Perizzites and the Rephaim, because Ephraim's hill country is too small for you."

¹⁶ But the descendants of Joseph said, "The hill country is not enough for us, and all the Canaanites who inhabit the valley area have iron chariots, both at Beth-shean with its surrounding villages and in the Jezreel Valley."

¹⁷ So Joshua replied to Joseph's family (that is, Ephraim and Manasseh), "You have many people and great strength. You will not have just one allotment, ¹⁸ because the hill country will be yours also. It is a forest; clear it and its outlying areas will be yours. You can also drive out the Canaanites, even though they have iron chariots and are strong."

Context

Consistent with the emphasis on Judah, Ephraim, and Manasseh that runs through the book, it is not surprising that the second inheritance account is for the Joseph tribes, Ephraim and Manasseh. The importance of these tribes is also evidenced by the fact that the only two individual allotments described, those of Caleb (14:6–15) and Joshua (19:49–51), are within these tribal allotments. It is characteristic of the land allocation narratives to refer to the tribe of Joseph (cf. 14:4), while outside of these chapters Ephraim and Manasseh are treated separately. The only exception to this (24:32) is because a reference to Joseph himself triggers a reference to his descendants; however, since it refers to their inheritance, it is consistent with the pattern of these chapters. By keeping the Joseph tribes together, Joshua is able to maintain a twelve-tribe structure even though the book is aware that Ephraim and Manasseh could be treated distinctly, and both are also called a "tribe" in this account (16:8; 17:1—a term never used for Joseph as a whole other than indirectly at 14:2). The importance of seeing Joseph as a whole is seen in the fact that references to the whole tribe bookend this section (16:1–4; 17:14–18), while a mingling of Ephraim and Manasseh is indicated by reference to Ephraim's cities being in Manasseh in 16:9. As such—made clear by their complaint to Joshua in 17:14—Ephraim and Manasseh together receive only one portion.

That Judah and Joseph receive the most prominence in Joshua can be traced back to Jacob's blessing of the tribes in Genesis 49:1–27, a passage that also treats Joseph as a single tribe. In that blessing, Judah (49:8–12) and Joseph (49:22–26) each receive five verses, while all the other tribes receive only one or two verses. Keeping Joseph as one tribe in Genesis 49 retains the twelve-tribe structure even though Genesis 48 had already made clear that Ephraim and Manasseh could be regarded as separate tribes when Jacob blessed Joseph's sons. This is because Jacob had claimed them for himself, placing them into the main tribal structure for Israel (Gen 48:5). The allocation to Joseph is thus a fulfillment of the ancient blessing, albeit one marked by a failure to claim the territory in full (Josh 16:10; 17:12–13).

This, however, raises questions about the genuineness of their claim for additional territory because of how God had blessed them (17:14). On the one hand, the numerical blessings are from God, but if they have not taken all the land God was giving, could they really claim additional land? Alongside this, the fulfillment of the promise to the daughters of

Zelophehad from Numbers 27:1–11 shows that God was indeed fulfilling his promises and that these promises could be claimed. But as Joshua 1 has made clear, the land was both a gift from God and something to be claimed. Moreover, placing this account at the heart of the Joseph allocation demonstrates that claiming the land was always a matter of taking up the promise of God.

Exegesis

16:1–4. The account of Joseph's allotment is patterned on Judah's through reference to the lot (גּוֹרָל). The language of the lot "coming out" for a tribe occurs in the introduction to the allocations of Simeon (19:1), Issachar (19:17), Asher (19:24), Naphtali (19:32), and Dan (19:40), with variations in the formulae used. For Benjamin (18:11) and Zebulun (19:10), the lot "came up" (עלה). Although reference will be made to Manasseh's "allotment" (17:1, also גּוֹרָל), this is understood as part of the one allotment to Joseph. As with the description of Judah's allotment (see on 15:1–12), key verbs are used to visualize an imaginary line that runs across a map. This initial description provides only the southern border for Joseph, across the central highlands from Jericho in the east to the Mediterranean Sea in the west. The route traced here leaves a space between Judah and Joseph that will be filled by Benjamin in 18:11–20.

Joseph's boundary begins at Jericho, near the point of Israel's entry into the land. The city's capture is recounted in Joshua 6. Since these chapters deal with the western allocation, it is appropriate that Joseph's boundary begins at its easternmost point, starting with the Jordan in the region of Jericho.[296] From there it moves to the "Waters of Jericho," which is perhaps a reference to the spring east of the city since Jericho itself would be allotted to Benjamin (18:21), though since there is no other reference to these waters in the Bible it is difficult to be certain. The balance of verse 1 is terse and the exact sense is not altogether clear, and we should probably assume that the preposition לְ ("to") attached to "the Waters" does multiple duty and covers both the wilderness and Bethel.[297] The wilderness is probably still in the vicinity of the Jordan, since from there the border line is described as "ascending" to Bethel. This reflects

---

[296] מִיַּרְדֵּן יְרִיחוֹ is lit. "from the Jordan of Jericho," but csb is probably correct to treat this a referring to a local point of the Jordan.

[297] On this possibility, see Ronald J. Williams, *Hebrew Syntax: An Outline* (Toronto: University of Toronto Press, 1967), 47 (§238).

the fact that Jericho (about 850 feet below sea level) is one of the lowest points on earth and it is quite a steep climb to Bethel (about 2800 feet above sea level) over thirteen miles to the west and slightly north.

A difficulty in verse 2 is that Bethel seems to be distinguished from Luz. Although this is perhaps the more normal translation of the text, elsewhere Luz is an alternate name for Bethel (Gen 28:19), and the continuing existence of both names for the site is reflected in Joshua 18:13.[298] Another solution is to follow NIV and understand "to Luz" as explanatory of the reference to Bethel and translate the start of verse 2 as, "It went out from Bethel (that is, Luz),[299] and proceeded." Perhaps, though, we should understand the older part of Luz as in some way distinguishable from the main part of Bethel.[300]

From Bethel, the boundary is then traced across the hills to the Archite boundary at Ataroth. Unfortunately, this town is elsewhere mentioned only in 16:7 when filling in Ephraim's border so its location is unknown.[301] Somewhat more significant is the mention of the territory (CSB "border")[302] of the Archites since it must fall within the boundaries of Canaan. The Archites may be the same as the Canaanite group mentioned in Genesis 10:17 (along with other Canaanite groups prominent in Joshua), though the spelling of the name there is different.[303] Even if they are not the same group, they appear to be a Canaanite group that is not eliminated from the land, and indeed David's friend Hushai was an Archite (2 Sam 15:32). Although the principal seven Canaanite groups were to be destroyed, Joshua also allows that some Canaanites were to remain in the land (Josh 11:20). If so, then this is also the most likely explanation for the Japhletites (v. 3). However, since we have no other information about them, less certainty can be attached to this.

---

[298] Another Luz is mentioned in Judg 1:22–26, but it is named after this Luz.

[299] Admittedly, the final ה on Luz is difficult since it is probably directional, but understanding it this way is better than regarding this as an alternative spelling for the toponym.

[300] Woudstra, *The Book of Joshua*, 258.

[301] Another Ataroth is mentioned in Num 32:3, 34, but this is east of the Jordan. Atarothaddar in v. 5 may be the same site, but this is not certain.

[302] Hebrew גְּבוּל can refer to a border, or as seems more likely here (and with the Japhletites in v. 3) to the whole territory of a group.

[303] In Gen 10:17 they are הָעַרְקִי, while here they are הָאַרְכִּי. But given the interchange between these letters (and that the pronunciation for these spellings would be virtually identical) this is not a significant issue, not least because this group is located within Canaan.

Although the territory of both these groups is probably small, this passage indicates that not all Canaanites were under the ban since these territories are apparently not taken over by the Joseph tribes. That the imagined line goes down westward toward the Japhletite territory is explained by the fact that it is in the region of lower Beth-horon (see on 10:10–11), a town in the Valley of Aijalon near where the coastal plain meets the hills, and then on to Gezer (see on 10:33), before ending at the Mediterranean. That this southern boundary covered two groups that are treated as one is made clear by the closing note of verse 4. Again, the syntax is terse, but the csb is probably right to understand "Ephraim and Manasseh" as explaining the identity of the sons of Joseph while also preparing for the treatment of each group separately in the following verses.

16:5–8a. Having sketched the southern boundary for Joseph, the account now turns to consider Ephraim. As is normal within the book, the allocation for Ephraim is according to the tribe's clans (see on 13:15). Like the territory of the Archites and Japhletites, the גְּבוּל ("territory") of Ephraim is to be understood as defining its borders in verse 5a, though in 5b it has the sense of "boundary." Here, the initial boundary in the south is described briefly since it is the same as that for Joseph from the previous verses. This makes it probable that Ataroth-addar is Ataroth in verse 2. Lower Beth-horon apparently belonged to the Japhletites, which is why Ephraim's own territory only covered the upper part of the town.

The northern boundary is then described in verses 6–7, again in a fairly abbreviated form. Defining this boundary with any precision is difficult because none of these sites can be identified with any confidence. In the case of Michmethath, it is not even clear that this is a toponym since it occurs only here and 17:7, both times with the definite article, so it could be a topographical feature. However, 17:7 places it in the area of Shechem, so we at least know roughly where it is. Taanath-shiloh is probably southeast of Shechem, with Janoah in much the same area. Apart from a passing mention of Janoah in 2 Kings 15:29, neither is mentioned elsewhere in the Old Testament. The border is then traced to Ataroth on the southern boundary (see on 16:2), presumably forming a loop as it heads back toward Jericho through Naarah, though again this site is not mentioned elsewhere so identification is uncertain. From Jericho, it is traced back to the Jordan as the easternmost point of Ephraim. The western boundary is also traced briefly from Tappuah (which is to be distinguished from the site with the same name in 15:34), a site about six miles northwest of Shiloh, and then along the Brook of Kanah to the Mediterranean. The relative vagueness of this boundary is reflected in the mention of Tappuah in Manasseh's allocation in 17:8.

16:8b–10. As with the description of Judah's boundaries in 15:12 (cf. 13:22, 28), a closing statement is given summarizing what has gone before, with the phrasing matching the opening of verse 5. Earlier occurrences of this formula serve as a conclusion to the tribal allotment, but this one is expanded to note that cities were also set apart for Ephraim, preparing for the wider use of a similar formula in 19:16, 23, 31, 39, and 48. No such formula occurs for Benjamin and Simeon, where a city list is provided; both Naphtali and Dan have both this extended formula and a (brief) city list. Manasseh is the only tribe for which such a summary is absent, probably because their inheritance is given in two groups, neither of which covers the whole allotment. In the case of Ephraim, the cities referred to here (along with their settlements) were somewhere within Manasseh, something not true of the other tribes.[304] It is possible that a list of these cities once stood here,[305] though given the terse language of the chapter as a whole it is not necessary.

As with Judah (15:63), Ephraim did not fully drive out the indigenous population (v. 10). This was apparently not a problem with the Archites and Japhletites (see on vv. 2–3). However, the continued presence of Canaanites in Gezer is similar to the situation of Judah with the Jebusites in Jerusalem; this community was still recognizably present at the time of the text's composition, except that they had become forced labor. We are not told how this happened, but it may reflect Solomon's actions referred to in 1 Kings 9:21, something made more probable by the fact that prior to this Pharaoh had captured the town and given it to his daughter as part of her dowry (1 Kgs 9:16).[306] The text makes no evaluation beyond the observation about the continued existence of this Canaanite group. However, given that Josh 13:6 only requires that Joshua allotted the inheritance to the tribes, it does not have to be taken as a failure.

---

[304] The uniqueness of this arrangement is apparent from the *hapax* הַמֻּבְדָּלוֹת. It is possible to understand 17:11 as indicating that some cities allotted to Manasseh were in Issachar and Asher (so NIV), but this is not necessary (agreeing with CSB).

[305] See Pitkänen, *Joshua*, 299.

[306] Pharaoh is said there to have killed the Canaanite population, but just as Joshua's defeat of the city in Josh 10:33 did not mean all had been killed, the same is probably true here.

Moreover, we know from the accounts of Rahab and the Gibeonites that some Canaanites had been accepted into Israel (the Gibeonites living in a form of indentured service, too). However, Gezer is also very close to the territory allotted to Dan, which that tribe failed to take (19:47). So this note could also prepare for that failure.

The note itself is ambiguous, as was also the case with initial presentations of both Rahab and Gibeon. So, this might be an indication of a significant failing on Israel's part in that Ephraim appears to have dealt with Canaanites in the way that Deuteronomy 20:16–18 allows only for peoples outside the land,[307] something worse than Judah's failure to remove the Jebusites from Jerusalem because Gezer had been defeated (Josh 10:33).[308] But it does not have to be, and it is also possible that Joshua's speech in 24:1–12 provides a mechanism by which they too might be included within Israel.

17:1–2. The narrative now turns to western Manasseh, since the allotment of the eastern half of the tribe was recounted in 13:29–31. Curiously, their allotment is recounted after Ephraim's even though Manasseh was Joseph's firstborn, as noted here.[309] But this reflects Jacob's blessing of Joseph's sons in Genesis 48:14–20, where he specifically put Ephraim before Manasseh even though the latter was the firstborn.

Before the western allocation is discussed, a summary of the allotment for Machir, Manasseh's firstborn, is recounted. Machir is described as a "man of war," a statement that looks back to Numbers 32:39–40 where his descendants had captured Gilead, so that he could be known as the father of Gilead.[310] In this instance, "father" probably means that he was the one who possessed the region, though there may also be a play on the fact that he was the father of a son with the same name.

---

[307] So, e.g., Harstad, *Joshua*, 558.

[308] Though as Rösel, *Joshua*, 274, notes, the earlier text does not claim the city was actually captured.

[309] Hebrew כִּי־הוּא בְּכוֹר יוֹסֵף could be taken to imply a causal relationship with the previous clause, but csb is correct to treat the conjunction concessively.

[310] Machir was also the father of a man named Gilead (Num 26:29), but the reference here is to הַגִּלְעָד, "the Gilead," and hence the region. With Howard, *Joshua*, 350, we should probably understand the region to have derived its name from the person. Place names in Manasseh are often associated with the names of individuals. A number of these names are mentioned in the Samaria Ostraca. Although it does not discuss place names, a helpful overview of the importance of the ostraca can be found in W. H. Shea, "The Date and Significance of the Samaria Ostraca," *IEJ* 27 (1977): 16–27.

Verse 2 focuses on the western allocation, noting again that the allocation was in accordance with the clans. But uniquely, in this case, we are actually given a listing of the clans. This is probably due to the fact that part of the tribe was east of the Jordan; therefore, it was important to know which tribes were west of the Jordan. Complicating the tribal history of Manasseh is that, according to Genesis 50:23, Manasseh's son Machir was to be treated as Joseph's own, akin to Jacob taking Ephraim and Manasseh as his own, except that Machir was Manasseh's only son. Machir too had only one son, Gilead, who was therefore the titular head of the clan of the Gileadites (Num 26:29). But according to Numbers 26:32–33, Gilead had six sons, each of whom was also head of a clan. These are listed here,[311] which suggests that some of these clans also had land east of the Jordan. The key variation to the list in Numbers is that Hepher is listed before Shemida. It is not clear which is the birth order, since in both passages the list prepares for the account of the daughters of Zelophehad, who was from the clan of Hepher. One passage has inverted the order of the sons, probably in order to highlight this link, but it is not possible to know which. In this case, reference to the "male descendants" who received the remaining land prepares for the story of Zelophehad's daughters since they too would inherit land.

17:3–6. The third of the land-grant narratives begins (see context discussion on Joshua 13–14), this one focusing on the daughters of Zelophehad. It is a striking feature of the land-grant narratives that they have a particular focus on women claiming land, through Achsah (15:18–19) and Zelophehad's daughters.[312] Apart from Caleb (someone of foreign descent), the male characters tend to be more muted whereas the women are quite forceful. The introduction to Zelophehad's daughters in verse 3 is largely taken over from Numbers 26:33, with the addition of three generations (Gilead, Machir, and Manasseh), which can be understood from context in the source text. This addition places the account squarely into the pattern of allotment of Manasseh's land by clans, while pointing readers back to the earlier genealogical note, which in turn prepared for the request of the daughters (Num 27:1–11) and the

---

[311] In Num 26:30, Abiezer is called Iezer, but these are clearly variants of the one name. Abiezer is a known place name within Manasseh, so it is likely that Joshua uses this fuller form to be consistent with this.

[312] Hawk, *Joshua in 3-D*, 209, accordingly highlights the fact that Israel could not be defined in male terms alone.

subsequent decision (Num 36). The importance of the clan structure for land in that account may be why Joshua is so careful to insist that each tribe received its land by clan. In any case, it certainly explains the focus in this particular account.

Zelophehad, son of Hepher, died in the wilderness without any male children. In Numbers, his daughters stressed that he had simply been part of the generation that died in the wilderness (Num 27:3), making clear that his death was not a special penalty. Whereas Caleb's claim was based on his exemplary service (see Josh 14:6–12), their claim is simply based on the fact that they were part of Israel. Up to this point, the assumption had been that inheritance would pass on through the male line; however, Zelophehad had only five daughters. With no sons, there was no clarity about what would happen. Therefore, the daughters assumed that this part of the family would effectively cease to exist. In response to this, God had indicated that, if there were no sons, land would in the first instance pass to daughters and then to other members of the family if there were no daughters (Num 27:5–11). Zelophehad's daughters are Mahlah, Noah,[313] Hoglah, Milcah, and Tirzah. Each of these names is also known as a toponym in western Manasseh (although not all are mentioned in the Old Testament), indicating a close link between the names and the region.

The five daughters approached Eleazar the priest and Joshua (see 14:1) to request their allotment. Eleazar and Joshua are also approached in 21:1 by the Levites. This note indicates that not only did the daughters have a legitimate claim to land, but they also claimed it in an appropriate manner. Like Caleb (Josh 14:6–9), the daughters' claim is rooted in a prior commandment of Yahweh issued by Moses (Num 27:6). This is perhaps why the detail of their claim can be reported so briefly, noting simply that they were to receive an inheritance among their male kin. Although CSB indicates that Eleazar and Joshua jointly gave the land to them, the verb is singular, which could indicate that Eleazar was the one who actually made the allocation.[314] In any case, the key point is that they have acted

---

[313] Although in English this is the same name as the Noah of Genesis 6–9, in Hebrew the name is quite different.

[314] The indirect object is להם, which is a masculine form, though some mss have the expected feminine form (להן), and the feminine form does occur later in the verse (אביהן). This may be a typical case of the less-common feminine plural being replaced by the masculine (something that happens more often than Hebrew grammars tend to suggest; see GKC §135o). However, there may be merit in the speculation of Harstad, Joshua, 560, that

exactly as God had directed. The daughters' claim was based on God's command, and this was how the land was allocated to them.

The allotment of land to the daughters had implications for the division of the land within Manasseh. Ten tracts in western Manasseh (aside from the two in the east, Gilead and Bashan) were allotted to the five daughters and the other five clans (Abiezer, Helek, Asriel, Shechem, and Shemida). It is unlikely that the allotment for the daughters was as large as the others, but since they had to marry within the larger clan structure, there needed to be some way of knowing which part of the land would be integrated into another part of Manasseh.

17:7-11. The text next turns to Manasseh's boundaries. Although most of the boundaries are difficult to draw with precision, Manasseh's is particularly challenging, even if the general region can be determined (from the central hill country to the coast). This difficulty is immediately apparent in the opening statement. If "Asher" refers to a city, then we have an otherwise unknown site. If it is the tribe, then it refers to the northwest of Manasseh and the shared border with Asher in the vicinity of Mount Carmel (see map at 15:1-12; for Asher's territory, see 19:24-30). This border runs across the heart of the highlands near Shechem, a site between Mount Gerizim and Mount Ebal that will be important for Joshua's final address in 24:1-28. In spite of the importance of Shechem, no narrative of its capture is provided. It would later become both a city of refuge (20:7) and a Levitical city (21:21). It is unclear whether the Michmethath near there is a place name or a geographical feature (see on 16:6).

From there, the border headed south toward En-tappuah, which is a spring at Tappuah. Reference to the inhabitants suggests there was an unwalled village at the spring. Because of possible confusion over control of Tappuah, an explicit comment confirms that the town belonged to Ephraim even though the region belonged to Manasseh. This represents the southernmost boundary of Manasseh and the northern border of Ephraim. This border is traced along the Brook of Kanah (see on 16:8) to the Mediterranean in the west. A further note is provided explaining its role as a boundary with towns south of the brook belonging to Ephraim and north belonging to Manasseh. The boundary is then traced along the

---

the masculine is used here because in inheritance terms they have taken on a traditionally masculine function. Butler, *Joshua 13-24*, 143, believes this story is included to show that Joshua did indeed carry out all that Moses commanded. But at most this is a subsidiary goal if the focus is on Eleazar.

north back to Asher and across to Issachar (see on 19:17–19), presumably reaching the Jordan somewhere south of the Valley of Jezreel.

Verse 11 could be interpreted as the remnant of a city list, though its interpretation is far from clear. Some translations (e.g., ESV) understand the towns as allotted to Manasseh but located within the territory of Issachar and Asher. However, the preposition used here (בְּ) could also locate these towns on the border. On balance, CSB is probably right that they were technically inside Manasseh's allocation.[315] Being reasonably well known, the towns provide some clarity on Manasseh's borders as they are all located relative to the Jezreel Valley.

Beth-shean is where the Jezreel Valley meets the Jordan Valley. Also called Beth-shan, it was where the Philistines hung Saul's body after his death on Mount Gilboa (1 Sam 31:10). Ibleam is about eight miles south of Jezreel itself and controlled a southern point of access to the valley. Dor is more or less due west of Jezreel on the coast. En-dor would presumably be nearby ("Spring of Dor"), though its exact location is unknown, and it may be on the south of the Jezreel Valley. En-dor would gain notoriety as the home of the spirit mistress Saul met on the night before his death (1 Sam 28:3–25).[316] Taanach, later a Levitical city (Josh 21:25), is about five miles southwest of Jezreel. Megiddo is about ten miles west of Jezreel and was one of the most important cities of northern Israel because of its location on a strategic crossroad. Like Shechem, we have no record of Megiddo's capture, though in Revelation 16:12–16 it is the site of a major eschatological battle. In each case we are told that their associated settlements were included, while reference is also made to the inhabitants for Dor, En-dor, Taanach, and Megiddo, though the significance of this is unclear. The last three are also described as the towns of Naphath, which means "heights." This may reflect the fact that they are on the spur of hills that runs from the central hills to the coast at Carmel; however, given the uncertainty over En-dor's location this is not certain.[317]

---

[315] However, the decision not to represent וַיְהִי לִמְנַשֶּׁה בְּיִשָּׂשכָר וּבְאָשֵׁר ("Now there was to Manasseh at Issachar and Ephraim") is difficult to understand.

[316] This would assume a location in the vicinity of the Jezreel Valley. If it is near Dor, then there would have to be two sites with this name. See Othniel Margalith, "Dor and En-Dor," ZAW 97 (1985): 109–11.

[317] Further, the MT of this verse shows some problems when compared to the parallel in Judg 1:27, which could suggest that we should read "Naphath Dor" at the end. See George

17:12–13. Manasseh's problem with the local Canaanite population was greater than Ephraim's in 16:10. Ephraim took control of their towns but were unable to expel the Canaanite population at Gezer. Manasseh was not able to possess these towns,[318] something that will point to the problems faced by the other tribes. Indeed, the Canaanites were resolved to remain in that part of the land. With the notable exceptions of Rahab and the Gibeonites, this was probably true of most of the Canaanites, but the verb here indicates that this group showed a particularly strong resolve that Manasseh was unable to overcome. Like the statements in 15:63 and 16:10, this one is ambiguous, as we are not told why they were so determined. It could be a military declaration, but they could also have opted to find a means of staying within Israel—similar to Rahab and the Gibeonites. If the resolve of these Canaanites was patterned after the Gibeonites, then Israel's putting them to forced labor makes sense, though we do not know how much later this happened.

17:14–18. Having focused on the constituent tribes within Joseph, the narrative returns to Joseph as a whole. The move is abrupt, with no introduction. Instead, we are simply presented with the tribe asking Joshua (Eleazar is notably absent) why he had given them only one allotment. The wording, literally claiming to have received only "one lot and one territory," suggests they believed that Joshua had made the decision himself rather than that he carried it out at God's direction (13:6–7). There is thus a strong hint that the Joseph tribes had misunderstood the nature of the allotment. When they introduced God's involvement, it was to point out that he had blessed them and made them a numerous people.[319]

If we take the census from Numbers 26 as a guide, then Joseph's combined size of 85,200 (Num 26:34, 37) is larger than any other tribe, with only Judah's 76,500 (Num 26:22) coming close. So they could legitimately point to their size, and the allotment was meant to take this into account (Num 26:53–54). However, a glance at the map of tribal allotments (see above at 15:1–12) shows that they actually received a substantial portion

---

Dahl, "The 'Three Heights' of Joshua 17.11," *JBL* 53 (1934): 381–83. Against this, the current reading can be understood, is the more difficult one, and should probably be retained.

[318] At 16:10, the verb is *hiphil* of ירשׁ, which has the sense of "dispossess." But here it is the *qal* of the same verb, and so it has the sense of "possess." The *hiphil* is used in v. 13, but the statement indicates that they still did not dispossess them.

[319] The Hebrew here is difficult, but the csb is a plausible rendering.

and, perhaps more importantly, some of the most valuable land since it included the northern coastal plain and access to the Jezreel Valley.

Joshua's response in verse 15 can therefore be taken in two ways.[320] Either he agreed with them and therefore directed them to clear the forest for additional land among the Perizzites and Rephaim, or he believed they were making an excessive claim and his subsequent directive was sarcasm. Since the best sarcasm is often not recognized by those receiving it, it is not altogether surprising that it is not clear which is meant. Unfortunately, the particular area to which Joshua referred is uncertain, but reference to the forest of Ephraim in 2 Samuel 18:6 indicates it is in the Jordan Valley. This would expand Joseph's usable territory (for agriculture) without greatly increasing the actual allotment by moving beyond Ephraim's allocation in the hill country. The Perizzites are one of the standard Canaanite peoples (see on 3:10), while other groups of Rephaim are mentioned in 12:4 and 13:12.

However we interpret Joshua's response to the Joseph tribes, their reply in verse 16 indicates that even though their initial request seemed innocent enough (modeled on the land-grant account of the daughters of Zelophehad), this was not in fact a claim based on faith. The descendants of Joseph contended that the hill country was not enough (ignoring the fact that they held more than that). They also pointed out that the Canaanites in the valley (referring to the Jordan) had iron chariots, highlighting the region around Beth-shean and from there access into the Jezreel Valley. Iron chariots were consistently regarded as dangerous weapons, though Israel had previously defeated a large chariot force in 11:1–9. Admittedly, this is the only time that "iron" chariots are

---

[320] Note that אִם can introduce either a real or unreal condition (Williams, *Hebrew Syntax*, 86–87). If a real condition, it is equivalent to "since" and agrees with Joseph. As an unreal condition, it would mean something like "if indeed," while implying that their claim was unreasonable.

mentioned in Joshua,[321] but, since Joseph did not attempt to defeat these Canaanites, whether or not God would grant them victory was unknown.[322]

This statement revealed a basic lack of faith on the part of Joseph's descendants; therefore, Joshua's response addressed this. Though they had expressed concern only with the hill country of Ephraim, the text makes clear that Manasseh was involved too, since Joshua replied to both tribes (v. 17). Joseph was granted an additional allotment, from the hill country through the forest, and given the assurance that they could indeed expel the Canaanites even with their iron chariots (vv. 17–18). But there is no evidence that they took this land or cleared the forest. Later, in the battle between Absalom and David's forces, the forest was responsible for more deaths than the fighting proper (2 Sam 18:8). That it would prove to be so dangerous suggests that this exhortation to clear the forest was never heeded. Moreover, Joshua never claimed that God was giving this land to Joseph; rather, he indicated that they could claim the land because of their own strength. From the perspective of the narrative, this is best understood as a parody of the land grants reported so far—something that looks like a claim based on God's promises but is in fact a subversion of it.

Bridge

Understanding these chapters requires that we place them within the larger movement of the biblical narrative to appreciate the ways it works with the faithfulness of God to his promises against the reality that his people often fail to take these promises up. These promises can be traced back to the blessings on the tribes announced in Genesis 49, in which Judah and Joseph were particularly prominent. It is therefore appropriate that these two tribes receive the most attention in the account of the land allocation. This is also important because it highlights not only that God

---

[321] But see Judg 1:19; 4:3, 12, where they were seen as a great threat. Exactly what is meant by "iron" chariots is uncertain, since this would be very early iron technology. Moreover, the bulk of the chariot would still have to be wood, or else it would be too heavy. Possibly, the term describes some of the weapons used by those on the chariot; it is conceivable that spears might at this point have had early iron tips. This is more probable than the suggestion of Robert Drews, "The 'Chariots of Iron' of Joshua and Judges," *JSOT* 45 (1989): 15–23, who believes it was a retrojection of the later Assyrian practice of attaching an iron tire to the wheel.

[322] As such, the Canaanites mentioned here would also survive. Cf. Mitchell, *Together in the Land*, 181.

was fulfilling his promise to Abraham from Genesis 15 (though he was), but also that God could be trusted to fulfill his commitments down to the lowest levels of Israel's community.

Joseph had received particular promises as a tribe, and God was faithfully fulfilling these, ensuring that (as Num 26:53–54 indicated) the most numerous tribes would receive the most land by lot. But God's promises could not only be traced to the tribe; they could also be traced below the level of the clan to the family. This is displayed in the example of the daughters of Zelophehad receiving the allotment promised to them through their father (Num 27:1–11). Indeed, by placing the story of the daughters at the heart of the Joseph account, the narrator emphasizes the possibility of the tribe as a whole receiving the promise of God. Thus, these chapters make clear that God was faithful to his promises and that this faithfulness was not simply expressed at a generic level but reached down to the family.

Against this, these chapters also demonstrate a consistent inability on the part of Joseph to live fully in light of the promise of God. This is evident in the inability of Ephraim to expel the Canaanites in Gezer and of Manasseh to possess the towns along the Jezreel Valley because of the determination of the Canaanites. That is, it was the Canaanite determination that was stressed, not an Israelite failure. Indeed, one of the curious features of Joshua is its apparent openness to some Canaanite groups continuing in Israel and this not being a problem, as is evident in the note about the Archites and Japhletites (16:2–3). Some Canaanites could continue to live among the Israelites and not be a threat. Whether the groups in Gezer or the Jezreel Valley could be understood that way is less clear. In the end, they were treated like the Gibeonites, placed under forced labor. Regardless of how we interpret these groups, Joseph is not fully enjoying the promise of God. Nowhere is this clearer than in the closing account (17:14–18), where Joshua's own words to Joseph seem to drip with irony. Joseph claims to be a great people because of God's blessing, but they are then unwilling to take additional land. Thus, Canaanites who are willing are allowed to remain, and Israelites who are unwilling do not take all the possible land. Of course, since Joseph did not actually take this land, we do not know if God was really going to support them. Perhaps Joshua knew that the offer of land would only be hypothetical because he recognized them as a people unwilling to take up the promise of God.

These verses are not picked up in the rest of the Bible. Nevertheless, it is worth reading them in light of Paul's presentation of the obvious power games that were being played out in the Corinthian church. Rejecting models of power and prestige that seemingly had taken hold, Paul points out that these believers had not come from positions of power or prestige (1 Cor 1:26–31). Indeed, God had chosen the weak (1 Cor 1:27), a label that his readers would no doubt not want applied to themselves. And yet, this church that had not come from power had received the promises of God, and this was not based on worldly wisdom. Joshua demonstrated that Joseph was following worldly wisdom and not living in the reality of God's promise to them, even as Zelophehad's daughters demonstrated an alternative possibility. Writing to the same church in a different context, Paul points out that in contrast to the uncertain reliability of human promises, all God's promises are "Yes" in Jesus (2 Cor 1:20). The God who promised in Genesis continues to promise in the gospel. God's faithfulness to his promise is at the heart of this passage, and that good news is taken up in the New Testament, though there too we see that not all God's people live in light of the reality of his promise.

D. Land Distribution at Shiloh (18:1–19:51)

18 ¹ The entire Israelite community assembled at Shiloh and set up the tent of meeting there. The land had been subdued before them, ² but seven tribes among the Israelites were left who had not divided up their inheritance. ³ So Joshua asked the Israelites, "How long will you delay going out to take possession of the land that the Lord, the God of your ancestors, gave you? ⁴ Appoint for yourselves three men from each tribe, and I will send them out. They are to go and survey the land, write a description of it for the purpose of their inheritance, and return to me. ⁵ Then they are to divide it into seven portions. Judah is to remain in its territory in the south and Joseph's family in their territory in the north. ⁶ When you have written a description of the seven portions of land and brought it to me, I will cast lots for you here in the presence of the Lord our God. ⁷ But the Levites among you do not get a portion, because their inheritance is the priesthood of the Lord. Gad, Reuben, and half the tribe of Manasseh have taken their inheritance beyond the Jordan to the east, which Moses the Lord's servant gave them."

⁸ As the men prepared to go, Joshua commanded them to write down a description of the land, saying, "Go and survey the land, write a description of it, and return to me. I will then cast lots for you here in Shiloh in the presence of the Lord." ⁹ So the men left, went through the

land, and described it by towns in a document of seven sections. They returned to Joshua at the camp in Shiloh. ¹⁰ Joshua cast lots for them at Shiloh in the presence of the LORD where he distributed the land to the Israelites according to their divisions.

¹¹ The lot came up for the tribe of Benjamin's descendants by their clans, and their allotted territory lay between Judah's descendants and Joseph's descendants.

¹² Their border on the north side began at the Jordan, ascended to the slope of Jericho on the north, through the hill country westward, and ended at the wilderness around Beth-aven. ¹³ From there the border went toward Luz, to the southern slope of Luz (that is, Bethel); it then went down by Ataroth-addar, over the hill south of Lower Beth-horon.

¹⁴ On the west side, from the hill facing Beth-horon on the south, the border curved, turning southward, and ended at Kiriath-baal (that is, Kiriath-jearim), a city of the descendants of Judah. This was the west side of their border. ¹⁵ The south side began at the edge of Kiriath-jearim, and the border extended westward; it went to the spring at the Waters of Nephtoah. ¹⁶ The border descended to the foot of the hill that faces Ben Hinnom Valley at the northern end of Rephaim Valley. It ran down Hinnom Valley toward the south Jebusite slope and downward to En-rogel. ¹⁷ It curved northward and went to En-shemesh and on to Geliloth, which is opposite the Ascent of Adummim, and continued down to the Stone of Bohan son of Reuben. ¹⁸ Then it went north to the slope opposite the Arabah and proceeded into the plains. ¹⁹ The border continued to the north slope of Beth-hoglah and ended at the northern bay of the Dead Sea, at the southern end of the Jordan. This was the southern border.

²⁰ The Jordan formed the border on the east side.

This was the inheritance of Benjamin's descendants, by their clans, according to its surrounding borders.

²¹ These were the cities of the tribe of Benjamin's descendants by their clans:

Jericho, Beth-hoglah, Emek-keziz, ²² Beth-arabah, Zemaraim, Bethel, ²³ Avvim, Parah, Ophrah, ²⁴ Chephar-ammoni, Ophni, and Geba—twelve cities, with their settlements; ²⁵ Gibeon, Ramah, Beeroth, ²⁶ Mizpeh, Chephirah, Mozah, ²⁷ Rekem, Irpeel, Taralah, ²⁸ Zela, Haeleph, Jebus (that is, Jerusalem), Gibeah, and Kiriath—fourteen cities, with their settlements.

This was the inheritance for Benjamin's descendants by their clans.

19 ¹ The second lot came out for Simeon, for the tribe of his descendants by their clans, but their inheritance was within the inheritance given to Judah's descendants. ² Their inheritance included

> Beer-sheba (or Sheba), Moladah, ³ Hazar-shual, Balah, Ezem, ⁴ Eltolad, Bethul, Hormah, ⁵ Ziklag, Beth-marcaboth, Hazar-susah, ⁶ Beth-lebaoth, and Sharuhen—thirteen cities, with their settlements; ⁷ Ain, Rimmon, Ether, and Ashan—four cities, with their settlements; ⁸ and all the settlements surrounding these cities as far as Baalath-beer (Ramah in the south).

This was the inheritance of the tribe of Simeon's descendants by their clans. ⁹ The inheritance of Simeon's descendants was within the territory of Judah's descendants, because the share for Judah's descendants was too large. So Simeon's descendants received an inheritance within Judah's portion.

¹⁰ The third lot came up for Zebulun's descendants by their clans.

> The territory of their inheritance stretched as far as Sarid; ¹¹ their border went up westward to Maralah, reached Dabbesheth, and met the brook east of Jokneam. ¹² From Sarid, it turned due east along the border of Chisloth-tabor, went to Daberath, and went up to Japhia. ¹³ From there, it went due east to Gath-hepher and to Eth-kazin; it extended to Rimmon, curving around to Neah. ¹⁴ The border then circled around Neah on the north to Hannathon and ended at Iphtah-el Valley, ¹⁵ along with Kattath, Nahalal, Shimron, Idalah, and Bethlehem—twelve cities, with their settlements.

¹⁶ This was the inheritance of Zebulun's descendants by their clans, these cities, with their settlements.

¹⁷ The fourth lot came out for the tribe of Issachar's descendants by their clans.

> ¹⁸ Their territory went to Jezreel, and included Chesulloth, Shunem, ¹⁹ Hapharaim, Shion, Anaharath, ²⁰ Rabbith, Kishion, Ebez, ²¹ Remeth, En-gannim, En-haddah, and Beth-pazzez. ²² The border reached Tabor, Shahazumah, and Beth-shemesh, and ended at the Jordan—sixteen cities, with their settlements.

²³ This was the inheritance of the tribe of Issachar's descendants by their clans, the cities, with their settlements.

²⁴ The fifth lot came out for the tribe of Asher's descendants by their clans.

> ²⁵ Their boundary included Helkath, Hali, Beten, Achshaph, ²⁶ Allammelech, Amad, and Mishal and reached westward to Carmel and Shihor-libnath. ²⁷ It turned eastward to Beth-dagon, reached Zebulun and Iphtah-el Valley, north

toward Beth-emek and Neiel, and went north to Cabul,
²⁸ Ebron, Rehob, Hammon, and Kanah, as far as greater
Sidon. ²⁹ The boundary then turned to Ramah as far as
the fortified city of Tyre; it turned back to Hosah and ended at the Mediterranean Sea, including Mahalab, Achzib,
³⁰ Ummah, Aphek, and Rehob—twenty-two cities, with
their settlements.

³¹ This was the inheritance of the tribe of Asher's descendants by
their clans, these cities with their settlements.

³² The sixth lot came out for Naphtali's descendants by their clans.
³³ Their boundary went from Heleph and from the oak in
Zaanannim, including Adami-nekeb and Jabneel, as far
as Lakkum, and ended at the Jordan. ³⁴ To the west, the
boundary turned to Aznoth-tabor and went from there
to Hukkok, reaching Zebulun on the south, Asher on the
west, and Judah at the Jordan on the east. ³⁵ The fortified
cities were Ziddim, Zer, Hammath, Rakkath, Chinnereth,
³⁶ Adamah, Ramah, Hazor, ³⁷ Kedesh, Edrei, En-hazor,
³⁸ Iron, Migdal-el, Horem, Beth-anath, and Beth-shemesh—
nineteen cities, with their settlements.

³⁹ This was the inheritance of the tribe of Naphtali's descendants
by their clans, the cities with their settlements.

⁴⁰ The seventh lot came out for the tribe of Dan's descendants by
their clans.

⁴¹ The territory of their inheritance included Zorah, Eshtaol, Ir-shemesh, ⁴² Shaalabbin, Aijalon, Ithlah, ⁴³ Elon,
Timnah, Ekron, ⁴⁴ Eltekeh, Gibbethon, Baalath, ⁴⁵ Jehud,
Bene-berak, Gath-rimmon, ⁴⁶ Me-jarkon, and Rakkon, with
the territory facing Joppa.

⁴⁷ When the territory of the descendants of Dan slipped out of
their control, they went up and fought against Leshem, captured it,
and struck it down with the sword. So they took possession of it, lived
there, and renamed Leshem after their ancestor Dan. ⁴⁸ This was the
inheritance of the tribe of Dan's descendants by their clans, these cities
with their settlements.

⁴⁹ When they had finished distributing the land into its territories,
the Israelites gave Joshua son of Nun an inheritance among them. ⁵⁰ By
the Lord's command, they gave him the city Timnath-serah in the hill
country of Ephraim, which he requested. He rebuilt the city and lived
in it.

⁵¹ These were the portions that the priest Eleazar, Joshua son of
Nun, and the family heads distributed to the Israelite tribes by lot at
Shiloh in the Lord's presence at the entrance to the tent of meeting. So
they finished dividing up the land.

Context

With the accounts of Judah and Joseph completed, the focus turns to the remaining west Jordan tribes. Since Judah and Joseph (especially Ephraim) would later dominate Israel, it is not surprising that more attention is given to them than the other tribes. But there is also logic internal to Joshua for this emphasis, demonstrated through the special allotments to Caleb and Joshua. Caleb's allotment is given first (14:6–15), but it will subsequently be made clear that his allotment fell within Judah's territory. Although Caleb's Edomite status is foregrounded in Joshua, his integration into Judah is not forgotten. Joshua's allotment within Ephraim is recorded last (19:49–50), so that the allotments of the two surviving spies provide a boundary for the whole of chapters 14–19. But even allowing for the prominence of these two tribes, it is still important for the book that all the tribes receive their allotment, and that provides the key focus of these chapters.

However, it is the focus on the tent of meeting that shows the theological importance of these chapters. Reference to it provides the boundaries for these two chapters (18:1; 19:51), though 19:51 serves double duty by also linking to 14:1 through its reference to the activity of Eleazar and Joshua in allotting the land. Whereas the previous allotments took place at Gilgal (14:6), the Israelites had now moved to Shiloh and set up the tent of meeting (see exposition on 18:1). Shiloh has not previously been mentioned in the book but will be the center for Israelite worship from this point until the destruction of the house of Eli (1 Sam 4:12–22). Its place as a worship center is particularly important, emphasized by the fact that when Israel gathered there they set up the tent of meeting.

Koorevaar has argued that this represents the theological heart of Joshua, the point where Yahweh's rule over the land is clearly demonstrated through the establishment of the central sanctuary required by Deuteronomy 12:5–14 and fulfilling the hope expressed in Leviticus 26:11 of Yahweh dwelling among Israel.[323] This perhaps claims slightly more for this text than is appropriate, but it is certainly the heart of the extended chiasm that runs through chapters 13–21 (see context discussion on Josh 13:1–14:15), so this is at least the theological heart of the land-allocation chapters. It makes clear the point that Moses argued in his dialogue with God in Exodus 33:12–17—that it can only make sense for Israel to be in

---

[323] Koorevaar, *De Opbouw*, 240, 255.

the land if God is truly present with them. The establishment of the tent of meeting, thus placing the worship of God at the center of Israel's life, amply demonstrates this. Moreover, it makes clear what had only been hinted at through the involvement of Eleazar (14:6), which is that the allocation of the land needed to take place within the context of worship.[324]

The material within these chapters is clearly looking back from a later date than the time of Joshua, since it knows of the failure of Dan to control the territory allotted to them and their subsequent move to the far north, to a site technically outside the boundaries of the land God had promised (19:47).[325] The gathering of this information at a later point would also explain the variances in form that we find in the information provided for each tribe (for the variances in content, see the context discussion on Josh 15:1–63). The introductory comments for how the lot was cast for each tribe take various forms. The verbs used are עלה ("came up," 18:11; 19:10) and יצא ("came out," 19:1, 17, 24, 32, 40), though without a significant variation in meaning. But even when the same verb is used, variances occur. A waw consecutive imperfect is used in both occurrences of עלה and the first three of יצא. But a qal perfect is used with Naphtali and Dan, and in both cases we have a sentence that begins with the relevant tribe as the indirect object. Zebulun is distinguished from the others as the only group not called a tribe—a term used in the opening statements for Benjamin, Simeon, Issachar, and Asher, but not Naphtali, for whom this information is provided in the closing statement.

This evidence suggests that the information has been derived from a range of source texts, which is why there are variations in presentation and why the boundaries for the northernmost tribes are not particularly clear. In spite of this, an attempt at uniformity has been made by the

---

[324] Horst Seebass, "Versuch zu Josua xviii 1–10," VT 51 (2006): 370–85, has argued that the Shiloh references come from multiple redactional layers (similarly Volkmar Fritz, Das Buch Josua [Tübingen: J. C. B. Mohr (Paul Siebeck), 1994], 178). Even if we accept this, and not all his arguments are equally persuasive since his doublets could also be examples of narrative resumption, the focus needs to be on the final form of the text since it is still demonstrably a coherent whole, and his wider conclusions about the appropriateness of the pericope being located at this point still support this. Moreover, with Butler, Joshua 13–24, 160, we should recognize that the Shiloh tradition is quite ancient.

[325] The various lists could conceivably come from different periods if they are not all from the one source, but still appear to be quite ancient. For example, Zecharia Kallai, "Simeon's Town List. Scribal Rules and Geographical Patterns," VT 53 (2003): 83, dates Simeon's list to the time of David.

narrator through the comments about the allotments being tied to the clans. This is consistent with the pattern demonstrated in the east Jordan tribes, Judah, and Joseph. So, although the material is drawn from a range of sources, there is a degree of literary unity and, more importantly, a theological coherence that holds these two chapters together along with the larger block of Joshua 14–19. This coherence can also be seen in that, with the intentional exceptions of Benjamin and Dan, the tribes are listed in birth order for their forebears.[326] Israel's life makes sense when they are a worshiping people, with each in the place God has allotted them but with a memory of how God has brought them this far. The sanctuary at Shiloh is the key demonstration of this.

Exegesis

18:1. Given that it has not been mentioned before, the statement that the whole Israelite community assembled at Shiloh is something of a surprise. The town is in the east of Ephraim, a little north of Bethel and east of a major highway (Judg 21:19). Although not mentioned previously, it will fulfill an important function subsequently, not only as the site from which the remaining tribes received their allocation, but also where the Levitical allotment was made (Josh 21:2) and as the center of the east-west rivalry (22:9, 12).

In the early chapters of Samuel (1 Samuel 1–4), Shiloh is still the center of Israel's worship life, the place from which the ark was captured. The Bible is silent as to when the sanctuary at Shiloh was destroyed, but it had clearly ceased to function as a worship center by the time of David's reign given his desire to establish a temple in Jerusalem (2 Sam 7:1–2). Jeremiah could later look back to its destruction as a well-known event that should have made clear that the simple presence of a central sanctuary was not in itself enough to guarantee its security (Jer 7:8–15).[327] But at this point all of that is in the future.

For Joshua, setting up the tent of meeting represents a crucial moment for the nation, a triumphal assertion that God had indeed journeyed with them into the land and was dwelling with them (Lev 26:11). This is why McConville and Williams regard Joshua 18:1 as one of the "most

---

[326] Matties, *Joshua*, 318.

[327] For a possible reconstruction of the history of the tabernacle, see Akiva Males, "Reconstructing the Destruction of the Tabernacle of Shiloh," *JBQ* 44 (2016): 8–12.

theologically pregnant" verses in the book.[328] Although it is never stated that Shiloh was the place that God had chosen (Deut 12), the subsequent narrative demonstrates his approval of it, and Shiloh was thus the place of the sanctuary until the early monarchy.

Notably, the sanctuary is called the "tent of meeting." In Exodus 33:7–11, this expression is used for a tent Moses used to set up outside the camp, but once the tabernacle was constructed, "tabernacle" and "tent of meeting" seem to have been used more or less interchangeably. As such, Israel was reminded that this was the place where God's glory had come to dwell (Exod 40:34–38).

Only after the declaration about the setting up of the tent are we told that the land had been subdued before Israel. Reference to the land being subdued (niphal כבשׁ) is relatively rare, and there is almost certainly an allusion here to Numbers 32:29 (cf. Num 32:22),[329] where Moses stipulated this as a key condition for the east Jordan tribes to return to their territory. This allusion demonstrates that the condition had been met even though all the land had not yet been allotted, and it also prepares for the importance of Shiloh in the events of Joshua 22 when those tribes do return to their possession.

18:2–7. The land was "subdued" before Israel, but that was not the same as being occupied or even fully allotted. So, although considerable attention has been given to the east Jordan tribes (Josh 13) and then to Judah, Ephraim, and west Manasseh (Josh 14–17), this leaves seven tribes (apart from Levi, who do not receive an allotment) without their allocation. More importantly, 13:6–7 indicates that Joshua was to divide (חלק) the land for the west Jordan tribes, but this had not yet been done for the remaining seven tribes. Since Joshua here approaches the remaining tribes, the assumption must be that he had created the context for each tribe to begin the division of their portion of the land, each division

---

[328] McConville and Williams, Joshua, 73.

[329] Apart from this verse and the two in Numbers 32, the only other occurrence of this verb form is 1 Chr 22:18, which is referring back to Josh 18:1. Harstad, Joshua, 578, is one of many who see a link to Gen 1:28, but the passive verb in Josh 18:1 seems to distinguish the two. In Genesis, it is a command to humans to subdue the earth, but here the fact that it "was subdued" points to God's action instead.

being the inheritance of that tribe. This is why Joshua asked them about their delay.[330]

The participle translated "delay" (v. 3) comes from a rare but important root (רפה) in Joshua. In 1:5, it was used by God to reassure Joshua that he would not abandon him; in 10:6 it was used by Gibeon to remind Israel of their commitment to them. These echoes make clear, then, that its use in 18:3 is not simply a "delay" (csb) but rather that these tribes had "put off" (esv) something that God had commanded.[331] God had not abandoned Israel; indeed, he was the one who had given them the land to possess. That the title "the Lord, the God of your fathers" is used here thus points back to the land promise that runs through Genesis (Gen 12:1–3; 15:18–21; 26:3; 28:13). That this promise reaches so far back into Israel's story demonstrates that God had not abandoned his people, which in turn highlights further the need for these tribes to divide the land he had given. Doing this would involve the seven tribes entering the land and so possessing it, thus alluding to Joshua 1:3, which had assured Israel that God would give them the land where they walked. As these seven tribes walked through the unallotted land they would effectively claim this promise as a local fulfillment of the promise to their ancestors. Once again, the book holds an important tension here between land as something God has already given and yet is still to be claimed.

Recognizing the need to claim the land, Joshua directed the seven tribes to appoint three men from each tribe so that he could send them out to write a report based on their walking through the land. Joshua acknowledged the lack of a detailed knowledge of the land, which is why the survey was needed. This may be why he uses the *hithpael* with this root (וְיִתְהַלְּכוּ), which typically means "to walk about"[332] and, thus, assumes they will wander through the land rather than go to specific sites.[333] In

---

[330] With Elie Assis, " 'How Long Are You Slack to Go to Possess the Land?' (Jos. xviii 3): Ideal and Reality in the Distribution Descriptions in Joshua XIII–XIX," *VT* 53 (2003): 7, this second stage of allocation is read as representative of the complex historical realities involved in Israel's emergence in the land.

[331] Given that there is no record in the Old Testament of the territory as described being fully settled, the choice of this term may also be a challenge to later readers to reflect on why parts of the land were not held.

[332] csb renders the verb "go," which (though not wrong) does not bring out the nuances of the *hithpael*.

[333] As Hawk, *Joshua*, 215, points out, this implies their walking through the land and, thus, ties this directive back to the promise of 1:3.

this way, they would develop a more complete knowledge of the land and of how it could be divided appropriately for the inheritance of the tribes.

A play on words occurs in verse 5, as the verb for "divide" (וְהִתְחַלְּקוּ) sounds very similar to the verb rendered "survey" in verse 4. But this time the effect of the *hithpael* is to indicate that the surveyors were to divide the land while recognizing the boundaries already allotted to Judah and the Joseph tribes. The surveyors could not allot the land; their task was to ensure that the land was divided into more or less equivalent portions. The actual allotments would happen at the sanctuary when they returned with their written reports to Joshua so he could cast the lot for the tribes. Doing so in the presence of God was a key means of demonstrating that, however much human involvement there was, the actual allotment was directed by God.[334]

Notably, the verb Joshua uses for casting the lot in verse 6 (ירה) is not used for this elsewhere in the book. It may be because the narrator is here drawing together a range of source materials, but perhaps a more likely reason is that this instance is focused on the act of casting lots (cf. the exposition on 14:2), whereas the other occurrences are concerned with its result. The seven tribes were also reassured that the seven divisions of the land they would receive were to be shared among them and with no others. Levi was excluded because their inheritance was the priesthood, and the east Jordan tribes had previously received their portions. They had received the allocation from Yahweh's servant Moses (v. 7), and the remaining tribes would receive theirs through Joshua, who was gradually moving toward the same status (see 24:29).

18:8–10. Verse 8 largely repeats the content of Joshua's speech in verses 4–7, except that there he addressed the tribes and outlined the process to be followed, whereas here he addresses the surveyors as they set out. Modern readers might find such repetitions unnecessary, but the narrative texts of the Old Testament frequently make use of repetition as an important mode for emphasis.[335] By closing this speech with reference

---

[334] Anne M. Kitz, "Undivided Inheritance and Lot Casting in the Book of Joshua," *JBL* 119 (2000): 601–18, has argued that the use of lots to determine inheritance reflects a pattern in ancient Near Eastern law. This shows that the pattern would have been intelligible to Israel, though the theological emphasis is still that God was making the allotment.

[335] See, e.g., Meir Sternberg, *The Poetics of Biblical Narrative: Ideological Literature and the Drama of Reading* (Bloomington: Indiana University Press, 1987), 365–440.

to the casting of the lot (this time using the verb שלך) at Shiloh, we are once again reminded that it is God's decision that matters.

The report of the surveyors' actions accords closely with Joshua's directives, with only small changes in the language used for variation. As directed by Joshua, their report divided the land into seven sections. An additional note indicates that they described the land by its towns, preparing us for the fact that several of the divisions would include city lists and that cities from across the land would subsequently be allocated as cities of refuge (Josh 20), taken from the larger list of Levite cities (Josh 21). The variation from strict repetition on this point demonstrates a consistent feature of the book, which is that even where specific instructions were given there was still scope for faithfully carrying them out in a number of ways.

Since the narrative is not interested in reporting the journey of the surveyors in any detail (even though such a journey would have taken some weeks), we quickly skip to the point where they had returned to Shiloh. There Joshua cast the lot before God and divided the land according to their divisions.[336]

18:11–20. The account of each tribal allotment begins with a statement about the lot (see discussion of context above). Although various verbs are used (here, עלה), there does not seem to be a significant difference in meaning. The allotments seem broadly grouped, so that those to the south (Benjamin and Simeon) are recounted first, followed by those to the north (Zebulun, Issachar, Asher, Naphtali). The obvious exception is Dan, whose allotment bordered Benjamin's. Since the account is told from a later point when Dan had failed to occupy their land and moved to the far north, keeping their report until last is a logical variant. The presentation of the tribes is thus relative to their location and does not necessarily represent the order in which the lots came out. As noted with Judah (Josh 15), the narrator is clearly better informed about southern sites, with the result that the northern allotments are not described in as much detail. Certainly, the report for Benjamin is more detailed than those of the other tribes.

Benjamin's report is broken down into two major sections, a description of the tribal boundaries (18:11–20) and a city list (18:21–28). Their

---

[336] With Harstad, *Joshua*, 585, we should probably understand the reference to Joshua here to include Eleazar even though he is not mentioned, since Joshua would have taken the lead.

report is roughly twice the length of any of those in chapter 19. It is further broken down according to the cardinal points: northern (18:12–14a), western (18:14b), southern (18:15–19), and eastern (18:20a) boundaries. The whole report is bounded by summary statements in verses 11 and 20b.

The opening summary in verse 11 aligns Benjamin's allotment to the earlier ones by noting that it was made according to their clans (see comments on 13:15), a pattern that continues in the remaining allotments. Reference to the lot also ties verse 11 to verse 10, making it clear that God directed the process; the lots were not random. Readers who have paid close attention to the boundary lists for Judah and Joseph (Josh 15–17) will note an unoccupied space between these groups. Verse 11 informs us that Benjamin would fill at least some of that gap. The balance would be allotted to Dan (19:40–46), though they would not retain it. That Benjamin fit between Judah and Joseph means that its borders mostly retrace areas discussed previously. It also means the allotment was spread wide from east to west but was quite shallow from north to south, which is why the eastern and western borders can be traced very briefly.

The northern border in verses 12–13 is traced from east to west, starting at the Jordan near Jericho. As is typical for the book, we follow an imaginary line around the border, which is shaped by the nature of the terrain. The locations match those in the account of Joseph's southern border (see comments on 16:1–4). The only addition is Beth-aven, a town previously mentioned in 7:2 when locating Ai, which lay east of Bethel. There was apparently a wilderness in the area, but given the uncertainty about these locations (see comments on 7:2) we cannot be certain what this means beyond the fact that it would have been sparsely populated.

The western border occurs as the central hills reach the Shephelah at Lower Beth-horon (see comments on 10:10) and is on the border with Joseph (16:3). The southward turn takes the boundary to Kiriath-jearim (also called Kiriath-baal), a town that appears in the boundary report for Judah (15:9) where a dual form of the name occurs (using the shorter form Baalah). The southward turn leaves space for the allotment to Dan.

Having reached Judah along the west, it is not surprising that the southern border (traced here from west to east back to the north end of the Dead Sea), is closely matched to that of Judah, with every place mentioned also noted in 15:5–11 (see comments there). The only exception is Geliloth, though with the Targum we should perhaps read "Gilgal" here (a word from the same root), in which case the difference is resolved on a text-critical basis.[337] Note that the borders are traced in opposite directions to one another.

The eastern border is simply the Jordan, but given the details of the other parts of Benjamin's border, we can easily recognize that it is only a relatively short stretch of the river, moving from the northernmost points of the Dead Sea to just east of Jericho. Thus, it is only about fifteen miles along the valley.

The summary note in verse 20 concludes the boundary description and indicates that, within these boundaries, each clan would receive its allotment. The remaining tribes receive a similar comment, though the closest parallel is with the tribe of Judah (15:12; see comments there), which also has a separate city list. By contrast, the comment for Ephraim and Manasseh is used to introduce the allotment for each of these tribes (16:5 and, in an expanded form, 17:1-2) since it was broken up between the two.

18:21-28. Benjamin also receives a city list (a feature it shares with Judah, the Joseph tribes, and Naphtali, though theirs is much briefer). This demonstrates the importance of Benjamin for the composition of the book, as well as the fact that the book in general displays more knowledge of the south and highlands. The city list is tied to the boundary list by the repetition of the statement that it was allotted to Benjamin by clans, again indicating that, although the cities belonged to the tribe as a whole, each clan could also identify its share within it. That may be why the allotment for an otherwise relatively small tribe breaks the city list into two groups, with twelve towns listed in verses 20b-24 and then another fourteen in verses 25-28a. Otherwise-unknown towns that receive no comment are:

Towns	Verse
Emek-keziz	21
Zemaraim	22
Avvim, Parah	23
Chephar-ammoni, Ophni	24
Mozah	26
Rekem, Irpeel, and Taralah	27
Haeleph, Kiriath	28

---

[337] "Geliloth" means "districts," and so is an odd place name.

The first list (vv. 20b–24) begins with one of Benjamin's best-known cities, Jericho (see comments on 6:1) in the northeast of the allotment, and the point where the boundary list had begun (18:12). Beth-hoglah (cf. 18:19) lies on the border with Judah (see comments on 15:6). Beth-arabah is also on Judah's border (15:6), a few miles north of the Dead Sea in the Jordan Valley. Bethel is a well-known town, near where Joshua set his ambush on Ai (18:9) and on the border with Joseph (16:1; 18:13). Ophrah (18:23) was raided by the Philistines in 1 Samuel 13:17. Geba (Josh 18:24), a town a few miles north of Jerusalem, will later become a Levitical city (21:17). These twelve cities and their associated settlements constitute the first group of Benjamin's cities. Certainty about some of the locations is not possible, but this group is probably in the east of Benjamin.

The second group (vv. 25–28a) begins and ends with some of Benjamin's better-known towns along with some more obscure sites. As with the first group, we cannot confidently identify them all, but based on those that can be recognized, this group appears to be to the west of Benjamin's allotment. Gibeon has already been central to the events of Joshua 9 (see comments on 9:3), and Israel's alliance with them triggered some of the conflict in chapter 10 (see comments on 10:1). The Gibeonites continued to live within Israel, an indigenous group that God had chosen to save (11:19). So, although the city fell within Benjamin's allotment, it was shared with the indigenous population, and readers know from the earlier passages that this was acceptable.

Ramah is a common toponym (meaning "height"; others are mentioned in 19:8, 29, 36). The exact location of this site is unknown, though it seems to be in the region of Gibeon, perhaps a little to the south since it (along with Gibeah) would be considered as an alternative resting place to Jerusalem in Judges 19:13. Beeroth is also in this area, having been already noted as a Gibeonite town (Josh 9:17). Mizpeh (meaning "watchtower") is also a common toponym, but this is not the valley mentioned in 11:3 since that is allotted to Judah (15:38). This site will later witness the tragedy of the Benjaminite war and forced marriages for the surviving members of the tribe (Judg 20:1; 21:1). It was also an important center in Samuel's ministry (1 Sam 7:5, 16) and the place where Saul was first publicly recognized as king (1 Sam 10:17). Even in the exile, it remained an important site—the place where Gedaliah established his administrative center (2 Kgs 25:23). However, although the general location is identifiable, a specific site has not been identified, suggesting that it was more useful as a meeting place than a major settlement. Chephirah has already been noted as a Gibeonite town (Josh 9:17).

Zela is where David would rebury the remains of Saul and Jonathan (2 Sam 21:14), but is otherwise unknown.[338] As before (Josh 15:8, 63), Jerusalem is associated with the Jebusites. Indeed, although the CSB renders this as a place name ("Jebus"), the MT actually has the gentilic ("Jebusite"), stressing the identity of those living there rather than the place name, unlike Judges 19:10, which does use this as a place name.[339] As with Judah's list, this suggests that the Jebusites were still resident when the list was initially compiled. Although the southern slope of Jerusalem was allotted to Judah (Josh 15:8), the city belonged to Benjamin. Both its continued Jebusite occupation and its location on the border of Judah made it an ideal site for David to establish his capital after capturing the city (2 Sam 5:6–10). Within these chapters, the reference to the Jebusites also downplays the importance of Jerusalem so that Shiloh remains the most important site.

Gibeah is another common toponym ("hill"), and this one is to be distinguished from those mentioned in Joshua 15:57 and 24:33. This site, probably a little northwest of Jerusalem, would be the most important one. It was the site of the outrage that triggered the Benjaminite war (Judg 19:10–30), but it would also be Saul's home (1 Sam 10:26; 15:34), a place from which he would later confront the Philistines (1 Sam 13:15–23). David would also hand over his grandsons to the Gibeonites there (2 Sam 21:5–6). This assumes that the CSB is correct in rendering this as a place name on its own, distinguished from Kiriath. The MT has the place name in the construct state, suggesting "Gibeath-kiriath" might be correct; however, feminine nouns can end in this form. Thus, the CSB is probably to be preferred since this also means the count is correct.[340] A closing note then stresses the point made in verse 11: The allotments were not just for the tribe as a whole, but also so that the clans would recognize their own portion within it.

---

[338] The LXX seems to join the first two towns of v. 28 into one place, "Zelah-haeleph." This is not impossible, and the fact that the number of towns in the list would then not agree with those listed is not an insuperable objection, as there is evidence elsewhere of textual problems in these lists. But as this would require multiple textual problems (notably the loss of another town), it seems best to stay with the MT.

[339] The LXX does have "Jebus," but this is most likely a smoothing out of the text.

[340] The rather different LXX here suggests that the challenge of this text has long been felt.

19:1–9. The second lot "came out" (יצא) for Simeon, the other southern tribe (v. 1). As with the others, this allotment is said to be for both
the tribe and the clans that made it up. But there is a difference for this
allotment: rather than being a separate territory, Simeon's allotment is
entirely within Judah, though the reason for this is not explained until
verse 9. The towns allotted to Simeon are identified (vv. 2–8) because,
even though the tribe would not have a definable boundary (a trait shared
with Dan), there was still a recognizable allotment for them.

This allotment was divided into two groups: a list of thirteen cities
(vv. 2–6) and a list of four cities (vv. 7–8). Many of the cities for Simeon
were listed in the allotment to Judah. This is most easily seen in tabular
form:

Town Name	Reference in Judah
Beer-sheba (also "Sheba")[341]	15:28
Moladah	15:26
Hazar-shual	15:28
Balah	
Ezem	15:29
Eltolad	15:30
Bethul	
Hormah	15:30
Ziklag	15:31
Beth-marcaboth	
Hazar-susah	
Beth-lebaoth	
Sharuhen	
Ain	15:32
Rimmon	15:32
Ether	15:42
Ashan	15:42

[341] I take the conjunction here as explicative (Williams, *Hebrew Syntax*, §434), so that
Sheba is not a separate town.

Among the towns with no direct match, Balah is probably only an apparent exception, as there is a Baalah in 15:29, indicating these may be variant forms of the one name. Bethul might also be a variant form for the Bealoth in 15:24 (this assumes a transposition too), though alternatively a case might be made for associating this town with Beth-lebaoth. None of the towns unique to this list in Joshua are mentioned elsewhere. From the eleven towns that can be identified through the parallel in Judah's listing, notably all but Ether and Ashan are drawn from the towns in the extreme south of Judah (15:20–32). Ether and Ashan are part of a district in the Shephelah, and these too are probably located in the far south.

Although Simeon did not have a distinct boundary, clearly the tribe as a whole was located within the one region of Judah so that it could still retain a degree of tribal unity. Nevertheless, the lack of a definable boundary prepared the way for a fulfillment of Jacob's blessing, which indicated that Simeon, along with Levi, would be scattered among the tribes (Gen 49:7). This blessing took a very different form for each of these tribes, but this allotment clearly presumes that the effect of this blessing was felt. Read solely against the background of the tribal blessings, Simeon's allotment within Judah could be seen negatively, a judgment on the tribe because of their ancestor's violence against Shechem (Gen 34).[342] But Joshua makes clear that Simeon received this allotment because Judah's was too large. This stems in part from the fact that Simeon was considerably smaller than any other tribe (Num 26:12–14). Yet the emphasis here is not that Simeon's need was less but rather that Judah had too much. Therefore, a just allocation of the land meant Judah needed to give up some of their initial allotment to ensure equity for all, fulfilling the directive of Numbers 33:54. Simeon's scattering is thus an expression of divine justice that can be viewed from two angles—negatively as a punishment for sin and positively as a model for the importance of equal provision for all. This allotment thus allowed Simeon the opportunity to flourish while still recognizing the effects of past sin.

19:10–16. From Simeon, we move to the northernmost tribes of Zebulun (vv. 10–16), Issachar (vv. 17–23), Asher (vv. 24–31), and Naphtali (vv. 32–39) before considering the anomaly of Dan (vv. 40–48). Less detail is provided for these tribes in comparison to those already treated,

---

[342] Cf. Howard, *Joshua*, 366.

suggesting that less information about the far north was available for this list's compilers.

The first of these tribes is Zebulun. Their territory lay north of Manasseh and bordered Issachar, Asher, and Naphtali (see tribal allotment map at 15:1–12). Zebulun's lot is said to have "come up" (עלה; cf. 18:11); as with the other tribes, their allotment was by clans. Zebulun does not have a separate city list, yet the presence of a count noting twelve cities (which is difficult to reconcile with the boundary list) suggests that there might once have been a city list. Uncertainty about the text means we cannot be sure what twelve cities are meant. Moreover, it is not always clear whether the towns mentioned belonged to Zebulun.

Their territory is initially tracked from Sarid, first westward in verse 11 and then eastward in verse 12. Although the border cannot be identified with certainty, it is probably on the northern side of the Megiddo Plain, and so represents a point where Zebulun bordered Manasseh. The westward movement from there is through Maralah and Dabbesheth toward the south of Asher. Although neither site is mentioned elsewhere, their general location on the north of the Megiddo Plain can be identified because of the reference to the brook east of Jokneam, which runs from Jokneam west to the Mediterranean south of Carmel. Jokneam was therefore also included in Zebulun, although it would later be part of the Levitical allocation (21:34).

The eastward movement is then traced through Chisloth-tabor and on to Daberath toward the north of Issachar. Chisloth-tabor is probably called Chesulloth in Issachar's allotment (19:18), but the name here suggests it is located in the region of Mount Tabor. Daberath is mentioned here as a border town, but as allotted to the Levites from Issachar (21:28), it did not belong to Zebulun. Japhia is also a border town (mentioned in the Amarna Letters), southwest of Nazareth.

Further east was Gath-hepher, best known as Jonah's hometown (2 Kgs 14:25). At this point the boundary is also heading north, since it is northeast of Nazareth. It is traced from there to the otherwise unknown Eth-kazin and Rimmon. Rimmon is another common toponym ("pomegranate"), so this town needs to be distinguished from that mentioned in Judah (15:32). Like Neah, it is unknown. Hannathon is not mentioned elsewhere in the Bible, but it does appear in the Amarna Letters and is on the northwest of the allotment along with the Iphtah-el Valley.

Verse 15 seems to trace the western border from north to south,[343] heading back toward Jokneam, but we cannot be certain. Kattah is not mentioned elsewhere unless it is the Kitron in Judges 1:30. While Nahalal is noted as a town allotted from Zebulun to Levi (Josh 21:35), according to Judges 1:30 Zebulun failed to expel the Canaanites from it (there spelled Nahalol). Shimron had been part of the attack on Israel in the northern campaign (11:1), but neither Idalah nor Bethlehem (to be distinguished from the famous town in Judah) are mentioned elsewhere. The listing ends by affirming that Zebulun's inheritance was allotted by clans. There is an additional note referring to "these cities, with their settlements," which is unclear and may be further evidence of textual corruption.

19:17–23. The fourth allotment is for Issachar, a tribe whose territory was bounded by the Jordan to the east, Manasseh to the south, Zebulun to the west, and Naphtali to the north (see tribal allotment map at 15:1–12). As with other tribes, the lot (which "came out," יצא) covers both the tribe as a whole and the clans within it (v. 17). Like Zebulun, Issachar has no clear city list, though reference to "sixteen cities" in verse 22 might suggest that one was once included. Sixteen cities are indeed mentioned, but it is not clear that they all belonged to Issachar since some seem to appear in other tribal listings. Thus, it is uncertain to what this "sixteen cities" refers.[344] Once again, defining the boundary exactly is difficult because of a number of unidentified sites.

The boundary starts at Jezreel, a well-known town north of the Megiddo Plain and about eighteen miles southwest of Chinnereth, near the border with Manasseh. This site is different from the one in Judah (15:56). The importance of controlling the Jezreel Valley (a major trade route) is reflected across the Old Testament. It was later the home town of Ahinoam, one of David's wives (1 Sam 25:43), and central to the final conflict between Saul and the Philistines (1 Sam 29). Ish-bosheth initially incorporated it into his realm (2 Sam 2:9), and Ahab used it as an

---

[343] Howard, *Joshua*, 369–70, regards it as a truncated city list. Given the awkwardness of the text, this is not impossible, but the conjunction at the start of the verse suggests a continuation of the boundary list from the previous verse. A more probable scenario is that a city list has fallen out of the text, perhaps by haplography.

[344] Howard, *Joshua*, 370, considers that the boundary list concludes at the end of v. 22, with the remaining towns comprising a city list. Certainly, the language in v. 18 is abrupt, so one could argue that a new topic is begun with no verb in v. 19, creating a separate city list. But the conjunction there is best read as continuing the border list, while v. 22 would suggest that the border list is being continued.

important center (1 Kgs 18:45–46), which is why he could so easily covet Naboth's vineyard there (1 Kgs 21). It later played a pivotal role in Jehu's revolt (2 Kgs 9–10), which formed the background to Hosea's creative use of the name (Hos 1–2).

As noted, Chesulloth is probably an alternative form for Chisloth-tabor (Josh 19:12). Shunem is another important site. The Philistines were encamped there, leading Saul to consult the spirit-mistress at En-dor (1 Sam 28:4). In David's old age, Abishag was brought to him from there to keep him warm (1 Kgs 1:1–15), and a wealthy woman there supported Elisha's ministry (2 Kgs 4:7–37).

By contrast, most of the other towns are obscure. Nothing certain is known of them, save that Kishion and En-gannim became Levitical cities (Josh 21:28–29), and Anaharath was apparently conquered by Thutmose III before Israel's arrival. En-gannim needs to be distinguished from the town with the same name in Judah (15:34). It is possible that Remeth is the Jarmuth that became a Levitical city (21:29). Verse 22 brings the border list to a close by tracing a line through Tabor, Shahazumah, and Beth-shemesh before reaching the Jordan. Tabor is presumably at the foot of Mount Tabor, an important site about twelve miles southwest of Chinnereth. Beth-shemesh is to be distinguished from the sites in Judah (15:10; 21:16)[345] and Naphtali (19:38).

19:24–31. The fifth allotment "came out" (יצא) for Asher. Their territory hugs the Mediterranean coast from Carmel to Tyre, with Zebulun and Naphtali to the east (see tribal allotment map at 15:1–12). As with the two preceding tribes we only have a boundary list, but the presence of a count (twenty-two cities) in verse 30 suggests that there may once have been a city list. If we understand all the place names as referring to towns and assume the repetition of Rehob refers to two different sites, there could be as many as twenty-seven cities mentioned in the boundary list as rendered by the CSB.[346] Some of them would have stood outside of Asher's territory since they represent points along the boundary, not necessarily cities allotted to them. The allotment is bounded with the typical statements indicating that it was for the tribe by their clans. Following the boundary line with any precision is not possible because of

---

[345] The "Ir-shemesh" allotted to Dan (19:41) is probably the same as the Beth-shemesh in Judah.

[346] There are numerous difficulties here, but on the whole the CSB's rendering can be defended, even if one or two might be challenged.

the uncertainty about where these sites were. Nevertheless, the general area can be recognized.

The difficulties in tracing the boundary are apparent in verse 25. We know that Helkath would become a Levitical city (21:35) and that Achshaph had been one of the cities in the northern coalition (11:1), but beyond this we know nothing certain of these cities, nor of Hali and Beten. The sites in verse 26 are similarly difficult to trace, since Allammelech and Amad are not mentioned elsewhere and Mishal is otherwise only known as one of the towns Asher would contribute to the Levites (21:30).

We are then told that the boundary headed west to Carmel (different from the town in Judah in 15:55), a prominent ridge that reached the sea, suggesting that these sites were south of Asher. This is presumably the region for the otherwise unknown Shihor-libnath. If we take Carmel as referring to the ridge rather than a town, then Shihor-libnath might have been a wadi in the region.

Since Carmel would be the westernmost point of Asher, it is necessary to turn east from there. It is likely that the boundary line is using Helkath as its reference point, in which case it would be on the southern boundary too. It moves from there to the otherwise unknown Beth-dagon (not the town allotted to Judah in 15:41), reaching the border with Zebulun. There, it turned north along the Iphtah-el Valley (noted as part of Zebulun's border in 19:14). The otherwise unknown Beth-emek and Neiel would be found in this area before the border headed further north to Cabul. This town, about nine miles southeast of Acco where the plain reaches some hills, is still known by this name.[347] Cabul may be the main town in an area Solomon later gave to Hiram, king of Tyre (1 Kgs 9:10–14), presumably as a means of covering debts he ran up during the construction of the temple.

Nothing is known of Ebron, Rehob, Hammon, and Kanah in verse 28. Given that the boundary has at this point reached Greater Sidon (presumably the area directly controlled by Sidon, a major port town about thirty miles north of Tyre), clearly the border has moved some distance when we realize that Acco is about the same distance to the south of Tyre as Sidon is north. Tracing the boundary back to Ramah (unknown, but not the sites mentioned in 18:25 and 19:36) and then to Tyre represents a significant move back to the south. In addition to being a major port city and trading center, Tyre is noted for its fortifications; this probably

---

[347] Usually spelled "Kabul."

refers to the main inhabited island and not just the region. Since Tyre is on the coast, the unknown Hosah must be further along. Although the idea of the border turning (שׁוּב) at this point might seem strange, it is most likely an idiomatic way of noting that the line has returned from the island of Tyre to the mainland and, thus, south of Tyre.

The final part of the border list seems to integrate a city list. The CSB "Mahalab" depends on the LXX, and it might be better to retain the MT and read "from Hebel," which could then be identified with Ahlab (by transposition) in Judges 1:31. Achzib is a coastal town south of Tyre (to be distinguished from the town in Judah in 15:44). Along with the two preceding towns, Ummah, Aphek, and Rehob might be the remnants of a city list (given that Rehob is mentioned in 19:28), but as the text now stands they are reference points for the boundary. Of these, Ummah is unknown (unless it is a corruption of Acco).[348] Aphek is a little north of Carmel, so it would make a natural reference point for tracing the boundary south from Tyre. This town is to be distinguished from the site mentioned in 1 Samuel 4:1 and 29:1, and it is one of the points from which Asher was unable to expel the existing population (Judg 1:31). As noted above, the uncertainty about Asher's boundary and the towns makes it impossible to know what "twenty-two cities, with their settlements" means (v. 30).

19:32–39. The sixth lot "came out" (יָצָא) for Naphtali (v. 32). As noted with the other tribes above, the report begins and ends with reference to the clans as a means of stressing the inclusive nature of the allotment. As with Asher, many of the details for Naphtali's allotment are difficult to trace. But in general the allotment ran along the hills inland from Asher's coast except for the southern area, which tapered to the west where it met the border with Zebulun. Naphtali's southern border ran along part of the northern border of Zebulun, while the eastern border extended along the upper Jordan Valley past Chinnereth (the Sea of Galilee) to Lake Huleh and then further north toward the region of Hermon (see the tribal allotment map at 15:1–12). The description of the boundary here is quite short, being traced in only general terms in verses 33–34. The lack of specificity means that although we have end points for it to the east, south, and west, no northern border is noted.

Complicating the process of tracing the border is the fact that the towns mentioned in verse 33 (Heleph, Adami-nekeb, Jabneel, and Lakkum)

---

348. So, Rösel, *Joshua*, 314, on the basis of the LXX.

are unknown (there is another Jabneel mentioned for Judah in 15:11, but it is to be distinguished from this site), and though the oak in Zaanannim is apparently intended to provide a further point of orientation, it too is unknown. However, that the border can be traced to the Jordan near Lakkum indicates that the town was in this area and should be located at the southern end of Chinnereth, thus forming an eastern boundary. From there, the border can be traced to the west. Beyond the points where Naphtali reaches the other tribes (Zebulun to the south; Asher on the west), however, little can be said with certainty since it is unclear whether Aznoth-tabor in verse 34 is describing a geographical feature near Mount Tabor (in the far south of Naphtali) or a place name. Hukkok may be southwest of Chinnereth, but it is perhaps to be equated with Helkath, a town assigned to Levi (21:31). Reference to the boundary reaching Judah at the Jordan as the eastern point is odd since Judah as a whole is too far south. It could be omitted (with the LXX), but this looks like an obvious correction. The best solution is probably to regard "Judah" here as a technical term for the point where Chinnereth flows into the main part of the Jordan on the basis that it runs down to Judah.[349]

From verse 35 we switch to a town list, though this time it covers fortified towns. Previously, fortification was mentioned in 10:20 (when some survivors fled in the southern campaign) and for Tyre (19:29), but this has not been a feature of the town lists. The significance of this is not clear, but given Tyre's earlier description it appears to be something that interested those who compiled the information about the far north. Ziddim could be a site a few miles northwest of Tiberias, modern Chattin. Zer is not known, but Hammath (which means "hot springs") can be identified with modern Hamman Tabariyeh, two miles south of Tiberias on the shore of the Sea of Galilee. If the list is regional at this point, then Zer presumably lay somewhere between the first two towns on the shore of Chinnereth. Rakkath may be in the same general area, especially since Chinnereth shared its name with the Sea of Galilee at the time and so was presumably on the shore. When the region of Naphtali was captured by Aram under Ben-hadad (1 Kgs 15:20), Chinnereth was particularly noted, though perhaps there the town also stood for the Sea of Galilee, and hence

---

[349] Fritz, *Josua*, 196, is open to this possibility but still omits the reference from his translation.

the region. The previous references to Chinnereth in Joshua (11:2; 12:3; 13:27) are all to the Sea of Galilee.

Adamah and Ramah in verse 36 are otherwise unknown (this Ramah is different from the one in 19:29), but Hazor was an extremely important town that was pivotal in the northern campaign (see comments on 11:1). In verse 37, Kedesh (to be distinguished from the town in Judah, 15:23) is presumably in the region of Mount Tabor. It will later become both a city of refuge (20:7) and a Levitical city (21:32). It could be the town included in the king list (12:22), but this is not clear. Later, it would be the home town of Barak and the launching point of his campaign with Deborah against Sisera (Judg 4:6–10). Edrei (not the site mentioned in Josh 12:4, 12, 31) and En-hazor are not mentioned elsewhere. None of the towns in verse 38 are known. Beth-shemesh is to be distinguished from the sites mentioned earlier (15:10; 19:22), and Iron could be modern Yaroun. As the text stands, only sixteen towns are listed, not nineteen as stated in verse 38, suggesting textual damage. As usual, the closing note stresses that the tribal inheritance was in accord with their clans.

19:40–48. The seventh lot "came out" (יָצָא) for Dan, an allotment that is again for the clans within the tribe. Dan does not receive a boundary list; however, the names of the cities make clear that it was on the coast, bounded by Judah to the south, Benjamin to the east, and Ephraim (with a small part of Manasseh) to the north (see tribal allotment map at 15:1–12). In essence, it fills the gap that the previous boundaries have implied. The fact that they had already been driven from this area by the time this chapter was compiled may also have meant that the provision of a boundary list was redundant. Rather, space is given to the longest indigenous population comment made for any tribe precisely because of the importance of their failure to settle in their territory. Although their site would later be important, it was always outside the boundaries that had been promised.

Dan's city list in verses 41–46 includes a number of towns known from the Samson narrative (Judg 13–16), reflecting the fact that these stories occurred before the tribe lost its allotment. As is common with the other lists, not all the sites mentioned can be identified. Indeed, the closest associations with the Samson narrative occur in the earlier part of the list, perhaps an intentional reflection on this narrative. Zorah (not the town in Judah in Josh 15:33) was Samson's hometown (Judg 13:2). It is perhaps Sar'ah (which retains the name with a slightly different transliteration), about thirteen miles west of Jerusalem. Eshtaol is probably nearby, as it is always mentioned in conjunction with Zorah. It was at the Camp of Dan, in between these sites, that the Spirit of God began to prod Samson (Judg 13:25), and he was also buried between these towns (Judg 16:31). This area was also the base from which the Danite spies were sent out in the Micah narrative (Judg 18:2). Ir-shemesh is not elsewhere mentioned but is most likely an alternative name for Beth-shemesh, about sixteen miles west of Jerusalem. This town was on the border with Judah (Josh 15:10) and would later be allotted to the Levites in 21:16, though in that passage it is said to have come from Judah. Thus, by the time the chapter was written, the town was effectively part of Judah.

Shaalabbin is possibly the same as Shaalbim (Judg 1:35), modern Selbit (about fifteen miles northwest of Jerusalem). Aijalon (the same consonants as Elon in v. 43 but with different vocalization) would later be allotted to the Levites (Josh 21:42); it was important in Joshua's southern campaign (10:12). Ithlah and Elon are otherwise unknown, but both Timnah and Ekron important in the Samson narrative. Timnah is about twenty miles west of Jerusalem, where the Shephelah meets the coastal plain. Ekron is about six miles further west on the plain. On the border of Judah (15:10), Timnah was the home of Samson's first wife (Judg 14:1) and a site of conflict with the Philistines who held it then. Ekron was one of the principal Philistine towns and, as a border town with Judah (Josh 15:11), was included in their allotment (see comments on 15:45–47).

Eltekeh would later be a Levitical town (21:23), and (though not mentioned elsewhere in the Bible) is included in Sennacherib's record of his campaign in 701 BC (on the Taylor Prism, held in the British Museum). Gibbethon, where Omri's men later proclaimed him king over the northern kingdom (1 Kgs 16:15–16) would also become a Levitical city (Josh 21:23), though its exact location is unknown. Baalath is probably on the coastal plain and would be rebuilt by Solomon (1 Kgs 9:18), but by then it was considered to belong to Judah. Jehud is unknown. Bene-berak is on the coastal plain slightly south of the modern town that bears this name. Gath-rimmon would later be a Levitical city. In Josh 21:24 it is said to have been given from Dan, whereas 21:25 says it was given from Manasseh. Most likely it lay around the Yarkon River, on the border between these tribes. Since both town and grazing land were allotted to the Levites, it could be said to come from both. Me-jarkon ("waters of

Yarkon") is unknown but was presumably in the same area. Rakkon is said to be facing Joppa and, if in the same region as the two preceding towns, would be on the coast to the north of Joppa. No count is provided for Dan's city list.

After the city list, the narrator provides a comment in verse 47 that historically looks back on the experience of the Danites and anticipates the Samson and Micah narratives (Judg 13–18).[350] This appears to be an insertion into the report for Dan since the closing note in verse 48 looks back to the city list, not the report of the northern migration. Clearly the note was important, since early readers would have known of Dan as a northern tribe. The Samson narrative mentions frequent conflicts with the Philistines, including the note that they ruled this area (Judg 14:4), anticipating Dan's move north when they captured Laish, made it their principal town, and named it "Dan" (Judg 18). The report here is much briefer. The originally allotted territory "slipped" (repeating the key verb יצא from v. 40) from Dan's control. After that they went up to Leshem (an alternative form for Laish, perhaps indicating that Joshua is using a different source from Judges), captured it, and renamed it. The site, Tel Dan, at the headwaters of the Jordan, has been rich for archaeological investigation. Settlement there considerably predates Israel, but there is good reason to understand the clear change in culture in the Late Bronze Age as indicative of the point when Israelites came to dominate.[351] A ninth-century inscription found there seems to be the earliest extra-biblical reference to King David.[352]

The closing note refers back to the city list of verses 41–46. In so doing, the final form of the text now offers a subtle critique of the northern move and capture of Leshem, a critique that will be more explicit in Judges 18:27. The relationship between Israel and the existing inhabitants of the land is ambiguous in comments elsewhere, but here it is clear that, although the allotment was appropriate for Dan, it was not where they lived.

---

[350] The LXX here is considerably longer, drawing on Judg 1:34–35 and Judges 17–18 along with elements not otherwise attested, but this seems clearly secondary.

[351] See Hawkins, *How Israel became a People*, 117–19.

[352] The interpretation has been a matter of considerable dispute, but this seems the most probable reading. See further Hallvard Hagelia, *The Tel Dan Inscription: A Critical Investigation of Recent Research on Its Paleography and Philology* (Uppsala: Uppsala Universitet, 2009).

19:49-50. The tribal allocations are followed by a special allocation to Joshua in verses 49-50. As noted (see context discussion on
Josh 13:1-14:15), this special allocation balances that given to Caleb
(14:6-15), so that the two faithful spies from Numbers 13-14 received an
allotment, providing a boundary to the report of the west Jordan tribes.
There may be a hint of the north-south division that would split the
country following Solomon's death (1 Kgs 12:16-24), since the text states
that the Israelites gave a special allocation to Joshua, whereas in Caleb's
case the request was initiated by Judah. This division was already clear by
the time of David (2 Sam 5:1-5). Although it is probably not understood
here in terms of the later rivalry, it may be an early hint of the distinction since otherwise a strictly parallel allocation for Joshua would have
come from Ephraim.

The inheritance was given to Joshua by the Israelites, but (like Caleb) it
stemmed from God's command (v. 50)—even if we have no other record of
this command. The importance of this gift is emphasized by the mention
of Joshua's patronym, something that usually marks points of significant
movement in the book (e.g., Josh 1:1; 2:1; 24:29). Joshua had apparently
requested Timnath-serah, a town in the hill country of Ephraim, which
was said to be north of Mount Gaash (24:30), though this mountain cannot be identified. In the parallel account in Judg 2:9, the town is called
Timnath-heres. Since the latter part of this name refers to the sun, the
narrator of Joshua has possibly reversed the letters to avoid associating
idolatry with Joshua. Therefore, the form in Judges is more likely original.
The town itself needed to be first rebuilt by Joshua, though it is unclear if
the damage was due to Israel's campaign. In any case, Joshua's settlement
points once again to his faithfulness and provides a clear contrast with
the Danites' failure to retain their allotment.[353]

19:51. Reference to Joshua, Eleazar, and the family heads in 19:51
provides a link back to the beginning of the western allotment in 14:1,
showing that this verse closes the larger account of the territory division
west of the Jordan (14:1-19:51). In addition, mention of the distribution
"by lot at Shiloh" means this verse also closes off the account begun at 18:1
with the setting up of the tent of meeting, followed by the allotments for
the seven tribes in these two chapters (18:1-19:51). The combination of
these elements means the whole land had been allotted, and that it had

---

[353] Similarly Hess, *Joshua*, 277.

clearly been done in the presence of God. Their actions west of the Jordan in dividing (חלק) the land matched those of Moses in dividing (חלק) the land east of the Jordan (14:5).[354] The completion of the land allocation was, therefore, not simply the end of a geographic process but rather one in which God had been intimately involved at every stage and for which the processes at every stage had been equivalent.

Bridge

Confronted by their lack of knowledge of the sites mentioned, most modern readers find these chapters difficult to read. So preachers face a challenge. It doesn't help that, especially in the far north, the boundaries and towns are fairly obscure. On the other hand, such an admission might indicate that, even when Joshua was being compiled, readers found these chapters difficult. Further evidence for this can be seen in the large number of points noted above in which we have reason to believe there has been textual corruption, suggesting that even learned scribes did not find these chapters easy. As interpreters of Scripture, we must acknowledge points where our knowledge is fragmentary, not least because this reminds us to focus on elements that are clear.

This approach is beneficial because it shows us that key themes running through the book come to a climax here. In addition, the passage looks back to key moments in the Pentateuch and looks forward to part of Israel's story to come. Israel needed to be God's people living in God's land, and this chapter makes clear that they were. This reality would enable them to live out what redemption meant. There is evidence for this in the fact that Simeon's allotment came out of Judah's. Such an arrangement ensured equity across the tribes so that none was made richer or more powerful than the others. Political forces and choices made by the people would subsequently impact this in a range of ways, but this would be contrary to how God established them. Such equity was what Paul expected in the celebration of the Lord's Supper (1 Cor 11:20–21). Local expressions of the church today will vary in the equity among members, but as we gather in worship we are reminded of the need for basic equity among us and for a concern to ensure sufficiency for all.

---

[354] Harstad, *Joshua*, 633, notes that in 14:5 the verb is *qal*, whereas here it is *piel*. The distinction is that the *piel* is resultative, highlighting the completed nature of the distribution.

Seeing these chapters in the context of worship is particularly important. Deuteronomy 12 indicates that Israel was to have a central sanctuary
around which they would gather, rather than numerous local sanctuaries
following the Canaanite model. By emphasizing the importance of Shiloh
as the central sanctuary, this section makes clear that God had provided
both the means for this sanctuary and a context for faithful worship going
forward. The equitable allotment of land at the sanctuary means all knew
that God had provided for their needs. This "all" went beyond the level of
the tribe and reached down to the clan, functionally the smallest group
in which households gathered. God's equity is not only for the powerful
but is something that all can experience. Moreover, the division west of
the Jordan is shown to be equivalent to that carried out through Moses
east of the Jordan. Shiloh would not endure as the central sanctuary, but
at this point in Israel's history it was the place where authentic worship
happened.

Christian worship naturally takes a rather different form and finds its
focus in Jesus as our temple (John 2:21–22), the one through whom we draw
near with confidence to God (Heb 10:19–23). But Christian worship also
understands something of the structure of what is presented here. This
is evident in Revelation 21:9–14 (which draws on the presentation here
through the grid of Ezekiel 48, which itself looks back to these chapters),
pointing to what our worship shall be. So, there are parallels that need to
be explored, not least the fact that the setting up of the tent of meeting
at Shiloh was a clear declaration of God's reign—of his presence among
his people. We do not express this today through buildings or a central
sanctuary, but rather through the abiding truth that Jesus continues to
be with us, most especially as we join him in his mission (Matt 28:16–20).
Although this is often treated in activist terms, the reality is that mission
finds its home within worship, and our worship is a declaration of Jesus'
presence and reign. Many (like Dan) do not hold onto this, and it slips
from their grasp. But the combination of faithful worship and mission
continues to be central to what it means to be God's people in Jesus Christ.

E. Levitical Distribution and Conclusion (20:1–21:45)

20 [1] Then the LORD spoke to Joshua, [2] "Tell the Israelites: Select
your cities of refuge, as I instructed you through Moses, [3] so that a person who kills someone unintentionally or accidentally may flee there.
These will be your refuge from the avenger of blood. [4] When someone

flees to one of these cities, stands at the entrance of the city gate, and states his case before the elders of that city, they are to bring him into the city and give him a place to live among them. [5] And if the avenger of blood pursues him, they must not hand the one who committed manslaughter over to him, for he killed his neighbor accidentally and did not hate him beforehand. [6] He is to stay in that city until he stands trial before the assembly and until the death of the high priest serving at that time. Then the one who committed manslaughter may return home to his own city from which he fled."

[7] So they designated Kedesh in the hill country of Naphtali in Galilee, Shechem in the hill country of Ephraim, and Kiriath-arba (that is, Hebron) in the hill country of Judah. [8] Across the Jordan east of Jericho, they selected Bezer on the wilderness plateau from Reuben's tribe, Ramoth in Gilead from Gad's tribe, and Golan in Bashan from Manasseh's tribe.

[9] These are the cities appointed for all the Israelites and the aliens residing among them, so that anyone who kills a person unintentionally may flee there and not die at the hand of the avenger of blood until he stands before the assembly.

21 [1] The Levite family heads approached the priest Eleazar, Joshua son of Nun, and the family heads of the Israelite tribes. [2] At Shiloh, in the land of Canaan, they told them, "The Lord commanded through Moses that we be given cities to live in, with their pasturelands for our livestock." [3] So the Israelites, by the Lord's command, gave the Levites these cities with their pasturelands from their inheritance.

[4] The lot came out for the Kohathite clans: The Levites who were the descendants of the priest Aaron received thirteen cities by lot from the tribes of Judah, Simeon, and Benjamin. [5] The remaining descendants of Kohath received ten cities by lot from the clans of the tribes of Ephraim, Dan, and half the tribe of Manasseh.

[6] Gershon's descendants received thirteen cities by lot from the clans of the tribes of Issachar, Asher, Naphtali, and half the tribe of Manasseh in Bashan.

[7] Merari's descendants received twelve cities for their clans from the tribes of Reuben, Gad, and Zebulun.

[8] The Israelites gave these cities with their pasturelands around them to the Levites by lot, as the Lord had commanded through Moses.

[9] The Israelites gave these cities by name from the tribes of the descendants of Judah and Simeon [10] to the descendants of Aaron from the Kohathite clans of the Levites, because they received the first lot. [11] They gave them Kiriath-arba (that is, Hebron; Arba was the father of Anak) with its surrounding pasturelands in the hill country of Judah. [12] But they gave the fields and settlements of the city to Caleb son of Jephunneh as his possession.

¹³ They gave to the descendants of the priest Aaron:

Hebron, the city of refuge for the one who commits manslaughter, with its pasturelands, Libnah with its pasturelands, ¹⁴ Jattir with its pasturelands, Eshtemoa with its pasturelands, ¹⁵ Holon with its pasturelands, Debir with its pasturelands, ¹⁶ Ain with its pasturelands, Juttah with its pasturelands, and Beth-shemesh with its pasturelands—nine cities from these two tribes.

¹⁷ From the tribe of Benjamin they gave:

Gibeon with its pasturelands, Geba with its pasturelands, ¹⁸ Anathoth with its pasturelands, and Almon with its pasturelands—four cities. ¹⁹ All thirteen cities with their pasturelands were for the priests, the descendants of Aaron.

²⁰ The allotted cities to the remaining clans of Kohath's descendants, who were Levites, came from the tribe of Ephraim. ²¹ The Israelites gave them:

Shechem, the city of refuge for the one who commits manslaughter, with its pasturelands in the hill country of Ephraim, Gezer with its pasturelands, ²² Kibzaim with its pasturelands, and Beth-horon with its pasturelands—four cities.

²³ From the tribe of Dan they gave:

Elteke with its pasturelands, Gibbethon with its pasturelands, ²⁴ Aijalon with its pasturelands, and Gath-rimmon with its pasturelands—four cities.

²⁵ From half the tribe of Manasseh they gave:

Taanach with its pasturelands and Gath-rimmon with its pasturelands—two cities.

²⁶ All ten cities with their pasturelands were for the clans of Kohath's other descendants.

²⁷ From half the tribe of Manasseh, they gave to the descendants of Gershon, who were one of the Levite clans:

Golan, the city of refuge for the one who commits manslaughter, with its pasturelands in Bashan, and Beeshterah with its pasturelands—two cities.

²⁸ From the tribe of Issachar they gave:

Kishion with its pasturelands, Daberath with its pasturelands, ²⁹ Jarmuth with its pasturelands, and En-gannim with its pasturelands—four cities.

³⁰ From the tribe of Asher they gave:

Mishal with its pasturelands, Abdon with its pasturelands, ³¹ Helkath with its pasturelands, and Rehob with its pasturelands—four cities.

³² From the tribe of Naphtali they gave:

Kedesh in Galilee, the city of refuge for the one who commits manslaughter, with its pasturelands, Hammoth-dor with its pasturelands, and Kartan with its pasturelands—three cities.

[33] All thirteen cities with their pasturelands were for the Gershonites by their clans.

[34] From the tribe of Zebulun, they gave to the clans of the descendants of Merari, who were the remaining Levites:

Jokneam with its pasturelands, Kartah with its pasturelands, [35] Dimnah with its pasturelands, and Nahalal with its pasturelands—four cities.

[36] From the tribe of Reuben they gave:

Bezer with its pasturelands, Jahzah with its pasturelands, [37] Kedemoth with its pasturelands, and Mephaath with its pasturelands—four cities.

[38] From the tribe of Gad they gave:

Ramoth in Gilead, the city of refuge for the one who commits manslaughter, with its pasturelands, Mahanaim with its pasturelands, [39] Heshbon with its pasturelands, and Jazer with its pasturelands—four cities in all. [40] All twelve cities were allotted to the clans of Merari's descendants, the remaining Levite clans.

[41] Within the Israelite possession there were forty-eight cities in all with their pasturelands for the Levites. [42] Each of these cities had its own surrounding pasturelands; this was true for all the cities.

[43] So the LORD gave Israel all the land he had sworn to give their ancestors, and they took possession of it and settled there. [44] The LORD gave them rest on every side according to all he had sworn to their ancestors. None of their enemies were able to stand against them, for the LORD handed over all their enemies to them. [45] None of the good promises the LORD had made to the house of Israel failed. Everything was fulfilled.

Context

Although all the land had been allotted to Israel's tribes, one important allotment remained—the provision of cities for the Levites. Within the structure of the book, there is good reason for this. Joshua 13 recounts the allotments that Moses had made east of the Jordan, while Joshua 14–19 describes the allotments west of the Jordan. All of the land had been distributed, even if all had not been settled (a problem explored in Judges 1). But whereas each of the other tribes was in a particular location, the tribe of Levi was to be scattered across Israel. Since their allotment was the priesthood (Josh 18:7), they were not to receive a division of the land but instead cities drawn from the whole land. This scattering of the Levites would enable them to carry out their work in all Israel, representing the priesthood throughout the nation, while being dependent on the nation through the tithe system (e.g., Deut 14:28–29).

Not all Levites were priests (though all priests were Levites), even if they supported the work of the sanctuary (Num 18:1–4). The role of the Levites who were scattered through the country is not clearly defined, perhaps because it was fairly fluid.[355] The fact that they were to receive the grazing land associated with their towns (Num 35:1–5), as well as support from the tithe system, indicates that they were expected to have some means of support in their towns. However, a key element of the Levites' role was the administration of the six cities of refuge where those who had accidentally slain someone could flee to escape the pattern of blood vengeance that was otherwise normative within the culture (Num 35:6–8).[356] Thus, they ensured a proper provision of justice. We should perhaps understand this as their principal focus even though their other forty-two cities were not places of refuge. The fact that the allocation of these towns occurred under God's supervision means that this element of their work was both divinely initiated and enabled.

These chapters are not concerned with explaining the role of the Levites but rather with demonstrating that the directives about providing them with towns and pasture, along with establishing the cities of refuge (outlined in Numbers 35), had been clearly fulfilled. Completion of this task meant that all Israel had truly received their land, providing the opportunity to reflect on God's faithfulness to his promises (Josh 21:43–45). This affirmation of divine faithfulness does not mean that all the tribes were settled in the land. The statement about Dan losing their allotment (19:47) and comments about the continued presence of the existing inhabitants make clear that Israel did not always live in a way that enabled them to enjoy God's fulfilled promises. Nevertheless, the allotment of the land

---

[355] See the list of tasks they undertook in Hubbard, *Joshua*, 464, including conscription of soldiers and workers, collection of taxes and tithes, serving as judges or in a local priestly role, teaching, and other roles that helped hold the nation together.

[356] Butler, *Joshua 13–24*, 199, has noted that this must be a particularly ancient practice since it assumes that homicide was dealt with locally rather than through a centralized justice system.

showed that God had been faithful. Not only is this celebrated here, but readers are also challenged to live in light of that faithfulness.[357]

Numbers 35 provides the principal background to both these chapters, but attentive readers will note an intriguing reversal here. In Numbers, the command to assign cities (and their associated pastureland) to the Levites is given first (Num 35:1–8), and only then are commands given about the cities of refuge (Num 35:9–34). But in Joshua, the cities of refuge are designated first and only then are cities given to the Levites. Moreover, in Numbers, the allocation of Levitical cities is treated relatively briefly, while the provision of the cities of refuge is treated at some length. In Joshua, though, the relative lengths are also reversed.

This variation in relative length is easily explained because the passage in Numbers details the law. Beyond some brief comments on process (Josh 20:4–6), there is no need for extended comment in Joshua. Conversely, although Num 35:1–8 indicates that forty-eight towns were to be allotted to Levi along with five hundred yards of grazing land around them, the actual towns could not at that point be listed. Therefore, the list of them in Joshua is fairly lengthy.

But the reversal of order is perhaps a more important element. In part, this is because Moses had allotted three of the required six cities of refuge east of the Jordan (Deut 4:41–43), so this was a process that had already begun. Joshua could then allot the remaining three, consistent with the requirements of Numbers 35:9–34 and Deuteronomy 19:1–13. The reversal here is also used so that the allotment to the Levites can serve as the climax of the land allocation. Their request for cities closely parallels that of Caleb and demonstrates that, although the worship of God was centered in Shiloh, the Levitical support for this was spread across the whole land.

Exegesis

20:1–2a. Save for the fact that God spoke to Joshua rather than Moses, this verse follows a standard pattern found in much of the legislation in the Pentateuch (e.g., Lev 4:1; 12:1; 17:1; 18:1; 19:1; Num 35:1, 9). According to the pattern, the first verse reports that God spoke to the lawgiver, and the second verse commences with an imperative of דבר ("speak"), directing him to address a designated group. The use of the formula stresses the

---

[357] Similarly Hubbard, *Joshua*, 451.

divine origin of the law while recognizing the importance of the mediator through whom God revealed it. This is the only time the formula is used for Joshua, and so it becomes an important step toward him being recognized along with Moses as a servant of Yahweh (Josh 24:29). He became the one who mediated the law to the Israelites, even though it was an expression of a law God had previously revealed through Moses (Num 35:9–34).

20:2b–6. Joshua's role was not to reveal a new law but to provide the details of how an existing law would be worked out. God had commanded through Moses that Israel was to set aside six cities of refuge, and Moses had overseen the setting aside of three cities east of the Jordan (Deut 4:41–43). This meant three were needed west of the Jordan (see above discussion of context).

These cities were designated as places of sanctuary for someone who had unintentionally taken a human life, so that they might escape the avenger of blood.[358] Such a sanctuary arrangement was (as far as we know) unique to Israel. The prohibition on killing in the sixth commandment lies in the background. Although the CSB translates the verb רצח as "murder" in Exodus 20:13 and Deuteronomy 5:17, it quite rightly uses the wider "kill" in verse 2 (the more common translation of הרג) before switching to "commit manslaughter" in verses 4–6. A difficulty we face is that the verb has a sense slightly narrower than our "murder," even though this is usually the most appropriate rendering.[359] There are contexts in which the taking of a human life is permissible even if undesirable (as in warfare or capital punishment), but רצח is never permissible and so generates the possibility of blood vengeance.[360]

An unauthorized taking of life was the trigger for blood vengeance, either through the intervention of the formal legal system or through the avenger of blood. The latter was a kinsman whose role was to execute the one who had killed in an unauthorized manner. Importantly, the law

---

[358] Similarly Fritz, *Josua*, 202, who sees this as an important legal status for the killer. However, his observation about its application in the monarchic period, using the example of Joab going to the altar (1 Kgs 2:28–35), misses the point. Joab was not claiming sanctuary for an accidental death; therefore, he stands outside of what is described here. Pitkänen, *Joshua*, 335, thus regards this account as dealing with political asylum.

[359] For a helpful overview of the linguistic evidence, see Mark F. Rooker, *The Ten Commandments: Ethics for the Twenty-First Century* (Nashville: B&H Academic, 2010), 123–29.

[360] Cf. W. R. Domeris, "רצח," *NIDOTTE*, 3:1189.

concerning the avenger of blood was intended to limit violence. Although Lamech claimed the right of unlimited violence in response to injury (Gen 4:23-24), the Old Testament as a whole aims to prevent violence spreading.[361] At the same time, it recognizes the massive significance of taking a human life, allowing for the avenger of blood (Gen 9:5-6), a role explained in reference to the cities of refuge.

Although warfare and capital punishment represented permissible forms of killing, the law also acknowledges the importance of intent. Instances of unauthorized killing in which there was no intent to harm should not receive the death penalty. Numbers 35:9-29 outlines a range of scenarios to distinguish between murder and unintended killing. These were not intended to cover all possibilities but rather to offer types of situations that could be used to determine whether a particular killing was unintentional.

The cities of refuge were places where those who had killed without intent could flee and be protected from the avenger of blood—with the stipulation that the killer had to stay in the city of refuge until the death of the current high priest. In effect, this would be a form of open detention since the killer could not return home even if the claim of manslaughter was accepted. The high priest's death was a symbolic end to this punishment,[362] though there is no direct evidence that the high priest's death was a form of atonement for the killer[363] or that the priest's death was a substitute for the killer since the period of detention was still served.

According to Deuteronomy 19:3, the Israelites were to measure the distances between the cities to ensure they were equally accessible, and the listing of the cities in Joshua 20:7 places them at roughly equal distances. Anyone who had unintentionally killed another would, therefore, be able to flee to one of these towns before being overtaken by the avenger. The use of the verb נתן in verse 2 (csb "select"; often translated "give") is probably intended to suggest that these cities were a gift that provided a mechanism for reducing violence.[364]

Although almost every element in this section is taken from the parallel passages in Numbers 35:9-34 and Deuteronomy 19:1-13, verse 4 adds

---

[361] Jerome F. D. Creach, *Joshua* (Louisville: Westminster John Knox, 2003), 103.

[362] Hess, *Joshua*, 279.

[363] Against Davis, *No Falling Words*, 151-52.

[364] Howard, *Joshua*, 381.

an additional element.[365] Numbers 35:12 presumes that the killer would stand trial before the assembly, a theme taken up here in verse 6. But this does not address the question of how the town would know someone should be given admission to claim refuge. That is clarified in verse 4. Those who fled to the city were initially only given access to the gate area (which, in a walled town, could still be secured from the avenger) and required to present their case to the town elders, who could then grant admission. The basis for this granting of refuge is outlined in verse 5, which summarizes the scenarios from Numbers 35. Even though this was not the final trial, as long as the killer was given refuge in the city the avenger could not gain access to him.

As verse 6 makes clear, the meeting with the elders in verse 4 was a kind of pre-trial, with the full trial happening before the assembly. The makeup of the assembly is not clear. Presumably, it consisted of a representative body that could hear witnesses not available in the hearing with the town elders and then confirm the validity of the claim of refuge. Although unmentioned, probably because the focus is on granting refuge, the trial before the assembly could presumably determine that refuge had been falsely claimed. But since the concern here is with a legitimate claim, verse 6 notes the period of detention and stipulates that the killer could return home without further penalty once the period had ended.

20:7-9. As the relevant cities are identified, there is a shift in the verb from נתן (v. 2) to קדשׁ (v. 7).[366] Although this verb can mean "designate" (csb), it is also commonly used to refer to that which is sanctified or made holy and thus can be translated "consecrate" (see 3:5; 7:13).[367] The point is that these are cities with a holy function, the provision of a mechanism for reducing violence in Israel. Use of this verb also allows for a play on

---

[365] Ludwig Schmidt, "Leviten und Asylstatde in Num. xxxv un Jos. xx; xxi. 1–42," VT 52 (2002): 105–6, uses this as the basis for identifying redactional layers within the text, but such expansions are perfectly understandable when explaining to a later generation how the system would work, making the criteria for his analysis unnecessary. The significant variances between the mt and the og for vv. 4–6 are thus better understood as a revision by the og that attempts to resolve repetitions in the mt that had failed to understand v. 4 as describing a preliminary hearing.

[366] Neither matches the verb in Num 35:11 (קרה), perhaps because it is relatively uncommon. Deuteronomy 19:2 uses בדל. Although partially synonymous, each verb highlights a different aspect of these cities.

[367] The *hithpael* is used in these passages, whereas here it is *hiphil*, but the basic point remains.

words, since the name of the first town, Kadesh in Naphtali (19:37), is derived from this root. This provided a city of refuge in the far north, west of the Jordan.

The remaining cities west of the Jordan were Shechem, from the hill country of Ephraim, and Hebron in Judah. Shechem was not noted in the allotment for Ephraim, though it is mentioned in the border report for Manasseh (17:7), from which it is clear that it fell to Ephraim. Although not named there, the covenant renewal in 8:3–35 happened near Shechem, and it would also be the site for Joshua's final speech (24:1). Located in the central highlands, it is more or less in the middle of Israel when moving from north to south. The final city, Hebron, is in the far south of Judah (10:3), thus ensuring that all had equal access to one of these cities west of the Jordan. Hebron is also called Kiriath-arba, a name otherwise associated with Caleb (14:15; 15:13).[368]

Having traced the western cities of refuge from north to south, the text then traces the eastern ones from south to north, following their listing in Deuteronomy 4:41–43. Bezer was in Reuben, though not mentioned previously in Joshua, and is probably southeast of Heshbon (see tribal allotment map at 15:1–12). Further north, Ramoth was in Gilead in the far north of Gad. Like Bezer, it is not mentioned before in Joshua, but it would later be an important site in the rise of Saul (1 Sam 11:1–11) and Jehu (2 Kgs 8:25–9:13). Golan in East Manasseh has also not been mentioned before in Joshua and is located in the center of their allotment. Thus, anyone east of the Jordan had good access to a city of refuge.

Verse 9 summarizes and includes the additional observation that these cities were available to both Israelites and aliens—stressing that this process also covered those who might not have others to protect them. Concern for the foreigner in these cities is consistent with the ceremony in Joshua 8:30–35, which included them in the covenant renewal near Shechem, and to Caleb's claiming of Hebron, especially important if he too was a foreigner (see on 14:6). Justice was to be provided to all who claimed a place within Israel, not just to those who were there by birthright.[369]

---

[368] On the issue of how Hebron could belong to both Caleb and the Levites, see on Josh 21:11–12.

[369] Similarly Robert R. Laha Jr., "Joshua 20," *Interpretation* 66 (2012): 195.

21:1–3. Although chapter 21 introduces a new topic (the allocation of the cities for the Levites), the fact that all the cities of refuge will also be given to the Levites binds it to chapter 20. The allocation of Levitical cities is also closely paralleled to the allotment of Hebron to Caleb, a city that will also serve the Levites (21:11). The approach of the Levites to Joshua and Eleazar follows the pattern of the earlier approach of Judah along with Caleb (14:6). Just as Caleb's request was based on a promise from God, so also the Levites' claim was in fulfillment of the divine promise.[370] Approaching Joshua, Eleazar, and the family heads was consistent with their responsibility to allocate the tribal inheritances (14:1). These repetitions are an important mechanism for emphasizing that the Levites' claim was just and that it was made within the framework God had established.

Moreover, just as the seven western tribes made their request at Shiloh—in God's presence at the sanctuary (18:9–10)—so also the Levites made their request at Shiloh. Given that the Levitical allotment could only be made after the other tribal allotments, it is logical that the allotment would be made at Shiloh. But by specifically mentioning it here, the narrative makes explicit the connection with the sanctuary and the process for the other tribes.

Remarkably, although Shiloh belonged to Ephraim, it is here described as being in the land of Canaan. This note is important since it reminds readers that, although the bulk of the land had been allotted to the tribes at Shiloh, it had not yet been taken at that point. Because of this, the Levitical allotment would also depend on the faithfulness of the other tribes in taking the remaining land. The land was an inheritance to be taken, not something already received, so in approaching the leadership and requesting their allotment the Levites were expressing their faith that it would be received.

The Levites' request is rooted in God's command to Moses in Num 35:1–8 that there were to be forty-eight cities given to the Levites, along with five hundred yards of pastureland around each of these cities. The Levites would have other responsibilities, but the provision of pasture meant that they would have space on which to graze livestock. Although they received some of the tithe (e.g., Deut 14:29), there is clearly an

---

[370] In English, there might also seem to be a parallel with the daughters of Zelophehad, but the verb translated "came before" in 17:4 (קרב) is different from the one rendered "approached" here (נגשׁ) and for Caleb (14:6). The link is there conceptually, but the linguistic link to Caleb makes this connection stronger.

expectation that they would also support themselves to some extent. Verse 3 provides a summary of the full allocation by noting that the Israelites did indeed honor God's command and provide for the Levites from their inheritance (נחלה). This term stresses that the cities were given from land that had not yet been taken but was yielded up in advance.

21:4-8. Whereas verse 3 summarized the whole, these verses provide a slightly more detailed summary before the full listing of the towns in verses 9-42. The reason for this is twofold. First, it establishes that (like the other tribes who received their allotment at Shiloh), the allotment for Levi was determined by lot. Casting the lot at the sanctuary was a mechanism for ensuring that the whole process was overseen by God and, therefore, that his justice would be worked out for the Levites (on casting lots, see on 14:2). Second, the tribe of Levi would also receive its allotment in terms of its clans, following the pattern for all the other tribes. But in their case, the scattering of the tribe throughout the nation meant it was more important that the specific location of each clan be known. The full list, therefore, indicates which cities were allotted to each clan, but the listing is dependent on the information provided in these verses.

The three Levitical clans were thus allotted their cities, with the order of the allotment following that of Numbers 4 (which outlines their roles relative to the sanctuary) rather than their birth order (which, according to Num 3:17, was Gershon, Kohath, and Merari). Because of their close association with the sanctuary, the Kohathites' allocation was broken into two groups. Thirteen cities from Judah, Simeon, and Benjamin were given to those who were descendants of Aaron (and thus priests); ten cities from Ephraim, Dan, and West Manasseh were given to the other Kohathites (vv. 4-5). The priests were obviously closest to the sanctuary, but the other clan members were associated with the process of moving the various elements of the tabernacle, especially the altar (Num 4:1-20). The priestly allotment meant that they were well placed when the temple was later established in Jerusalem. But at this point they were some distance from Shiloh, though the non-priestly Levites were close.

The Gershonites had primary responsibility for the coverings and curtains of the tabernacle (Num 4:21-29). They were allotted thirteen cities from the far north in Issachar, Asher, and Naphtali west of the Jordan and in the Bashan region of East Manasseh. Merari, who had primary responsibility for the tabernacle's framework (Num 4:29-33), received twelve cities from Reuben and Gad east of the Jordan and from Zebulun to the west. As most of these cities are mentioned elsewhere in the book, comment will only be provided where towns not previously mentioned are included.

Just as verse 3 provides a summary of the opening approach to the leadership, so verse 8 summarizes the allotment process, stressing once more that it was overseen by God and in accordance with his commands through Moses. Such summaries are a key feature of this chapter, with verses 41-42 summarizing the allocation of the cities and preparing for the summary of the whole process of Israel's claiming the land in verses 43-45.

21:9-19. The cities are now listed in accordance with the outline in verses 4-8, with those from Judah, Simeon and Benjamin listed first. As the initial listing had only indicated the number of cities given (thirteen), the cities are now listed according to the tribe of origin (but with Judah and Simeon combined, consistent with 19:9) with the number from each that contributed to the total.

Consistent with the first lot falling to the priestly Kohathites (designated as descendants of Aaron), their cities are outlined first. Although their allotment came from three tribes, Simeon's was merged into that of Judah because they had received their portion within Judah (19:9), and so a combined listing for these two tribes is given first in verses 9-16 before Benjamin's is listed in verses 17-19. Before the main listing, the particular issue of Hebron is addressed. Joshua 14:13-15 stated that this city had been given to Caleb, but in 20:7 it was listed as a city of refuge and, therefore, was to be a Levitical city (consistent with Num 35:6-8). How could both these things be true? The answer to this conundrum is provided before the main listing by noting that the city and its immediate pasturelands were given to the Levites, but the settlements and their fields were given to Caleb. That is, the region around Hebron belonged to Caleb as his special allotment, but the city itself and its immediate pastures belonged to Levi.

Since information on each town is provided in the discussion of the tribal allotments for Judah (15:20-63), Benjamin (18:11-28), and Simeon (19:1-9), readers need to refer to the treatment there for information known about these towns. Of Benjamin's towns, Anathoth and Almon were not mentioned in Benjamin's city list (18:21-28). Anathoth, a few miles northeast of Jerusalem, would later gain prominence as the city to which Solomon would banish Abiathar (1 Kgs 2:26) and as the hometown of the prophet (and priest) Jeremiah (Jer 1:1). Almon (called "Alemeth" in 1 Chr 6:60) is presumably in the same region.

21:20–26. Since only one line among the Kohathites were priests, it is also necessary to record the allotment for the rest of this clan. Their ten cities, as noted in verse 5, came from Ephraim, Dan, and West Manasseh. Again, see the allotment accounts for Ephraim (17:5–10), Dan (19:40–48), and Manasseh (17:1–13) for details about these towns. The following comments only address towns not previously mentioned or ones that raise interpretive issues.

Kibzaim's location is uncertain, though given that Beth-horon (16:3) is also in the west of Ephraim, it may be in the same area. Gath-rimmon is problematic since a town with that name has just been allotted from Dan. For the counts to be correct (both here and the forty-eight cities in the whole list), these need to be separate cities. The parallel list in 1 Chronicles 6:70 (MT 6:55) has Aner and Bileam as the two cities here, the latter of which could be a mis-transcription through transposition of Ibleam (hence the CSB note). Two main possibilities emerge from this— either there were two different cities called Gath-rimmon[371] or there is a series of textual errors. Either of these is possible as there are numerous cases in Joshua of towns with the same name, and equally numerous cases of textual corruption in the city lists. Of the two, preference should be given to the possibility of textual error, though this has affected both Chronicles and Joshua. The accidental reuse of the name "Gath-rimmon" from earlier in the list in Joshua is easily explained since a scribe could accidentally have copied from the wrong line. In English, Aner and Taanach look quite dissimilar, but the initial "T" (Heb. ת) of Taanach could have been accidentally omitted since the previous word also ends with this character. Furthermore, the final "ch" (ך) could have occurred through the downstroke of the final letter (ר) being a little too short, producing the "r" (ר). Such transcriptional errors can easily occur. This approach has the benefit of explaining how each reading emerged, and it would indicate that the relevant towns are Taanach and Ibleam, both of which are mentioned in 17:11.[372]

---

[371] See Harstad, *Joshua*, 656–57.

[372] The larger issue of the text-critical relationship between Josh 21:1–42 and 1 Chr 6:54–81 (MT 6:39–66) cannot be resolved here. However, against A. Graeme Auld, "The 'Levitical Cities': Text and History," *ZAW* 91 (1979): 194–206, it still seems better to understand Joshua 21 as the source text and not the other way around, and also to accept that textual

21:27–33. Continuing to expand on the outline from verses 4–8, the allotment to Gershon is now described. Their allotment came from East Manasseh, Issachar, and Naphtali. The count of thirteen cities matches the list of towns here and also the initial summary for the Gershonites in verse 6. East Manasseh is outside of the region allotted in the book, but readers should consult the discussion of the allotment for Issachar (19:17–23) and Naphtali (19:32–39) for information on these towns.

Gershon received two towns from East Manasseh. The first of these, Golan, was also the northernmost city of refuge east of the Jordan (20:8) and so a Levitical town by definition. Beeshterah is not mentioned elsewhere, but 1 Chronicles 6:71 (MT 6:56) has "Ashteret," a reading also found in the Syriac here. Perhaps we should understand the town's correct name to be Beth-ashterah, also called Ashteroth in Joshua 12:4. The remaining allotment was from west of the Jordan, all in the north. Four cities each were given from Issachar and Asher. Abdon (v. 30) is not mentioned elsewhere but is probably a variant for Ebron, noted in 19:28. Finally, three cities were given from Naphtali. Neither Hammoth-dor nor Kartan (v. 32) are mentioned elsewhere, though Hammoth-dor could be a variant for Hammath (19:35). Kartan becomes Kiriathaim (an easily explained byform) in 1 Chronicles 6:76 (MT 6:61) but has not been identified.

21:34–40. The final element in the expansion of verses 4–8 is the Merarite allotment of twelve cities and their pastureland. Their allotment was from Zebulun, Reuben, and Gad, meaning they had a higher concentration east of the Jordan than the other Levitical clans.

Merari received four towns from Zebulun, their only allotment west of the Jordan. Kartah and Dimnah (vv. 34–35) are not mentioned elsewhere, unless Dimnah is a variant of Rimmon (19:13),[373] an easily explained transcriptional error.

A further four cities are allotted from Reuben, in the south of the land east of the Jordan.[374] Bezer (20:8) was the southernmost of the cities of

---

issues between the two passages have influenced one another and that priority cannot be given to either. Rather, the two should be seen as variants that need to be weighed against each other.

[373] This would be supported by 1 Chr 6:71 (MT 6:56), which reads "Rimmono," though there are also significant textual problems in that verse.

[374] Anyone using *BHS* will note that these verses are in smaller type. The reason for this is that they are missing from the Leningrad codex that *BHS* uses as its base text, but this is a clear error in the manuscript since they are present in the majority of Masoretic manuscripts as well as the versions. Rather than placing this in a footnote, these verses have

refuge east of the Jordan and so a Levitical city by definition. Jahzah is listed as Jahaz in Reuben's allotment (13:18), where it is also listed with Kedemoth and Mephaath.

The last four cities are from Gad, in the central region east of the Jordan. Ramoth in Gilead was also a city of refuge (20:8) and so automatically a Levitical city. Mahanaim is noted in Gad's allotment (13:26), as also is Heshbon, though this town is more commonly noted with reference to its famous inhabitant Sihon (9:10; 13:10). Jazer is listed in 13:25.

21:41–42. While verses 4–8 initially summarized the Levitical allotment, a closing summary is provided in verses 41–42. The count of forty-eight cities matches the counts within the chapter and the directive in Numbers 35:6–8. According to the latter passage, the number of cities from each tribe was to be based on the size of their allotment to ensure that the responsibility for providing for the Levites was shared equally among the tribes. Joshua does not mention this stipulation. Nevertheless, Judah's contribution was more than the other tribes (Josh 21:13–16), and Naphtali's was less (21:32), indicating that this principle was at work. Greater emphasis is placed on the fact that the towns included associated pastureland, which shows the importance of enabling the Levites to be partially self-supporting.[375] Thus, the Israel described here was an ideal, with provision for all. This ideal presented both to the initial generation and to subsequent generations God's intention of what they could be.[376]

21:43–45. With the land fully allotted, we come to the first of two key summaries of God's faithfulness within the book. In verses 43–45, the summary is provided by the narrator; the second summary is provided by Joshua in his speech to the nation's leaders (23:14). In the latter case, the provision of rest for Israel is noted in the setting for the speech (23:1). The similarities between these passages indicate that we are to read them

---

been placed in the main text on the basis of the other manuscripts—but with the smaller text indicating they are not part of the Leningrad codex, and the evidence supporting this provided in the footnote.

[375] The LXX offers a much longer text here, but with Harstad, *Joshua*, 660, it is probably best to consider this an expansion based on 19:49–50 rather than something accidentally omitted by the MT.

[376] Ehud ben Zvi, "The List of the Levitical Cities," *JSOT* 54 (1992): 77–106, sees this as evidence that this listing is postexilic, but the use of an ideal can also point forward. Admittedly, there is evidence of editing within the list (the various counts could have been useful for administrators during the united monarchy), but there is nothing here that requires that editing to be later than the time of Solomon.

in light of one another, though it is also clear that they have different rhetorical functions. In Joshua's speech, the emphasis falls on the need for Israel to continue trusting God on the basis of his faithfulness. In the current passage, it is important to establish the fact of God's faithfulness while laying the foundation for an exhortation for the future.

As a reflection on God's faithfulness, this summary has two points of reference. First, in verse 43 it pauses to consider the fact that God had given all the land he had sworn to give to Israel's ancestors, a promise that reaches back to Genesis 12:1–9 and that will feature in Joshua's speech in Joshua 24. This statement looks back on chapters 13–21, in which the land was given to Israel. A key element running through these chapters, especially chapters 18–21, is that the land was given before Israel had actually taken it all. Even in the opening chapters of the allotment west of the Jordan, it is clear that Israel had not yet taken full possession of the land in spite of the success of Joshua's military campaign (13:1–7). In fact, apart from allotting the land, nothing had physically changed since God's speech to Joshua telling him to allot the land. The sanctuary had been set up in Shiloh, but much of the land remained to be possessed. Nevertheless, this one change marked the fundamental shift for Israel because at this point they worshiped Yahweh in the land, confessed that the land was truly his, and allotted it in his presence.

Therefore, the statement in verse 43 manages both to look back and to look forward. It looks back because God had indeed given the land to the tribes and their clans; on that basis it could be allotted. Each tribe, each clan, had received its land. But it also looks forward as a statement of faith, one that recognized the need for Israel to not only possess the land by divine grant, but also to possess the land by physically living in all of it. They had received the promise of God, but they also needed to live in light of that promise.[377]

---

[377] Robert Polzin, *Moses and the Deuteronomist: A Literary Study of the Deuteronomic History. Part 1: Deuteronomy, Joshua, Judges* (New York: Seabury, 1980), 132 (see also R. B. Coote, "Joshua," 701), misses the subtlety of this when he claims there is an irreconcilable contradiction between this statement and those passages emphasizing that much of the land remained to be taken. Both elements can be true at the same time because the giving, possession, and dwelling can simultaneously be partially and fully true, depending on whether we focus on God's faithfulness or Israel's current experience. See also T. A. Clarke, "Complete v. Incomplete Conquest: A Re-examination of Three Passages in Joshua," *TynBul* 61 (2010): 100–103.

The second point of reference for this summary is the actual process of Israel taking the land up to this point. This is the principal focus of verses 44–45. These verses continue to reflect on the promise to the ancestors, but they do so with reference back to Joshua 1. God's promise of rest was particularly important in Joshua's speech to the eastern tribes (1:10–15). He stressed that they had already been granted rest in their inheritance (1:13) and that the western tribes were still to receive theirs by taking possession of the land (1:15). His language there is close to the language in verse 44, except that now he could say that God had granted rest to the whole nation. This language anticipates Joshua's speech to the eastern tribes in 22:4 when they were to return to their land and the narrator's reflection in 23:1 on the rest God had given. Just as God spoke of the inability of the peoples of the land to resist Israel and reaffirmed his promise to their ancestors in 1:5–6, these ideas are echoed in 21:44.[378] The whole of Israel's entry to the land is thus seen as the fulfilment of God's promises—indeed that not one of his promises had failed (v. 45).

As with the reflection in verse 43, the statements in verses 44–45 need to be seen from two perspectives at the same time. At every point where Israel had claimed God's promise, they had received it. So it could be said that he had given them rest. But there are also points where Israel made no such claim on the promise, most notably in Dan's failure to keep the land allotted to them (19:47). Therefore, at a second level, these verses also function as an exhortation to faithfulness which claims God's promises. This second level will be more prominent in Joshua 23, which is why the writer to the Hebrews (via Ps 95) can say that Israel did not receive rest under Joshua (Heb 4:1–13), whereas the first level is more prominent here. However, both levels are always true in Joshua. This is perhaps nowhere clearer than in the allocation of the Levitical cities since most of them were in land that had already be given by God but had not yet been taken.

Bridge

As noted previously, the chapters detailing the allotment of the land (Josh 13–21) are difficult for modern readers. Apart from the brief comments about the cities of refuge (20:1–6) and the doxological reflection on

---

[378] Though there is a change of verb about the inability of the peoples to resist: from יצב in 1:5 to עמד in 21:44.

God's faithfulness (21:43–45), they are basically a listing of towns, many of which cannot be identified with any certainty. They do not readily suggest themselves as texts for reflection,[379] and preachers will need to prepare themselves thoroughly if they are to help their congregations to appreciate them. Nevertheless, once we understand these chapters within their context, we will appreciate that they are a rich theological source. The real difficulty for modern readers is that they do not often encounter texts such as these. Preachers will most likely want to take them to Hebrews 4, but we would be wise to teach them this text in its own context first.

There are several reasons for doing this. First, chapters 20–21 are an extended reflection on the importance of taking seriously the promises of God and remembering his faithfulness. The theme of God's faithfulness obviously emerges in the closing summary (Josh 21:43–45), but this is because the preceding chapters describe how God's faithfulness was worked out in the allotment of the Levitical towns and the cities of refuge. Taken out of this context, it is all too easy to think of God's promises in an abstract manner, but they are instead rooted to a particular time and place. Those promises can be traced back to the call of Abram (Gen 12:1–9), are repeated throughout the Pentateuch, and come to focus in Joshua 1. Seen in this light, we can appreciate that the fulfillment of God's promises can be a long-term process (especially if Abram was called about seven hundred years before entry into the land). But they were indeed fulfilled—and fulfilled in detail. These chapters thus provide an important opportunity to pause and consider what God had previously promised.

Second, these chapters highlight the fact that God's faithfulness was not merely something expressed in the past but also a reality to be experienced through time. This is evident in the cities of refuge. They served as continuing evidence of how God provided for his people, preventing a cycle of violence from developing. God knows the human heart; its deceit (Jer 17:9) leads to further sin and violence. This pattern can be traced to the time of Noah (Gen 9:21) and further back to the spread of violence that followed Abel's murder (Gen 4). The gift of the cities of refuge provided a means of preventing violence from spiraling out of control—though

---

[379] Indeed, this view finds a scholarly supporter in Earl, *Reading Joshua*, 177, who considers the context of these chapters so different that they have "rather little development in the Christian context."

Jesus taught that the heart continued to be a source of sin (Mark 7:21). God's provision was also evident in the distribution of the Levites across the land to fulfill a range of functions, including the administration of justice. Yet with God's provision of the Levites, there was also the need for Israel to provide for them. This pattern continues in the support that believers give to clergy today, a theme that lies behind Paul's injunctions in 1 Timothy 5:18.

Third, these chapters demonstrate that God's faithfulness in turn calls for faithfulness from his people. This is implied by Israel's provision of cities and pastureland for the Levites to (at least partly) sustain them in their work. But this faithfulness of God's people is also seen in the need for Israel to take all of the land God was giving them, making the gift of rest real in their experience. The fact that these cities could be allotted, even though many of them were still outside territory Israel had entered, demonstrates this quite clearly. God was faithful to give the cities—and with them rest—but Israel still had to take them. Israel's eventual failure to do this, hinted at already in Dan's failure to keep their land (19:47), prepared the way for the reflections we find in Psalm 95 and Hebrews 4.

So, we can indeed bring modern readers to Hebrews 4 via Psalm 95:11, but we need to do this within the terms set out in these chapters first. The declaration in Psalm 95 about the people not entering God's rest refers in the first instance to the wilderness generation. But in taking up this text and Joshua, the writer to the Hebrews sees a repeated pattern, albeit one tied to God's rest in the Sabbath. Israel's failure to live out the rest God had given under Joshua means there was still a rest to be claimed, and it is this rest that is available to us in Jesus. Israel still had to strive to live out the rest God was giving, and Christians are likewise called to strive to live in the Sabbath rest God gives us in Christ. We recognize that this repeats the pattern in Joshua. God has already objectively given the rest in Christ;[380] however, we are also called to make this rest real in our experience. Only as we appreciate these chapters in their own context can we understand how their themes are developed in the rest of Scripture.

---

[380] See further §7 ("Rest") and §8 ("The Promise of God").

IV. Preparations for Life in the Land (22:1–24:33)

A. The Jordan Altar (22:1–34)

¹ Joshua summoned the Reubenites, Gadites, and half the tribe of Manasseh ² and told them, "You have done everything Moses the Lord's servant commanded you and have obeyed me in everything I commanded you. ³ You have not deserted your brothers even once this whole time but have carried out the requirement of the command of the Lord your God. ⁴ Now that he has given your brothers rest, just as he promised them, return to your homes in your own land that Moses the Lord's servant gave you across the Jordan. ⁵ Only carefully obey the command and instruction that Moses the Lord's servant gave you: to love the Lord your God, walk in all his ways, keep his commands, be loyal to him, and serve him with all your heart and all your soul."

⁶ Joshua blessed them and sent them on their way, and they went to their homes. ⁷ Moses had given territory to half the tribe of Manasseh in Bashan, but Joshua had given territory to the other half, with their brothers, on the west side of the Jordan. When Joshua sent them to their homes and blessed them, ⁸ he said, "Return to your homes with great wealth: a huge number of cattle, and silver, gold, bronze, iron, and a large quantity of clothing. Share the spoil of your enemies with your brothers."

⁹ The Reubenites, Gadites, and half the tribe of Manasseh left the Israelites at Shiloh in the land of Canaan to return to their own land of Gilead, which they took possession of according to the Lord's command through Moses. ¹⁰ When they came to the region of the Jordan in the land of Canaan, the Reubenites, Gadites, and half the tribe of Manasseh built a large, impressive altar there by the Jordan.

¹¹ Then the Israelites heard it said, "Look, the Reubenites, Gadites, and half the tribe of Manasseh have built an altar on the frontier of the land of Canaan at the region of the Jordan, on the Israelite side." ¹² When the Israelites heard this, the entire Israelite community assembled at Shiloh to go to war against them.

¹³ The Israelites sent Phinehas son of Eleazar the priest to the Reubenites, Gadites, and half the tribe of Manasseh, in the land of Gilead. ¹⁴ They sent ten leaders with him—one family leader for each tribe of Israel. All of them were heads of their ancestral families among the clans of Israel. ¹⁵ They went to the Reubenites, Gadites, and half the tribe of Manasseh, in the land of Gilead, and told them, ¹⁶ "This is what the Lord's entire community says: 'What is this treachery you have committed today against the God of Israel by turning away from the Lord and building an altar for yourselves, so that you are in rebellion against the Lord today? ¹⁷ Wasn't the iniquity of Peor, which brought a plague on the Lord's community, enough for us? We have not cleansed ourselves from it even to this day, ¹⁸ and now would you turn away

from the Lord? If you rebel against the Lord today, tomorrow he will be angry with the entire community of Israel. [19] But if the land you possess is defiled, cross over to the land the Lord possesses where the Lord's tabernacle stands, and take possession of it among us. But don't rebel against the Lord or against us by building for yourselves an altar other than the altar of the Lord our God. [20] Wasn't Achan son of Zerah unfaithful regarding what was set apart for destruction, bringing wrath on the entire community of Israel? He was not the only one who perished because of his iniquity.' "

[21] The Reubenites, Gadites, and half the tribe of Manasseh answered the heads of the Israelite clans, [22] "The Mighty One, God, the Lord! The Mighty One, God, the Lord! He knows, and may Israel also know. Do not spare us today, if it was in rebellion or treachery against the Lord [23] that we have built for ourselves an altar to turn away from him. May the Lord himself hold us accountable if we intended to offer burnt offerings and grain offerings on it, or to sacrifice fellowship offerings on it. [24] We actually did this from a specific concern that in the future your descendants might say to our descendants, 'What relationship do you have with the Lord, the God of Israel? [25] For the Lord has made the Jordan a border between us and you descendants of Reuben and Gad. You have no share in the Lord!' So your descendants may cause our descendants to stop fearing the Lord.

[26] "Therefore we said: Let's take action and build an altar for ourselves, but not for burnt offering or sacrifice. [27] Instead, it is to be a witness between us and you, and between the generations after us, so that we may carry out the worship of the Lord in his presence with our burnt offerings, sacrifices, and fellowship offerings. Then in the future, your descendants will not be able to say to our descendants, 'You have no share in the Lord!' [28] We thought that if they said this to us or to our generations in the future, we would reply: Look at the replica of the Lord's altar that our ancestors made, not for burnt offering or sacrifice, but as a witness between us and you. [29] We would never ever rebel against the Lord or turn away from him today by building an altar for burnt offering, grain offering, or sacrifice, other than the altar of the Lord our God, which is in front of his tabernacle."

[30] When the priest Phinehas and the community leaders, the heads of Israel's clans who were with him, heard what the descendants of Reuben, Gad, and Manasseh had to say, they were pleased. [31] Phinehas son of Eleazar the priest said to the descendants of Reuben, Gad, and Manasseh, "Today we know that the Lord is among us, because you have not committed this treachery against him. As a result, you have rescued the Israelites from the Lord's power."

[32] Then the priest Phinehas son of Eleazar and the leaders returned from the Reubenites and Gadites in the land of Gilead to the Israelites in

the land of Canaan and brought back a report to them. [33] The Israelites were pleased with the report, and they blessed God. They spoke no more about going to war against them to ravage the land where the Reubenites and Gadites lived. [34] So the Reubenites and Gadites named the altar: It is a witness between us that the Lord is God.

Context

With this chapter, the process of bringing the book of Joshua to a close begins. This process is marked by three speeches from Joshua, each one longer than the one before. Each represents an element of Joshua's farewell. The speech in 22:1-8 is given to the east Jordan tribes as they are sent from Shiloh back to their possession across the Jordan. It will be followed by the speeches focused on Israel's leaders (23:1-16) and the people at Shechem (24:1-28). Joshua's death and burial is then related (24:29-30). The first and third speeches conclude with Joshua sending the relevant group back to their territory (22:6-8; 24:28). Central to each speech is the need to remain faithful to Yahweh so that the people's future can be shaped by such obedience. In this, there may be an intentional parallel with Moses since Deuteronomy is also broadly divided up into three speeches (Deut 1-4; 5-28; 29-33) before the report of Moses' death (Deut 34). Joshua's receipt of the title "Servant of Yahweh" at his burial certainly represents a parallel to Moses, so the use of three speeches would also stress Joshua's importance since no other Old Testament figure gives three farewell speeches. This feature is reinforced by the fact that at least the first two speeches are saturated in the language of Deuteronomy.

At the same time, the farewell speeches do more than just associate Joshua with Moses since they must also contribute to the book's narrative arc. The placement of this chapter is particularly important because it simultaneously begins the book's closure (chapters 22-24) while also closing off the issue of the relationship between the eastern and western tribes. The importance of this relationship, one in which Israel's unity was paramount, has lain in the background in the last two chapters as both the cities of refuge (Josh 20) and allotment for the Levites (Josh 21) were concerned with territory on either side of the Jordan. These chapters have not problematized the issue of the river as a barrier between the two groups, but the possibility of this was certainly hinted at in the crossing of the river (Josh 3-4), while Joshua's initial charge to the eastern tribes had stressed the importance of the nation's unity in anticipation of crossing the Jordan (1:10-18). Indeed, that Manasseh's contribution of four cities to the Levites came from both sides of the river (21:5-6, 25, 27), while all the Levitical groups apart from the priests were given towns on both sides of the river, clearly indicates that the river was not intended to divide the nation, even if it could be a significant boundary in the spring of each year. Equally, there were three cities of refuge on each side of the Jordan, stressing that everyone living in Israel had equal right of access to this element of the justice system. All of this depended on the nation's unity—which would be challenged here.

More immediately, there is a close relationship between the closing affirmation of the reliability of God's promises (21:43-45) and Joshua's speech in 22:1-8 since the theme of rest (נוח), which also finds an important parallel in Joshua's opening speech (1:13, 15), is prominent here (22:4). This theme is also important at the start of Joshua's next speech (23:1). Perhaps more subtly, the claim of the eastern tribes that their altar is a witness to the unity of the nation, something reflected in the naming of the altar (22:35), also anticipates the stone that Joshua set up after the covenant renewal (24:26-27), which was a witness to the events of that day. The importance of these themes indicates how this chapter establishes links across the book as a whole, with particularly significant connections also made with the Achan story (22:16, 20, 22, 31).

Beyond this, there is an intriguing interplay in terms of the main pentateuchal texts that lie in the background to the various elements of this narrative, and this too echoes the earlier parts of the book. Joshua's speech (22:1-8) deliberately echoes the language of Deuteronomy, but the balance of the chapter draws its main themes from a variety of passages in Numbers even as it echoes earlier passages in Joshua. This parallels the main structure of pentateuchal references in the rest of the book, with Joshua 1-12 principally drawing on Deuteronomy, whereas Numbers is the principal point of reference in chapters 13-21. To a certain extent, this interplay between Deuteronomy and Numbers was already anticipated in Joshua 1, since 1:1-9 draws from Deuteronomy whereas the rest of the chapter interacts more with Numbers. In 22:1-8, though, Joshua's speech (which is in the language of Deuteronomy) refers quite heavily to the latter part of Joshua 1, which is the section of that chapter most heavily dependent on Numbers.

All of this indicates that this narrative is a carefully composed whole.[381] It directs readers back to the book's beginning to see how its themes interact with it, reflects on the declaration of divine faithfulness at the end of the previous chapter, and prepares readers for the passages that follow. It is thus an important distillation of key themes across the book as well as an important narrative in its own right. Only by reading the text in light of the references it makes to the rest of the book (as well as Numbers and Deuteronomy) are we able to understand what the unity of the nation means.[382]

Exegesis

22:1–3. The whole of this chapter is bounded by the use of the verb "to call" (קרא). As in English, the Hebrew verb can mean "to summon" or "to name." The chapter opens with Joshua "summoning" the east Jordan tribes of Reuben, Gad, and the half tribe of Manasseh; it ends with the tribes of Reuben and Gad "naming" the altar. Joshua's addressing of these tribes also echoes the initial speech to them (1:13–15). The parallels are then made stronger when in verse 2 Joshua refers to the fact that the eastern tribes had done all that Moses had commanded them—in addition to obeying Joshua himself. This deliberately reflects the wording of the earlier speech, which focused on God's command to the eastern tribes through Moses that they could only return to their own possession (and thus their families and livestock) after God had granted rest to their kin who were to settle across the Jordan. The link between obedience to Moses and Joshua had already been established by the eastern tribes in their response to Joshua (1:16–18), so Joshua's reference to himself further ties this speech to the book's opening. Although the campaign to this point has run for many days—and Caleb's statement in Josh 14:10 could suggest it took five years from entry into the land to the point

---

[381] This does not deny the possibility of discrete source materials that have been brought together, since historians typically do this, but this is a different approach to that of Fritz, *Josua*, 220–21, who tracks redactional developments within the narrative, thus losing its clear integration. With Butler, *Joshua 13–24*, 246, we can agree that "syntax and content thus render the entire chapter as a single unit."

[382] See especially Elie Assis, "The Place and Function of Jos 22 in the Book of Joshua," *ZAW* 116 (2004): 528–41. All of this stands rather against the assertion of Rösel, *Joshua*, 346, that this story "does not seem appropriate in the book of Joshua."

of allocation of the land—the eastern tribes had remained faithful. Just as God had not "abandoned" Joshua (1:5), so also these tribes had not "deserted" (עזב) the western tribes. Joshua could thus commend them for their faithfulness because they not only had obeyed Moses and Joshua, but they had also obeyed God.

22:4–6. The repetition of "and now" (וְעַתָּה) in verse 4 points to the significant change that had come about. The eastern tribes could not return until God had granted rest to the western tribes, but that rest had now been given. In a statement that is effectively a summary of the narrator's earlier comment (21:43–45), Joshua stressed that God had been faithful to his promise to these tribes to give them rest in the land. In referring to Yahweh as "your God," Joshua reminded them that they served the same God as the western tribes. The God who had promised rest to the western tribes was also the God of the eastern tribes, stressing therefore that worship was the element that bound the nation together. Moreover, this God was one whom they had found was faithful to his promise. In light of this, the second "and now" points to the appropriate action for the eastern tribes, which was to return to their homes (lit., "tents") in the land of their possession, which Moses had given them across the Jordan. As in 1:1, Moses is again referred to here as God's servant, thus emphasizing God's involvement in the granting of this territory.

Within Joshua, the language of "across the Jordan" depends on the perspective of the speaker. Sometimes it refers to the area west of the Jordan (e.g., 5:1; 7:7), whereas here (as in 1:15) it refers to the land east of the Jordan. There may be a hint of the unusual nature of the eastern tribes holding that territory since it is referred to in verse 4 as their possession (אֲחֻזַּתְכֶם). This term is otherwise used only of Caleb's special holding (21:12) or the allocation of the Levites (21:41), both elements that stood outside of the standard division of the land but that nonetheless were God's gift. The term is used for the eastern tribes' territory throughout this chapter (22:9, 19), though by the time it occurs in Phinehas' speech (22:19), there is perhaps more emphasis on it being an irregular territory than a divine gift. At this stage there is no such hint.

What the eastern tribes needed to do as they returned was continue to obey all that had been revealed through Moses (v. 5). Joshua's language about loving God evokes a number of passages from Deuteronomy (especially Deut 10:12–13; 11:13, 22), all passages in which Moses exhorted Israel to faithfulness through wholehearted covenant loyalty. Just as the eastern tribes had demonstrated this in assisting their western kin to receive rest west of the Jordan, so they were to continue to demonstrate it when they returned to their own territory.

Having charged the eastern tribes to obedience, Joshua then sent them away with a blessing.[383] The content of the blessing is not stated yet (it is deferred until v. 8), but the important point is that parting with a blessing indicates that there was no conflict between east and west as the eastern tribes left to go home. Their faithfulness to the western tribes was replicated in the western tribes' commitment to them expressed in Joshua's blessing.

22:7–8. With Joshua's speech complete, there is now a brief editorial comment about the tribe of Manasseh as one that had territory on both sides of the Jordan—the eastern territory given by Moses (13:29–31) and the western by Joshua (17:1–13). Although this note might seem odd in terms of the development of the narrative since it recounts information that has frequently been noted in the book, it has an important narrative function in preparing for the conflict that would emerge once the eastern tribes have built their altar. The fundamental issue was whether the people on both sides of the river would be recognized as Israel. This had a particular effect for Manasseh since they (like the nation as a whole) lived on both sides of the Jordan. Manasseh thus became a microcosm of Israel: a people who were one and yet potentially separated by the river. In the same way that the land allocation consistently localized the tribal allotment by referring to the clans, so also the division of Israel into east and west was localized in the tribe of Manasseh.[384]

The division is further hinted at by noting that Joshua had given land "across" the Jordan. Whereas the reference in verse 4 meant land east of the Jordan, in verse 7 the addition of יָמָּה ("the west side") means the land west of the Jordan. The different ways in which Israel could perceive the land are thus subtly placed to prepare readers for the conflict over who Israel is and where they live, all of which would find its focus in the altar.

With this narrative focus prepared, we return to Joshua's blessing of the eastern tribes. In this case, the blessing was not asking for something extra for the eastern tribes so much as it was recognizing that God had

---

[383] Although "blessing" was a priestly task, as Harstad, *Joshua*, 686, notes, it was also something a father did within his household, and that is the appropriate analogy for understanding Joshua here.

[384] Nelson, *Joshua*, 247, appropriately refers to them as a "bridge people."

provided them with considerable wealth in the form of livestock, precious metals, and clothing. Three of these items—clothing, gold, and silver—had been the sources of temptation to Achan, whose story echoes through much of this chapter. Here, Joshua could understand them as good things that God had given his faithful people (rather like the Israelites who plundered Egypt as they left in the exodus; Exod 12:35–36), but their mention also prepares readers for the more obvious references to Achan later in the chapter. Indeed, the spoils at Jericho had tempted Achan (Josh 7:21), but here the spoils were God's gift that could be divided among the families of the eastern tribes, even as Joshua had divided up the land among the western tribes. Rösel believes these verses do not suit their context well,[385] but it seems more likely that we are dealing with a careful narrator who deliberately provides information that, although standing outside of the main narrative arc of the chapter, is important for its interpretation.

22:9–12. The focus shifts from Joshua to the eastern tribes as they left Shiloh to return to their own territory. But even the language of their departure creates deliberate uncertainty about the identity of the nation and its land. The note that the eastern tribes left "the Israelites" (בְּנֵי יִשְׂרָאֵל) raises immediate questions. Are not the eastern tribes also Israelites? Had the narrator wanted to avoid this implication, then the text could have said that they left their "kin" (אֲחֵיכֶם, as in v. 3). But the term used in verse 9 points to a possible fissure in the nation, one in which its identity is less clear.

Moreover, that they left from "Shiloh in the land of Canaan" also raises questions. At one level, it simply repeats the note from 21:2, but it also means that they were leaving the land that had actually been promised, something that makes the repetition of "possession" language (אֲחֻזָּה) for these tribes intriguing. They are outside of the land that was promised, the land where (strictly speaking) Yahweh's sanctuary was found. Are they therefore dwelling outside of the area where God's people are meant to dwell? It was a land they had received by God's command through Moses (Gilead being shorthand for the whole region, even though Reuben was further south), so it was not outside God's purposes. But it was still somewhere outside the territory God had actually promised.

---

385 Rösel, *Joshua*, 346.

Following the narrative technique of 1:1–5:12,[386] in which the narrator provides important information but refrains from commenting on its meaning, we have these issues laid before us, but none of this fully prepares us for the surprise of verse 10, which reports the large altar that these tribes built when they came to "the region of the Jordan."[387] Indeed, its size is particularly stressed, suggesting perhaps that it was larger than the one at Shiloh.

Therefore, it is no surprise that word came back to the Israelites about its existence (v. 11). Once again, "the Israelites" (בְּנֵי יִשְׂרָאֵל) refers only to those living west of the Jordan since they distinguished themselves from the eastern tribes. What was initially only hinted at becomes a reality, at least as the western tribes defined themselves. The report aimed to provide more clarity about exactly where the altar was built and seems to suggest that it lay right on the frontier, presumably on the bank of the Jordan. Curiously, they are said to have heard of this altar, not seen it, though this is likely because the narrator wanted both verses 11 and 12 to begin with a reference to Israel hearing about the altar. Verse 11 provides a report that would have been conveyed beyond those in the region who could have seen it, and verse 12 indicates the actions taken.

The first time the Israelites had assembled at Shiloh (18:1), all the tribes were present, but now only the western tribes were gathered. In a scene that would have a tragic echo in Judges 20 when the tribes would combine against Benjamin, the western tribes prepared to go to war against the eastern tribes. Beyond the report of the altar, no reason for this is yet given, but this is consistent with the narrative technique that refrains from providing interpretative clues. Numbers provides the principal background for this part of the chapter, but the prohibition of the multiplication of altars in Deuteronomy 12 probably also lies in the background, though in fact it will not feature in any of the discussion about the altar.[388] Nevertheless, Israel stood on the verge of civil war.

---

[386] See further Firth, "Disorienting Readers in Joshua 1.1–5.12," 413–30.

[387] The csb note indicates that the reference to the "region" of the Jordan both here and in v. 11 could be the toponym "Geliloth." Although possible, both here and in 13:2 it is more probable that it is used as a common noun.

[388] Deuteronomy 12 is often understood as prohibiting any altar but the central one (at this point, Shiloh), but as Peter C. Craigie, *The Book of Deuteronomy* (Grand Rapids: Eerdmans, 1976), 217, has shown, this is not the primary focus here; up to this point, or indeed even until the time of Josiah, a plurality of altars had not been problematic (see Woudstra, *The Book of Joshua*, 320). Rather, the issue is the appropriate worship of Yahweh. For a fuller

22:13–14. Although the western tribes were ready for war, this story will not follow the devastating path taken in Judges 20. Instead, the western tribes (again, "the Israelites") decided to send Phinehas, the son of the high priest Eleazar, along with ten other leaders to the eastern tribes in Gilead. As is typical for this chapter, "Gilead" is a shorthand term for the region east of the Jordan. As a member of the high priestly family (stressed here), Phinehas was an obvious delegate, someone who would carry a degree of authority in his negotiations with the eastern tribes. But he is also someone remembered from the events of Shittim in the plains of Moab, where he had decided to spear an Israelite man and Moabite woman to stop the plague (Num 25:1–13). He is thus a man of action; there is no evidence of his negotiating. However, the fact that he had previously stopped a rebellion was likely central to his appointment in this case.[389]

Since the mission was to represent the whole of the western tribes, a further ten leaders were sent with him, each representing a tribe (and thus their clans). These leaders will be prominent at later points in the chapter, though they are always subservient to Phinehas (22:21, 30). However, there are two distinctive features about their appointment that should be noted. First, the appointment of ten leaders means that Manasseh is included since the eastern group is a "half tribe." The bridging function of Manasseh is thus emphasized through this element and may prepare for the fact that only Reuben and Gad are involved in naming the altar (22:34).

Second, the term translated "clans" here (אֶלֶף) is different from the one used in the land allocation (מִשְׁפָּחָה); elsewhere in the book it means "thousand," either as a measure (e.g., 3:4) or as a reference to a military unit (23:10). The term can mean "clans" (e.g., 1 Sam 10:19), but there is probably at least a militaristic hint in its use here, so that the leaders who accompanied Phinehas may have been commanders of militia units as well as important figures in their clans. The group sent by the western tribes was not necessarily there to make peace, even though this would be the outcome of the visit.

---

treatment, see Peter T. Vogt, *Deuteronomic Theology and the Significance of Torah: A Reappraisal* (Winona Lake, IN: Eisenbrauns, 2006), 160–203.

[389] Firth, *The Message of Joshua*, 200. See also Barbara E. Organ, "Pursuing Phinehas: A Synchronic Reading," *CBQ* 63 (2001): 212–14.

22:15-20. The possibility of conflict certainly lies behind the speech of Phinehas' group when they address the eastern tribes in Gilead. We are not told who spoke, since this would distract from their role as representing the message of the assembly. Indeed, they did not claim to represent simply the western tribes but "the entire community" of Yahweh (v. 16), implying that the eastern tribes were now not part of this community (though the presence of Manasseh among the representatives could have served to invite the rest of that tribe to take a different stance).

Through a series of rhetorical questions and accusations, Phinehas' group presented their challenge to the eastern tribes. They consistently indicated that the eastern tribes were out of a proper relationship with God because of the construction of the altar, and tied this to the fact that they dwelled outside of the land that had been promised.

The first of the rhetorical questions is posed in verse 16. Rather than arguing that the eastern tribes had acted treacherously, the question served indirectly to accuse them of treachery. There is a clear link to the Achan story, since the word rendered as "treachery" occurs elsewhere in Joshua (outside of chapter 22) only at 7:1 (the csb obscures the link by translating it "unfaithful" there). In 7:1 the treachery was corporate, even though it was technically the act of one person. The link between the two stories probably suggests that the western tribes were concerned that rebellion by the eastern tribes would have a corporate effect.

The treachery was said to be against "the God of Israel" and described as "turning away" from Yahweh. Such a turning was contrary to Joshua's earlier directive (v. 6). This language most commonly refers to the worship of other gods, but here it is defined as the act of building an altar for themselves and so being in "rebellion" (מרד) against God. The issue as presented is, therefore, not that the eastern tribes had built an additional altar, but rather that they had done so without divine authority.[390] This second verb for rebellion is relatively uncommon in the rest of the Old Testament, with six of its twenty-four occurrences in this chapter. There is an important echo of the speech of Joshua and Caleb after the spies had gone through the land in which they urged the people not to rebel (מרד) against God (Num 14:9). The allusion thus points to pivotal moments of failure in Israel's past that involved Joshua, suggesting to the eastern tribes that this is the tradition in which they stood.

---

[390] Butler, *Joshua 13-24*, 259.

Verses 17–18 include further rhetorical questions that build on verse 16, moving toward a climax: the actions of the eastern tribes were placing the whole community of Israel at risk. Mention of the "iniquity" of Peor refers to Numbers 25:1–13 (see also Ps 106:28–31), in which worship of Moabite gods included sexual relations with Moabite and Midianite women as well. This sin triggered the plague that was only stopped by Phinehas' zeal for God that led him to spear an Israelite man and Midianite woman. This reference once again suggests a flaw in the worship of the eastern tribes, implying that the purpose for the altar could only be to worship other gods. Although the plague had been stopped in the wilderness, the western tribes claimed in verse 17 that Israel had still not been made clean from it. Howard is right that this indicates Israel had always flirted with the worship of other gods and that stopping one plague had not changed this.[391]

The speech moves from rhetorical questions with clear implications to direct accusation at the end of verse 18. The eastern tribes had rebelled against God, and this in turn would provoke him to be angry with the whole community. The contrast between "today" and "tomorrow" should not be pressed into twenty-four-hour periods but instead indicates that the current actions of one group had future implications for the others. The western tribes feared that they would be caught up in the sin of the eastern tribes. Whereas no action had been taken against Achan until the damage had been done, the western tribes were attempting to stop the perceived sin before it affected them.

These themes come together in verses 19–20, the climax of the speech. Although questions continue to be used (understanding v. 19 as indirect questioning), only the reference to Achan in verse 20 is still rhetorical. Instead, the opening question is intended to offer a means of resolving the problem, though in doing so it again raises questions about the boundaries of the land in which Israel is to live. This is immediately apparent in their question about the land possessed by the eastern tribes.

The suggestion that the land might be "defiled" in verse 19 contrasts with the problem of the people being "clean" after the sin of Peor in verse 17. This introduces an important distinction in Priestly texts (the natural home for Phinehas) between the "clean" (טהר) and the "unclean" (or "defiled," טמא). Distinguishing between these two states and teaching the people the difference between them was a key priestly task (Lev 10:10–11).

---

[391] Howard, *Joshua*, 409.

The question (as posed here) does not say that the possession of the eastern tribes was necessarily unclean. Nevertheless, contrasting it with Yahweh's possession certainly implies that it might be and indicates that it might not be appropriate for the eastern tribes to live across the Jordan. The result of a defiled land is that it leads to defiled worship, whereas the land of Yahweh's possession is where his tabernacle is found and thus where appropriate worship occurs. So the eastern tribes were invited to cross the Jordan to the area that the western tribes regarded as definitely belonging to God (not least because it had the sanctuary) and to take a possession there instead.

There may be a contrast here with the portion that the western tribes had received, with the eastern tribes therefore to be scattered through them just as the Levites had been. Certainly, such a scattering could represent the idea of living "among" the western tribes. If so, this would indicate a lesser status for the eastern tribes. Whether or not this was intended, the western tribes challenged the eastern tribes not to continue in rebellion against both God and the western tribes by building the altar. The clear implication is that construction of an altar other than the one in Shiloh had put the eastern tribes out of fellowship with both God and the rest of Israel.

In verse 20, the figure of Achan, who has so far been alluded to but not mentioned by name, comes to the fore. His unfaithful action with the devoted items from Jericho had brought God's wrath on the whole community so that many others died—not only his immediate family (7:22–26) but also those killed when Israel first attacked Ai (7:5). The eastern tribes were thus challenged to avoid bringing God's wrath on the whole nation and, instead, to abandon their sin, leave the altar, and come dwell west of the Jordan.

22:21–23. We might imagine that these verses would recount the repentance of the eastern tribes, much as Achan had done after he was discovered (albeit too late to avoid his punishment). But to this point the narrator has carefully avoided providing information about why the altar was built. All the reader knows is what the western tribes saw and the implications they drew from it. Of course, the problem with any artifact is that it has to be interpreted. Without all of the information, any interpretation may not only be partial but also incorrect. We have been able to feel the anger build among the western tribes but without any other perspective to challenge it until now.

The claim of the eastern tribes was that the western tribes' partial perspective was fundamentally flawed. Their response came in three stages. The first stage, in verses 21–23, was in effect to swear an oath of innocence. Such oaths seem to be evident at certain points in the psalms (e.g., Ps 7:4–6), though those oaths were presumably in the sanctuary. Since they addressed the clan leaders (אֵלֶּה), they may have felt they were responding to a military threat.

The key element in their response is the declaration of verse 22. The CSB takes אֵל אֱלֹהִים (lit., "God of gods") as a single title, "the Mighty One," which is then clarified as Yahweh. This is entirely possible, and no one English rendering does full justice to the language here. But there is much to commend Hess's suggestion that we render the whole phrase, "The LORD is the greatest God."[392] Perhaps we should keep both translations (the CSB note "The LORD is the God of gods" hints at the latter). The point is to stress both God's incomparable power and authority, while admitting the reality that Israel lived in a world that acknowledged the existence of many gods. Even if those gods had no actual substance, Israel had no other language than to describe them as "gods." Yahweh is the Mighty One, the one who is supreme above all others, and the eastern tribes invoked him twice as they made their defense.

For the eastern tribes, such an affirmation was not an abstract statement of theology. Rather, it was something they immediately applied, insisting that God knew their intentions. And in light of this, they wanted Israel to know. Since they included themselves within this label, clearly they were claiming to be a legitimate part of Israel.[393]

The oath of innocence proper begins with their insistence that, if they were indeed guilty of any form of rebellion (whether like the failure of the tribes to enter the land or like the treachery of Achan), then the western tribes should not spare them. The nature of the rebellion is then specifically characterized as the suggestion that they built the altar to turn away from God and serve other gods. But the possibility of rebellion is then turned in a somewhat surprising direction by their assertion that God himself should hold them accountable if they had intended to offer on the altar burnt offerings, grain offerings, or fellowship offerings—the

---

[392] Hess, *Joshua*, 292. For other possibilities, see Dallaire, "Joshua," 1029. Fritz, *Josua*, 224, points to the parallel in Ps 50:1, though the significance of this is unclear.

[393] See also Creach, *Joshua*, 112.

basic options for sacrifice outlined in Leviticus 1–3. In other words, this altar was *not* for offerings. English speakers might not be troubled by this, but in Hebrew the word for an altar (מִזְבֵּחַ) comes from the root meaning "to sacrifice" (זבח). Thus, an altar is literally a place of sacrifice, and it is hard to imagine that the western tribes could have conceived it in any other way.[394] This, perhaps, was why the eastern tribes began with such a strong oath formulation.

22:24–26. In a culture that couldn't think of an altar as anything but a place of sacrifice, the second stage of their response explained why the altar had been built. This stage is also introduced by an oath formulation: וְאִם־לֹא. The phrase can be used in a number of ways, but one of the most important is to introduce a strong declaration.[395] csb's "We actually did this from a specific concern" moves in this direction, though the language is perhaps more forceful than this. "It was indeed because of a specific concern" would be slightly clearer. The formulation also indicates that the oath was contrary to what would be expected, and this is certainly true in any discussion of an altar not used for sacrifice.

The particular concern was a fear that the western tribes would prevent the descendants of the eastern tribes from worshiping God in the future. Indeed, the particular issue (already hinted at in the questions posed by the western tribes) was that the western tribes would regard the eastern tribes as outside of the purposes of God precisely because the Jordan was a barrier between them. The western tribes might conclude that only those dwelling in the land promised to Abraham could be the people of God.[396]

Notably, the eastern tribes only mentioned Reuben and Gad (v. 25), the two tribes solely outside the land, again indicating Manasseh's "bridge" status within this chapter. It is not altogether clear how the western tribes would cause the descendants of the eastern tribes to turn to other gods, but perhaps the implication is that they could control the crossings of the Jordan and prevent them from coming to the sanctuary to worship. Although not focused on the issue of worship, the end of the Jephthah

---

[394] N. H. Snaith, "Altar at Gilgal: Joshua xx 22–29," *VT* 38 (1978): 331, insists therefore that the narrative is effectively covering the fact that the eastern tribes did erect an altar for sacrifice. But this misses the narrative's subtlety, in which we are initially allowed to see and feel what the western tribes did, not necessarily what was really happening.

[395] *GKC* §149.

[396] See also Hawk, *Joshua in 3-D*, 228–30; Earl, *Reading Joshua as Christian Scripture*, 178–83.

story indicates that the crossing points of the Jordan could be controlled
to limit access to the land (Judg 12:1–7).

22:26–29. Only in the third stage did the eastern tribes explain their
purpose, again insisting that this altar (i.e., "place of sacrifice") was not, in
fact, for any form of sacrifice. Rather, anticipating the naming of the altar
in verse 34, the purpose was that it should serve as a witness between the
eastern and western tribes, so that the eastern tribes could continue to
worship God. This could be done in God's presence with burnt offerings,
sacrifices, and fellowship offerings, repeating the three categories that
the eastern tribes had denied were the function of the altar in verse 23.
These offerings could only properly be offered in God's presence, and that
meant in the sanctuary in Shiloh. In some way, the altar was intended as
a witness to this reality, so that the western tribes would not in the future
deny that the eastern tribes had any portion in Yahweh.

Verse 28 presents an imagined future conversation in which the
descendants of the eastern tribes would point out the presence of the
altar as a replica of the real altar, not for any form of offering, but as a
witness between them. The idea of a replica (תַּבְנִית) is important because
it could refer to a plan from which something was built, most obviously
the tabernacle itself and its implements (Exod 25:9). So, although this
altar was large, it was intended as a replica of the actual altar. By insisting
that the altar was not for sacrifice but rather to serve as a witness, the
eastern tribes hoped to resolve potential conflict. Exactly how this would
happen is unclear. That the western tribes clearly did not see it this way
indicates that the plan was not as thoroughly conceived as it might have
been. Nevertheless, the implication seems to be that once the western
tribes realized the eastern tribes had no means of worshiping God other
than by going to the Shiloh sanctuary, then they would not prevent them
from crossing the Jordan to worship.

This is reaffirmed in the closing declaration of verse 29. The eastern
tribes insisted they would never rebel or turn away from the proper
worship of God by building another altar for sacrifice. The only one appropriate for this was the altar in the tabernacle. This final declaration is
introduced by an oath formula (חָלִילָה לָּנוּ), which is perhaps slightly more
forceful than csb's "We would never" and could be better rendered, "Far
be it from us!" Though it was a strong declaration, later generations reading this text would know that, for all the eastern tribes' insistence, this did

not prove true. No resistance from the western tribes was required for the eastern tribes to fall into the worship of other gods in the years to come.

22:30–31. We are never told if the claims of the eastern tribes were correct. Given that Phinehas' group accepted their claim (doubtless because of the various oath formulae), we are presumably to do likewise, even though an altar not intended for sacrifice remains an odd concept within the Bible. The opening verb of verse 30 is singular, indicating a particular focus on Phinehas. His status as a priest is again emphasized, perhaps because one of the key roles of a priest was in fact to judge difficult cases.[397] His judgement in favor of the eastern tribes was endorsed by the rest of the group. If the other leaders were also potential militia commanders, then their support for this decision was important and suspended military action.

Since the speeches reported in this chapter were all spoken by groups, it is significant that Phinehas alone spoke and rendered a judgement on the case (v. 31). His status to do this is emphasized. In verse 30 he is simply "the priest," but in verse 31 he is "son of Eleazar the priest" and thus successor to the position of high priest. The use of this full title points to the importance of his judgment. Addressing the eastern tribes, he reported that his group now knew that God was present with them. The use of the verb "know" (ידע) echoes the hope expressed by the eastern tribes in verse 22 that all Israel would know the truth of their claim. Phinehas could affirm God's presence in the area east of the Jordan because it was clear the eastern tribes had not committed treachery like Achan. God's presence "among us" must, therefore, include both eastern and western tribes.[398] If so, then the Israelites (בְּנֵי יִשְׂרָאֵל) who were delivered from God's power must be those on both sides of the river, because an inappropriately triggered civil war would mean all God's people had placed themselves under divine judgment. A people at war among themselves

---

[397] See Deut 17:8–13. In this Deuteronomic text, consideration is given only to individual crimes and the assumption was that they would be brought to the central sanctuary. But a broader role in overseeing justice can be assumed, and a case such as the one in Joshua could clearly not have come to the sanctuary.

[398] John S. Kloppenborg, "Joshua 22: The Priestly Editing of an Ancient Tradition," *Biblica* 62 (1981): 355, argues that the narrative finally sees the salvation of the western tribes, but this seems to miss the various elements that finally overcome the divisions within the nation.

is a people living outside of a relationship with God and thus needing to be rescued from his judgment.

22:32–34. With the conflict resolved, the narrative moves to its conclusion as Phinehas' group returned to the west. Again, the principal focus is on Phinehas, though the whole group brought back their report to the Israelites in Canaan. The Hebrew is slightly ambiguous, but it seems best to understand verse 32 as indicating that the report came back to the Israelites in Canaan, thus suggesting that those outside of Canaan could also be considered Israelites.

The report is presumably a brief summary of all that had happened. Just as it had proved satisfactory to Phinehas' group, so it was also satisfactory to the western tribes who no longer spoke of going to war against Reuben and Gad. Manasseh again is absent from this statement, either by abbreviation or (more likely) because of their bridging function between east and west. Closure for the western tribes meant an end to the plan for war, and they therefore blessed God. Joshua had blessed the eastern tribes when they left, but now the western tribes blessed God. In this context, "blessing" God means to worship him. It certainly includes the element of praise, but thanksgiving would appear to be the dominant element.

For the Reubenites and Gadites, closure was expressed in the naming of the altar.[399] There is some uncertainty in the manuscript tradition (see CSB note) about whether the altar was simply called "Witness" or whether the full statement as represented in the CSB text was the title.[400] We could also read it as saying that they named the altar but that the name has not been recorded, only the reason behind it. Of these options, preference should probably be given to the CSB note since this makes good sense in context. Thus, the altar was probably called "Witness." Regardless, the important point was the presence of the altar as a continued reminder that Yahweh was God. This truth held together the people of God as a worshiping community and mattered far more than location.

Bridge

This chapter manages to be both charmingly simple and yet also remarkably complex. Preachers who reflect on it will find that believers can be

---

[399] In the LXX, Joshua named the altar, but this seems to be a late correction to a perceived absence of Joshua in the latter part of the chapter.

[400] On the main possibilities for understanding the MT, see Harstad, *Joshua*, 716–18.

encouraged to read it at various levels, each of which is valid and contributes to its meaning within Joshua and to its place within the larger message of the Bible.

At a simple level, this chapter can be read as an exhortation to continued faithfulness to God, faithfulness that is expressed in authentic worship.[401] The importance of this can be seen in Joshua's speech to the eastern tribes as they prepared to return to their possession across the Jordan. This speech, with its allusions to Deuteronomy (see comments on vv. 1–8) is consciously linked to the importance of serving God alone and expressing this through faithfulness to what he has commanded. These links also prepare us for the allusions to Deuteronomy 12 that, in part at least, lie behind the conflict that emerges over a seemingly unauthorized altar.

Even at the simplest level, this is a chapter that expects us to read it in light of other texts, a process that is enriched in the important allusions to Joshua 1 as we explore how faithfulness in one setting is intended to lead to faithfulness in others. That is, just as the eastern tribes had been faithful in enabling the western tribes to settle (at least partially) in their allotment, so also were they challenged to continue in faithful worship. Indeed, this faithfulness and how it was to be expressed drives the exploration of the conflict between the western and eastern tribes. This is of particular importance given the assumption of the western tribes that the altar was a call to inappropriate worship. Instead, as the narrative demonstrates, appropriate worship becomes the means by which the nation as a whole was held together.

The model of appropriate worship and how it holds the people of God together is developed across large portions of Scripture.[402] In the books of Kings, for example, kings are routinely assessed on whether they led the people to worship more appropriately. Only Hezekiah (2 Kgs 18:3–8) and Josiah (2 Kgs 22:2) are given a wholly positive assessment because of their commitment to proper worship. Others such as Asa (1 Kgs 15:9–15) are given qualified approval because, although they established positive patterns for worship, it was not wholly as it should have been. Finally,

---

[401] For a helpful exposition on these lines, see Davis, *No Falling Words*, 165–75.

[402] Particularly helpful resources in this respect are Daniel I. Block, *For the Glory of God: Recovering a Biblical Theology of Worship* (Grand Rapids: Baker Academic, 2014); and Timothy M. Pierce, *Enthroned on Our Praise: An Old Testament Theology of Worship* (Nashville: B&H Academic, 2008).

some were regarded as evil (e.g., Manasseh in 2 Kgs 21:1–9) because they encouraged the worship of other gods. The consistent theme of a king's responsibility to lead in faithful worship is evident in the books of Chronicles as well. Particularly important for the Chronicler was the fact that the celebrations of Passover by both Hezekiah (2 Chr 30) and Josiah (2 Chr 35:1–19) enabled all Israel to worship, in spite of the division between north and south. In Hezekiah's case, intent mattered most (2 Chr 30:13–22), just as intent was crucial to resolving the challenges in Joshua 22. More briefly, Psalm 133 is a wonderful celebration of the blessing found in the unity of God's people.

That worship brings together the diverse people of God, uniting us in spite of our differences, is also a key theme in the New Testament. Worship that does not properly attend to our differences can still cause difficulties, as is evident in the conflict that arose in Acts 6:1–7 or in the background problems to which Paul alludes in 1 Corinthians 11:17–22. But the unifying power of worship is particularly evident for Paul in Ephesians 2:11–22, where the language of Christ as our sanctuary means that worship is where Jew and Gentile come together. Worship that is properly grounded in the character of God, now made known to us in Jesus and through the indwelling of the Spirit, provides a proper means for holding the diverse people of God together. This reality continued to be explored in Christian tradition (e.g., 1 Clem 19:2–3) and is evident in shared worship gatherings today.

This issue of how worship creates unity points also to the more complex issues that are woven into this narrative. Put simply, how do we know who the people of God are so that we can be one? What criteria enable us to know this? Beyond a willingness to worship God in a manner consistent with how he is known from Scripture, there is perhaps no one simple answer. But what can be much more problematic is the ease with which God's people have divided, often on the basis of a misunderstanding rather than any authentic basis for division. Clearly, a desire to worship other gods (such as was effectively introduced by Jeroboam in 1 Kgs 12:25–33) means that we are not countenancing authentic worship. But these are not the difficult cases. Much more complex is the human desire to classify and separate, often on the basis of perceptions.

These complex issues are vital to this chapter and are made clear in the ways in which the western tribes variously took the title of "Israelite" to themselves while excluding the eastern tribes from this identity. The presence of the Jordan, and the relationship of the eastern tribes to the land that God had promised, became a mechanism for effectively excluding the eastern tribes.[403] The eastern tribes' cause was perhaps not helped by the fact that they did not communicate effectively about the reasons for their altar on the Jordan, but the fact that the western tribes went prepared for war makes clear that the issue of the identity of God's people is vital here. In essence, they were prepared to exclude a group that was viewed with suspicion, with the reasons for this only emerging in their accusations (e.g., Josh 22:19). In making their allegations, the western tribes constantly arrogated for themselves the language of "Israelite," subtly indicating that the eastern tribes did not bear this label. Moreover, in suggesting that they might need to settle west of the Jordan, they further indicated the eastern tribes were living outside of God's land and, therefore, outside of God's purposes. In the end, the issue was resolved; neither tribal affiliation nor land could truly divide God's people. But a division came perilously close, even though both sides would have said they were indeed being faithful.

A text like this can thus helpfully inform our response to a passage such as John 17:20–26, in which Jesus offers a prayer for unity among his followers, a prayer that continues to be important for the church today. Jesus prays that through this authentic worshiping community the world would believe the Father had sent the Son, something that also lies behind Paul's concerns in 1 Corinthians 1:10–17. Such unity is often understood in structural terms. But reading Jesus' prayer in light of Joshua 22 suggests that there can be both unity and diversity, provided our diversity exists within the bounds of true worship , which holds us together.[404] Granted the problems of communication that always affect human interaction, this passage challenges us to realize that we tend to divide too easily and express this division through our language. Yet, in affirming the true identity of God (now made known to us in Jesus Christ) and seeing worship as that which unites us, we see that this unity becomes an important way in which Jesus' prayer continues to be worked out among us.

---

[403] As Hawk, *Joshua*, 242, helpfully notes, the western tribes constructed a boundary that God had not.

[404] For Paul in Rom 10:9, this can be expressed in the simple confession that "Jesus is Lord."

B. Joshua's Farewell (23:1–16)

¹ A long time after the Lord had given Israel rest from all the enemies around them, Joshua was old, advanced in age. ² So Joshua summoned all Israel, including its elders, leaders, judges, and officers, and said to them, "I am old, advanced in age, ³ and you have seen for yourselves everything the Lord your God did to all these nations on your account, because it was the Lord your God who was fighting for you. ⁴ See, I have allotted these remaining nations to you as an inheritance for your tribes, including all the nations I have destroyed, from the Jordan westward to the Mediterranean Sea. ⁵ The Lord your God will force them back on your account and drive them out before you so that you can take possession of their land, as the Lord your God promised you.

⁶ "Be very strong and continue obeying all that is written in the book of the law of Moses, so that you do not turn from it to the right or left ⁷ and so that you do not associate with these nations remaining among you. Do not call on the names of their gods or make an oath to them; do not serve them or bow in worship to them. ⁸ Instead, be loyal to the Lord your God, as you have been to this day.

⁹ "The Lord has driven out great and powerful nations before you, and no one is able to stand against you to this day. ¹⁰ One of you routed a thousand because the Lord your God was fighting for you, as he promised. ¹¹ So diligently watch yourselves! Love the Lord your God! ¹² If you ever turn away and become loyal to the rest of these nations remaining among you, and if you intermarry or associate with them and they with you, ¹³ know for certain that the Lord your God will not continue to drive these nations out before you. They will become a snare and a trap for you, a sharp stick for your sides and thorns in your eyes, until you disappear from this good land the Lord your God has given you.

¹⁴ "I am now going the way of the whole earth, and you know with all your heart and all your soul that none of the good promises the Lord your God made to you has failed. Everything was fulfilled for you; not one promise has failed. ¹⁵ Since every good thing the Lord your God promised you has come about, so he will bring on you every bad thing until he has annihilated you from this good land the Lord your God has given you. ¹⁶ If you break the covenant of the Lord your God, which he commanded you, and go and serve other gods, and bow in worship to them, the Lord's anger will burn against you, and you will quickly disappear from this good land he has given you."

Context

In this chapter we come to the second of Joshua's three farewell speeches (see context discussion on Joshua 22:1–34). As with the previous speech, this one reflects the concerns of the narrator's summary in 21:43–45, interacting with the themes of rest (נוח, see also 22:4) and the reliability of God's promises.[405] The speech in 22:1–8 did not indicate any particular challenge that Israel faced, but that is largely because the rest of the chapter explored the hazards posed to the nation when worship was not authentic and they failed to recognize their unity. The dangers presented by life in the land were essentially internal to Israel.

In this speech, the dangers came from outside the people of Israel but from within the land because of the nations who continued to live among Israel. This reflects the important theme of the partial nature of Israel's occupation of the land to this point. As with the summary in 21:43–45, Joshua's speech here asserts that God had indeed faithfully fulfilled all his promises about the land and that Israel still had much of the land to claim. These two perspectives consistently sit side by side throughout Joshua. Reference to Joshua's age reinforces this point since it directs readers back to 13:1–7, where the need to claim the rest of the land was stressed precisely because Israel had only partially taken the land. Although it had been allotted in the intervening chapters, it had still not been taken. There was sufficient rest for the eastern tribes to have returned to their territory because God was the one who was giving the western tribes the balance of the land, even if it still had to be taken.

As with Joshua's speech in 22:1–8, the form of this speech is heavily influenced by language and themes from Deuteronomy,[406] which are applied to develop a theological commentary on Joshua.[407] This is important to note in light of the issues dealt with in the previous chapter. The balance of that narrative had shown how Israel nearly self-destructed through the western tribes' effective denial that the eastern tribes were truly Israel, an issue that was particularly complex for Manasseh as a tribe on both sides of the Jordan (22:7). Through Joshua 22, the question of who truly constituted Israel gradually emerged in importance. Thus, when Joshua addressed "all Israel" (23:2), we now know he meant both the eastern and western tribes, and also that absolute loyalty to God was required wherever the Israelites lived.

Internal disunity, expressed in inappropriate worship, was no longer the issue. Instead, a new threat was identified, which was simultaneously internal and external, though worship remained central. The problem was

---

[405] See further §7 ("Rest") and §8 ("The Promise of God").

[406] Note the table of terms from Deuteronomy in Butler, *Joshua 13–24*, 269–71.

[407] Similarly Earl, *Reading Joshua as Christian Scripture*, 183.

internal because the partial occupation meant that the various peoples of the land continued to live among them. But the problem was also external because these peoples stood outside the people of Israel. Immediately, therefore, we need to appreciate the difference between those like Rahab and her family, or the Gibeonites, who had integrated into Israel and were thus fully internal. The concern here is rather with those, such as the initial occupants of the territory assigned to Dan, who continued living within Israel (19:47). Peoples can be geographically internal but theologically external.[408]

This fact creates an important additional link to the previous chapter, because there the western tribes had suggested that the possession of the eastern tribes could be "defiled" (22:19) since it was not within the promised boundaries. But now it becomes clear that the problem could not be tied to a specific location. The language of defilement is not used in this speech,[409] but the focus on the need for absolute loyalty to God (23:8) and the possibility of kindling divine wrath against the nation (23:16) reflect this concern. Indeed, that the faithfulness of God to his promises now becomes a threat rather than a word of encouragement is crucial to the speech. By highlighting this, Joshua showed the whole nation that they placed themselves in the position of the Canaanite population if they did not continue to hold to God alone and worship him. If the whole nation had received God's rest (21:43–45) and could not be divided (Josh 22), then the whole nation needed to remain in a state of committed faithfulness.

The form in which this faithfulness was to be expressed was by keeping covenant (23:16). The danger of breaking the covenant relationship between God and Israel provides a link to the Achan story (7:11, 15), the only other point in the book where covenant was broken.[410] Such a parallel is particularly important given the prominence of allusions to Achan in the previous chapter. At the same time, this reference forms a bridge

---

[408] See further §2 ("Identity of the People of God"). This possibility is recognized in a slightly different form in Deuteronomy 13.

[409] Apart from the passing references in Deut 21:23 and 24:4, it is not a theme that occurs in Deuteronomy.

[410] In both Joshua 7 and 23, the verb used is עבר rather than the more common verb used to describe covenant breach, פרר.

to 24:25 when Joshua made a covenant with the people at Shechem.[411] Combined with allusions to chapter 1 in the introduction to the speech, this chapter thus asks us to reread the preceding parts of the book while preparing us for key themes to emerge in Joshua 24.

Exegesis

23:1–2a. Although the opening of chapter 22 is tied fairly closely in time to the preceding events, the opening of this chapter is chronologically looser. The elapsed time is not stated specifically, but enough time had passed for the tribes to have at least begun the process of settling in their allotted portions. Reference to God having "given Israel rest" refers back to 21:44; therefore, verse 1 simply indicates that a considerable period had elapsed between then and when Joshua spoke here. More important for this chapter, this opening picks up the earlier note that the rest God had given was from their surrounding enemies—that is, those external to Israel.[412] But a consistent theme of the land allocation was that other groups continued to live *within* Israel. It is the issues posed by these peoples on which Joshua focused his speech.

Though an appropriate observation prior to this speech, the note about Joshua's advanced age repeats the opening words of 13:1. Since 13:1 and the comments about God granting rest to Israel in 21:43–45 provide the boundaries for the whole land allocation (Josh 13–21), this introduction in Joshua 23 points readers back to the land allocation as the context for what follows.

The four groups of leaders summoned in verse 2 are also summoned in 24:1, providing a further link with that chapter. The exact distinction between these groups is not always clear,[413] and depending on the role

---

[411] These links suggest that Joshua 22–24 is a carefully composed unity; therefore, there is no need to relegate Joshua 24 to a later redaction—as suggested, for example, by Richard D. Nelson, *The Double Redaction of the Deuteronomistic History* (Sheffield: JSOT Press, 1981), 94–98. Therefore, although this chapter probably has a redactional history of its own, there is no need to pursue this in terms of the putative Deuteronomistic History (though for a positive assessment of this option, see Joachim J. Krause, "The Book of the Torah in Joshua 1 and 23 and in the Deuteronomistic History," *ZAW* 127 [2015]: 412–28, and the literature cited there).

[412] Indeed, Creach, *Joshua*, 115, suggests that an advantage of the loose chronology is that it highlights the theme of rest.

[413] For probable interpretation, see Philip S. Johnston, "Civil Leadership in Deuteronomy," in *Interpreting Deuteronomy: Issues and Approaches*, ed. David G. Firth and Philip S. Johnston (Nottingham: Apollos, 2012), 137–56.

being fulfilled at a given point in time different labels might well be applied. "Elders" were generally older people within a clan, and "judges" decided legal cases (though without a formal court structure, so judges could also be elders). "Leaders" and "officers" are less clear, as both could be civil or military roles depending on circumstances. Rather than attempting to identify these groups, we are probably better off recognizing the terms as a means of indicating that the summons was given to as broad a cross-section of Israel's leadership as possible.

More importantly, we should note that three of them (elders, officers, and judges) were also present in the covenant ceremony recorded in 8:33. In light of the prominence given to covenant at the close of Joshua's speech, the inference is that these people needed to come because they were present for the previous ceremony. But we should also note that it had been the officers of the eastern tribes who had organized those tribes to cross over ahead of the western tribes (1:10), and their inclusion here provides a small link back to that chapter too—and through that to Joshua 22. This careful arrangement of links to the rest of the book means we read this chapter in light of the whole, ensuring that it provides the context for interpreting it.

23:2b–3. The link with 13:1 is strengthened by the opening to Joshua's speech. There, once the narrator points out Joshua's age, God repeats his age as the opening of his speech. In 23:2, Joshua himself repeats the point made by the narrator, emphasizing the importance of his advanced years. But by switching to what God had done, Joshua turns the focus away from himself to God, because this was something the leaders could see from their own experience.

Indeed, Joshua highlights this point through an emphatic use of the pronoun "you" in verse 3. Since the verb "you have seen" (רְאִיתֶם) is marked to indicate a second-person subject, the Hebrew pronoun is unnecessary. Nevertheless, it can be included for emphasis. "You yourselves have seen" is slightly clumsy English, but it brings out the point that these leaders had personally experienced what God had done. This is important, because the verb "see" (ראה) could mean that they understood this reality (as is also true of the verb "see" in English), but Joshua wanted to stress that this was something they knew because they saw it happen.

They did not take the land because they were stronger than the nations they defeated. Their experiences at Jericho (Josh 6) and in the southern and northern campaigns (Josh 10–11) demonstrated that they had faced more powerful military forces. But God had fought for them. The initial defeat at Ai (7:2–5) had shown how powerless Israel was when God did not fight. The clearest parallel to this affirmation in verse 3 is found in 10:14, a point at which God's fighting for Israel was particularly stressed. But in verse 3, that reality is extended to the whole of Israel's entry into the land. All the peoples within it had been defeated because God had fought for Israel. This insight is vital to remind the leaders not to think their own might had brought them rest. It was the work of God, and this in turn provides the foundation for the rest of this speech, most notably in verse 10. This theme will also be of particular importance for Joshua's speech in the next chapter (24:8–11).

23:4–5. Because God had fought for Israel, Joshua was able to allot the inheritance to each of the tribes, which included the nations who remained in the land. Joshua's speech picks up the key verb "see" (ראה) from the previous verse. The usage in verse 3 pointed to what Israel had seen, but in verse 4 it is an imperative that directs them to see (and so understand) what Joshua had done in allotting the tribal inheritance.

Other nations continued to live within the inheritance, something generally true for the western tribes. This too draws on themes from earlier in the book, covering groups like the Rahab clan (Josh 6), the Gibeonites (Josh 9), or Canaanite groups (15:63; 16:3, 10; 17:12–13; 19:47). It should also be noted that the allotment to the tribes in the far north covers territory where Israel had not, to any significant extent, gone. Therefore, we would expect other peoples to be there too.

What is striking is that Joshua said he had allotted these nations to Israel as their inheritance, so the focus is not so much on the land that they occupied as on the people within the land who were to form Israel's inheritance. This inheritance also included the nations that God had destroyed (כרת, not חֵרֶם) in the region between the Jordan and the Mediterranean. The verb in verse 4 does not mean that they were necessarily completely destroyed; thus again the focus was on the continued existence of these nations. Yet this was not to be a problem for Israel, since God would force them out before his people.[414] The point is that just as God had previously acted to give the land, so he would continue to act and the presence of the nations should not trouble Israel. As a general statement, it does not attend to the exceptions (such as Rahab

---

[414] The verb "force back" (הדף) is unique in the book.

or the Gibeonites) whose existence within Israel was assured, but rather focuses on the nations who would continue to oppose Israel. Nevertheless, Joshua could still assure the people that God would be faithful to his promises. Just as he had kept his promise to give the territory west of the Jordan (1:2–5), so also would he be faithful to his promise that Israel would possess the balance of the land.

23:6–8. Given that God would remain faithful to his promises, how should Israel act? It was to this that Joshua turned, and in so doing drew on the words of encouragement that he had himself received in 1:6–9. In that passage, God commanded Joshua to be strong (חזק) three times (a theme picked up again by the eastern tribes in v. 18). Furthermore, when confronting the southern coalition, Joshua commanded the people to be strong (10:25). Within the book, therefore, such commands provide an important frame in which Joshua's experience is mirrored by that of the nation. Moreover, the narrative to this point has shown that not only Joshua, but also the nation as a whole, could rely on God to fulfill his promises, providing a reason for continued faithfulness to him.

The strength required was not, however, military. Rather, it was the strength needed to continue to do all that was commanded in the law (תּוֹרָה) of Moses, again matching what God had told Joshua in 1:6–9. As in that passage, the "law" in 23:6 is principally Deuteronomy. This is clear given the extent to which the language of this chapter echoes Deuteronomy, though that would not discount other parts of the law (especially in light of the importance of Numbers for Joshua 13–21).

Although faithfulness to the law could be thought of in positive terms (things Israel might do), verses 6b–7 define this in terms of what Israel must not do. As the CSB shows, these prohibitions change their form through verse 7. The prohibitions in verses 6b–7a are structured in the same way using the negative לְבִלְתִּי plus an infinitive: respectively, סוּר ("to turn aside") and בּוֹא ("to go in"). The CSB's "to associate with" for the latter is perhaps too general; inappropriate mingling is meant here. These represent the key goals in being faithful to what is written in the law.

The balance of verse 7 includes four prohibitions with the negative לֹא plus an imperfect verb. These are enduring prohibitions, but their key purpose is to indicate what turning aside from the law and mingling with the nations might entail. Each addresses a breach of the first two commandments (Exod 20:3–6; Deut 5:7–10), and indicates that the concern about the nations is fundamentally focused on the issue of worship.

Anything that led Israel to worship other gods (whether by invoking their name and swearing by them, or through some formal expression of worship) was to be avoided.

Verse 8 then expresses the same reality positively. If other gods were to be avoided, then the only appropriate task for Israel was to live in loyalty to God. In spite of Israel's failures recounted in the book, they could still be said to have lived faithfully so far, an assessment based on overall trajectory. Joshua's call to loyalty echoes his earlier directive to the eastern tribes (Josh 22:5), and in turn draws on similar calls for loyalty in Deuteronomy (Deut 10:20; 11:22; 30:20). Joshua, like Moses, called for loyalty, a further step toward him receiving the title "the LORD's servant" (Josh 24:29).[415]

23:9–13. Having outlined the basic shape of loyalty to God, Joshua turns to consider how God had been loyal to Israel and why they should continue to express loyalty to him. This call pivots on the phrase "to this day." In verse 8 it points to how Israel had lived, whereas in verse 9 it looks to how God has acted for them during the same period. Although Israel had clearly fought battles, the repeated emphasis of the book is that God had fought for Israel; therefore, he was the one who had driven out the stronger and mightier nations before them. Because of this, no one had been able to resist them, fulfilling his promise to Joshua (1:5).

The result in verse 10, with one Israelite routing a thousand (i.e., a large military unit), echoes the Song of Moses (Deut 32:30), in which Moses wonders how one could put a thousand to flight unless it was God who fought. For Joshua, this was not simply a rhetorical flourish but something grounded in God's promise (Josh 1:3–5), which had been worked out in the rest of the book and, thus, experienced by his audience.

The implication is then spelled out in verses 11–13. Israel was to love God, fulfilling the call of Deuteronomy (Deut 6:4–5; 10:12; 11:1, 13, 22). Loving God required not becoming involved with the nations among them; therefore, it was primarily an action of covenant fidelity rather than an emotion. Again, this needs to be understood with care. The book as a whole has shown that people who committed themselves to God posed no problem to Israel, and verses 7–8 have already indicated that the key concern was with the worship of other gods. So, to express loyalty to

---

[415] Krause, "The Book of the Torah," 416, rightly notes that Joshua's speech is effectively a small-scale example of Moses' in Deuteronomy.

these nations would be to turn away from God—summarized in verse 12 by intermarriage and undefined intermingling.[416] Clearly, the result would be Israel losing their identity as the people of God.

If this happened, Israel could be certain that God would not continue to drive out the nations before them. Their ability to enjoy the gift of the land was dependent on their loyalty to him. Should they cease to be loyal, God would not drive out the nations, which would become a snare, trapping Israel into their way of life and bringing pain to them.[417] The pain would not merely be that experienced by a trapped animal but would result in Israel being destroyed from the land, effectively making them Canaanites. This destruction echoes the curses of Deuteronomy 28:20–22, making clear that Israel's possession of the land[418] was dependent on their commitment to God.

23:14–16. Joshua next looks forward to his coming death, using his own mortality to persuade the nation to continue in its loyalty to God. Joshua's phrasing, "going the way of the whole earth," has become proverbial in English, but this is the only time it occurs in the Old Testament,[419] though its meaning is clear from context. Israel knew from its own experience that God had been absolutely faithful, keeping all his promises. This statement immediately echoes the comment in 21:45 (see commentary there) about God's faithfulness to his promises. That affirmation reflected on events thus far, but Joshua's statement now includes God's continued faithfulness through the events of chapter 22. Giving the land had demonstrated God's faithfulness, and now it could be seen that his faithfulness included protecting the nation from its own inclinations to violence and division. Israel knew they could easily fall into patterns of rebellion, but God's faithfulness meant this did not lead to its logical conclusion.

---

[416] As in v. 7, the CSB again renders בוא as "associate with." But the parallel with "intermarry" suggests a stronger form of relationship, especially when we note that the verb is often used as a euphemism for sexual intercourse.

[417] Exactly what is meant by some of the terms (e.g., שׁטט occurs nowhere else, though [with Fritz, *Josua*, 228] it may be a textual corruption from שׁטים) here is uncertain, but the general tenor of the passage is as rendered by the CSB.

[418] Although both ארץ and אדמה are often used interchangeably in the Old Testament to refer to the land, in Joshua אדמה occurs only here and v. 15. In contrast, אדמה occurs thirty-nine times in Deuteronomy. It is difficult to draw clear conclusions from this distribution, but perhaps we are to understand the references here as to the land as a sustaining environment, whereas the more common ארץ (171 times in Deuteronomy; 91 times in Joshua) refers to the geography more broadly.

[419] First Kings 2:2 is similar in English, but the Hebrew is slightly different.

But if God's good promises were fulfilled, then Israel could be assured that his promised judgments for unfaithfulness would come about as well (v. 15). All of God's promises are certain and are dependent upon the relationship of his people to him. To become indistinguishable from the nations among whom they dwelled, especially when their distinctiveness was their faith, would be for Israel to incur the curses promised in Deuteronomy 28:15–68.

Israel's religious distinctiveness is highlighted in verse 16, when Joshua points to the worship of other gods as the means by which they might break their covenant with God. Within their covenant relationship, such actions have promised outcomes. The example of Achan (7:11) showed that the covenant could be broken in more subtle ways, but the issues remained the same. Israel was reminded, therefore, that the land belonged to God—not to them. Therefore, their continued enjoyment of it was tied to their continued loyalty to him. They would not always have someone like Joshua to lead them. Israel needed to remember that, as important as human leaders are (and we should not lose sight of the fact that Joshua was addressing Israel's leaders), their relationship with God would ultimately shape their future.

Bridge

Most Christians are familiar with the importance of the promises of God. They have played an important part in our formation as believers and can be expressed in the familiar hymn:

> Every promise in the Book is mine,
> Every chapter, every verse, every line.
> All are blessings of His love divine,
> Every promise in the Book is mine.

Yet as comforting as such expressions might be, they are not actually true to the Bible, and in particular to what Joshua said here. The natural tendency behind such thinking is that every promise from God is one of blessing. But, as this chapter has emphasized, the faithfulness of God to his promises means we cannot treat them simply as points of reassurance. Most assuredly, not every promise of God is one of blessing, even if God's intent is to lead his people to experience blessing (Gen 12:1–3). Joshua's warning makes this particularly clear. God is indeed faithful to his promises, but those promises included judgment if Israel failed to maintain their distinctiveness as the people of God and instead became indistinguishable from the peoples who lived among them. These are not promises that anyone wants to claim.

Understanding the consistency of God's character is central to this. God had indeed promised Israel the land, and none of his promises had failed. Israel's sin, as at Ai, had created barriers to this, but it did not stop God from keeping his promises. Thus, Israel now enjoyed rest, albeit a rest that needed to be extended into subsequent generations. But the promises of God are contingent upon the loyalty of his people. Israel was part of his mission to restore creation to himself, and his blessings served this. If they claimed the name of God but were otherwise indistinguishable from others, they were not serving his mission and stood under the promise of punishment.

God's faithfulness means both elements of his promise must always be true—a path of blessing where his people are loyal and a path of punishment where they are not. Joshua's urgent aim was to encourage the nation to follow the path of blessing after his death by remaining true to God and his word.[420] But in doing so, he did not flinch from highlighting the alternative precisely because the evidence of God's faithfulness meant he would not leave unfaithfulness unpunished. Those who read this chapter in the exile would certainly have understood the truth of this, and the book of Kings also highlights how this truth became a reality in the fall of the northern kingdom (2 Kgs 17:7–23).

But is this not simply an Old Testament theme? Not if we take Jesus seriously, because he too emphasized the importance of his people retaining their distinctiveness if the promise of blessing was to become a reality.[421] His comments on salt which loses its savor (Matt 5:13) show that he wanted his disciples to continue living in a way that was distinctive and pointed to him. As he developed that theme, he summoned believers to let their good works be seen so that all may glorify the Father. The distinctiveness of the Christian community is thus specifically centered on that which glorifies God, and arguably this is central to Joshua's warnings too.

---

[420] Similarly, Matthias Ederer, *Das Buch Josua* (Stuttgart: Verlag Katholisches Bibelwerk, 2017), 328.

[421] We will not note the importance of Psalm 95 and Hebrews 4 since these have already been highlighted in reflecting on Joshua 20–21, but the themes noted there continue to be important here.

This theme is especially important in the letters to the churches in Revelation (Rev 2–3) where the seven churches are encouraged to faithfulness expressed in distinctive commitment to him. For each church there are also promises, though those promises might warn of punishment for lack of faithfulness (e.g., Rev 2:5, 16; 3:3). This theme climaxes in the declaration that the Lord punishes those whom he loves (Rev 3:19) and in promises of encouragement for faithfulness (Rev. 2:9, 3:11–12). The future of God's people is always shaped by their loyalty to God in Christ, and it is because of this that Joshua's warnings continue to resonate.

C. Covenant and Conclusion (24:1–33)

[1] Joshua assembled all the tribes of Israel at Shechem and summoned Israel's elders, leaders, judges, and officers, and they presented themselves before God. [2] Joshua said to all the people, "This is what the LORD, the God of Israel, says: 'Long ago your ancestors, including Terah, the father of Abraham and Nahor, lived beyond the Euphrates River and worshiped other gods. [3] But I took your father Abraham from the region beyond the Euphrates River, led him throughout the land of Canaan, and multiplied his descendants. I gave him Isaac, [4] and to Isaac I gave Jacob and Esau. I gave the hill country of Seir to Esau as a possession.

" 'Jacob and his sons, however, went down to Egypt. [5] I sent Moses and Aaron, and I defeated Egypt by what I did within it, and afterward I brought you out. [6] When I brought your ancestors out of Egypt and you reached the Red Sea, the Egyptians pursued your ancestors with chariots and horsemen as far as the sea. [7] Your ancestors cried out to the LORD, so he put darkness between you and the Egyptians, and brought the sea over them, engulfing them. Your own eyes saw what I did to Egypt. After that, you lived in the wilderness a long time.

[8] " 'Later, I brought you to the land of the Amorites who lived beyond the Jordan. They fought against you, but I handed them over to you. You possessed their land, and I annihilated them before you. [9] Balak son of Zippor, king of Moab, set out to fight against Israel. He sent for Balaam son of Beor to curse you, [10] but I would not listen to Balaam. Instead, he repeatedly blessed you, and I rescued you from him.

[11] " 'You then crossed the Jordan and came to Jericho. Jericho's citizens—as well as the Amorites, Perizzites, Canaanites, Hethites, Girgashites, Hivites, and Jebusites—fought against you, but I handed them over to you. [12] I sent hornets ahead of you, and they drove out the two Amorite kings before you. It was not by your sword or bow. [13] I gave you a land you did not labor for, and cities you did not build, though

you live in them; you are eating from vineyards and olive groves you did not plant.'

¹⁴ "Therefore, fear the Lord and worship him in sincerity and truth. Get rid of the gods your ancestors worshiped beyond the Euphrates River and in Egypt, and worship the Lord. ¹⁵ But if it doesn't please you to worship the Lord, choose for yourselves today: Which will you worship—the gods your ancestors worshiped beyond the Euphrates River or the gods of the Amorites in whose land you are living? As for me and my family, we will worship the Lord."

¹⁶ The people replied, "We will certainly not abandon the Lord to worship other gods! ¹⁷ For the Lord our God brought us and our ancestors out of the land of Egypt, out of the place of slavery, and performed these great signs before our eyes. He also protected us all along the way we went and among all the peoples whose lands we traveled through. ¹⁸ The Lord drove out before us all the peoples, including the Amorites who lived in the land. We too will worship the Lord, because he is our God."

¹⁹ But Joshua told the people, "You will not be able to worship the Lord, because he is a holy God. He is a jealous God; he will not forgive your transgressions and sins. ²⁰ If you abandon the Lord and worship foreign gods, he will turn against you, harm you, and completely destroy you, after he has been good to you."

²¹ "No!" the people answered Joshua. "We will worship the Lord."

²² Joshua then told the people, "You are witnesses against yourselves that you yourselves have chosen to worship the Lord."

"We are witnesses," they said.

²³ "Then get rid of the foreign gods that are among you and turn your hearts to the Lord, the God of Israel."

²⁴ So the people said to Joshua, "We will worship the Lord our God and obey him."

²⁵ On that day Joshua made a covenant for the people at Shechem and established a statute and ordinance for them. ²⁶ Joshua recorded these things in the book of the law of God; he also took a large stone and set it up there under the oak at the sanctuary of the Lord. ²⁷ And Joshua said to all the people, "You see this stone—it will be a witness against us, for it has heard all the words the Lord said to us, and it will be a witness against you, so that you will not deny your God." ²⁸ Then Joshua sent the people away, each to his own inheritance.

²⁹ After these things, the Lord's servant, Joshua son of Nun, died at the age of 110. ³⁰ They buried him in his allotted territory at Timnath-serah, in the hill country of Ephraim north of Mount Gaash. ³¹ Israel worshiped the Lord throughout Joshua's lifetime and during the lifetimes of the elders who outlived Joshua and who had experienced all the works the Lord had done for Israel.

³² Joseph's bones, which the Israelites had brought up from Egypt, were buried at Shechem in the parcel of land Jacob had purchased from

the sons of Hamor, Shechem's father, for a hundred pieces of silver. It was an inheritance for Joseph's descendants.

³³ And Eleazar son of Aaron died, and they buried him at Gibeah, which had been given to his son Phinehas in the hill country of Ephraim.

Context

Readers will note a significant overlap between this chapter and the preceding one as both present speeches from Joshua to the people encouraging faithfulness to God. The degree of overlap has led to extensive discussion as to which was the original ending of the book, the assumption being that to have both is unnecessary.[422] However, although the material that makes up these chapters could reasonably have come from different sources,[423] the more important task is to focus on how they work together in the book that we have, since there is no evidence that Joshua ever existed without both chapters 23 and 24.

As noted (see context discussions for Josh 22 and 23), the end of the book is built around three speeches from Joshua, each longer than the one before. In addition, although each speech is an exhortation to faithful obedience to God, each develops this in a different way and for a different audience. These variations are crucial for us to understand the function of this chapter as it brings the book to a close. Joshua's challenge to his audience to commit themselves to God becomes a continuing challenge for each new generation to do the same.

The repetitions across the chapters are not necessarily a problem for an ancient audience, for whom repetition was an important means of emphasis. But the distinctive audience for each address should be noted:

---

[422] See Thomas Römer, "Das doppelte Ende des Josuabuches: einige Anmerkungen zur aktuellen Diskussion um, 'deuteronomistisches Geschichtswerk' und 'Hexateuch,' " *ZAW* 118 (2006): 523–48; and Krause, "The Book of the Torah."

[423] Note, e.g., the analysis of S. David Sperling, "Joshua 24 Re-Examined," *HUCA* 58 (1987): 119–36, who argues for the independence of this chapter at a source-critical level and that this source is no later than the eighth century BC. Although there is much value to this (though perhaps with a slightly earlier dating), our concern is with how this works in the finished text. For a more comprehensive summary of the various critical analyses of this chapter, see William T. Koopmans, *Joshua 24 as Poetic Narrative* (Sheffield: Sheffield Academic, 1990), 1–164.

Speech	Audience	Site
22:1–8	eastern tribes	Shiloh
23:1–16	national leaders	Shiloh (?)
24:1–28	all tribes	Shechem

As can be seen, although each of Joshua's farewell addresses is a call
to faithfulness, the audience is expanded each time. This development
makes the final speech a suitable conclusion because of its inclusive
nature.[424] Although the two earlier speeches were clearly addressed to a
significant part of the nation (in chapter 23 the point of addressing the
leaders was to convey the message to the nation), the note that Joshua
"assembled all the tribes of Israel at Shechem" (24:1)[425] is a conscious
extension of the message of the previous chapter.

The change of location is also important, though care on this point is
needed. Shiloh was clearly the location for Joshua's speech to the eastern
tribes (22:9), but the site for his speech in Joshua 23 can only be implied
given that the events from 18:1 occurred at Shiloh. However, the site for
chapter 24 is clearly Shechem, about eight miles north of Shiloh. The
latter location had been important because it was the site of the sanctuary, but in light of the tensions exposed in Joshua 22 over the altar, a
different site made sense for a gathering of all the tribes so that there
was no sense of favoring the western tribes.

Within the book, Shechem itself has played a relatively minor role,
being noted as a Levitical city (and city of refuge) in Manasseh's allotment (17:7; 20:7; 21:21).[426] However, though it is not named there, the
covenant ceremony described in 8:30–35 was clearly near Shechem (see
context discussion for those verses). That covenant ceremony was notable
for its inclusive nature, and the themes of covenant and the inclusive
nature of God's people are likewise important here. Thus, within the
narrative structure of the book, the move to Shechem for this chapter
is an important signal concerning the events about to unfold and links

---

[424] The language here is somewhat elevated, and even if this cannot be classified as
poetic, as Koopmans, *Joshua 24*, 165–80, has argued, the affect within a rhetorical close to
the book is noteworthy.

[425] The LXX reads "Shiloh" (also v. 25), but this is surely a secondary conforming of this
text to 18:1.

[426] The clan of Shechem was also noted in 17:2.

the covenant established in Joshua 24 (a covenant to be faithful to God) to the covenant ceremony commanded in Deuteronomy 27 and carried out in Joshua 8:30–35.

That a sanctuary is noted as being at Shechem (24:26) also points to the suitability of the site for the ceremony at the climax of Joshua's speech, though the fact that the sanctuary was marked by an oak tree may also indicate this as an example of Israel repurposing a Canaanite site.[427] If so, this is a subtle extension of the model of inclusion that has developed through the book. It should be noted that although a covenant is established here, and that at points Joshua's speech reflects characteristic elements of ancient covenant texts,[428] this chapter is not a record of the covenant itself but rather of its establishment.[429]

Although it is possible to overstress this element, there are also important differences in emphasis in each speech. All three are a summons to faithfulness, but the form of that faithfulness is explored differently in each chapter.[430] In chapter 22 the speech itself does not address the nature of faithfulness in any detail, but by reporting it in the context of the dispute about the altar it becomes clear that the chapter addresses the issue of *where* the people of God were. The answer that emerged is that God's people are not restricted geographically to the regions originally promised.

In chapter 23 the principal issue was *how* Israel was to be faithful to God. The answer was by maintaining their religious distinctiveness and not becoming like the nations who remained with them. In both cases, the threat to Israel was largely internal. In Joshua 22 it was Israel's own

---

[427] McConville and Williams, *Joshua*, 89, thus believe this is an important site for reflecting on the whole of Israel's relationship with Yahweh.

[428] Most notably its recital of covenant history, though note also the leaving of the covenant text at the sanctuary. On this pattern, see Delbert R. Hillers, *Covenant: The History of a Biblical Idea* (Baltimore: Johns Hopkins University Press, 1967), 47.

[429] With Earl, *Reading Joshua*, 193, we need to move beyond attempts to trace back a distinctive historical creed here without reference to Sinai, and see instead that even this element is shaped by Joshua's rhetorical concerns. These, rather like Paul in Romans 4, need to go back to the inclusive nature of the Abrahamic material rather than the more particular focus of the Sinai material.

[430] For example, Mitchell, *Together in the Land*, 115, notes that the two earlier speeches had introduced the concept of illegitimate worship, but its decisive development occurs here.

sense of identity that was problematic, while in Joshua 23 the problem was the continued existence of the nations that had not been expelled.[431]

Both of these issues continue in Joshua 24, but the problem is now internalized to the threat faced by all Israel—the possibility that they might be drawn to worship other gods, forgetting what Yahweh had done for them. This is why Joshua's challenge is not only that they worship Yahweh alone but that they do so "in sincerity and truth" (24:14). The central question here is *who* is to be worshiped.[432] The answer is that God alone is to be served, and that cannot simply be a matter of form. Rather, it must arise out of a genuine commitment to God.

In noting these issues, we should also note that the book does not end with this covenant ceremony but rather with the deaths of Joshua and Eleazar, along with the interment of Joseph's bones. Although this might seem anticlimactic for modern readers, the report of these deaths provides an important point of closure to the book and also places its story within the larger narrative of what God has done (and so matches Joshua's own speech in vv. 2–13). Joshua's death at the end points back to the report of Moses' death at the beginning of the book (1:1), while Eleazar's death takes us back to Aaron's death (Num 20:22–29). Placing these on either side of Joseph's interment links the book back to Genesis 50:22–26, and reminds us that the story of Joshua stands within the grand narrative of redemption that has been recounted since Genesis. In addition, the deaths of Joshua and Eleazar prepare us for a new story, though how that will work out is the subject of the book of Judges.

Exegesis

24:1. There are no obvious chronological links among any of Joshua's farewell speeches; therefore, exactly when Joshua summoned the tribes of Israel to Shechem is unclear. If the events of chapter 24 occurred after those of chapter 23 (and it is not necessary that they did because the material could be presented thematically), then the gap between them could not have been great because of Joshua's age. However, the narrative

---

[431] It is worth noting that although these nations continued, now that God had given rest there was no scope for the application of חרם (total destruction), even though the prohibition on intermarriage clearly references the law of חרם from Deuteronomy 7. Again, this makes clear that this was a time- and context-limited law.

[432] See also Nelson, *Joshua*, 268; Hawk, *Joshua in 3-D*, 239.

is not especially concerned with establishing a chronology internal to the book beyond the broad point that Joshua is now an old man.

The important development in chapter 24 is that Joshua assembled all the tribes of Israel. Naturally, this would include the eastern tribes, the western tribes, and the leaders summoned in chapter 23. By noting those assembled, the narrator makes clear that the issues of the two previous speeches are brought together here, linking this chapter to the preceding two. We also face the possibility that some of the peoples still in the land were included in this assembly. Although this is only implicit in verse 1, the probability of this increases when we note the ways in which Joshua deliberately merges the generations in his recount of Israel's history (24:2-13), so that a people who were clearly not present at certain key points in the past are spoken of as if they were.

The people were not simply assembled before Joshua—they presented themselves before God (אֱלֹהִים). Although this term for God occurs sixty-five times in Joshua (forty-nine so far), to this point only in 9:23 and 14:6 is it not made immediately clear that this is a reference to Yahweh, and these two passages are only apparent exceptions because the larger context makes clear that Yahweh is the one meant. But this chapter changes that significantly. Though the reader knows that Yahweh is intended, the verse does not have to imply that those gathering did. Indeed, a central theme that runs through the whole of the covenant ceremony is the need to identify Yahweh as God—as opposed to the gods worshiped by some in the assembly or by their ancestors. The worship of other gods has not been a theme in the book thus far, though it will be in Judges. But it comes to special prominence here, and the presentation of the tribes before God is a subtle preparation for this.

24:2-4. Since Joshua was building toward an appeal to serve Yahweh alone in the new setting of life in the land, it was necessary to provide evidence to support this appeal. Thus, he provided a review of covenant history. As noted, a key rhetorical feature of this is that Joshua blurred the gap between the present and the past, placing his audience in situations in the past.[433] This is not confusion on his part but rather a deliberate rhetorical move that shows his audience (and all who read this chapter)

---

[433] This is not unique to this passage. See, e.g., Deut 5:3. But the crucial point is always to attend to the rhetorical force of such an approach in its own particular setting.

that they are included in God's acts in the past through their commitment to him.[434]

The broader scope of Joshua's address is also highlighted by the fact that he is said to have spoken to all the people and not just the leaders. Although it has not been a significant part of his presentation previously (cf. 3:9), Joshua is presented as a prophet, employing the messenger formula in which he indicates that the words he speaks are not his own but rather the words of Yahweh, "the God of Israel."[435] This title occurs commonly enough in the Old Testament (ninety-nine times), but its importance here becomes apparent as Joshua's speech progresses. Those who make up Israel will be those committed to this God and no other.

The balance of these verses focuses on Israel's ancestors recounted in Genesis. These events were already in the distant past for Joshua's audience, but they still formed a crucial part of their own story. Furthermore, they took place outside of the promised land, an important point in light of the conflict over this issue in Joshua 22, something highlighted by the sentence order in Hebrew, which points to this first. The "river" in verse 3 is not defined, and one might first think of this as the Jordan, but the wider context makes clear that the Euphrates is intended (hence the csb includes this in its translation).

In going back to Terah, the father of Nahor and Abraham, Joshua reached back to Genesis 11:27–32. This is important because these people lived outside of the land before there was a land promise. Making them even more unsuitable was the fact that they served other gods. In spite of this, God had taken Abraham from that region and brought him through the land of Canaan (Gen 12:1–9). The nature of Abraham's religion at this point is unclear, though throughout Genesis 12–50 patriarchal religion clearly cannot be equated with Israel's later practice even though they were worshiping Yahweh.[436] However, the events described in Genesis 12 occurred before the formulation of the covenant with Abraham in Genesis 15 and 17. It is important, therefore, to note that Joshua was not suggesting any merit on Abraham's behalf that would have justified his call. Emphasized instead is that God took the initiative and in so doing

---

[434] Something similar occurs in Samuel's speech in 1 Sam 12:6–15.

[435] As Ederer, *Josua*, 329, emphasizes, this means that the review of history is from God's perspective, thus contrasting with the review in Joshua 23.

[436] See the helpful discussion of R. W. L. Moberly, *The Old Testament of the Old Testament: Patriarchal Narratives and Mosaic Yahwism* (Minneapolis: Fortress, 1992), 79–104.

began a process that would lead to Israel inhabiting the land purely as an act of grace with those who might have otherwise seemed unsuitable.

God's grace was not limited to Abraham's initial call but was extended by his multiplying Abraham's descendants. The term rendered "descendants" (זֶרַע) can also be translated "seed" and is an important term in Genesis. Like the English "seed," it can be both a collective noun and singular, and it is not always possible to bring this out in translation. Concerning this "seed," Abraham challenged God and had his faith reckoned as righteousness (Gen 15:1–6). Abraham had numerous sons (cf. Gen 25:1–6), but only one could be truly counted as the "seed" through whom God's promises were to find their fulfillment: Isaac. Isaac receives comparatively little attention in Genesis, and the same is true here as Joshua moves on to his two sons, Esau and Jacob. A common feature of the patriarchal narratives is that the elder son was passed over for the younger, and this was true in the case of Isaac's sons. Esau's receipt of Edom (the hill country of Seir) is noted so that Joshua can follow the main contour of the biblical narrative as Jacob and his sons traveled down to Egypt (Gen 37–50). By the end of the patriarchal story, the people were once again outside the land.

24:5–7. With Israel in Egypt, Joshua turns to the exodus, with the clear focus on what God had done. Israel was never strong enough to defeat Egypt; therefore, God sent Moses, struck Egypt with plagues, and brought his people out in the exodus. Notably, Joshua merges the generations. Rather than claiming that God brought out the previous generation, Joshua says God brought out his current audience. At one level, this is untrue; the exodus generation (save Joshua and Caleb) died in the wilderness. But at a more profound level, this is a fundamental reality, because even though Joshua's audience was not physically present, the continuity of God's people means that they *were* there. Only because of this could they be gathered before Joshua.[437]

Joshua is fully aware of what had happened and switches to their ancestors in describing the exodus in verse 6. The purpose of the shift is as much rhetorical as it is historical. Joshua focuses on the response of the exodus generation as the Egyptians pursued them with chariots

---

[437] This same strategy is employed in the African American spiritual, "Were You There (When They Crucified My Lord)?" According to hymnary.org, it was first published in William Barton's *Old Plantation Hymns* (1899) but was known to predate this.

and horsemen—a force that Israel could not overcome on their own. The presentation shifts from the first person, with God recounting events through Joshua, to the third person, as Joshua describes the response of the earlier generation to emphasize their experience of God. Retelling the events of Exodus 14:19–29 in a highly compressed way, Joshua describes how God brought darkness on the Egyptians and engulfed them by the Sea after the Israelites cried out to him. But because this experience is fundamental to the presence of the people at Shechem, Joshua switches back to his current audience, pointing out that their eyes had seen it all. As before, this is a rhetorically charged move that stresses the continuity of the experience of God's saving acts by his people.

After this deliverance came the wilderness period. For this too, Joshua blurs the generations. Both the judgment and the deliverance experienced in the wilderness were not simply past occurrences; they are the reality of his audience—and of course of every audience that comes to read this text.

24:8–10. Joshua returns to the first person as his prophetic speech continues to recount God's actions for the people. The "you" addressed in verse 8 partially refers to the immediate audience, though not exclusively so. Joshua focuses on the end of Numbers and the victories in the regions east of the Jordan, especially the defeats of Sihon and Og (Num 21:21–35). These victories would lay the foundation for the settlement of the eastern tribes in that area; therefore, Joshua's speech begins moving to include the eastern tribes. He stresses that, although the Amorites attacked Israel, God gave them into their power so that Israel took over their land. It was not Israel but God who destroyed (שמד) these people who opposed them, anticipating the pattern that would be stressed earlier in Joshua.

This pattern was already evident in the crossing of the Sea, but it is stressed more clearly here. Such an attack was something Israel would have recognized, but that is not true in the case of Balaam (Num 22–24), through whom Balak fought against Israel on the plains of Moab. In Numbers, there is no evidence that Israel was aware that Balak had hired Balaam to curse them, nor that God had changed it to a blessing. In this we see a further reflection on Genesis 12:1–3, since the verb "curse" (קלל) also occurs there. The one who cursed would himself be cursed because of God's intention of bringing blessing through Israel. In light of this background, Balaam's curse clearly could not be effective, which was why God was unwilling to hear it. Instead, he changed the circumstances such that Balaam continually blessed Israel (much to Balak's chagrin).

24:11–13. Joshua's merging of communities continues. He says "you" were brought across the Jordan and came to Jericho. Although this was the experience of most of those addressed, the book has made clear that various others had become part of Israel. As those groups (such as the Rahab clan and the Gibeonites) had integrated themselves, they received the blessing that flowed from that integration and so could be said to have been there.

The statement that Jericho fought against Israel has often been taken as indicating a different tradition from that recorded in Joshua 6, in which Israel captured the city miraculously.[438] However, Joshua 6 makes clear that fighting occurred after the walls collapsed. Moreover, a city locked up in readiness for a siege was clearly engaged in battle, even if not yet participating in hand-to-hand combat. Jericho's citizens, along with the seven Canaanite groups, all fought in various ways against Israel. Joshua here effectively summarizes the whole of chapters 6–11 before leading to the central conclusion of his speech: God had given these nations into Israel's control. The means by which God did this is not specified, but the background of chapter 6 has already made this clear.

More difficult to understand is the claim that "hornets" had been sent before Israel. This reference alludes to Exodus 23:28, in which God had promised to send the "hornet" and so drive out the Canaanite population.[439] This has been variously interpreted. The CSB's "hornets" understands this in natural terms, taking the singular noun "hornet" as a collective, and hence that there was some sort of insect plague. This is a perfectly plausible reading, though nothing else in Joshua would confirm this interpretation. It would, however, be consistent with the events of the plague narrative (Joshua has just mentioned the exodus) in Exodus 8–10 in which frogs, flies, gnats, and locusts all terrified the Egyptians.[440]

Alternatively, the "hornet" could be understood as a metaphor for "panic."[441] This approach can be supported by the fact that in Exodus 23:27

---

[438] E.g., Nelson, *Joshua*, 274–75.

[439] This theme is elsewhere taken up in Deut 7:20, but the language in Joshua is closer to that of Exodus, so although Deuteronomy also lies in the background, the Exodus text is the primary source.

[440] Cf. Harstad, *Joshua*, 773. The LXX interprets the text this way.

[441] So Koopmans, *Joshua 24*, 332.

God promised to send terror on the existing population to confuse them and lead them to flee before Israel. Reference to the hornet in the next verse would then be understood as parallel to this and so becomes a metaphor for the terror God would bring on the Canaanites. Although the language is different, this would be consistent with Rahab's confession (Josh 2:10–11). In broad terms, it also lines up with the statement of 11:20 in which God's hardening of the Canaanite hearts would reflect the sort of confusion promised. On balance, this interpretation is marginally more likely since it does not depend on something not otherwise narrated in the book.

A further difficulty is the reference to "the two Amorite kings." Since Joshua is speaking of the period after the entry into the land, this cannot mean Sihon and Og (Num 21:21–35), who were already alluded to in verse 8, even though they would otherwise be the most obvious candidates.[442] In any case, neither of these kings was driven from their land. But since "Amorite" can sometimes stand for all the indigenous population,[443] there is no need to find two kings who were specifically identified this way. Within the narrative flow of the book, we should perhaps consider these two kings to be Adoni-zedek (Josh 10:1) and Jabin (11:1), the kings who had respectively led the southern and northern coalitions against Israel.[444] By defeating them, God had thus driven them from the land.

Although Israel had been present in the various battles of Joshua 10–11, the constant emphasis is that God fought and won, a theme picked up by David when he challenged Goliath (1 Sam 17:47). Having cleared the land, God gave his people a land for which they did not labor, cities they did not build, and agricultural products they had not planted. This listing echoes Deuteronomy 6:10–11, reminding Israel that not only had God won this for them, but he had also promised to do so beforehand. However, Deuteronomy 6 also serves as a warning to Israel in Joshua's day not to forget God. This context provides a useful background for Joshua as he transitions to his next point.

---

[442] Rösel, *Joshua*, 369, claims that the appearance of two kings here is faulty, but that is because he reads them as Sihon and Og. This difficulty is already felt in the LXX, but its reading of "twelve" rather than "two" seems a self-evident correction to the text. See also Diana V. Edelman, "Are the Kings of the Amorites 'Swept Away' in Joshua xxiv.12?," *VT* 41 (1991): 281–82.

[443] Cf. Fritz, *Josua*, 242, though he still regards the reference as a gloss.

[444] See also Koopmans, *Joshua 24*, 256.

24:14–15. Joshua abandons the mode of prophetic speech in which his words and God's are joined and instead challenges Israel to faithfulness. The allusion to Deuteronomy 6:10–11 in the previous verse set this up. In Deuteronomy, Moses had warned the people not to forget God when they were settled in a good land. Israel had now reached that point, so Joshua picks up the themes of the earlier text and calls his listeners to fear God and worship (עבד; perhaps better, "serve") him.

The opening "therefore" (וְעַתָּה) clearly signals the change in focus, indicating that Joshua is drawing conclusions that follow from the review of covenant history. But the implications Joshua draws are not new. Instead, they continue to reflect Deuteronomy 6, specifically 6:13, which insisted that Israel's life in the land be shaped in these terms. Although "fear" can refer to being afraid of something (e.g., Deut 20:1), in worship contexts it is associated with a life lived in conformity with God's will (cf. Deut 10:12, 20). Joshua goes beyond his source in Deuteronomy by stressing that service to God should be rendered in sincerity and truth. A decision to worship God alone must not simply exclude the worship of other gods but also demonstrate a genuine life lived (cf. John 4:23–24).

Joshua's focus on the service of God alone is made clear by his call to remove the gods that their ancestors had served and to worship Yahweh. That Joshua had to direct them to do this indicates that some of them continued to worship these gods, even if they also claimed to worship Yahweh. Two contexts for these gods are imagined—beyond the Euphrates and in Egypt. Reference to the Euphrates picks up the statement in verse 2 about Abraham's family and their worship of other gods, while Egypt refers to the period leading up to the exodus. Since the exodus account makes clear that a "mixed crowd" had come out with Israel (Exod 12:38), we know that not all those present could trace their biological descent back to Abraham. So, for some of the audience, the gods of their ancestors would have been those of Egypt; for others it would have been the gods of Abraham's family.

Regardless, we are probably not to imagine that these were the only gods worshiped by those present. Rather, these options were a way of summing up all the possibilities, suggesting in effect that whatever gods they served were to be put aside (something that could be done physically with idols). Thus, the Gibeonites were not to continue worshiping their old deities as they served at the sanctuary. Likewise, other groups who had been incorporated into Israel were not to think they could serve

Yahweh and their gods. The first commandment (Exod 20:3) applied to all who lived the life made possible by the exodus, irrespective of whether their ancestors had been in Egypt.

This local possibility is made explicit by Joshua as he challenges his audience to choose whom they would serve: either Yahweh or the gods of their ancestors, which in this case included the Amorite deities (cf. Judg 6:10) instead of those of Egypt. Joshua insists that he and his family would worship Yahweh. At one level, Joshua's challenge is more rhetorical than actual. His family had not decided that day to serve Yahweh alone, but this language is used to heighten the urgency of making such a decision.

This urgency also lies behind the alternative he poses, imagining that serving God alone might be displeasing to his hearers. Hebrew tends to express alternatives in absolute terms where English does so in comparatives, so we might render this as an option of preference ("if you would rather not worship Yahweh"). But in this rhetorical context that summons a decision, it is right to keep the stronger language because this is a vital choice, equivalent in its own way to Moses calling his hearers to choose life (Deut 30:19–20). Joshua and his family had set the pattern, and now everyone else had to make a choice. Moreover, it was at Shechem that God had issued the same challenge to Jacob (Gen 35:1–4), making it even more appropriate that Joshua issues his challenge in the same location.

24:16–18. The people's response seems on first reading to be exactly what Joshua had requested. Indeed, they open with the same oath formula (חָלִילָה לָּנוּ) the eastern tribes had used to deny that their altar was intended to promote false worship (22:29). As strongly as possible, they claim they will not forsake Yahweh to worship other gods.

The reason for their answer is expressed in their own brief recounting of covenant history, focusing on the exodus and wilderness wanderings. Like Joshua, they collapse time so that they speak as if they had been present with their forebears when God brought them up from slavery and performed great signs. These signs are not enumerated in such a brief statement but probably include the events of the exodus itself, since the confession then moves to the wilderness wanderings and the entry into the land when God drove out the Amorites (as a representative of the Canaanite peoples). God had guarded them in the wilderness and had driven out the peoples before them.

In all cases, they attribute their ability to stand before Joshua at Shechem to God's mighty deeds. Accordingly, they affirm that they will worship (עבד) Yahweh because he is their God. On the surface, therefore, it seems as if they are responding exactly as Joshua had challenged them to. However, as will be apparent, their declaration (for all its solemnity) is not true to Joshua's summons. As becomes clear in verse 23, the people had not yet acted to remove their foreign gods, a vital part of Joshua's challenge (Josh 24:14). The people had not put their words into practice through the removal of these gods. Worship in sincerity and truth required this practical step.

24:19–20. Unless we note that the people's response failed to include the removal of other gods, we might find Joshua's rejoinder surprising.[445] After all, their words were entirely orthodox, acknowledging God's mighty acts in salvation and committing themselves to worship him. But Joshua recognizes that orthodox words only make sense when aligned with orthodox practice. When we understand his starting point, we can understand why he concludes that they are unable to worship God.

His reason for this—God's holiness—might also seem surprising. Elsewhere in the Old Testament, God's holiness is something to be imitated by his people (Lev 19:1–2), but it also points to the absolute nature of his claim on them. This is because holiness was often a reason for separating God and people, as at Sinai (Exod 19:1–2), or in the fact that the most holy place was separate from the rest of the tabernacle (Lev 16:2). Only once we understand that the holiness of God means his separation from all that is unholy do we appreciate that his holy people must be absolutely committed to him.[446] God's holiness in verse 19 stresses his uniqueness, and this is why a people who wished to serve him and other gods could not succeed.

God's jealousy is also understood positively in passages such as Exodus 34:14, in which it points to the need for his people to commit absolutely to him. Indeed, the context there refers to the entry into the land, so Joshua probably refers back to that text precisely because of the presence of other gods. In Nahum 1:2, God's jealousy is why he acts against

---

[445] In part, this is why Fritz, *Josua*, 246–48, treats vv. 19–24 as a redactional accretion.

[446] See further Robin Routledge, *Old Testament Theology: A Thematic Approach* (Nottingham: Apollos, 2008), 105–6.

his adversaries. Thus, it serves as a word of reassurance for his people but also highlights why it is important to commit absolutely to him.

Joshua's startling conclusion is the announcement that God will not forgive the people's transgressions and sins. This statement echoes God's self-revelation in Exodus 34:7, in which he declares that he forgives iniquity, transgression, and sin, but that he will not clear the guilty. By evoking this text, Joshua is able to address the implicit flaw in the people's claim of loyalty to God. Forgiveness in the Exodus text is not unconditional but presumes a basic loyalty to God. Joshua recognizes that the failure to remove other gods means the people are effectively disqualifying themselves from receiving God's forgiveness. Therefore, this statement reflects the particular circumstances of the people and is not a general statement about God's forgiveness. That is why Joshua proceeds to highlight the danger caused by abandoning God to serve foreign gods (the gods of foreign peoples). Exodus 34:7 implies that God would turn against them and destroy them, even though he had been good to them thus far. Forgiveness is available, but it cannot be presumed upon.

24:21–24. The people respond to Joshua by declaring their intent to worship God. The implication is that they would serve Yahweh alone, though this fact needs to be teased out. The solemnity of this statement is probed as Joshua points out to them that they had become witnesses against themselves of the fact that they were to worship Yahweh alone. The people immediately agree to this.

The language of "witnesses" draws on the image of the law court, but witnesses were also commonly part of covenant ceremonies.[447] There is no need to choose between these elements, as both can be present. By agreeing that they were witnesses to their choice, the people effectively agreed that, if they were ever charged with worshiping foreign gods, they would have to testify as witnesses for the prosecution against themselves for breaking their commitment to God. However, at this point the people had merely given verbal assent to their decision to worship God; they had not removed the foreign gods that Joshua recognized were still present among them. Therefore, he calls them to action.

Joshua's statement in verse 23 is stronger than in verse 14, when he referred to these gods only in terms of historical practice. This time,

---

[447] Although it is neither a courtroom nor a covenant ceremony, one might note the similar use of testimony language in 1 Samuel 12.

he makes clear that such gods (perhaps in the form of household idols) were present at Shechem, which was why their removal was so urgent. Removing them was to be balanced by a realignment of the people's hearts toward Yahweh, "the God of Israel," a title that strongly contrasts to "foreign gods." Israel existed as a people only because of what God had done, and thus the people could worship only him. Although an actual removal of the gods is not narrated, the larger context indicates that the people's declaration to worship and obey "Yahweh our God" makes clear that these gods have been removed. After all, they could not otherwise obey.

24:25–26. Having heard the people's testimony, Joshua established (כרת; lit. "cut," though this is a standard idiom) a covenant with them. Much of the Bible is structured around key covenants (Noah in Gen 9:1–17; Abraham in Gen 15 and 17; Sinai in Exod 19; David in 2 Sam 7:1–17; the new covenant in Jer 31:31–34), but there are a number of other covenants made in the Bible. A "covenant" (בְּרִית) is an agreement of some sort, a means of regulating a relationship. In a case such as this, it was a means for Joshua and the people to commit themselves to each other, a mechanism for stressing the solemnity of this commitment when no other external mechanism existed for enforcing it. In other words, the covenant itself was what regulated this relationship between God and Israel, which is why it could be regarded as a "statute and an ordinance" for Israel (v. 25). It was not part of Israel's law from the Torah on which Joshua was to meditate (Josh 1:8), but it functioned on this pattern.

Leaving it at Shechem, which had a sanctuary, was a means of demonstrating that this covenant was enacted before God, the key witness to it. Although the details of the covenant are not laid out for us, the essence would be that the people were to serve no God but Yahweh and to remove all foreign gods. However, the text of the covenant is not the main concern but rather that Joshua wrote it out in the book of the Torah. It is not impossible that this means he wrote it at the end of the scroll on which he was initially called to meditate. But if so, we need to recognize that what he wrote was in effect an addendum to the Torah and not part of it.[448] Rather, those reading the scroll at the sanctuary would be reminded that a covenant had been established at Shechem to worship Yahweh alone and

---

[448] Against Harstad, *Joshua*, 804.

specifically acted on through the removal of foreign gods. This covenant was thus dependent on Torah and expressed what faithfulness looks like.

In addition, Joshua set up a stone in the sanctuary at Shechem. This signified an important change to the site. It was here that God had appeared to Abraham in what was then a Canaanite sanctuary (Gen 12:6–7; note the reference to the oak in both texts since these were typical markers of Canaanite shrines), but that site had had a change of character as it was now claimed for Yahweh.[449] The significance of the large stone is not initially explained, but the idea is parallel to the stones beside the Jordan (Josh 4:19–24) and the stone altar on nearby Mount Ebal (8:30–35), which attested to the greatness of Yahweh to all the peoples of the earth. Even the negative example of the cairn raised over Achan (7:26) functions toward this goal. This stone was thus not only a marker of the sanctuary where this covenant was established, it was also a marker of God's greatness to all.

24:27–28. The function of the stone is explained as a witness against the people. The language of "witness" draws on the law court (cf. Exod 20:16), largely because the existence of a covenant indicated a formalized relationship, and that a breach of this can be pursued in law. At the same time, the solemnity of the covenant should mean that it was largely self-enforcing. Moreover, since a stone could not in reality testify in a court case concerning a breach of the agreement, we have to understand its testimonial function as providing a continual reminder to the people of their commitment to serve Yahweh alone.

God's greatness in Joshua is for all the peoples of the earth, and a people representative of that has begun to form as the book has progressed. But that people is not yet complete, and Israel's history will attest that they were not always committed to God's greatness (2 Kings 17). Nevertheless, anyone who saw that stone would be reminded of the covenant established at Shechem and its meaning.[450]

With this accomplished, Joshua sent the people to their inheritance. Within the structure of the book, the term "inheritance" (נַחֲלָה) is important. It first appears in 11:23 as part of a summary of the conquest and appears fifty times overall, mostly in the tribal allotments. Just as the

---

[449] Judges 9, however, will demonstrate the longevity of Canaanite worship patterns at Shechem.

[450] This is closely paralleled by the stone "Ebenezer" set up by Samuel (1 Sam 7:12).

term serves to close the first half of the book, so here it brings the main narrative to its close. Much of the inheritance was still to be claimed (18:2), but the basis for claiming it was now established.

24:29–31.[451] Just as Joshua 12 followed the summary statement about the inheritance (11:23) with the list of defeated kings (12:1–24), so this list of three important burials (vv. 29–33) follows the reference to inheritance in verse 28. The first burial is Joshua's (cf. Judg 2:6–9), whose death balances Moses' death at the beginning of the book (Josh 1:1–2). The exact point of Joshua's death relative to the rest of the chapter cannot be determined, but since both 13:1 and 23:1–2 stress Joshua's advanced age we are probably not to imagine a significant period of time has passed.

Description of Joshua as "son of Nun" matches his introduction in 1:1, except that instead of Moses' attendant he has become (like Moses) "the servant of Yahweh."[452] Only Moses (Deut 34:5; Josh 1:1), David (2 Sam 7:8; Isa 37:35), and Eliakim (Isa 22:20) receive this title, besides the anonymous servant figure introduced in Isa 42:1. Joshua's 110 years fall short of Moses' 120 (Deut 34:7), but unlike Moses he was able receive his inheritance within the land (Josh 19:49–50). So, whereas Moses' burial place was unknown (Deut 34:6), Joshua's was in his inheritance in Timnath-serah (see comments on Josh 19:49–50).

More importantly, the people are said to have served God throughout the lifetime of Joshua and the elders who outlived him, because these people had all seen what God had done for Israel. At one level this might seem a strange assertion to make, because clearly Israel has not destroyed all the indigenous population but rather incorporated them in various ways (e.g., Rahab in Joshua 2 and 6; the Gibeonites in Joshua 9). But this statement is also closely matched by 11:15, which insists that Joshua had done everything God had commanded through Moses. These statements are provided as hermeneutical guides to read all that has happened to this point.[453] They suggest that Joshua understood the intent of the commands as indicating, not the minimum, but the maximum that

---

[451] The text for 24:29–33 in the LXX is very different from the MT. The CSB follows the MT, as do most English translations. See Butler, *Joshua 13–24*, 335–37. With Nelson, *Joshua*, 261, it seems likely that the MT represents the earliest recoverable text, so the variations in the LXX are not treated here.

[452] See further §3 ("Joshua and Jesus").

[453] On this see Rachel M. Billings, *"Israel Served the Lord": The Book of Joshua as a Paradoxical Portrait of Faithful Israel* (Notre Dame: University of Notre Dame Press, 2013).

could be accomplished in order for Israel to be deemed faithful. Both the midpoint of the book and its close point to Israel's faithfulness, even though the narrator knows it did not remain this way. Nevertheless, we are encouraged to now reread the book and understand how faithfulness was worked out, so that those who had not witnessed these events could also learn about faithfulness.

24:32. A brief note ties Israel's entry into the land back to the patriarchs. In Gen 50:22–26, Joseph had asked to be buried in the land God promised to Abraham, Isaac, and Jacob. That hope had now been fulfilled, since Israel has taken that land. Jacob had purchased a parcel of land near Shechem, within the territory now allotted to the Joseph tribes (Gen 33:19), though that initial settlement had led to violence and murder (Gen 34).[454] Nevertheless, we discover that Israel had brought Joseph's bones with them in the exodus, allowing him to be buried in the land that had become part of his descendants' inheritance. As Joshua's death had been matched to Moses', covering the period from the end of the exodus to the end of the conquest, Joseph's burial is an enduring reminder that Israel's claim to the land reached much further back.

24:33. The final burial notice is that of Aaron's son Eleazar. Like Joshua's, this is tied to the end of the exodus. Eleazar's importance within the book is seen in his allotment of the land with Joshua (14:1; 19:51; 17:4; 21:1). The record of his death shows that this period of Israel's story has concluded. He too would be buried within Ephraim, at a site allotted to Eleazar's son Phinehas. "Gibeah" is commonly rendered as a proper noun, but no town in Ephraim is called that in Joshua. Therefore, we may be wise to follow the csb note and read "the hill of Phinehas," since the word can also be a common noun. There is no record of Phinehas receiving a particular hill, but as he was the high priest it is plausible. Eleazar differs from Joshua and Joseph in that there is no reference to his inheritance, since his inheritance was the priestly work of his family. The final words indicate that this particular priestly heritage did indeed continue through Phineas.

Bridge

Joshua 24 is a careful and intentional conclusion, gathering together key themes developed throughout the book. Joshua's speech presents

---

[454] The value of one hundred qesitahs (csb note) is unknown (cf. Job 42:11).

a challenge to readers of future generations to make the same choice to put aside all other gods and serve God alone.

We should note that the chapter begins and ends with reasons for this. The beginning, Joshua's account of covenant history, tells the story of God's faithfulness across all of Israel's story. This story has consistently included other peoples because, although God was working through Israel, his election of them never excluded others. God was faithful, and each generation could discover the reality of that faithfulness for themselves.

The closing report of three burials also serves to encourage service to God alone, reminding readers that God continued to be faithful. Joshua was buried in his inheritance, which God had given to Israel, while Joseph's burial in his tribal inheritance reminds readers that God's promises were longstanding. Furthermore, just as God had worked through Eleazar as high priest, so the role would continue through his son Phineas. This was already signaled in the allotment of the cities of refuge and Levitical towns (Josh 20–21). God had thus faithfully given the land as an inheritance to Joshua and Joseph, but the work of life in the land would continue. God's faithfulness was not something relegated to the past but a living reality.

If God is faithful, then a covenant relationship with him is the right response, requiring one to serve him alone and live as he requires. Joshua's call to "choose this day" thus echoes down through the ages. However, to be clear, the call is for those who already know God—that they might set aside distractions and serve only him with a faithful life. Second Kings 17 will make clear the tragic results of not doing this. The book of Joshua, however, shows that, not only could it be done, it could integrate outsiders into God's people in the process.

Such themes are particularly prevalent in the letter to the Hebrews. Having listed the heroes of the faith in chapter 11, the writer exhorts readers to "lay aside every hindrance and the sin that so easily ensnares us" (Heb 12:1). The image is of runners competing in a race. Likewise, as believers we need to fix "our eyes on Jesus" (Heb 12:2), the faithful one who has gone before us. In running this race, we know that we cannot have anything that distracts from the requirements of faithful discipleship in the midst of a challenging and often hostile world. Likewise, the believers in Acts 19:19 destroyed the markers of their old religious life, a situation not dissimilar to what Paul addresses in 1 Corinthians 8–10 where he encourages believers to "flee idolatry" (1 Cor 10:14). The gods that Joshua urged Israel to put aside would always distract them from a life of faithfulness—in the same way that holding on to various hindrances prevents us from staying the course with Jesus (Heb 12:1–2). Although the author of Hebrews does not necessarily allude to Joshua 24 here, the structure of the letter as a whole has emphasized God's faithfulness to us in Jesus Christ and our need to remain faithful. Within the new context of Christian faith, Joshua's call echoes down through the ages to us, insisting that only a life given wholly to Jesus makes sense.

For believers, it is not a stone in Shechem that attests to this but the cross of Christ. Every time we look to the cross, it testifies of God's faithfulness. Baptism, likewise, continues to testify to believers of the need to live out a life consistent with God's faithfulness to us in Christ (Rom 6:1–14), since we have been brought from death to life. But that life is not a one-time choice but a life of continued discipleship. The challenge for the church is to model this corporately so that, as gathered believers, we pursue faithfulness to God in Christ while working out what that faithfulness looks like in new contexts.

BIBLIOGRAPHY

Allen, Leonard. "Archaeology of Ai and the Accuracy of Joshua 7:1–8:29." *ResQ* 20 (1977): 41–52.

Assis, Elie. "A Literary Approach to Complex Narratives: An Examination of Joshua 3–4." Pages 401–414 in *The Book of Joshua*. Edited by E. Noort. Leuven: Peeter, 2012.

Auld, A. Graeme. *Joshua Retold: Synoptic Perspectives*. Edinburgh: T & T Clark, 1998.

Ballhorn, Egbert. "Die Gestaltung des Gilgal (Josua 3–4): Das Buch Josua als Heterptopie." Pages 415–429 in *The Book of Joshua*. Edited by E. Noort. Leuven: Peeter, 2012.

Beck, John A. "Why Do Joshua's Readers Keep Crossing the River? The Narrative-Geographical Shaping of Joshua 3–4." *JETS* 48 (2005): 689–699.

Begg, Christopher T. "The Function of Josh 7,1–8,29 in the Deuteronomistic History." *Biblica* 67 (1986): 320–334.

Berman, Joshua. "The Making of the Sin of Achan (Joshua 7)." *Biblical Interpretation* 22 (2014): 115–131.

———. "Law Code as Plot Template in Biblical Narrative (1 Kings 9:26–11:13; Joshua 2:9–13)." *JSOT* 40 (2016): 337–349.

Billings, Rachel M. *"Israel Served the Lord." The Book of Joshua as a Paradoxical Portrait of Faithful Israel*. Notre Dame: University of Notre Dame Press, 2013.

Block, Daniel I. *The Gods of the Nations: Studies in Ancient Near Eastern National Theology* (2nd ed.). Leicester: Apollos, 2000.

Boda, Mark J. *'Return to Me': A Biblical Theology of Repentance*. Nottingham: Apollos, 2015.

Boling, Robert G. *Joshua: A New Translation with Notes and Commentary* (Introduction by G. Ernest Wright). Garden City: Doubleday, 1982.

Brueggemann, Walter. *Divine Presence Amid Violence: Contextualizing the Book of Joshua*. Milton Keynes: Paternoster, 2009.

Butler, Trent C. *Joshua*. Waco: Word Books, 1983.

———. *Joshua 1–12*. Grand Rapids: Zondervan, 2014.

———. *Joshua 13–24*. Grand Rapids: Zondervan, 2014.

Campbell, K. M. "Rahab's Covenant: A Short Note on Joshua ii 9–21." *VT* 22 (1972): 243244.

Chambers, N. "Confirming Joshua as the interpreter of Israel's *Tôrah*; The Narrative Role of Joshua 8:30–35." *BBR* 25 (2015): 141–153.

Creach, Jerome F. D. *Joshua*. Louisville: Westminster John Knox, 2003.

Coote, Robert B. "Joshua." Pages 553–720 in *The New Interpreter's Bible*. Edited by Leander E. Keck. Nashville: Abingdon Press, 1998.

Copan, Paul and Matthew Flanagan. *Did God Really Command Genocide? Coming to Terms with the Justice of God*. Grand Rapids: Baker Academic, 2014.

Craigie, Peter C. *The Book of Deuteronomy*. Grand Rapids: Eerdmans, 1976.

Crowell, Bradley L. "Good Girl, Bad Girl: Foreign Women of the Deuteronomistic History in Postcolonial Perspective." *Biblical Interpretation* 21/1 (2013): 1–18.

Dallaire, Hélène. "Joshua." Pages 815–1042 in *The Expositor's Bible Commentary* (Rev. ed., vol. 2). Edited by Tremper Longman III and David E. Garland. Grand Rapids: Zondervan, 2012.

———. "Taking the Land by Force: Divine Violence in Joshua." Pages 51–74 in *Wrestling with the Violence of God: Soundings in the Old Testament*. Edited by M. Daniel Carroll R. and J. Blair Wilgus. Winona Lake: Eisenbrauns, 2015.

Davis, Dale Ralph. *No Falling Words: Expositions of the Book of Joshua*. Grand Rapids: Baker Book House, 1988.

Dawkins, Richard. *The God Delusion*. London: Black Swan, 2006.

Den Braber, M. E. J. " 'They Keep Going On…': Repetition in Joshua 6:20." Pages 489–500 in *The Book of Joshua*. Edited by E. Noort. Leuven: Peeter, 2012.

———. *Built from Many Stones: An Analysis of N. Winther-Nielsen and A. G. Auld on Joshua with Focus on Joshua 5:1-6:26*. Bergambacht: 2VM Uitgeverij, 2010.

den Hertog, Cornelis G. "Ein Wortspiel in der Jericho-Erzählung (Jos 6)?" *ZAW* 104 (1992): 99–100.

de Prenter, Jannica A. "The Contrastive Polysemous Meaning of חרם in the Book of Joshua: A Cognitive Linguistic Approach." Pages 473–488 in *The Book of Joshua*. Edited by E. Noort. Leuven: Peeter, 2012.

Dozeman, Thomas B. "Joshua 1,1–9. The Beginning of a Book or a Literary Bridge?" Pages 159–182 in *The Book of Joshua*. Edited by E. Noort. Leuven: Peeter, 2012.

Dus, Vikar Jan. "Die Analyse zweier Ladererzählungen des Josuabuches (Jos 3–4 und 6)." *ZAW* 72 (1960): 107–134.

Earl, Douglas S. *The Joshua Delusion? Rethinking Genocide in the Bible*, with a response by Christopher J. H. Wright. Cambridge: James Clarke & Co, 2010.

———. *Reading Joshua as Christian Scripture*. Winona Lake: Eisenbrauns, 2010.

Ellis, Robert R. "The Theological Boundaries of Inclusion and Exclusion in the Book of Joshua." *Review & Expositor* 95/2 (1998): 235–250.

Eybers, I. H. *A Geography of Biblical Israel and its Surroundings*. Pretoria: NGK Boekhandel, 1988.

Faley, R. J. *Joshua, Judges*. Collegeville: Liturgical Press, 2011.

Firth, David G. "The Spirit and Leadership: Testimony, Empowerment and Purpose." Pages 259–280 in *Presence, Power and Promise: The Role of the Spirit of God in the Old Testament*. Edited by David G. Firth and Paul D. Wegner. Nottingham: Apollos, 2011.

———. "Passing on the Faith in Deuteronomy." Pages 157–176 in *Interpreting Deuteronomy: Issues and Approaches*. Edited by David G. Firth and Philip S. Johnston. Nottingham: Apollos, 2012.

———. *The Message of Joshua: Promise and People*. Nottingham: IVP, 2015.

García-Alfonso, Cristina. *Resolviendo: Narratives of Survival in the Hebrew Bible and in Cuba Today*. New York: Peter Lang, 2010.

Gangel, Kenneth O. *Joshua*. Nashville: Broadman & Holman, 2002.

Goldingay, John. *Joshua, Judges and Ruth for Everyone*. London: SPCK, 2011.

Gray, John. *Joshua, Judges, Ruth*. Grand Rapids: Eerdmans, 1986.

Gundry, Stanley N., ed. *Show them No Mercy: Four Views on God and the Canaanite Genocide*. Grand Rapids: Zondervan, 2003.

Hall, Sarah Lebhar. *Conquering Character: The Characterization of Joshua in Joshua 1-11*. London: T & T Clark, 2010.

Harris, J. Gordon. "Joshua." Pages 1–119 *Joshua, Judges Ruth*. J. Gordon Harris, Cheryl A. Brown, and Michael S. Moore. Peabody: Hendrickson, 2000.

Hawk, L. Daniel. *Every Promise Fulfilled: Contesting Plots in Joshua*. Louisville: Westminster John Knox, 1991.

———. *Joshua*. Collegeville: Liturgical Press, 2000.

———. *Joshua in 3-D. A Commentary on Biblical Conquest and Manifest Destiny*. Eugene: Cascade, 2010.

Hawkins, Ralph K. *How Israel Became a People*. Nashville: Abingdon, 2013.

Hess, Richard S. *Joshua: An Introduction and Commentary*. Leicester: IVP, 1996.

———. *Israelite Religions: An Archaeological and Biblical Survey*. Nottingham: Apollos, 2007.

Hillers, Delbert R. *Covenant: The History of a Biblical Idea*. Baltimore: Johns Hopkins University Press, 1969.

Hofreiter, Christian. "Genocide in Deuteronomy and Christian Interpretation." Pages 240–262 in *Interpreting Deuteronomy: Issues and Approaches*. Edited by David G. Firth and Philip S. Johnston. Nottingham: Apollos, 2012.

Howard, David M. Jr. *Joshua*. Nashville: Broadman & Holman, 1998.

———. "Three Days' in Joshua 1-3: Resolving a Chronological Conundrum." *JETS* 41/4 (1998): 539–550.

Hubbard, Robert L. Jr. "'What Do These Stones mean?': Biblical Theology and a Motif in Joshua." *BBR* 11 (2001): 1–26

———. *Joshua: The NIV Application Commentary*. Grand Rapids: Zondervan, 2009.

Johnston, Philip S. "Civil Leadership in Deuteronomy." Pages 137–156 in *Interpreting Deuteronomy: Issues and Approaches*. Edited by David G. Firth and Philip S. Johnston. Nottingham: Apollos, 2012.

Keil, C. F. and F. Delitzsch. *Joshua, Judges, Ruth, I & II Samuel*. Grand Rapids: Eerdmans, 1956.

Koorevaar, H. J. *De Opbouw van het Boek Jozua*. Heverlee: Centrum voor Bijbelse Vorming-Belgie, 1990.

Krause, Joachim J. "Der Zug durch den Jordan nach Josua 3–4: Eine neue Analysis." Pages 383–400 in *The Book of Joshua*. Edited by E. Noort. Leuven: Peeter, 2012.

———. "Vor wem soll die Auskundschaftung Jerichos geheim gehalten warden? Eine Frage zu Josua 2:1." *VT* 62/4 (2012): 454–56.

———. *Exodus und Eisodus: Komposition und Theologie von Josua 1–5*. Leiden: Brill, 2014.

———. "Aesthetics of Production and Aesthetics of Reception in Analyzing Intertextuality: Illustrated with Joshua 2." *Biblica* 96/3 (2015): 416–427.

Lilley, J. P. U. "Understanding the ḤEREM." *Tyndale Bulletin* 44 (1993): 160–177.

Livingston, D. P. "Location of Bethel and Ai Reconsidered." *WTJ* 33 (1970): 20–44.

Longman, Tremper III and Daniel G. Reid. *God is a Warrior*. Grand Rapids: Zondervan, 1995.

Lunn, Nicholas P. "The Deliverance of Rahab (Joshua 2, 6) as the Gentile Exodus." *Tyndale Bulletin* 65/1 (2014): 11–20.

———. "Allusions to the Levitical Leprosy Laws in the Jericho Narratives (Joshua 2 and 6). *JESOT* 4/2 (2015): 131–144.

McCarthy, D. J. "The Theology of Leadership in Joshua 1–9." *Biblica* 52/2 (1971): 165–175.

McConville, J. Gordon and Stephen N. Williams. *Joshua*. Grand Rapids: Eerdmans, 2010.

Magyarosi, Barna. *Holy War and Cosmic Conflict in the Old Testament: From the Exodus to the Exile*. Berrien Springs: Adventist Theological Society Publications, 2010.

Matties, G. "Reading Rahab's Story: Beyond the Moral of the Story." *Direction* 24 (1995): 57–70.

———. *Joshua*. Harrisonburg: Herald Press, 2012.

Madvig, Donald H. "Joshua." Pages 239–374 in *The Expositor's Bible Commentary*. Edited by Frank E. Gaebelein. Grand Rapids: Zondervan, 1992.

Mann, Thomas W. *The Book of the Former Prophets*. Eugene: Cascade, 2011.

Merling, David Sr. *The Book of Joshua: Its Theme and Role in Archaeological Discussions*. Berrien Springs: Andrews University Press, 1997.

Mitchell, Gordon. *Together in the Land: A Reading of the Book of Joshua*. Sheffield: JSOT Press, 1993.

Moberly, R. W. L. *Old Testament Theology: Reading the Hebrew Bible as Christian Scripture*. Grand Rapids: Baker Academic, 2013.

Motyer, Alec. *The Message of Exodus: The Days of our Pilgrimage*. Leicester: IVP, 2005.

———. *Discovering the Old Testament*. Leicester: Crossway, 2006.

Nelson, Richard D. *Joshua: A Commentary*. Louisville: Westminster John Knox Press, 1997.

Noort, Ed (ed). *The Book of Joshua*. Leuven: Peeters, 2012.

Peckham, Brian. "The Composition of Joshua 3–4." *CBQ* 46 (1984): 413–431.

Pitkänen, Pekka M. A. *Joshua*. Nottingham: Apollos, 2010.

Polzin, Robert. *Moses and the Deuteronomist: A literary study of the Deuteronomic history. Part 1: Deuteronomy, Joshua, Judges*. New York: Seabury Press, 1980.

Prouser, O. Horn. "The Truth about Women and Lying." *JSOT* 61 (1994): 15–28.

Provan, Iain, V. Phillips Long, Tremper Longman III. *A Biblical History of Israel*. Louisville: Westminster John Knox, 2003.

Robinson, B. P. "Rahab of Canaan–and Israel." *SJOT* 23 (2009): 257–273.

Rösel, Hartmut N. *Joshua*. Leuven: Peeters, 2011.

Rowlett, Lori L. "Inclusion, Exclusion and Marginality in the Book of Joshua." *JSOT* 55 (1992): 15–23.

———. *Joshua and the Rhetoric of Violence: A New Historicist Reading*. Sheffield: Sheffield Academic Press, 1996.

Schreiner, T. R. *Commentary on Hebrews*. Nashville: B & H, 2015.

Schwienhorst-Schönberger, Ludger. "Josua 6 und die Gewalt." Pages 433–472 in *The Book of Joshua*. Edited by E. Noort. Leuven: Peeter, 2012.

Seebass, Horst. "Das Buch Josua als literarisch nicht zu erwartende Fortsetzung des Buches Numeri." Pages 249–258 in *The Book of Joshua*. Edited by E. Noort. Leuven: Peeter, 2012.

Sherwood, Aaron. "A Leader's Misleading and a Prostitute's Profession: A Re-examination of Joshua 2." *JSOT* 31/1 (2006): 43–61.

Soggin, J. Alberto. *Joshua: A Commentary*. London: SCM Press, 1972.

Spero, Shubert. "Why the Walls of Jericho Came Tumbling Down." *JBQ* 34 (2006): 86–91.

Stec, David M. "The Mantle Hidden by Achan." *VT* 41 (1991): 356–359.

Stek, John H. "Rahab of Canaan and Israel: The Meaning of Joshua 2." *CJT* 37 (2002): 28–48.

Stone, Lawson G. "Ethical and apologetic tendencies in the redaction of the Book of Joshua." *CBQ* 53 (1991): 25–36.

Van Wieringen, Archibald L. H. M. "The Literary Function of the Joshua-Reference in 1 Kings 16,34." Pages 501–508 in *The Book of Joshua*. Edited by E. Noort. Leuven: Peeter, 2012.

Vogt, Ernst. "Die Erzählung vom Jordanübergang Josue 3–4." *Biblica* 46 (1965): 125–148.

Wagenaar, Jan A. "The Cessation of Manna: Editorial frames for the Wilderness Wandering in Exodus 16,35 and Joshua 5, 10–12." *ZAW* 112 (2000): 192–209.

Wenham, J. W. "Large Numbers in the Old Testament." *Tyndale Bulletin* 18 (1967): 19–53.

Williams, Ronald J. *Hebrew Syntax: An Outline*. Toronto: University of Toronto Press, 1967.

Williams, Stephen N. "Could God Have Commanded the Slaughter of the Canaanites?" *Tyndale Bulletin* 63 (2012): 161–178.

Winther-Nielsen, Nicolai. *A Functional Discourse Grammar of Joshua*. Stockholm: Almqvist & Wiksell, 1995.

———. "Stones on Display in Joshua 6: The Linguistic Tree Structure as a 'PLOT' Tool." *Journal of the Hebrew Scriptures* 12 (2012): 1–29. http://www.jhsonline.org/Articles/article_179.pdf.

Wiseman, D. J. "Rahab of Jericho." *Tyndale Bulletin* 14 (1964): 8–11.

Wood, Bryant G. "The Search for Joshua's Ai." Pages 205–240 in *Critical Issues in Early Israelite History*. Edited by Richard S. Hess, Gerald A. Klingbeil and Paul Ray Jr. Winona Lake: Eisenbrauns, 2008.

Woods, Edward J. *Deuteronomy: An Introduction and Commentary*. Nottingham: IVP, 2011.

Woudstra, Marten H. *The Book of Joshua*. Grand Rapids: Eerdmans, 1981.

Wright, Christopher J. H. *The Mission of God: Unlocking the Bible's Grand Narrative*. Nottingham: IVP, 2006.

———. *The God I Don't Understand: Reflections on Tough Questions of Faith*. Grand Rapids: Zondervan, 2008.

Zehnder, Markus. *Umgang mit Fremden in Israel und Assyrien: Ein Beitrag zur Anthropologie des "Fremden" im Licht antiker Quellen*. BZWANT, Stuttgart: Kohlhammer, 2005.

———. "The Annihilation of the Canaanites: Reassessing the Brutality of the Biblical Witness." Pages 263–290 in *Encountering Violence in the Bible*. Edited by M. Zehnder and H. Hagellia. Sheffield: Sheffield Phoenix, 2013.

Zevit, Ziony. "Archaeological and Literary Stratigraphy in Joshua 7:1–8:29." *BASOR*, 251 (1983): 23–35.

SCRIPTURE INDEX

OLD TESTAMENT